Ethics and the Clinical Encounter

Richard M. Zaner

Ann Geddes Stahlman Professor of Medical Ethics
Vanderbilt University

Prentice Hall
Englewood Cliffs, New Jersey 07632

LIBRARY OF CONGRESS
Library of Congress Cataloging-in-Publication Data

Zaner, Richard M.
    Ethics and the clinical encounter / Richard M. Zaner.
        p.   cm.
    Bibliography: p.
    Includes index.
    ISBN 0-13-290545-0
    1. Medical ethics. 2. Physician and patient. 3. Humanistic
psychology.   I. Title.
    [DNLM: 1. Ethics, Medical.   W 50 Z28e]
    R725.5.Z36 1988
    174'.2--dc19
    DNLM/DLC
    for Library of Congress

Cover design: Lundgren Graphics, Ltd.
Manufacturing buyer: Margaret Rizzi

For Pruett Watkins, M.D., and Edmund D. Pellegrino, M.D.,
who in different ways were providential

Printed in the United States of America
10 9 8 7 6 5 4 3 2 1

ISBN 0-13-290545-0   01

Prentice-Hall International (UK) Limited, *London*
Prentice-Hall of Australia Pty. Limited, *Sydney*
Prentice-Hall Canada Inc., *Toronto*
Prentice-Hall Hispanoamericana, S.A., *Mexico*
Prentice-Hall of India Private Limited, *New Delhi*
Prentice-Hall of Japan, Inc., *Tokyo*
Simon & Schuster Asia Pte. Ltd., *Singapore*
Editora Prentice-Hall do Brasil, Ltda., *Rio de Janeiro*

Acknowledgment is gratefully made for permission to use material from the following
sources:

E. J. Cassell, *The Healer's Art: A New Approach to the Doctor-Patient Relationship* (Cambridge,
Mass.: MIT Press, 1976). Excerpts reprinted by permission of the publisher. Copyright ©
1976 by Eric J. Cassell, M.D.

These acknowledgments are continued on page 328, which constitutes an extension of the copyright page.

Contents

Foreword: Progress in Ethics *by Eric J. Cassell*   vii
Preface   x

CHAPTER 1

Medicine's Challenge to Ethics   1

The Initial Idea 1   The Philosopher's Response 4   Applied Ethics 6
The Backlash Against Ethics 9   The Backlash Continues 11
"Clinical" Versus "Biomedical" Ethics 13   A Clinical Example 14
Critique of the Case 14   Heterogeneity of Moral Views 16
Medicine's Dilemma 18   The Challenge: A First Look 19
Toward Another Approach: A Case Study 21   Developing
a Responsive Ethics 27

CHAPTER 2

The Moral Dimension of Medicine:
Preliminary Reflections   29

The Complex Field of Medical Work 30   An Illustrative Case 32
The Social Context of Patients 34   Several Clues to Being Morally
Responsive 36   The Moral Resolve and Its Specifications 38
Sources of Moral Conflict 41   Review: Case and Comment 44
The Moral Basis of Medicine: Another View 50

CHAPTER 3
"How the Hell Did I Get Here?": The Patient's Place in the Therapeutic Dyad 53

A Phenomenology of Illness: Outline 53   Patients Present Themselves 56   "What's Wrong with Me?" "Do You Really Care?" 62   Tears in the Fabric of Daily Life 65 Unavoidable Trust 69   The Experience of Being Cared For 71 Soundings at Uncertain Levels 75   Who Is My Stranger? 80 Power and Vulnerability 84   The Helping Relation as Promise 86 "Telling" Illness: Gratitude and Luck 88

CHAPTER 4
Patient Discourse and Medicine's History 92

The Complexity of the Field 92   Medicine's Two Sides: A Historical Irony 94   The Text of the Clinical Context 96   The Stages of Clinical Judgment 99   Deficiency of the Received View 102 The Displacement of the Patient 104   Cartesian Dualism 106 The Cartesian Puzzle 108   Descartes as Medical Consultant 110 Descartes's Anatomy and Physiology 112   Dualism Revisited 114 The Body-Machine Analogy 117   The Living Body, the Dead Cadaver: The "Subtle Hoax" 120   The Oddity of Ordinary Life 123 The Post-Cartesian Context 126   The Elusive Everyday: A Historical Theme 127

CHAPTER 5
Themes from Medicine's History: Interpretive Reconsiderations 130

Human Anatomy: A First Look 132   Between Descartes and Bichat 135   Conflict of Interpretation in Ancient Medicine 137 The First Clue: Interpretation of Symptoms 140   The Dogmatic Doctrine 142   The Empiric Tradition 146 The Descartes-Bichat Difference Revisited 150

CHAPTER 6
The Anatomist's Conceit, the Body's Cunning 154

Reductivism and Dualism in Current Medicine 155   The Anomaly of Gallows Humor 157   The Soma and the Corpse 159 The Historical Thematic 162   The Postmortem in Medieval Medicine 164   Mind and Body as Historical Artifacts 165 The Corpse and the Soul 168   The Empiric-Dogmatic Dispute Revisited 170   The Therapeutic Dyad Reconsidered 172 A Review of the Terrain 174

CHAPTER 7
Skepticism in Medicine 177

Hellenistic and Hippocratic Empiricism 177   Medical Methodism 180 The Skeptic's Circumstantial Understanding 182   The Historical Irony of the Human Corpse 184   The Place of Galen 188   Anatomy in the Ancient World 190   The Retreat of Life (Soul) 197 The Improvement of Man 199

CHAPTER 8
Ethics in Ancient Medicine 202

Medical Morality and Medical Power 202   The Hippocratic Oath and Medical Morality 205   Hippocratic Morality 210   The Ethics of Methodism 219   Summing Up 221

CHAPTER 9
Clinical-Liaison Ethics: Part I 224

"Why Won't You Let Me Die?" 225   Everyone Did What They Could, Right? 234   What Went Wrong? 236   Ethics as Clinical Liaison 242   Enablement 248

CHAPTER 10
Clinical-Liaison Ethics: Part II 251

The Work of Helping Strangers 251   Dilemmas of Necessary Distancing 255   The Aftermath of Distancing: Good Times and Bad 259   Addressing Aftermaths 263   Clinical Conversation: A Clue 266   Description in Clinical-Liaison Ethics 267 A Rule of Method 269   Interpretation in Clinical-Liaison Ethics 270 A Second Rule of Method 272   Understanding Moral Themes 273 Topical, Interpretive, and Motivational Schemata 275 The Documentary Method 279

CHAPTER 11
Trust and Care: Toward a Moral Foundation 283

Review of the Terrain 283   The Idea of the Autonomous Moral Agent 285   Assumptions Underlying Autonomy 288 A Case in Point: The Dialysis Patient 293   Falling Ill 295 The Idea of "Moral Chance" 297   "Accident of Birth" and Moral Imbalance 300   Awakening a Moral Sense: "Good Fortune Obligates" 303   Awakening a Moral Sense: Gratitude and Response 305   The Twofold Meaning of Awakening a Moral Sense 307   The ESRD-Dialysis Patient's "Good Fortune" 308 Illness and the Moral Order 310   Intent in Patient-Physician Discourse 312   Affiliative Feeling: "Put Youself in My Shoes" 315 A Final Word 319

Bibliography 321

Index 329

Foreword: Progress in Ethics

Eric J. Cassell

This book is a pleasure to read, rich in ideas, intellectually generous, and immediately applicable to clinical medicine. Its worth, however, goes beyond these qualities, rare as they may be in books about medical ethics. It is generally accepted that medical science, *because* it is science, consistently generates new ideas. A similar expectation of continued advancement is too often lacking in medical ethics. That Richard Zaner does not share this view is amply demonstrated by his work, which represents important progress in the basic concepts of the field. To understand what an interesting book this is, and the importance of Professor Zaner's contribution, it is necessary to view the book from the perspective of medical history.

No one would argue with the notion that the dominant characteristic of twentieth-century medicine is the fundamental position of science. But as the noted Spanish medical historian Pedro Lain-Entralgo has pointed out, there is another equally characteristic theme of the medicine of our times: the central importance of the patient's perspective. Francis Peabody's paper "On the Care of the Patient" (*Journal of the American Medical Association*, March 1927) can be considered an early landmark in medicine's concern with the patient *as a patient*, not merely as a container of disease. The social medicine movement of the 1930s, which stressed the importance of socioeconomic factors in sickness, furthered the emphasis on the patient. The idea was strengthened by Freud and other depth psychologists, who convincingly demonstrated the influence of emotional factors in illness. By the 1950s, the slogan "Treat the patient as a person" was firmly ensconced in American medicine, although not often honored in day-to-day practice. The social changes of the 1960s pushed to prominence the notion that medicine must be *relevant* (a common word of the times) to the needs of its patients, while at the same time giving added meaning to the word *person*. Where the sameness of people had been stressed, now differences between individuals assumed primary importance. People had become proud of every facet of their distinctiveness. As a result, patients came to demand treatment as the unique persons they were, not just as livers or lungs.

By the late 1960s and early 1970s, it was clear that the major biomedical and technological advances could harm as well as benefit the persons for whom they were intended. In this setting, the current intense interest in ethics arose.

Although much ethical theory has its origins in antiquity, many of our ideas about the object of ethics—the individual—arose in the same historical period during which the basic concepts of modern science were formed. Thus it is not surprising that the "objects" of science (things in nature) and the "object" of ethics (the person) should be conceived of in ways that are strikingly similar. Both disciplines have classically understood their objects to be atemporal, separate, free-standing, and essentially unchanging. As noted above, for medical science the objects were diseases viewed in their original sense. For ethics there was the individual seen as an autonomous, reasoning creature, essentially uninfluenced by time, the body, or illness. In the current era, as ethics entered medicine, it did so in the form of these ethical theories of the past.

One of the major contributions of Professor Zaner's work is to demonstrate that attempts to apply classical ethical theories to medicine do not work. The profession requires a new understanding of ethics, developed in the light of medicine's special activity—the care of sick persons by physicians.

Professor Zaner is clearly aware that in recent decades medical science has been changing, and his book presents a conception of moral thought comprehensive enough to deal with the expanded ideas about illness that have recently been emerging. As the patient *as sick person* has become more important, the notion of diseases as things with independent existence has begun to recede. Instead, illness is coming to be seen as a process, a concatenation of events. Moreover, if the chain of happenings in illness is important, why stop at the body? Why not expand this pathophysiologic thinking to include the whole person, the family, and even the community? This is the kind of understanding of medicine that is present throughout this book.

It has become evident in recent times that the person's background and identity influence the presentation, course, and outcome of the disease. Pneumococcal pneumonia in indigent alcoholics differs from pneumococcal pneumonia among the comfortable. Type I insulin-dependent diabetes mellitus is different in an intelligent, conscientious, food-conscious, exercising, family-supported person than in a rebellious, slow-witted, slothful, single ne'er-do-well. And so it is with almost any disease one can think of: sick persons cannot be seen apart from their bodies or from the settings of their illnesses. Nor can patients be understood as moral agents apart from their relationships (or the conspicuous absence of certain relationships) with family and others, because all of these factors have an effect on the person's choices, behaviors, and illness experiences. In like manner, the relationship between doctor and patient can never be dismissed from consideration, because all medical care flows through it and is influenced by it.

I believe that many ideas about the individual embodied in classical ethics—autonomy and paternalism, for example—are as unreal and inapplicable to sick persons as are the ideas about diseases as objects. Practically speaking, there are no sick persons who are entirely independent, who look, feel, and act in exactly the same manner as when they are healthy, and who have true freedom of choice. The implication of many current notions about self-determination and paternalism—that if sick persons merely had their physicians' knowledge and access to technological power, they could be their own doctors—is, to be charitable, pure mythology. Some ethicists, acknowledging the impact of illness on the patient's autonomy and relationships with others, speak of autonomy as an ideal to be sought after in the care of the sick. While this idea is acceptable as far as it goes, it is an inadequate guide to action. Richard Zaner's text, on the other hand, goes beyond classical ideas about autonomy to provide new concepts for dealing with the rich network of human relationships and with the other realities of the sick person's condition.

Sick persons are subject not merely to fate or the caprice of disease but to the actions of other people, and nowadays the actions of some of these people carry enormous technological and scientific power. If our ideas of persons have moved forward, and if medicine has also changed, it seems reasonable that medical ethics should advance in order to guide this powerful technology. Professor Zaner never loses sight of that goal. He focuses on the actual clinical setting and on the participants in the drama of medical care, and he shows us how the patient's interests can be brought to bear on medical decisions. Because he is writing about real medicine and real people, he never neglects the network of relationships in which care takes place: the family, other caregivers, the institution, and sometimes the community. Richard Zaner's book makes its greatest contribution by giving a modern meaning to concepts like autonomy and self-determination, allowing them to be employed in the real world of contemporary medicine.

Preface

The medical enterprise has in recent years been the occasion of widespread public moral concern and, along with that, a kind of formal ethical deliberation almost unprecedented in its history. Not surprisingly, this has resulted in the emergence of a new field of professional inquiry—medical, or biomedical, ethics. At the same time, issues more broadly associated with clinical medicine and its burgeoning new technologies have attracted the notice of philosophers and others, giving rise to a more comprehensive kind of professional concern. Here, traditional questions of the nature of knowledge (epistemology), method (methodology), concepts and theoretical frameworks (philosophy of science), and basic assumptions about and implications for human life, death, and destiny (ontology, metaphysics) have received important new impetus from reflections about the medical enterprise.

We have witnessed, in short, the emergence of a new discipline, the medical humanities. These developments have been understandably accompanied by controversy and confrontation, with both professionals and the public divided on ethical and philosophical grounds.

Even so, not only have refinements in inquiry and insight occurred—for instance, on the nature and requirements of beneficence as a key to medical morality—but progress has also been won on other fronts—for instance, on issues presented by medical treatment for multiply handicapped infants with life-threatening conditions (so-called Baby Does). It is now an accepted part of public policy that one does not have to engage in futile or even virtually futile therapies. Although it may well not have been the aim of those who urged legislation in response to what they believed were abuses, the result has in part been to clarify the process and content of decision making on behalf of these infants. There is also now a recognition of the significant (if still somewhat ambiguous) place of parents in deciding about their own imperiled babies.

Despite such hard-won achievements, much about medicine remains perplexing. For example, at least since the early nineteenth century medicine has been an enterprise mainly of *discovery*—with regard to the human body (its interactions with its own internal or external environments) as well as research into new chemical substances, development of surgical regimens, and the like. With its remarkable successes—especially since the discovery of the penicillins in the 1930s and the new knowledge of the body's physiology and neurology since the 1960s—medicine has been shifting from an emphasis on discovery, with its consequent harvest of therapies, to one on *intervention*.

Focused first on *acute* traumas, this interventional emphasis has in the past few years been shifting more and more to *chronic* and *preventive* issues. Problems presented by the elderly and long-term illnesses (e.g., the malignancies), as well as those presented by the rest of us, in many ways raise basic questions about the doctor's relationship to the patient. Many of these questions are new and were generally ignored or poorly heeded so long as medicine was conceived of and practiced primarily as a science of discovery and diagnosis. Considering the main illnesses of our times—arteriosclerotic heart disease, diabetes, degenerative bone disease, hypertension, AIDS, and cancer—it is clear that doctors have had to contend increasingly with the sick or injured person as regards personal life and values (of every sort) and social circumstances, as well as in the light of legislative and legal considerations designed in general to articulate and enhance the rights of individuals to make decisions.

This gradual change—detectible since at least the late 1960s—has become a tangible factor to be reckoned with. On the other hand, the educational development of the medical intelligence and skills needed to make diagnostic and therapeutic interventions effective and humane has generally lagged behind.

Sensitivity to these personal and social dimensions of illness and injury, especially to ordinary language and conversations (so much a part of daily life and clinical encounters), has only slowly come to be recognized as a central component of that medical intelligence in dealing with people as patients. Even more slow to develop has been the understanding that these conversational interchanges can themselves be therapeutically significant, not to mention morally and socially compelling, parts of the doctor-patient relationship. What a patient believes and says about what is important can be as decisive a part of medical knowledge and skillful clinical practice as anatomy, physiology, or biochemistry, and as integral to diagnosis and therapy as scientific knowledge.

Just as there are systematic requirements for medical education and practice regarding effective and humane interventions, the nature and extent of which have yet to be fully examined, so too are there important implications in this shift for the medical humanities, and even more directly for biomedical ethics. At first generally thought to be an exercise in philosophical analysis of concepts, rules, and applications, biomedical ethics has gradually, and only with much resistance, been forced to realize that this approach simply has not had much bite or relevance for the actual contexts of doctors' clinical practices and interventions into the lives of real patients struggling to restore or maintain themselves in the face of painful, highly emotional, and wholly individual decisions within their own respective moral and social frameworks.

Here again, though in somewhat different ways, sensitivity to conversational usages and interchanges between doctors and patients assumes major importance for understanding which issues (moral, social, medical, and others) are actually at stake for the various participants in each clinical situation. In short, what has become suggested is a *project of work* focused on ethics (and other issues) presented within these specific clinical encounters. That project is given its impetus and direction by a governing question: What do we have to know and do if we wish to be truly responsive to the moral and other issues occasioned by and presented within the actual clinical encounters between doctors and patients?

Expressed a bit differently, the issue concerns whether or not there is a proper place for philosophers (or their like) in the clinical situations involving doctors (and other health professionals) and patients and their families. In still different terms, the question is whether or not the increasingly voiced idea of a "clinical ethics" is at all sensible and possible and, if so, what it actually involves, what its inherent requirements are, and what if anything justifies it. This, it seems to me, is a project of work at the cutting edge of the medical humanities (including so-called biomedical ethics). It is in any event what this book explores, even if only in a preliminary way.

TOPICAL ORDER OF THE STUDY

To think about the requirements inherent in that project is to find oneself faced with an immensely complex field surrounding the central phenomenon, the clinical encounter of doctor and patient, or what is called the therapeutic dyad. After a brief overview of some typical responses to medicine's challenge to ethics, certain of these demands become clearer, and the need for a different approach is suggested (Chapter 1). It is also evident that if a clinical ethics is to make sense we must gain a much finer understanding of clinical medicine itself (including its complex social arrangements) (Chapter 2), as well as the many levels of patient life and the human meaning of illness (Chapter 3).

Cautious probing of these regions of the dyad makes it apparent, however, that there are several peculiarities that need special attention. On the one hand, medicine has incorporated a view of the human person in ordinary life (whether as ill or healthy) that subtly but definitely textures and influences even routine medical encounters with patients. The talk between physicians and patients is shaped by a historically inculcated viewpoint that tends to distort and even to preclude much of what a patient in fact says or intends to say. On the other hand, closely tied to that, modern medicine has incorporated a historical understanding of the human body that is at once internally questionable and at odds with the ordinary person's actual experiences; yet this understanding has become remarkably authoritative for how people are encouraged to conceive of their own bodies (and the relationships between these persons and their own bodies).

So integral to modern medicine are these anomalies, it seems to me, that they call for careful historical study, especially as regards the intriguing themes within the so-called Cartesian dualism (Chapter 4). These themes in turn suggest other fascinating and important topics in the earlier history of medicine (Chapter 5), especially as regards human anatomy and dissection (Chapter 6). As the analysis proceeds through these themes, it seems necessary to probe still further, in particular to gain firmer purchase on issues in ancient medicine that turn out to be formative for the subsequent history of medicine and its deeply imbedded self-understanding: the ancient disputes among the dogmatics (rationalists), empiricists, and methodists (skeptics), in both classical Greek and Hellenistic times (Chapter 7).

These inquiries shed important light on medicine as a moral enterprise (a phrase often repeated in our times by physicians and others). This was understood to be the case even in the critical inaugural stages of medical history, with the Hippocratics. However, this has not been generally appreciated, and determining the exact sense of ancient medical theories requires considerable caution (Chapter 8).

It may be that not all my historical reflection is essential to the problem that initiates this study. Perhaps I have allowed myself to become too enamored by this utterly fascinating history, even though I've merely scratched a few of its wonderful surfaces. Such enthusiasms (for instance, regarding Cartesian dualism or the "divided legacy" within ancient and later medical history) will, I hope, be indulged by my readers. I plead only that these themes are enchanting and, in the end, very suggestive for the many issues that so preoccupy us today.

However that may be, I am then led back to my original problem, what I have come to believe is indeed the cutting edge of the medical humanities. The project of work and the implications of what is called clinical ethics or ethics in the clinical encounter (as I prefer to say) lie at that cutting edge. To pose as serious a challenge as I can to that project, I develop a single case in considerable depth and detail, and suggest through this means that there does indeed seem to be a proper, legitimate, and necessary place for such an ethics (Chapter 9). That problematic is a tough one, especially for philosophers, and needs to be worked out in serious detail with attention to the important questions of method and aim (Chapter 10).

Having gone this far, I then found it unavoidable to suggest a moral foundation for clinical medicine and its accompanying ethics (Chapter 11). While this attempt is undertaken seriously, although with trepidation, I must note here that its results, initial and tentative as they must be, leave much to be done.

This is one person's attempt to make sense of the systematic and historical bases of the phenomenon of medicine in our times and thereby to begin laying a foundation for understanding and contending with the many difficult moral issues within its practices, technologies, and therapies. The project of a clinical ethics seems to me imperative. Learning how to be as responsive as possible to these issues within their clinical situations is demanding and complex yet also rewarding. It is also, I believe, imperative that our responses to these issues be at all times *responsible*: responsive to the people and their situations, and responsible for what we say to and about them and their specific problems. There is at the heart of the idea of a clinically informed ethics a compelling demand for full *accountability*, without which we serve neither patients, doctors, nor ourselves.

ACKNOWLEDGMENTS

I am indebted to many good people who gave gladly of their time and insights. While they are in no way responsible for what is finally said here, I warmly acknowledge each of them.

A. Gene Copello, one of the first students in the program, suffered through a good many of my early efforts to work out the project. My colleague for the past two years, he was my cohort in bringing the project's vision to fruition through our Center for Clinical and Research Ethics (C-CARE) and, after our appointments as clinical ethicists, our consultation Service for Vanderbilt University Hospitals and Clinics. With his unusual curricular talents, he more than anyone was responsible for the articulation of the project into an actual program, our Clinical Ethics Training Program. He read the study in its early versions, contributed important suggestions (especially to the methodology sections), and was courageous (or, perhaps, foolish) enough to use portions of the study in his teaching and clinical work, thanks to which central parts of the basic conception were given serious and ongoing tests.

Eric Cassell, whose own writings were crucial to my understanding of clinical medicine, contributed directly to the study by reading it in several versions, discussing it with me on several occasions, and making very sound suggestions during the rewriting. Eric has been steadfast in his encouragement and sensitive in his criticisms. I am delighted and honored that he agreed to write the Foreword.

Paul Dokecki, Professor of Psychology and of Special Education in Vanderbilt's Peabody College (and Co-director of its deservedly well-known Kennedy Center), proved to be invaluable, especially as I was struggling (as philosophers must struggle) to get a handle on the demands of empirical research into moral issues (so integral, I have had to realize, to the work of a clinical ethics). Our many discussions, and his helpful comments after reading the text, were always on target and at times crucial in the development of my thinking.

I also acknowledge the encouragement and suggestions from Robert Romanyshyn and Calvin Schrag, both of whom read the manuscript in an earlier version. In addition, discussions with my adjunct colleague, Robert H. Crumby, concerned with developing an "outreach" consultation program for outlying hospitals, have been important by giving this project a second perspective—health care in community settings—from which it has greatly profited.

Many students contributed to shaping the project, and I warmly acknowledge them here, especially those who were so supportive of the project early on: Ann VanDervoort, Marian "Shug" Yagel, Shelton Smith, and, in particular, Harriet Able. Two other students more recently involved should also be recognized: Janet Vice and Donna Patterson. Each of them, and many others, are gratefully acknowledged for their patience, encouragement, and belief in the project.

I am grateful, too, for the chance to express my deep appreciation to the many physicians, nurses, health professionals, and administrators at Vanderbilt University Medical Center for their willingness to suffer my presence, to be responsive to my desire to be seriously involved within the remarkably rich tapestry of clinical and research medicine for which this institution is deservedly known. The list is a long one. Many have been very supportive from the day I first arrived in 1981, and well over 50 of them have agreed to serve as Clinical Associates of C-CARE's programs, working at times in considerable detail with me, my colleagues, and our students. Several contributed to this study in direct ways and deserve special mention: Mildred Stahlman, Robert Cotton, John Flexner, Bruce Sinclair-Smith, Virgil LeQuire, Frank Boehm, Dinesh Shah, Jayant Shenai, Richard Stein, Ann Wentz, A. Everette James, Stephen Entman, Tom Hazinski,

William Hartmann, and Fred Gorstein. These individuals were strongly supportive of my efforts and were always open to serious conversation about their work and mine. They helped in many significant ways to convince me that this project was both worthwhile and possible.

For the sabbatical leave which allowed me to complete the writing of the project, I am grateful especially to John E. Chapman, Dean of the School of Medicine. Dr. Chapman has been uncommonly understanding and appreciative of my work and the evolving program in ethics. Through his efforts, and those of Grant Liddle, who was Chairman of the Department of Medicine when I first arrived, many doors were opened and numerous difficulties I faced as a veritable alien in this world were eased. My gratitude goes also to John A. Oates, present chairman of my department, and Roscoe R. Robinson, Vice-chancellor for Health Affairs, for their continuing encouragement and support.

The list of people who have in various ways enabled me to complete this study and develop the programs at Vanderbilt is long and impressive. One remains to be mentioned, my wife, Junanne. I mention her not simply because she, in word and deed, has endured my complicated and too often consuming preoccupations; nor simply because she has had to live through the many dark times of depressive doubt which accompanied those preoccupations; but more because she has been throughout a source of insight and strength, a person and artist of remarkable dimensions.

R. M. Z.

CHAPTER 1

Medicine's Challenge to Ethics

To run into a philosopher in a hospital or other health-care setting is often the occasion for a question. The question, although perhaps obvious, may be felt as too embarrassing to ask aloud: What, exactly, is a philosopher doing here? If you happen to be that philosopher, the question is disconcerting and sharply edged. Not only is it frequently on the minds of health professionals, patients, and the families of patients, it is also an issue for the philosopher's daily life and work in health-care settings. Working in a health-care setting is hardly traditional or natural for philosophers.

THE INITIAL IDEA

To understand what has come to be called biomedical ethics, it is helpful to know what prompted physicians, over twenty years ago, to call on philosophers for help. It seemed, to physicians at least, fairly straightforward: Considerable help from persons trained in ethics was seen as critical. Historically, their presence in medicine was prompted mainly by physician-educators who found themselves facing severe conceptual and moral dilemmas, conflicts, and enigmas occasioned by the remarkable developments in medical knowledge and technology.

With the new technologies and knowledge already at hand in the late 1950s and early 1960s, and even more prospects on the immediate horizon (see Taylor, 1968), physicians had good reason to be troubled. New diagnostic tools and techniques promised more accurate and earlier detection of both present and possible damage. Also emerging were new surgical practices, pharmacological interventions (Farber and Wilson, 1961), anesthesias, and other treatments for conditions not previously treatable (or, at least, not as effectively). Resuscitative techniques and more refined biological and biomedical knowledge showed that different physiological systems functioned and ceased to function in different ways, rates, and stages, and that some of these systems (pulmonary, cardiac, renal, and others) could be artificially supported.

These innovations raised awesome, wholly new issues and gave a new force and content to many perennial problems. For instance, with the development of the pill, which permitted the separation and control of sexual functions as regards their recreational and procreational aspects, society for the first time had to reckon with brand-new issues impacting family life and planning, rearing and educating of children, and even such exotic new issues as whether certain classes of persons should be allowed to procreate or whether the yet unborn have effective rights comparable to actual persons. On the other hand, many perennial issues acquired new significance. With effective psychopharmacological substances (mind expanders, mood depressants), for instance, the ancient dispute over whether people are basically free or determined took on wholly new directions (see Gorovitz et al., 1976).

Not only was it increasingly possible to maintain patients who only a few years before would have died, often very painfully, but the horizons of life's beginnings (the double helix of DNA, genetic research) and ceasings (mechanical ventilators, brain functioning) were becoming better understood (Burnet, 1978; Eccles, 1970, 1979; Penfield, 1975). When life begins and when death occurs seemed to become matters for definition or redefinition, but not without problems, however. Perceptive physicians and researchers agonized over the value and moral issues inherent to these developments. For example, with five patients and only one dialysis machine, who should receive treatment? When is a person dead, so that organs can be harvested for transplantation to save another's life?

Many physicians and scientists continued to be haunted by the horrors of the Nazi concentration camps. After the Nuremberg Trials and ratification of the United Nations Charter, they were anxious to reaffirm the existence of inalienable human rights, especially in connection with the medical sciences and the need for experimentation with human subjects. However, recognizing their lack of training in handling such issues, physicians and researchers quite naturally turned to others whose credentials seemed to bespeak competence in this area.

To be sure, already in the 1940s and 1950s, the physician Otto Guttentag was urging greater appreciation by physicians of the moral issues intrinsic to medicine and biomedicine (see Guttentag, 1968). Earlier, and well before Paul Ramsey made the phrase common (Ramsey, 1970), Francis Peabody was moved to deliberate on the need for physicians to "treat their patients as persons" (Peabody, 1927). During the late 1950s, the president of the University of Texas Medical Branch at Galveston, Chauncy Leake (himself the author of several books concerned with "what we are living for" [see Leake, 1976]), brought in the philosopher Patrick Romanell to teach, participate in clinical settings, and advise on moral and other issues (Romanell, 1956, 1972, 1974).

In the early 1960s, under the leadership of Samuel Banks (a psychologist and theologian), Al Vastyan (a hospital chaplain who had worked with Chauncy Leake and Patrick Romanell), and Edmund D. Pellegrino (a physician and educator), the first formal but still tentative courses and programs on human values appeared, and the initial meetings of what came to be the Society for Health and Human Values (SHHV) were held. By the early 1970s it appeared that the trappings of a veritable movement were at hand. By 1981 an SHHV survey of 125 medical schools in the United States (122 responding)) disclosed that 114 of the schools were actively engaged in some form of human values teaching (Pellegrino and McElhiney, 1981; Pellegrino et al., 1985).

Along with that movement, of course, came the not unexpected growth of literature, journals, societies, conferences, training programs and centers, and the other accoutrements of recognized academic fields. A study of this whole development would be quite interesting, but this is not the place to undertake that. The lingo of the times, in any event, is suggestive. The bureaucratic organization of the modern health science centers and hospitals, with their increasingly sophisticated technologies, was regularly regarded as being "dehumanizing" to people. The specialization in medicine after World War II seemed inevitably to fragment "the whole person," prompting more focus on "diseases" and "organ systems" than on "persons." Staying abreast of the new developments often meant that while physicians were obliged to be and to remain technically competent, they rarely had the time or inclination to be alert to moral issues, religious values, or social concerns (see Cassell, 1973; Pellegrino, 1970, 1979b).

The "new physician" being discussed as the agenda for the 1970s and beyond, it was thought, needed to be "humanized," as the physician Samuel P. Martin expressed it when he spoke at the first meeting of the Institute for Human Values in Medicine (of SHHV) in 1972. The complex, specialized social organization of health care and the dramatically new developments in medical and biomedical technology made it necessary to ask, "How can we humanize the present-day physician so he can be prepared to approach the problem" created by the ever-widening gap between physician and patient? Physicians' attention had become too focused on diseases and organs, diagnostic capabilities, and treatment protocols, and too little on the persons receiving them. Thus, Martin continued, a second question became necessary: "How can we humanize the physician who is now in training and who will be in practice" in the near future? Inevitably, this raised a third question, "How can we humanize the teachers so as to affect students who will be physicians of the future?" These issues were dependent on a fourth, more difficult question concerned with the "humanist," the one "who must help us all." Too many of the "humanists," Martin thought, were "trying to outscience our scientists," and thus it had become critical to understand just what the humanities are all about, and especially how most effectively to transmit their art (Martin, 1972).

These "humanists" were thought to be "experts in human values," not unlike, say, a physician who is an expert in pulmonary diseases. A new name was concocted for this breed: "ethicist," an occupation as unlikely as the name is awkward to pronounce. Such ethicists had to be persuaded to help, for the pressing moral issues and the mounting public pressures had already begun to make the physician's situation quite difficult—and the increasing threats of malpractice, to say the least, gave a decidedly painful edge to clinical practice.

Philosophers have responded several ways both to the issues and to the appeal from physicians. Since their responses set the context of discussion for the next few years (roughly, since the early 1970s), it will be helpful to examine them in some depth.

THE PHILOSOPHER'S RESPONSE

At first, in the 1960s, only a few, rather venturesome philosophers responded; in the early 1970s, a few more. Most of them found the world of clinical medicine bewildering and puzzling, yet compelling. The existential cut of Martin's jibe about what makes a "humanist" was a keenly felt, daily reality. Separated from a comfortable home base (a philosophy department in a college or university), philosophers were utter *naifs* in this new milieu, literal aliens listening in on a recondite babel of technical lingos and observing wholly unfamiliar actions, equipment, and contexts. When in deference to our lack of understanding of technical, often acronymic, conversation, some of it was translated ("What does PTA mean?" "Oh, that's prior to admission!"), our initial embarrassment was later overcome by the awesome meaning of other terms ("PDA?" "Yes, patent ductus arteriosis, which if untreated means certain death for this baby!").

At times, we were encouraged to talk or offer an opinion about a case—for instance, about whether a child born with developing hydrocephalus secondary to myelomeningocele should be operated on. We then found ourselves babbling in an equally alien tongue, about persons and potential persons who could in all likelihood never become persons, but yet who should not only be treated as persons but accorded all the rights and privileges of actual, real-life persons.

At these times, many of us felt acutely out of place and recoiled in shock and dismay. Our reaction often was that *this* is simply no place for a philosopher, whose training and disposition include nothing that could prepare one for rendering judgments, much less definitive, possibly irreversible, moral decisions. Even if one could begin to untangle some of the moral issues implicit to such cases, one had neither the time to do so properly nor the appropriately prepared audience to hear the discourse or participate in a philosophical discussion designed to clarify issues.

Nor did gradual familiarity with clinical settings, specific cases and patients, technical jargon, and exotic technologies help to ease the sharp sense many felt that the philosopher remains an interloper, a *theorist* in the land of *therapists*—an opinion shared by a great many physicians (see Fleischman, 1981b). The philosopher's stock-in-trade is principles, concepts, and theories—not therapy or guidance counseling. The philosopher is concerned with foundations, arguments, and logic, not with, as often seemed the real agenda for physicians, sensitizing health professionals to values, ethics, and morals.

Despite that, some physicians continued to call for a far greater, deeper involvement by philosophers. One pediatrician, Tomas Silber, lamented "the absence of these professionals from our daily lives" in neonatal intensive care units (NICUs) and pediatric wards (Silber, 1981). He and others believed that ethicists could be of real help to physicians, but to do so they must make the effort to understand the meanings of medical diagnosis, therapeutic protocols, prognoses, and the rest of the basic medical armamentarium of methods, concepts, and procedures. Otherwise, ethicists may quite literally not know whereof they speak and write—for instance on abortion, on euthanasia, or on the many problems presented by an infant with multiple congenital anomalies. Ethicists "who have never been in an intensive-care nursery" inevitably "lose an important dimension" for dealing with the ethical problems encountered in the daily, routine practices within such a unit, in the hospital, and elsewhere in medicine. For their part, Silber concluded, physicians, pressured by training and an increasingly secular culture into being "only scientists," must undertake the adventure of learning philosophy and theology (ibid.).

Silber's conclusion echoed the appeals made earlier by Pellegrino, Cassell, Martin, and other physicians. But philosophers were quick to point out in return that the difficulties in being responsive to these appeals could be insurmountable. After all, medicine and philosophy, arguably among the most complex and demanding of human enterprises, are fundamentally different. Consider simply the central place of clinical work in medicine. No form of clinical experience or knowledge is native to the training or disposition of philosophers; nor would most philosophers be inclined to say that it should be. Furthermore, while the physician's relationship to patients is basically therapeutic, that between the philosopher and students or auditors is not, at least not in the same sense. For instance, a patient's well-being, health, and mental stability depend directly on the actions, words, and work of the physician; the philosopher's relationship to students is certainly not as immediately critical.

Indeed, most philosophers would probably agree with Fleischman's view, and not with Silber's or Pellegrino's. If anything, Fleischman reflects the accepted, received view of philosophy's proper role. While philosophers certainly think about the great moral questions and while many of them would agree with Aristotle's claim that ethics is a practical discipline, the work of philosophy is theoretical and does not include the attempt to solve the specific, practical questions raised by specific cases. The philosopher can only provide clarification of issues and assumptions, analyze arguments, trace out and assess the various concepts employed by physicians, and help to sort out the differences between medical and evaluative factors. It was widely thought that the fascinating and demanding social and moral problems presented by medicine could only be properly addressed in philosophy's usual ways.

Thus, medicine became viewed as merely one of several fields (engineering, nursing, social work, and business were others) to which ethical principles, analysis, and argument could be "applied." Biomedical ethics came to be conceived as one of several "applied ethics" fields.

APPLIED ETHICS

Alan R. Fleischman's report on a medical ethics teaching component in a pediatric residency program in several New York City hospitals provides a good example of what the typical "applied ethicist" does in a clinical setting (see Fleischman, 1981b).

After a case that is "interesting" to the resident is presented, in nontechnical language (with a history, diagnoses, tests, alternative therapies), the social worker will often be asked to fill in pertinent social data about the family. The resident, after formulating the ethical issue he or she believes needs response, calls on the ethicist for comments and questions. Seeking to help the medical and nursing staffs clarify the ethical bases for their respective opinions about alternatives in the case, the ethicist will try to help them understand the ethical principles upon which their various opinions are or might be based and possibly justified. The ethicist thus seeks to clarify the principles underlying proposed actions and the ways of justifying the actions. The physicians, on the other hand, must actually decide the course of action (although, at times, and for certain kinds of issues, patients or their families will be asked to participate).

The program is reported to have been a success in every way. Residents consistently felt that they had learned a great deal about their own moral positions, that they were better able to use their now clarified moral views, and that this kind of program was an important exercise that should be replicated elsewhere. The ethicist was said to have been most helpful, and his presence was reported to have constituted no threat to the physician's role in decision making.

The program, designed expressly as an educational activity having no bearing on actual patient care and decisions, convinced physicians that "medicine is an inherently moral enterprise" (Fleischman, 1981b)—a judgment that had already been made much earlier by Eric Cassell (1973), to whom I shall return at a later point.

The reported success serves only to make the oddity more pronounced. The residents apparently learned that "their decisions were based on ethical principles," yet they reported that they "felt that the neonatal ethics rounds did not specifically affect medical care." Some of the "most frequently presented issues involved the rights of the fetus and of the newborn" and the "right to decide" by the parents, yet these same issues and the principles applied to them were just as frequently "found to have little relevance in actually determining what was the right decision." Finally, the residents stated that "they did increase their understanding of ethical principles and the process of ethical analysis," yet they also stated that "they felt that their general moral and ethical views had not been changed" as a result of the program (Fleischman, 1981b).

Very significant things were learned. It is, after all, no small thing to have learned not merely that one's decisions are actually based on certain ethical principles (something not known beforehand) and to learn a good deal about the rights of fetuses, infants, and parents (again, not known beforehand), but also to understand ethical principles and how to conduct ethical analysis! Yet, apparently at no point did any of this significant learning influence actual decisions nor in any important way alter any moral or ethical viewpoint. This is odd, as is the fact that the discrepancy received no comment in the report. While the "process of ethical analysis" was designed to have no effect on medical decision making, it is in a sense understandable that it was subsequently found to have so little "relevance" to it. Yet, when "value conflicts" arose, as they did quite often, these were supposedly handled by that very same "process of ethical analysis"! This is surely not trivial, especially in view of the important claim that "medicine is an inherently moral enterprise."

It seems quite clear that this "process" could hardly lead to very much in the way of "value conflict resolution." Simply to help people see how their respective opinions are based on one or another ethical principle leaves quite untouched the problem generated by a conflict of opinions or principles. The residents may well have been left in an unsuspected, but very acute, moral dilemma: appreciating that conflicting values and principles were at hand, but having no way to resolve them.

Thus, while reporting "success," it seems that the work of medical ethics was, in Alasdair MacIntyre's words, "relatively fruitless" and "often frustrating":

> It is, I believe, a common experience for doctors, nurses, and others to become very excited when discussion of these problems is first opened up and past silences are broken. There follows a short period of increasing clarity during which disagreements and divisions are formulated. And then nothing or almost nothing. Where everyone had hoped to move towards a constructive resolution of these disagreements, instead they find themselves merely restating them. (MacIntyre, 1977, p. 197.)

It is interesting to view this program from the side of the philosophers who designed and worked within it. Reading the report (Ruddick, 1981), it quickly becomes clear that a part of the problem was impatience: No one, philosophers least of all, can be reasonably expected to have ready-to-hand answers to immensely complicated medical issues or their inevitable social and moral dimensions. On the other hand, no one should expect to be able to learn ethics, or even to become more sensitive to the subtle and complex moral dimensions of medical situations, in contexts such as working or teaching rounds in a hospital. It takes time, concentrated devotion, and hard intellectual labor to achieve either moral sensitivity to or expert knowledge of ethical phenomena.

Just as clearly, however, the problem cannot be laid simply at the feet of impatient physicians, nor even at the feet of philosophers frustrated by the peculiar, unfamiliar demands of clinical work and the constraints inherent to life in medical institutions. "Perhaps," William Ruddick advised after having directed this project, "philosophers are well advised to limit their role as classroom or clinic casuists" (ibid., p. 17). If they become concerned for actual cases, whether in the classroom or in the NICU, and especially if they attempt to influence the management of cases within the hospital, "philosophers can lose the critical distance they have assumed since Socrates drew off from the Sophists," and will then cease to view issues "*sub specie aeternitatis*" (ibid.).

Ruddick also worries that philosophers involved in the routines of clinical practice "will be absorbed into the medical center ethos and become collaborators in a flawed system" (ibid.). Stereotyping, of course, exaggerates the differences and distances between medicine and philosophy. Even so, "the worlds of hospital medicine and academic philosophy are too far apart for a commuter shuttle service," or any other attempted compromise—for what threatens to get compromised is the discipline of philosophy itself. Despite their efforts to work alongside physicians—serving on hospital committees, team teaching with clinicians and lawyers, and helping to clarify unusually "hard cases"—the philosophers involved in this program eventually came to the gloomy conclusion that

> like midwives, philosophers may be dismissed by physicians as amateurish invaders of well-governed territory. Professionals resent those who do not accept the technical routines by which professional practice is defined and justified. And institutions resist those who do not easily fit into the hierarchical routines by which daily life is ordered. (Ibid.)

On the other hand, if philosophers are not alongside physicians, medical routines may tend to become "self-serving rather than client-serving." Yet, if philosophers do participate, they risk being co-opted by the medical ethos—not only giving in to a "flawed system" but also becoming alienated from their own colleagues and departments. These are powerful temptations, and if subtly seduced the philosopher may well wind up merely indulging himself in "casuistry without theory"—as superficial in its way as dermatology without physiology. If not co-opted, the philosopher runs the risk of becoming schizophrenic—split between the familiar things of "home" and the strangeness of medicine. What is at stake is losing professional credibility in both fields.

The Philosophers in Medical Centers Project (1976–80), then, is both a poignant lament and an expression of remarkable optimism. For, despite all these risks and threats to the integrity of philosophy itself, Ruddick concludes that "physicians, we immodestly claim, need philosophers to enable them to remain therapists, despite professional and institutional pressures to become functionaries" (ibid.). The claim, however, does not seem matched by the reality, for no satisfactory ways of resolving these painful tensions and dilemmas were found, but on the other hand they seem endemic to such a project. Philosophers are, in the end, theorists and not therapists, and therefore must ultimately remain aliens in those domains.

THE BACKLASH AGAINST ETHICS

That response, in general, for all the disputes and problems it both encountered and generated, has certain key characteristics. The challenge was accepted as presenting a set of moral issues seen as quite typical for philosophy. Moral philosophers are already in possession of a number of theories (with their various principles, concepts, rules, and methods) that can be applied to the practical issues occasioned by medicine. In principle, these practical issues are no different from those raised in other spheres of practical life. And, the various theories (principles, concepts, rules, and methods) that are to be applied are no different from those characteristic of philosophy more generally.

Thus, for these philosophers, biomedical ethics is not a special kind of ethics; it does not include some special set of moral principles or methods specific to the field of medicine. Ethics is ethics, whatever its particular applications. The practical field of medicine—its various "facts"—are morally neutral, and the clinician's conduct is governed by the same normative principles and rules as those in other spheres of human life. There are no norms specific to medicine (see Caplan, 1982, pp. 158–62).

By the mid-1970s, in large part because of the recognition of this, a good many physicians were coming to the conclusion that, as Franz Ingelfinger, the distinguished former editor of *The New England Journal of Medicine*, expressed it in an editorial (1975, p. 44), "the intrusion of Big Ethics into medical research and practice" was unfortunate. In 1975, Daniel Callahan also noted this "ethics backlash" and identified four factors in this unhappy development. First, many physicians suspected that biomedical ethics was actually a disguised form of anti-technological, even anti-scientific, feeling. Second, they felt that it was really an attack on the personal morality of physicians and scientists. Third, bioethicists seemed concerned more about harms to individuals than about the public good. Finally, there was "a sense that much of what is labelled 'ethics' represents a casual and irresponsible mischief-making, led by people with little understanding of research or practice" (Callahan, 1975, p 18).

In direct response to this backlash within medicine against the "intrusion of Big Ethics," a major conference on medical ethics was held in 1975. One of the principal speakers, Richard M. Hare, put the challenge directly at the beginning of his address:

> I should like to say at once that if the moral philosopher *cannot* help with the problems of medical ethics, he ought to shut up shop. The problems of medical ethics are so typical of the moral problems that moral philosophy is supposed to be able to help with, that a failure here would be a sign either of the uselessness of the discipline or of the incompetence of the particular practitioner. (Hare, 1977, p. 49.)

Philosophers cannot be supposed to possess magical elixirs for solving complex moral problems, for physicians or for patients. The reason for this is to be found in the very different relationships between the philosopher and someone having a difficult ethical problem and between the physician and the patient (ibid., p. 50). Whereas a patient suffering from heart ailment can be treated by a physician, for a person with a moral dilemma ethics or "philosophy itself is the medicine, and it has to be understood, to some degree at any rate, by the patient himself, in a way that medical science does not" (ibid.).

The main, and possibly the only, contribution philosophers can make to the solution of biomedical ethics problems concerns the meaning and logical properties of the many key terms used in moral discourse—"right," "wrong," "good," "bad"—as well as such notions as "persons," "justified killing," "confidentiality," and "consent."

> Philosophy is a training in the study of such tricky words and their logical properties, in order to establish canons of valid argument or reasoning, and so enable people who have mastered it to avoid errors in reasoning (confusions or fallacies), and so answer their moral questions with their eyes open. It is my belief that, once the issues are thoroughly clarified in this way, the problems will not seem so perplexing as they did at first and, the philosophical difficulties having been removed, we can get on with discussing the practical difficulties. (Ibid., p. 52.)

Being able to avoid the verdant underbrush of confusions, ambiguities, and fallacies so characteristic of everyday life and much technical language, physicians will be in a far better position to understand their own moral views and issues, to assess their implications, and in general to act in an informed and competent manner.

Consistent with this, Tom Beauchamp argues that philosophers have much to contribute. First, they can perform "conceptual analysis," through which needlessly tangled disputes can be clarified, many of whose concepts "cry out for philosophical analysis" (Beauchamp, 1982, p. 14). Second, philosophers can expose the inadequacies and unexpected consequences of arguments about abortion, euthanasia, and other controversial issues in medicine. Third, with scholars and researchers in other fields, they can help provide a better basis for policy development and evaluation and work toward important institutional reforms. Then, by participating in institutional and policy decision making, philosophers "can assist in various ways with policy decisions" (ibid.). Although there are no guarantees that conflicts can be finally resolved, there are a number of "strategies" that are useful in clarifying options and assumptions (Beauchamp and Walters, 1982, pp. 6–7).

THE BACKLASH CONTINUES

Many of the concerns expressed by physicians and researchers seem to have been redressed. Even so, there has been concern that the philosopher's response makes it appear that medical ethics is a kind of new "profession," with its own "ethics experts" (Beauchamp, 1982, p. 12). Cheryl Noble argues against such claims, for they seem to imply that "moral error is in significant degree produced by logical and conceptual obtuseness" and even that "the claim to expertise is a claim to the possession of a neutral skill in evaluative reasoning" (Noble, 1982, p. 15). It is this claim of neutrality that seems troublesome, for it hardly seems reasonable to suppose that philosophers can so readily strip themselves of moral commitments.

Physicians and researchers have if anything become more sharply critical and skeptical. First, Robert S. Morison recently lamented, while it is true that "biomedical ethics has shown the academy that interdisciplinary scholarship really is possible" and may be its greatest achievement to date, recent developments work against precisely that. Prominent among these is "the growing tendency to professionalize the field," with the result that it is less and less "the product of interdisciplinary discussion" (Morison, 1981, p. 9). Clearly concerned about what Noble later criticized, Morison suggests that the tendency is even more strongly present today than it was in the previous decade. That is why "some of us worry that medical ethics has recently recruited far more representatives from academic ethics than from the profession of medicine" (ibid., p. 12).

Furthermore, too many people in the now well-established field of biomedical ethics have too little knowledge of, and respect and preparation for, actual clinical work. Physicians worry deeply about the prospect of academic, theoretical interests displacing such practical clinical experience.

A primary reason for that concern forms the third direction of recent criticism. While it may be that philosophers are interested in establishing ethical principles, and as Noble said, "pride themselves" on their commitment to various theoretical positions (while presuming their "neutrality" on issues of "skills"), the fact is that there is not one but a heterogeneity of rival positions and principles. Singer and others (1982, pp.11–14) believe that it does not really matter which "point of view" a philosopher adopts. However, it matters very much to the clinical practitioner, who faces a wholly different problem: Which, among the competing principles, is the one that *ought* to be applied in a particular case? As Morison says, "Perhaps the most serious difficulty with the general principles underlying such matters as abortion, euthanasia, suicide, or genetic engineering is the lack of general agreement about them" (ibid., p. 12).

But there is an equally difficult issue the physician has to confront. Many of the issues with which clinicians must contend in their routine practices are not addressed by philosophical disputes (Siegler, 1979, pp. 914–15). No amount of linguistic or logical clarification of key terms or of the canons of valid argument can provide the clinician, or the patient, with the kind of moral assistance needed to make decisions about cases such as these.

Even if it were possible, unlikely as it may seem, to settle the vexing question about the nature of "person" or "human being," it must still be clinically determined whether or not a specific infant or a specific comatose old man is a case in point. Since there is a plurality of views about "persons," the clinician faces the awesome question of trying to figure out which view is the one to apply in each specific case—or else, trying to figure out who should decide that issue. Decisions about presumable "persons" (or "nonpersons") *are* made anyway: To decide to "let nature take its course" (which some may erroneously think is a way not to decide), is quite obviously a decision, with consequences for all those affected by it.

"CLINICAL" VERSUS "BIOMEDICAL" ETHICS

Many physicians and researchers, then, have been more inclined to reject the idea that medicine needs "help." Picking up on this, Mark Siegler argues that the major problem with that response is that it has involved non-physicians almost exclusively. He agrees with Eric Cassell (1973, p. 53) that medicine "is inherently moral," but contends that only the physician is in a position to understand and address the moral issues within medical practice and research (Siegler, 1979, pp. 914–15). The physician alone has actual experience in and appreciation of the nature, demands, and responsibilities of clinical work. Hence, the proper response to the many dilemmas and conflicts mentioned is for physicians to become seriously trained in ethics.

Those in what Siegler terms "the establishment of BME [biomedical ethics]" have interests that are "quite different from those of the medical-scientific community" (ibid., p. 914). Frequently anti-scientific and anti-medicine, they have rarely been concerned with the issues of routine clinical practice. They have, in fact, "actually expressed their disdain for traditional, Hippocratic, bedside medical ethics, which, since Hippocratic times, have been overwhelmingly physician-and-patient-oriented" (ibid.).

Siegler finds nothing wrong with philosophers discussing the ethics of medical situations, but, he insists, they can be merely *observers*. The physician, to the contrary, "is never a mere observer" and can never rely on the "counterfeit courage" of the noncombatant, as must the BME theoretician (ibid., p. 915). While the philosopher knows theories, principles, concepts, and rules in ethics, the physician is the one who must apply them. It is the physician who is on the firing line, who is accountable to, and held accountable for, patients. Without that clinical experience and accountability, the philosopher can have no idea, in Kierkegaard's parable, "of the change that takes place in the knower when he has to apply his knowledge" (Kierkegaard, 1978, p. 38).

Siegler has given expression to a prominent feeling among physicians: clinical ethics must be clearly distinguished from biomedical ethics; that is, there must be an awareness of what physicians must do and what philosophers can offer. He does not, he says, wish to appear "reactionary." He is not suggesting "that the judgment of medical professionals is correct merely because of their medical expertise" (Siegler, 1979, p. 915). So far as BME is concerned, Siegler merely wants to "infuse a higher degree of contact with clinical reality into the debate that has characterized BME in the past" (ibid.). In the end, it is his sense that much of the BME emphasis on ethics is an exaggeration and a misrepresentation of medicine. All things considered, indeed, the very term, " 'clinical ethics' is redundant, because good clinical medicine is necessarily ethical medicine" (ibid.).

A CLINICAL EXAMPLE

It is easy to admit that the field of medicine is quite different from other fields. However, the response to moral quandaries from physicians such as Siegler, Morison, and Fleischman has its problems as well. It in fact adopts the very same view of the nature of ethics as the philosophers criticized, with this difference: Physicians have to do the work of applying moral principles (albeit with some help from philosophers). Consider one clinical example, from the book *Clinical Ethics* (Jonsen-Siegler-Winslade, 1982), expressly designed as an "in-the-pocket" guide to moral decision making within clinical situations.

> An elderly man is suffering from a chronic, lethal disease. He lapses into a coma at home and is brought into a hospital emergency room. Admitted for treatment of a urinary tract infection, he also presents with gram-negative septicemia, shock, and adult respiratory distress syndrome (ARDS). Therapy is instituted with fluids, antibiotics, and blood pressure agents. The attending physician, however, hesitated before intubating the man for placement on a respirator (ibid., p. 25).

The authors' discussion is intended to provide practical guidelines for clinical practitioners. Admittedly somewhat complex, the case nevertheless seems clear to them: The patient's recovery from sepsis and ARDS is "low to the vanishing point." Return to adequate lung function might be "remotely possible," but medical experience suggests that the man has entered the terminal phase of ARDS. His survival will in all likelihood not exceed several weeks, and he is unlikely to emerge from his coma. Prolonging his life will actually only prolong his dying. Therefore, the authors conclude, "it is ethically permissible not to intubate" (ibid., p. 27).

As they see the issues, it is the "principle of beneficence" that is applicable to this case—a principle "expressed in the history of medicine by the Hippocratic maxim: Be of benefit and do no harm" (ibid., p. 11). This principle or maxim does not require that useless or futile actions be performed if they would merely prolong dying.

CRITIQUE OF THE CASE

To make their "handbook" useful to clinicians, the authors deliberately try to inform the ethical discussions with medical details and seriously attempt to keep philosophical jargon to a minimum. Written by a theologian

(Jonsen), a philosopher-lawyer (Winslade), and a physician (Siegler), the discussions are importantly multidisciplinary (giving credibility to Morison's point mentioned earlier). Still, several matters have to be brought out, at the risk of appearing, unavoidably, I fear, uncharitable.

In the first place, for all the real force of the "backlash" and Siegler's own rather heavy remarks about "the BME establishment," what is offered here seems little different from what is found in BME. A "principle" is "selected" and then "applied" to the practical, clinical situation. The discussions are clearly sensitive to the many problems associated with non-physicians (Jonsen, Winslade) making, or appearing to make, decisions about patients. While rich in medical details, the "cases" are not actual ones, but constructed on the basis of actual cases. Furthermore, the authors emphasize, "it was in the application of our differing perspectives to each case that we grew confident enough to offer counsel" (ibid., p. x). Even then, of course, the "counsel" is only that not intubating is "ethically permissible," not that it is required or obligatory.

The difference between this case discussion and what might be expected of a bioethicist is only that the authors do "offer counsel," that is, actually apply a principle to a specific case. In all other respects, however, what is termed "clinical ethics" is the same as what is in other respects criticized as "biomedical ethics."

Other matters in their discussion call for comment. Nothing is mentioned about the wishes or needs of the patient's family or circle of intimates. After all, someone found him comatose, called the ambulance, and had him brought to the ER. To take beneficence as implying ethical permissiveness not to intubate, in the absence of discussions with the family or friends (possibly even foreclosing their wishes or decisions), is surely odd at best. Nor do the authors even suggest that the physicians in the case should try and contact the family or friends.

Furthermore, in such cases, no physician faces a series of clear givens. Rather, cases like this present numerous probables, along with some range of uncertainty and ambiguity. An appeal to beneficence, however, cannot of itself tell the physicians how to act when matters are not clear or certain—how to weigh the probables and possibles, the ambiguities and uncertainties, so as to reach an "ethically permissible" recommendation. Suppose, for instance, that even a brief recovery of alertness would provide the man with what he, at least, believes is a highly significant period in which he can "settle accounts." Would not beneficence in this case require intubation (i.e., just the opposite of what the authors recommend)? Or, suppose that his family believed that they needed additional time with the patient. Wouldn't beneficence then require physicians to try and give them that time?

The appeal to beneficence, in other words, could just as readily yield the *opposite* recommendation as that given by the authors, which suggests that, despite the medical details, much has been left out of consideration in this case (and others in the handbook)—details or "facts" that, it could turn out, are central to its moral assessment.

In general, there are two major flaws to this approach. First, the appeal to an apparent moral principle (beneficence) is not enough to permit the "counsel" (recommendation, decision) offered. More than one conclusion can follow from the principles and data given, and these conclusions can well be quite contradictory. The "counsel" could be disastrous. Second, it has to be asked just why and how beneficence is appealed to. The authors say that it was "selected," which implies that there were alternatives that were rejected. Does this make sense?

For that matter, when we think about the mainline philosophical response to these problems, the very same oddity arises. It is common knowledge that there are numerous moral points of view on the scene. This circumstance alone has to make things awkward at best: Given a pluralism of points of view, how does one know which one to apply to a particular case?

HETEROGENEITY OF MORAL VIEWS

In his wonderfully lucid study *After Virtue* (1981), Alasdair MacIntyre directly confronts the implications of the heterogeneity of moral beliefs, practices, and concepts. He suggests, first, that each of them can be shown to be internally consistent; conclusions follow logically from the respective basic premises accepted by each. Not only are there many such viewpoints, however, but each of them is a rival of every other point of view, contending for our adherence and making claims on our conducts. While Veatch's advocacy of a sort of Hobbesian "social contract" model of society is dubious (1981), it may nevertheless be true that our current social and moral milieu shows a kind of modern-day Leviathanism—a war of each (moral viewpoint) against all (other moral points of view), and of all against each. It often seems that to think morally is to think of war and rivalry, of ways of defending one's own viewpoint and of attacking the others.

It is in any case one of the more striking features of current moral discussion that it frequently takes the form of argument and dispute, defense and attack. As MacIntyre emphasizes, a striking feature of these debates is that they seem utterly unsettlable. They go on interminably and rarely if ever reach a point of mutual agreement or resolution. The disputes over right to life, Baby Doe, abortion, or definition of death are surely clear cases in point.

The reasons for these characteristics are not hard to find. In fact, MacIntyre maintains that there is a "conceptual incommensurability" among the various moral views. While each is or can be shown to be internally consistent, each is also at war, and incommensurable, with the others. Yet, each viewpoint assumes at least the guise of rationality and objectivity:

Each appeals to standards or norms of reasoning that are supposedly impartial and independent and that command the adherence of every rational moral agent precisely by virtue of that rationality. These rational standards or basic premises, however, are conceptually at odds with one another.

This makes clear another striking characteristic of contemporary moral life and discourse:

> The rival viewpoints are such that we possess no rational way of weighing the claims of one as against another. For each premise employs some quite different normative or evaluative concept from the others, so that the claims made upon us are of quite different kinds. (MacIntyre, 1981, p. 8.)

This is true of our common moral discourse and also at the level of ethical theory. Every theory makes the same sort of rival, incommensurable claims on us and provides rival ways for us to understand the key phenomena of moral life. Each defines a moral universe and prescribes an entire moral vocabulary for handling it: what it means to be a "moral agent" or "moral problem," as well as such key notions as "good," "evil," or "right." These terms, too, are conceptually incommensurable.

Upon close inspection, MacIntyre suggests, it becomes evident that each theory makes use of basic concepts that on the other hand have been stripped of their original historical contexts, within which they had their systematic placement and significance. Our current pluralism seems in fact little more than an "unharmonious melange of ill-assorted fragments," which appeal to concepts and norms without the rich, historical contexts that gave them force, significance, and moral persuasiveness (ibid., pp. 9–11).

Even if we suppose that each moral viewpoint has been well formulated, we merely discover that it is rivaled by other, also well-formulated viewpoints. At no point, however, do we discover any culturally acceptable or logically compelling ways by which to weigh and consider the rival claims made on us by each of them. Even more, the very fact of this heterogeneity serves to present us with an absurd issue: Does being a "moral" person require that one has to choose among the rivaling points of view? Are these views in fact alternatives?

Certainly, this seems to be the view underlying the case discussions in *Clinical Ethics*, as we saw. It is also Veatch's view, when he sets about to "invent" a basic moral universe by having presumably "reasonable" folks get together and "contract" with one another (Veatch, 1981, pp. 113–26). Is morality, as Singer intimates (1982, p. 11), a matter of "adopting" (i.e., choosing) one or another of the theories presented in a typical undergraduate or graduate college course in "ethics"?

MacIntyre makes it painfully clear that such questions are quite incoherent. Each rival viewpoint appeals to standards (principles or rules) that are supposed to be, or are posited as, impartial and thus independent of any individual moral agent. Yet, to present the matter as an issue of choosing among alternatives is to say that each moral agent would have to choose what shall be impartial, objective, and authoritative for himself. But the moral sphere is supposed to include principles that are in themselves already authoritative, independent of our own attitudes, preferences, choices, and feelings. If that were coherent, then of course nothing whatever prevents a person from arbitrarily and even whimsically deciding to reject that very same principle. In short, if moral heterogeneity is taken to imply choice among alternative principles, rationality and objectivity are simply lost.

MEDICINE'S DILEMMA

These matters should probably be brought down to earth. Suppose a physician is faced with the problem of whether to withdraw one or more life-supports from a patient, whether to withhold others that might or could be instituted, or whether not only to continue those already in place but also possibly to initiate still other measures should an acute episode occur. The physician, we can suppose, seeks to do the right thing for the patient—to be fair or act correctly on the patient's behalf. Different moral concepts and approaches will suggest different conducts for the physician, along with different concepts expressing what is "right" and "fair." What the patient's "best interests" are, clearly, will vary for each approach. To act in one way is not only to adopt a specific point of view on the issues, but it is also to reject other possible points of view and their respectively implied concepts, conducts, and claims. Since the very point here is the patient's best interests, how are these to be determined in the most rational, objective, morally appropriate, and correct way?

Here, MacIntyre's analysis is keenly felt. There simply is no culturally acceptable, logically compelling way to answer that question, no way to choose among conflicting viewpoints, even though the medical situation itself, along with the current structural modality that defines the requirements of decision making, requires that the attending physician (along with the patient and possibly the family) do precisely that—answer the question. To "let nature take its course," as was pointed out earlier, is to decide the question in a specific way, just as much as if one were to decide for some other alternative. If the attending physician does not directly answer the question, he or she is no less liable and accountable for the results than were a direct answer attempted. There is no way to avoid answering what on the other hand is an incoherent, absurd question!

Suppose further that, sensing that acute dilemma, the attending physician calls on an ethicist for help (see Purtillo, 1984). What is the ethicist supposed to do? The ethicist is not morally neutral, any more than is the patient or the physician. Thus, there seems no way to provide any clear-cut and coherent way of resolving what must perforce be resolved: What are the patient's best interests, and who is to decide that?

Are a patient's best interests, however, really a matter of choice? After all, to ask, Who is to decide? is already to recognize that the different people who might decide often hold quite different moral views. Thus, to decide that one of them should decide what the best interests are, is in fact to decide for one, as opposed to another, point of view. But if, as was argued, the heterogeneity of moral viewpoints cannot coherently be taken as presenting moral agents with choice, then neither is the question, Who should decide? coherent. Frustration, dismay, possibly even power plays over decisions, then, seem the texture of moral life, especially in the context of clinical situations.

THE CHALLENGE: A FIRST LOOK

There are many valuable contributions from those on both sides of the backlash. Siegler's and others' criticisms of BME cannot be ignored. Moral issues, we've suggested, are presented solely in the contexts of their actual occurrence: within clinical contexts and research settings. On the other hand, Hare's, Beauchamp's, and others' insistence that there are positive contributions to these discussions from philosophical circles (one might chance to call them identifiable "skills" even) cannot be denied. Still, there are fundamental flaws in both responses to the challenge of grappling significantly with the pressing, often depressing, moral issues within medicine and biomedical research.

It is doubtlessly true that philosophers must become more sensitive to the routines of clinical work; it is also true that greater understanding of the rigors of ethical reasoning could only help the work of physicians. Still, Siegler's claim that "good clinical medicine is necessarily ethical medicine" obviously begs the key questions. It is also quite impractical to expect physicians to become competent in medicine and research, specialized in a very particular subdiscipline, and at the same time to become experts in ethics in any serious sense of that problematic phrase. On the other hand, while it is surely not true that moral philosophers must "close up shop" (Hare), it is unfortunately true that, however well intentioned, they have not been very well informed about clinical work and have as a consequence not been significantly responsive to the challenge from medicine.

There is in fact even more to the challenge, as can be readily appreciated when one takes into consideration the fact that medical practice is hardly ever merely a matter of one physician treating one patient—the fabled one-to-one physician-patient relationship, which today is mainly the stuff of nostalgia. As will be seen, medical practice includes other health professionals (nurses, social workers, consultants) and is conducted within certain kinds of social institutions (hospitals, clinics, offices) that present their own sort of moral complexity and variety. It is conducted within a highly complex network of rules, regulations, laws, and professional standards, which again present special moral issues for that practice and its moral assessment. Finally, every society incorporates into its various health systems and socially legitimated conducts a number of basic values that contribute to the meaning of such key notions as health and disease, and within whose shadow all social practices (including those of medicine) go on and which help to determine just what are permissible, impermissible, or obligatory conducts.

An ethics responsive to medicine must be capable of discerning the range of issues lying at these different levels and occurring within different contexts, each of which presents its own peculiar kind of complexity and difficulty. Beyond this, of course, medical practice involves patients, families, friends and associates, communities, and social groups. Complex in themselves, these contexts are also complicated by the fact that patients (families, friends) are affected by the presence of health professionals, by the institutions of practice, by the rules and regulations governing that practice, as well as by the social, religious, and other types of value. It thus remains to be determined in each case just which levels and kinds of moral issues are presented in each case, and how they impact the variety of decisions that are to be made at each stage of an illness or injury.

Beleaguered by the emergence of profound moral issues in the very midst of its own research and practice, medicine appealed to philosophy and others of the humanities for help. In their attempt to respond to this extraordinary challenge, philosophers have been often bewildered by its complexities. Also challenged has been the usual understanding of what philosophy itself is, as a social practice within the same social world as medicine. Certainly, philosophy's place within the world of clinical and research medicine must be reconsidered.

Ruddick's reference to that "critical distance" philosophers have "assumed since Socrates drew off from the Sophists" (1981, p. 17) may have an unexpected point. While it is in a sense true that Socrates "drew off from the Sophists" ("those hired rhetorical aides of the Athenian elite" [ibid.]), this does not take note of the fact that Socrates remained within the "marketplace" in constant critical dialogue with common folks as well as the Sophists. Indeed, the "unobtrusive art" of Socratic midwifery (in Ruddick's phrase) has its place, not so much in the cloistered halls of philosophy departments, but specifically in the "marketplace" of issues as and where they actually occur, that is, within the world of clinical medicine. Grappling with these issues will have to be a matter, too, of constant dialogue with those settings and the people in them. The problem we face is to determine just what that clinical "marketplace" is and what being within it requires of us.

TOWARD ANOTHER APPROACH: A CASE STUDY

We have to learn from clinical situations. Suppose we granted, however unlikely this may be, that we knew, with full clarity and even certainty, that a particular infant could not benefit from any of the possible therapies currently at hand in the most sophisticated NICU, or that the medical risks of using any therapies far exceeded any possible benefit the infant might realize from them. In the language of the Final Rule (1985) for the Amendment to the Child Abuse Prevention and Treatment Act (1984), all potential treatments are either "futile" or "virtually futile" in terms of the infant's survival, and the treatments themselves are therefore "inhumane."

Here is a clear-cut social policy coupled with several rather obvious moral principles. If "reasonable medical judgment" indicates that an infant cannot "medically benefit," or would be put to more "risk" than "benefit," or would merely have its life prolonged needlessly with additional pain and suffering, then otherwise therapeutically indicated medical or surgical procedures need not be used. Neither beneficence nor dignity requires foolish or pointless treatments; rather, they suggest withholding or withdrawal of all treatments except those that meet the minimum requirements of dignity (routine medication, hydration, and nursing care) while the baby is allowed to expire.

> Now suppose, knowing all this, we are presented with a 27-week gestational age female infant weighing 970 grams at birth. Born at a local hospital by cesarean section because of fetal distress, the infant's Apgar score at birth (assessment of heart rate, respiratory effort, muscle tone, reflex irritability, and color) was extremely poor (2 at 1 minute, 6 at 5 minutes; a score of 10 is normal). The mother was a 17-year-old woman married to a 22-year-old man. This was their first child, and although the pregnancy was unplanned, it seemed welcome. The infant was immediately transferred to the pediatric surgical unit of the regional tertiary, acute-care center, for correction of an omphalacele (mid-line abdominal wall defect resulting in the visceral organs lying exposed); a diaphragmatic defect (partial absence on both sides) was noted during surgery. The surgical team only closed the abdominal skin (mainly for cosmetic purposes), as the infant had multiple congenital anomalies requiring evaluation prior to any further surgical efforts; nothing could be done to correct the diaphragmatic defect.
>
> The infant was admitted to the center's NICU at about two weeks of age for evaluation and treatment. The diaphragmatic defect had indicated mechanical ventilation from birth; indeed, resuscitation during surgery had been required because of a hypoxic incident. Other respiratory problems seemed present, along with other anomalies. To permit medical evaluation, the ventilator was maintained at very high settings: respiratory rate of 100, oxygen concentration of 100 percent, and very high airway passage pressures. Over a period of days the following prominent problems were diagnosed:
>
> 1. Mid-line abdominal defect, with partial absence of diaphragm, suggesting possible additional neurologic deficits;

2. Multiple heart defects, including several holes permitting reverse shuntings of bloodflow, overriding aorta, and patent ductus arteriosis (PDA), with cardiological outcome judged very poor;

3. Central nervous system (CNS) evaluation with EEG showed diffuse faulty brain-wave activity (encephalopathy) and abnormal seizure activity, due to congenital problems or secondary to hypoxia during surgery, and neurological outcome judged very poor;

4. Gastrointestinal feeding was not possible because of abdominal problems and use of mechanical ventilation, and the infant was placed on total parenteral nutrition (TPN: "tube feeding"), which could not be replaced, with resultant inadequate caloric intake;

5. Pulmonary status required mechanical ventilation at the highest settings, which had to be maintained because of diaphragmatic defect, poor oxygenation, and other problems.

Having at hand, as we've supposed, a clear-cut social policy and several moral principles, what should be done for this infant? For instance, several times during her hospitalization she developed airway infections (not unexpectedly, due to the use of the ventilator). Does the policy require treatment of the infections? Do the moral principles? The patent ductus arteriosis (PDA) can be closed with indomethacin, and if not closed could well be lethal. Do the policy and/or the principles require treatment? Possibly, too, the holes in the walls of the heart could be closed surgically. Should they be? Should additional surgery on the mid-line abdominal wall defect be done? It eventually became clear that the infant was totally ventilator dependent, and at the highest settings. The only way to stop the lung damage would be to wean her to lower settings; since she could not be weaned, what should be done about the ventilator?

We should examine this case in light of the 1984 Amendment to the Child Abuse Prevention and Treatment Act (Pub. L. No. 98-457, [K]4[b][2]), which also invokes the moral principles already noted (beneficence and dignity), as the Department of Health of Human Services (DHHS) stated in its Final Rule (Fed. Reg., 45 C.F.R. pt. 1340, Apr. 15, 1985).

The basic criterion governing treatment for infants with multiple congenital anomalies is the attending physician(s) "reasonable medical judgment," which is based on the "medically beneficial standard." To ask whether treatments should be provided this infant is to ask whether the physician's reasonable medical judgment" is that the envisioned treatments would be "medically beneficial."

The amendment created a new category of child abuse and neglect concerned with "withholding" of treatment, defined as

the failure to respond to an infant's life-threatening conditions by providing treatment (including appropriate nutrition, hydration, and medication) which, in the treating physician's reasonable medical judgment, will be most likely to be effective in ameliorating or correcting all such conditions.

Certain exceptions to the requirement are given, but do not include exceptions to medication, hydration, and nutrition. Treatments, the amendment states, may be "withheld" when

1. the infant is chronically and irreversibly comatose;
2. the provision of such treatment would merely prolong dying or not be effective in ameliorating or correcting all of the infant's life-threatening conditions, or otherwise be futile in terms of the survival of the infant; or
3. the provision of such treatment would be virtually futile in terms of the survival of the infant and the treatment itself under such circumstances would be inhumane.

During the infant's course, the attending neonatologist and primary care staff, knowing the new law and guidelines, faced a number of acute problems. Several were especially difficult.

1. Neither the amendment nor the rule distinguish between two different medical procedures involving the use of life-supports: (a) to allow for "special" medical evaluation (required by the rule), and (b) to provide therapy (either corrective or ameliorative). While this distinction may not always be critical, in cases like this it is vital. Evaluation may take days (to allow for neurological, cardiological, ultrasonographic, and other diagnostic evaluations) and may disclose that initially noted anomalies (the omphalocele) are associated with underlying impairments (neurological defects). It may also identify other life-threatening anomalies (heart defects) that may also be incompatible with intact survival, or even survival with major compromise.

As these conditions are diagnosed, the use of medical or surgical procedures designed to be therapeutic may then become problematic. For instance, given the infant's "overall condition" (consideration of which is required by the DHHS rule) and outlook, should the PDA be closed, airway infections treated, or fluid electrolyte imbalances corrected? Such treatments as mechanical ventilation, initially used to allow evaluation (as distinct from therapy), can present a harsh dilemma. If this shows the kind of prognosis as it did for this infant, should the ventilator or other therapeutic measures be kept in place or be removed? The problem becomes even more difficult if the infant continues to require extremely high ventilator settings over a long period, and weaning is not possible; then, chronic lung disease may set in, as it did with this infant. Since no distinction between evaluation and therapy was made by the amendment or guidelines, the physicians were left not knowing what was permissible and what was not. Since, finally, neither beneficence nor dignity distinguishes between these very different purposes of treatments, appeal to them would be pointless. We do not know what they require.

2. This problem was even more acute in another way. The exception language mentions only "withholding" of treatments. It does not mention

either withdrawal or discontinuation (whether full or partial). It is stated that if "reasonable medical judgment" indicates that treatments are "futile"—they can neither "correct" nor "ameliorate" all of the "life-threatening conditions"—then they may be "withheld." Does "treatments" refer to those which are *already in place* (such as the ventilator), or to those which *might* be used but are *not yet in place* (such as indomethacin, antibiotics, heart surgery)? Specifically, may the ventilator (used to stabilize and permit evaluation) be *discontinued* after evaluation shows poor prognosis? Or, to the contrary, must it be kept in place, and only *contemplated* treatments "withheld"?

The ambiguity of "withhold" can be clinically significant: Does it refer to the future or to the past? While clinicians frequently make this distinction (even between partial and full withholding, and partial and full withdrawal), the failure to do so by Congress and DHHS results in grievous problems for physicians exercising their "reasonable medical judgments." Neither "beneficence" nor "dignity" are of much help, either; they do not speak to the issue of determining which action, withholding or withdrawing, is the "beneficent" thing to do out of respect for the infant's "dignity" as a human being.

3. This ambiguity could become further problematic, even eerie, when the third exception is considered. If a treatment is "virtually futile in terms of the survival of the infant," then the "treatment itself under such circumstances would be inhumane" and presumably could be "withheld." According to the Final Rule, the statute specifies that the "balance is clearly to be between the very slight chance that treatment will allow the infant to survive and the negative factors relating to the process of the treatment" (p. 14892). That is, "virtually futile," and "inhumane" refer strictly to "the treatment itself"; thus, the Final Rule "does not sanction decisions based on subjective opinions about the future 'quality of life' of a retarded or disabled person" (p. 14880).

Suppose it is medically determined that mechanical ventilation is "virtually futile." After several months, weaning has proven impossible, the highest settings are still required, and progressive and irreversible lung damage (chronic lung disease) is occurring. As "virtually futile," the ventilator's use would be "inhumane," and as merely prolonging the infant's dying, its use is clearly a violation of the infant's dignity and thus is not beneficent. To continue the ventilator would be immoral and possibly even illegal, specifically contrary to "reasonable medical judgment" and thus fitting the third exception. But, if "withholding" is distinct from "withdrawal" and only the former is "intended by Congress," the dilemma is striking and eerie: The physicians are required to ventilate this infant, which is an "inhumane" and possibly criminal act!

4. Parents are not mentioned in the amendment, either as decision makers, participants in decisions, or even as having to be consulted by phy-

sicians. The sole criterion is "reasonable medical judgment." Initially, in its Interim Rule (Fed. Reg. 45 C.F.R. pt. 1340, Dec. 10, 1984), DHHS did not include parents in exception decisions; nor had parents been included in any of the previous guidelines to Baby Doe regulations.

However, in response to numerous objections, DHHS changed its interpretation of the amendment. The Final Rule states that "the decision to provide or withhold medically indicated treatment is, except in highly unusual circumstances, made by the parents or legal guardian," although it must be "based on the advice and reasonable medical judgment of their physician (or physicians)" (p. 14880). Neither a state's child protection service (CPS) nor any hospital's infant care review committee (ICRC) can make decisions about the care and treatment of the imperiled infant. "This is the parents' right and responsibility," which must be supported "unless they choose a course of action inconsistent with applicable standards established by law" (ibid.).

But the Final Rule did not fully clarify matters. One possible scenario consistent with the rule, for instance, is this: If physicians wanted to continue and parents to withhold treatment, the latter would be legally inconsistent with "reasonable medical judgment." Presumably, this would be one of those "highly unusual circumstances" affecting the "right and responsibility" of parents to make decisions for their own infant: If parents insisted, it would be proper for physicians to notify the state CPS and institute appropriate legal proceedings, if necessary, to ensure that the infant was treated.

But consider another scenario equally consistent with the rule: Physicians' "reasonable medical judgment," say, is that continued treatment is "futile" or "virtually futile," yet parents want them to continue with treatment. What should be done? Would it be proper to notify the state CPS and possibly institute legal proceedings to ensure that treatments be "withheld"?

The case being considered was a good example of that second scenario. The parents' decision was not based on the physician's reasonable medical judgment. At no point was it suggested that the disagreement had to be adjudicated either through the ICRC or the state CPS or in court. Rather, the parents' wishes were followed. In short, for this type of conflict, neither the amendment nor the rule seemed in the least relevant. The conflict signaled, instead, the need to work carefully and patiently with the parents, to help them come to understand and accept (intellectually and emotionally) their infant's actual condition and poor prospects.

During the infant's hospitalization, the ventilator was continued at the highest settings; weaning proved impossible. With the heart problems, CNS deficits, and pulmonary difficulties, the outlook for intact survival was judged to be nil. If the infant survived at all, it would suffer from major neurological, cardiac, pulmonary, and other compromise. Severe chronic lung disease did occur, and progressive and irreversible lung damage ensued. By itself, this would eventuate in death, although no exact prediction could be given; if treatments were continued, the infant might survive for several months or longer, but eventually would die from pulmonary and cardiac failure.

After lengthy discussions with the parents, the attending wrote a DNR (do not resuscitate) order: If a cardiac arrest occurred, no resuscitation would be attempted (no cardiac massage, no drugs, and no machines); no further tests for electrolytes would be done, and fluid management would be done empirically; efforts to comfort would be used (for instance, fever would be treated empirically, with no effort being made to diagnose its cause). However, the ventilator was kept at the highest settings to maintain pulmonary functioning. The infant managed to survive in the NICU another two months before succumbing to an episode of bradycardia (cardiac arrest from diminished heart rate).

The six months' hospitalization cost, physicians' fees excluded, was over $270,000. No insurance covered the infant; thus, the cost became part of the hospital's "charity care" commitment, which totals over $12 million annually.

I am not suggesting that clarity and even certainty about moral standards are pointless, undesirable, or an idle pursuit. Nor do I want to judge, much less condemn, this minor, married girl or her young husband for getting pregnant, having almost no prenatal care, and having no insurance—even though there are surely important moral and social issues here and elsewhere in such cases.

It ought to be clear that restricting moral discourse to the formal level of principles, or that of social policy, fails in several ways to be responsive to the real, clinical demands of such a case. However caring one might want to be, it is simply not clear just what that requires of us in this case, nor are there any clear guidelines for determining just what the moral principles and policies imply for clinical decision making. The fact is that the ambiguities of the infant's initial condition, the uncertainties about her future (short or long-term), and the multiplicity of problems she presented throughout her long course of treatment, make it improbable if not impossible to know what beneficence requires. We simply do not know what caring amounts to, since otherwise contradictory actions (continuation or discontinuation) could both be consistent with it. Even when the prognosis is much clearer, communication problems as well as apparent disagreements among staff and between staff and parents (not to mention the murky regions of legal deliberations and decisions, which in any case may not be appropriate when it comes to moral dilemmas) severely complicate such cases to the point where action can be, and often is, highly problematic.

Moreover, since, as everyone, including DHHS, acknowledges, medical judgments can and do differ in such cases; what the amendment and guidelines require is by no means obvious. After all, infants suffering from even more severe complications than these have been known to survive. It is not at all obvious that beneficence requires treatment (she "is able to live"), since it might also require withholding (she "is dying"). When we are in doubt, appeal to principles or policies does not help us decide what to do; yet it is precisely such cases that prompt such appeals in the first place. It is only when we have few if any doubts about what to do that appeals like these seem at all clear, but by then the appeals are pointless (Gorovitz, 1982).

DEVELOPING A RESPONSIVE ETHICS

This point could be illustrated in numerous ways—in fact, by any specific case, and not necessarily one like that just considered. In every instance, we face quite special issues and requirements as we try to be responsive to the concerns of clinicians, patients, and the families of patients. To face issues such as those presented by the infant or other cases is to realize that we have neither the wisdom nor a sort of moral calculus to instruct us on what any set of moral principles may or may not require of us in the concrete, clinical situations of medical practice.

Reviewing the terrain covered thus far, several additional things come to mind in trying to think through how best to respond to the challenge to ethics from clinical medicine. In the first place, such an ethics must become well informed about the facts of the case—not only the medical facts but other facts as well. Or, to the extent that only some facts and not others are considered (or, are at hand at the time one is asked to consider a case), the range of moral deliberations will be correspondingly limited—and so, too, for proposed moral judgments. *Moral issues are presented solely within the contexts of their actual occurrence.* Hence, it is not possible to know just which issues are actually presented by a specific case in advance of knowing the actual circumstances of their occurrence, much less to know how they might best be handled or how best to propose possible resolutions in advance of having the facts well in hand. We shall have to consider this in greater depth later.

A second requirement also seems quite obvious: A good deal more has to be understood about the practice of medicine—its history, thematic nature, and connections with biomedical science. Most especially, it is necessary to think about medicine itself in respect of its moral dimensions: In just what sense is it, as Cassell and others remark, "an inherently moral enterprise"? Again, this topic will occupy us later, as regards both physicians and patients.

A third requirement is also clear: A responsive ethics must somehow be *accountable* for its deliberations and recommendations. In a sense, Siegler is quite right; ethical deliberation removed from the "field of com-

bat" can only be somewhat artificial ("counterfeit" seems too strong), remote from the issues needing consideration. The rationale for this must be
carefully probed as the demands of a clinically responsive ethics become
more fully laid out. For now, I want only to observe that ethical deliberations here, with real people facing very real moral dilemmas and problems,
must be accountable. *A responsive ethics must be a responsible ethics*—
responsible for being well informed and responsible both to the providers
and to the patients and their families.

Is there a legitimate place for the ethicist within the context of clinical
(or research) practice? If not, direct contact with such cases is not a legitimated activity. In another sense, this may be understood as the critical test
of a proposed responsive and responsible ethics within medicine. The test
here is precisely that prompted by physicians themselves when they called
(and continue to call) on ethicists for assistance in dealing with the complex
issues of contemporary medicine, biomedicine, and technology. So, let it
stand this way for now: The presumption I want to make is that such an
ethics is possible, and the test is to find out if the presumption is correct.

CHAPTER 2

The Moral Dimension of Medicine: Preliminary Reflections

A philosopher taking up the challenge by physicians to "become involved" in clinical medicine may find himself in a confusing situation. Upon entering a sophisticated health-care center, for instance, one finds all sorts of people doing all manner of busy things; speaking many languages, some highly technical and mysterious-sounding; using lots of exotic-looking machines and other contraptions ticking, beeping, pulsing, zigging, and zagging; and performing all manner of curious and even intimate actions on, to, and with people in beds and on carts, some looking quite bad off, while others seem fine.

Still, this profusion of people, actions, things, and places is not a total confusion for most of us. Each of us has had some experience with doctors, nurses, social workers, and dietitians (and their respective students), as well as with hospitals, drugs, and video screens. So, when a would-be ethicist enters such a place, much is already somewhat familiar while much else is quite strange.

But now the ethicist is there in a quite different way, unlike any previous experience, save, perhaps, for what has been picked up through media portrayals, books, or conversations. The ethicist is there as an actual part of it, as his hospital badge (if not also white coat) proclaims. This is quite enough to make the ethicist a real neophyte, to whose inexperienced eye nothing seems familiar or obvious. Not only is there now access to hitherto forbidden places (No Admittance: Staff Only) and talk, but not even the once relatively familiar world of sick people is exactly the same. The ethicist is not someone visiting relatives or friends in the hospital. Now, this world is seen from the quite different perspective of one who works there. This perspective, however, is decidedly complicated by the fact that what counts as "work" is itself a matter of considerable uncertainty for everybody, including the ethicist.

THE COMPLEX FIELD OF MEDICAL WORK

For the ethicist seeking to understand issues in the contexts where they actually occur, it nevertheless quickly becomes apparent that there is a kind of order in the field of medical work.

Consider again that critically ill baby whose case we studied in the last chapter. In a sense, there is a kind of one-to-one encounter in the NICU between the physician(s) and the infant (and, periodically at least, the parents). As will become clearer later on, this encounter has its own inherent norms, values, and array of conducts. It is, however, immediately apparent that this encounter goes on within a specific context: the NICU, which includes numerous other providers who are also present (some directly caring for this infant, others doing so periodically or for special purposes, and still others preoccupied with other infants or other activities), as well as residents, interns, social workers, technicians, and students. Moreover, it is also apparent that the NICU is but one among many units in pediatrics, which is in turn but one among many other hospital units and departments. Like other institutions in our culture, this one, too, functions within the context of prevailing social policies, legislative enactments and established legal norms at the local, state, regional, and federal levels. Furthermore, listening to the talk going on in the NICU, it becomes evident that it goes on within our particular culture, in this particular historical period with its economic and other conditions, and that there are detectable sociocultural values presented, though sometimes subtly and indirectly, in this talk.

There is, in short, a specifiably complex field of work here. Note the health provider's side of it: the *physician* (who, like anyone else, has a specific biographical situation, which includes attitudes, habits, and values); the other *health professionals* (with their specific biographical situations); the particular unit within which the physician practices (with its own personnel, protocols, regimens, written and unwritten rules and codes of conduct); the particular *hospital* as a socially legitimated institution (and its complex of rules, codes, regulations, specific charter and mission, committee structure); the particular *state* and region in which the hospital is located (with its set of regulations, licensures, laws, policies); the *federal government* (and its rules, regulations, mandates, policies). This complex is, of course, but one feature of our culture—with its particular complex of folkways, mores, laws, institutions, history, and values.

Although the phenomenon (this physician treating this infant) turns out to be immensely complex, my point is quite simple. All of these levels relate directly and indirectly to what goes on at the bedside of the infant. In the course of a single day, this critically ill newborn will be seen (in a medical sense alone) by as many as thirty or more health professionals, all of whom work within and are governed by those various rules and policies.

What these observations signify for the attempt to be ethically responsive is that we face a most complex situation on each occasion. To be well informed becomes almost unmanageable in many cases. The attending physician's judgments, parents' wishes, consultant's reports, nurses' views, social workers' findings, unit policies and protocols, hospital policies, state and federal laws and regulations, prevailing social and religious values—all are impacted within the boundaries of a single case. Knowing "what's going on," merely from the side of the providers of care, requires a good deal of out-and-out "detective" work to discern just how the various views and policies bear on the case and to determine their relative weight, as well as to interpret all the data concerning possible or likely outcomes. To become involved in clinical situations as an ethicist is to realize that one never knows in advance just which issues are going to be presented, at what level they have their source, how the various levels interrelate, and just how to weigh matters, much less just what to say or even to whom it should be said. One must rather probe, always gently, for the range of surrounding data, merely to become aware, always gradually, of just which issues need attention and how and why.

Ethics practiced within clinical situations must cultivate a kind of deliberate vigilance or circumspect alertness to these intrinsic complexities, as well as watchful patience, avoiding second-guesses of either patients, their families, or providers. This complexity can be diagrammed as shown in Figure 1.

Figure 1 does not exhaust the complex structural lines and organizational relationships within health care. For instance, it must be recognized that actual work at these various levels goes on in tacit, taken-for-granted ways impossible to chart in such a diagram (see Schutz, 1973). Institutional contexts such as hospitals, and medical units are characteristically like other social groups in many ways; the "unspoken" recipes of action govern quite as much as the written codes and often even more powerfully, as Wieder has noted (1974). In an obvious way, therefore, the ethicist's work must be supported by sensitive ethnomethodological, sociological, and other forms of empirical study.

There is another way that Figure 1 is not exhaustive. Consider, for

Social Values

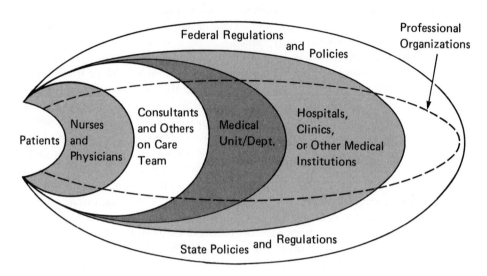

FIGURE 1. The medical side of patient care.

instance, how drugs and medications are made available for use (and subject to misuse, abuse, and failure to use); the variety of medical review boards, committees, and informal groups and conversations within the hospital (see Starr, 1982); the problems of quality control regarding the array of equipment, appliances, machines, and instruments with which physicians, nurses, units, and institutions are outfitted; and the multiple lines of connection or interrelationship obtaining between and among different departments or units (governing diagnoses; standard, investigational, or experimental therapies; intra- and inter-institutional referrals of patients).

Thus, significant moral issues can and do arise from any of these sources. Accordingly, the ethicist has as his or her "subject-matter" not simply patients or providers, but that entire complex. To "practice" ethics, then, requires that these various levels and their sundry interrelationships be understood at every point in the course of a particular case—which requires that peculiar form of detective work mentioned earlier.

AN ILLUSTRATIVE CASE

Considering specific cases means encountering a variety of impacted issues arising at different levels, in different ways among different individuals or groups, each of which may have important and different bearing on a patient's condition, diagnosis, routine care, proposed therapies, and outcomes. Merely to illustrate some facets of this point, consider the following case.

A boy had been diagnosed at age two months as having a degenerative and progressive form of neural disease, accompanied with degenerative muscle disease. Now 4½ years old, he had been hospitalized for all but the first few weeks of life, and had been transferred at about age two from the intensive to the intermediate care unit.

A recent consult with a pediatric neurologist and a pediatric psychiatrist suggested that the boy, a ward of the state since birth, be placed on DNR (do not resuscitate), as he was effectively "dead below the neck" and soon perhaps would be dead even "above"—though this was still a bit unclear since certain body functions associated with the brainstem were still present (e.g., gag reflex). He was thus not "whole" brain-dead: Tests continued to show brainstem activity, but the neural pathways to the neocortex, the neocortex itself, and the centers governing vision and audition seemed to have been irreversibly damaged.

His primary care nurses, however, were not convinced that the boy was "dead": His eyes seemed at times to "track," even to focus on the TV screen beside his bed; he seemed to respond with smiles when talked to; and though he could move no part of his body, his skin had a "different feel" from that of persons who are clearly brain-dead.

A resident reported that "the nurses have bonded with him." A nurse reported that "the residents are just frustrated because they can't cure him, can't do anything except comfort him—and that's something they have trouble doing." Another nurse reported that "the attending physician never comes around anymore; he's given up, too." Because there was no DNR order, the frequent episodes of bradycardia brought on full-scale resuscitation efforts, all of them successful. The social worker reported that "there simply is no place to send him, no place to keep him except here, and this is just not the place for him." Apparently, the boy's dependency on the ventilator (as well as the neuropathy and myopathy) prevented his being transferred to a chronic facility in the area, and his being a ward of the state prevented his transfer out of state.

A physician stated that with all the cutbacks on funds for crippled children, there was just no way to justify the enormous outlay of funds for this child: "He's dead anyway; or at least, he'll be *completely* dead in a few months. The disease is clearly irreversible and progressive, and soon his heart and breathing will go, too, when the disease hits the brainstem." A resident declared: "This is an *acute-care* center; we just can't handle this kind of chronic, drawn-out, hopeless, long-term case." A medical student remarked: "Why do we have to keep resuscitating this kid when his heart slows down? Does the law, or morality, force us to keep plugging away with him?"

The law in that state included a definition of death with a focus on "irreversible cessation of the functioning of the whole brain, including brainstem functioning." The providers were advised that they would run "serious legal risks" were they to discontinue the life-supports then in place, or fail to resuscitate. A physician asked: "Who the hell would sue us in the first place?" "Who knows?" the hospital attorney replied, "Our society is very litigious—look at Baby Doe and Baby Jane Doe!"

To conduct an "ethics consultation" is to confront highly complex, compacted issues, not all of which are on the face of it obviously "moral" to those involved in caring for patients. Rather, moral issues of very different sorts and levels are found implicit to and interlaced with medical, legal, social, economic, and other issues. Contending with these, simply to help patients and providers sort out the confusions, ambiguities, and multiplicity of problems, requires coming to grips with the layered interrelationships among the different levels (of people, activity, institution, legal norms, federal and state statutes and polices), with communication difficulties, and with intra- and inter-professional issues—not to mention more traditionally recognizable moral problems (such as truth telling, personhood, terminal illness, confidentiality, and damaged children).

THE SOCIAL CONTEXT OF PATIENTS

The aforementioned complexities arise just on the side of the providers. That, of course, is hardly the only thing to be considered, for all these strata, people, instruments and machines, and regulations and laws are directed to and oriented around a quite specific patient and patient family. This obviously introduces further complexities bearing directly on "what's going on" and "what can be done" for each patient and patient family.

On the one hand, there is this patient with his or her own specific biographical situation and its distinctive values, attitudes, history, linguistic usages, and habits. But the patient is only rarely without some immediate family or friends (circle of intimates). Moreover, each is a member of social, business, political, or religious groups, each of which has its own specific traditions, values and usages. Just like the providers, each patient is part of the same (or at the very least, part of some) culture with its prevailing nexus of social values, mores, and folkways.

FIGURE 2. The patient's side of patient care.

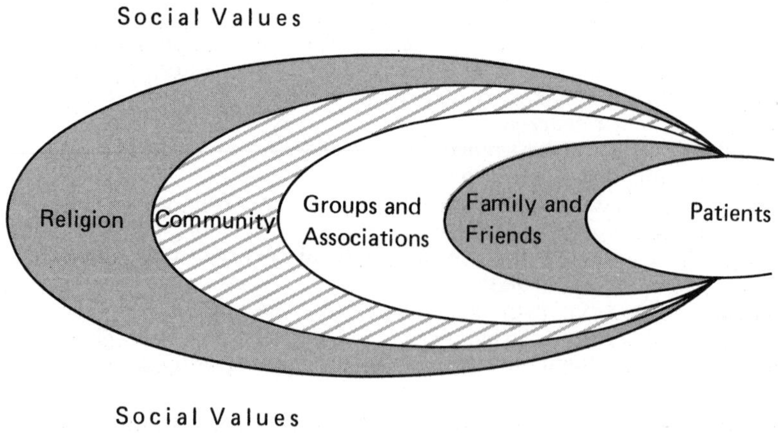

Social Values

Religion   Community   Groups and Associations   Family and Friends   Patients

Social Values

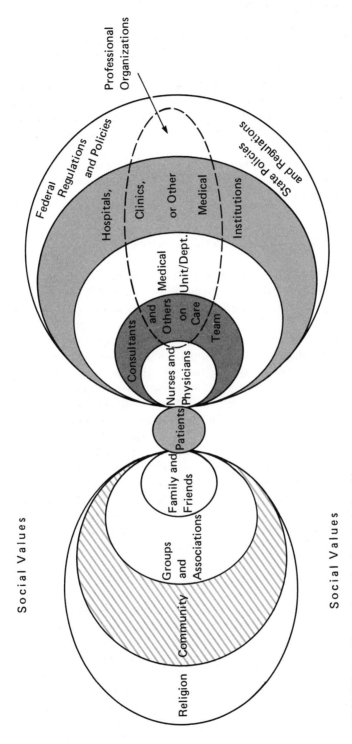

FIGURE 3. The patient-physician relationship.

Suffice it to say here that a graphic look at any patient reveals strata of adherence, influence, belief, custom, and conduct, all of which can and do texture every medical encounter (see Figure 2).

To be sure, the relative weight these personal and social contexts receive for any given individual will vary at any given time according to circumstances and the individual's personal biography. Each case, however, presents a complex of these sorts of influences on an individual's beliefs and values.

Figures 2 and 3 together help us to appreciate that every medical encounter is thoroughly contextualized (keep in mind that these diagrams are inevitably incomplete).

SEVERAL CLUES TO BEING MORALLY RESPONSIVE

To seek an ethics responsive to the demands of health-care situations is to propose that such an ethics be conceived as a clinical discipline, integral to the settings of health care. Such an ethics needs to incorporate respect for the rigors of clinical work and, along with that, cultivate its own clinical methods for discerning, interpreting, and weighing moral phenomena—thereby, developing a body of empirical experience and knowledge.

It is necessary to recognize, however, that such a proposal runs considerably contrary to the prevailing understanding of ethics in our times as a philosophical discipline and topic. Still, what I am suggesting may well be, in some core way, at least as ancient as Aristotle's *Nicomachean Ethics* (1962).

Pointing out that "precision cannot be expected in the treatment of all subjects alike" (1962, part 1, sec. 3), Aristotle insisted what "when the subject and basis of a discussion consist of matters that hold good only as a general rule, but not always," as is the case with politics and ethics, "the conclusions reached must be of the same order" (ibid.). Concerning moral actions, "although general statements have a wider application, statements on particular points have more truth in them: actions are concerned with particulars and our statements must harmonize with them" (1962, part 2, sec. 7).

Ethics concerns emotion and action (1962, part 2, sec. 3), and here "there are no fixed data in matters concerning action and questions of what is beneficial, any more than there are in matters of health" (1962, part 2, sec. 3). The treatment of particular problems will thus be characteristically imprecise. "The agent must consider on each different occasion what the situation demands, just as in medicine and in navigation" (ibid.).

The cases mentioned earlier provide a number of clues for drawing the outlines of this ethics. First, clinical medicine is premised on conscientious, competent, technically scrupulous diagnosis, therapy, and prognosis. Unlike preventive medicine (which is a topic of its own), it is focused on distressed or damaged persons, to whatever extent distress or damage is presented. It is designed to be "in the best interests" of each individual patient (as well as groups or populations, as the case may be). Whether or not this is only a cultural phenomenon, this kind of clinical medicine at the present time is primarily focused on acute care; it is crisis-oriented medicine for the most part. Thus, while chronic and preventive medicine are surely significant, they pose somewhat different issues that should be tackled on their own. However that may turn out, it should be recognized that medical education, residency training, and much medical practice (not to mention investigational, experimental, and research medicine) have this predominant focus, and it is this focus that provides the context for the rest of this study.

A second clue is also at hand: Clinical medicine is *not* value-free. As Pellegrino lucidly emphasized, the altogether central feature of this form of medicine (that is, clinical judgment) incorporates an inherently moral dimension, an end that in a sense is the whole point of the enterprise:

> The end of the medical encounter, and the process of clinical judgment through which it is achieved, then, is restoration and healing—some corrective, remedial or preventive action is directed at what the doctor and the patient perceive as a diminution of the patient's wholeness, each in his/her own fashion. (Pellegrino, 1979a, p. 172.)

"Perhaps," Cassell remarked some time ago, "medicine is called an art, not a science, because a necessarily inherent part of it is decision-making linked to human values" (1973, p. 54). Each of these decisions or clinical judgments is a unique and terminal event. Settling on one regimen or another is simply the point of the encounter, legitimated by the patient's turning to the physician in the first place, whether the decision is made by the physician alone, by the patient, by the family and the patient, or through some combination of these.

Clinical judgment is the outcome of a complex process involving chains of reasoning (some perhaps deductive, some perhaps inductive, others more like informed hunches and guesses, and still others involving other elements). These are typically serially organized around and modified by recourse to "facts" and observations, often uncertain in their way:

> Truth and certitude are, therefore, almost always problematic. Out of the uncertain conclusions of earlier syllogisms, a decision to act must be taken which has a different character from the conclusions that precede it. The conclusions of the earlier reasoning chains become premises for further reasoning . . . a cumulative and progressive series of hypotheses and conclusions, always open to further recourse to fact and experiment. (Pellegrino, 1979a, p. 172.)

Thus, medicine is an inherently fallible discipline (Gorovitz and MacIntyre, 1976) that inherently invokes numerous moral and other issues. In its therapeutic and prognostic moments, clinical judgment comes closer to its inherent goal—the right action for a specific patient—and therefore "involves more questions of value by far, than diagnosis" (Pellegrino, 1979a, p. 179). Therapeutic judgment is thus far more "dialectical," less "scientific" and quantitative, and even more intertwined with moral themes and issues than diagnosis.

To be concerned with healing and restoring is to be governed by a basic moral resolve to help afflicted persons, regardless of whether the "helping" is done well or poorly. To be responsive to clinical medicine, then, is to be obliged to recognize this moral resolve, to take it into account precisely as it is present in any particular instance.

A third clue may now be introduced. Situations involving human affliction are invariably charged with feeling—passion, emotion, desire. On the one hand, the providers no less than patients and families (or friends, associates, and communities) want "to do the right thing" for the patient—to be helpful, fair, just, honest, and right. On the other hand, patients themselves, precisely in respect of their specific distress or injury, are not only the occasions of these feelings, not only the continuing orientations for the attention and feelings of providers and others, but are also in their very condition presentations of moral demands.

While each of these themes or clues (and there are others, as we will shortly see) must be carefully studied, it is important at this stage to note that we face a kind of complex dyad at the center of which is the provider-patient relationship. This relationship, as was already indicated, is highly complex. It is contextualized within numerous explicit and implicit social levels that variously impinge on and influence it. But it is also complex in a historical sense: The self-understanding on the part of physicians is highly charged with a certain tradition that itself carries a kind of moral thematic within it.

THE MORAL RESOLVE AND ITS SPECIFICATIONS

That moral theme seems, indeed, governing for medical practice. As the medical historian Harrison B. Coulter (1973, 1975, 1977) expresses it, this motif is the effort to make sense of the healer's experience with the patient. This effort has two basic aspects: to make sense of the healer's experiences (to interpret "symptoms") and to do something positive about it ("provide therapies"). This is to recognize that clinical medicine is deeply historical, specifically as regards what it views as its Hippocratic tradition. Although this self-understanding may be, perhaps even commonly is, only implicit and poorly articulated by individual physicians—and often incomplete, even when more amply understood—the underlying motif is this therapeutic experience and clearly embodies a moral theme. There is, however, much more to this historical motif, and we shall preoccupy ourselves with it at a later point, simply to make good sense of it.

Medical practice is guided by the moral resolve of physicians to put their knowledge, experience, time, and talents at the disposal of distressed or damaged persons, individually or as groups. *The resolve to help other people* (who are in need of help, ask for help, or are unable to help themselves) is governing: to interpret an afflicted person's presenting symptoms with the aim of attempting to correct, restore, or comfort, to the extent possible in particular circumstances. As the physician Grant Liddle expresses it, "First, the physician must do no harm. Second, the physician must do whatever is within his power to protect and improve the health of his patient" (Liddle, 1967). Or, to use Pellegrino's terms, the physician's clinical judgments are governed by the goal of medicine, namely, to do "the right action" for each specific patient.

What Liddle calls "duties," it seems clear, are two of the main ways in which the physician is to be at the disposal of afflicted persons and thus may be understood as its main *situational specifications*, ways in which that resolve becomes specified according to the demands of the person's particular circumstances. While primary, "doing no harm" and "protecting and improving health," understood situationally, are not the only specifications of that theme. In fact, Liddle's discussion suggests several others that can serve as illustrations. Whenever the physician is faced with a situation in which his own limitations (of whatever sort) make "the best course of action" uncertain, the physician "has an obligation to augment his knowledge so that the benefits and risks of a particular regimen are as predictable as possible" (ibid.). Given that moral resolve, each physician is specifically obligated to be the best possible physician for each and every patient, by augmenting knowledge of whatever sort each patient's condition requires.

When the physician is faced with a situation "in which there is doubt as to what to do because social values are ill defined, the physician should consult not only other physicians but also responsible lay people in trying to arrive at a morally acceptable course of action" (ibid.). When a physician faces issues lying outside medical competence in a strict sense, he or she is responsible for arranging appropriate consultations about these issues, precisely because they directly bear on the care appropriate for that patient.

Further specifications of the moral resolve within therapeutic experience could, and in particular cases must, be demonstrated. To make lively, coherent sense of any specific medical case, it is necessary to take into account the presence of the therapeutic theme and its guiding moral resolve, as well as the ways in which they are (well or poorly) understood by the particular physician in each case. Attention must also be paid to the specific commitments that may be invoked by the specific patient in his or her particular circumstances.

While it may be possible to interpret this theme and resolve as involving a sort of "ethical principle" (Veatch, 1981; Jonsen, Winslade, Siegler, 1982), two things must be emphasized. First, even if it is a principle it is not found somewhere outside medicine in some ethereal heaven of moral ideas. Rather it is embedded within medicine itself, and in its special history, as the basic sense of its therapeutic theme. Therefore, second, dealing with the moral issues within medicine is by no means a matter of starting from such presumable principles and then trying to apply them to the practical situations of medical practice. Rather, as it is *within* these concrete, clinical situations themselves that one finds this theme and its moral resolve, so it is *within* these situations that one finds a variety of specifications of that resolve appropriate (or, presumably appropriate) to the different conditions and circumstances of each patient. Therefore, acute-care, clinical medicine is an already committed moral enterprise, and it is precisely this value-laden characteristic that, among other features, defines these clinical situations.

Finally, elucidating all these dimensions has to be *contextural.* Every physician practices within multiple contexts, and thus the therapeutic theme of practice is also deeply and multiply contextured. There are mores, rules, norms, regulations, and laws that configure and impact every form of medical practice, from those within intra- and inter-professional relationships, to those at work within the units and institutions of practice, to those set down in legislative enactments and policies, and to broad social values and expectations. No assessment of a case is even remotely adequate if it fails to give due consideration to these contexts, as well as to those belonging to the individual patients and their families and to the specific ways these contexts variously shape, determine, constrain, or enable various practices. There also has to be assessment of which particular specifications for practice are morally required at any given time.

We are thus able to proceed further toward outlining an ethics responsive to clinical medicine. Medical situations are marked by a number of orders, or levels, of moral issues. Not all of these are noted by the persons involved, of course; indeed, it is perhaps rare to find more than minimal awareness of them, or at least of some of them. It thus becomes imperative to submit each case to a kind of clinical inspection, to be a kind of detective, as was earlier suggested, or to perform a kind of differential moral diagnosis—discerning, testing, probing, and interpreting in an effort to find out "what's going on" in each case.

My emphasis on the moral resolve should not obscure the fact that at least some physicians may well be more interested in engaging in "good business" or "good research" than in being sensitive to the needs of patients. Rather, all I want to emphasize here is the fundamental moral character of the therapeutic dyad at the heart of medicine. On the one hand, every physician has deliberately taken on a network of responsibilities, principally those generated by that moral resolve of therapeutic work. On the other hand, everyone who undergoes some disease process, discomfort, injury, or other noxious experience presents as needing to be relieved or restored, whether this is done (and to whatever extent it is done) by self-treatment or through placing himself or herself in the care of some professed healer, allopathic physician or otherwise.

Thus, if a distressed person presents to a professed healer and the healer agrees to try and help, then that physician's knowledge, technical skills, experience, and time, beyond being (in our culture) legally contracted, are morally *covenated* in at least two important ways. First, there is the commitment to do whatever can be done to relieve that person's *present* condition (e.g., pain medication, surgery, respirator); second, to do what can be done to determine, among the possible *futures* available for this patient in this condition, that which is *preferable* (restore health, attain successful pregnancy, correct vision). The physician covenants to care for this patient—and that is the point, whether or not a particular physician (or, for that matter, particular patient) does this well or poorly.

SOURCES OF MORAL CONFLICT

Acute-care clinical medicine is thus based on a contextually specifiable therapeutic theme with its underlying moral resolve to be at the disposal of afflicted persons, with the aim of trying at least to enable them to be restored, healed, or comforted. Its focus is at once on the patient's present condition and on the future(s) available for the patient, thus requiring alertness to the different circumstances that are present in each case and how these require one or another specific modality of caring or helping.

At the same time, each medical encounter occurs within multiple contexts that frame and specify the therapeutic theme and moral resolve. Hence, establishing what are the "best interests" or "right action" in a particular case may, in view of the prevailing circumstances, vary from what otherwise similar cases might suggest.

Situations involving human affliction are invariably charged with feeling, on the part of patients and families and on the part of providers. While there is a pronounced tendency in our times to interpret moral life in terms of feelings, such feelings are seldom if ever understood as themselves moral in nature. Even though we get into serious confusions and conflicts about the nature of moral phenomena, physicians quite as much as patients and their families, still want, sometimes desperately and passionately, to "do the right thing"—to be morally fair, good, right, and honest.

Feelings, most often strongly and vividly presented, are evoked by and orient attention to the patient in terms of the patient's presented condition and possible futures; thus they are related to both "what's wrong" and "what can be done about it." Despite the pervasiveness of heterogeneous moral beliefs and practices and despite considerable confusion and doubt about "what is best to do," persons of all sorts feel strongly on occasions of affliction and distress. A key component of that feeling is the fervent desire to do the right thing, even while there may be, and often is, severe disagreement about what that may be. There are, in fact, many sources of conflict.

A major one is the heterogeneity of moral beliefs, practices, conducts, and concepts, which MacIntyre and others have stressed. I have tried to take into account that in clinical medicine conflicts of this sort invariably occur within the context of the therapeutic theme and its underlying moral resolve. So far as medical practice is socially conditioned by the different levels impacting it (professional, institutional, governmental, societal), as well as by those that contexture each patient (personal, familial, community, religious), conflicts arising from moral heterogeneity may occur not only at these different levels, but also between or among the different socially conditioning levels on either side of the dyad.

For example, what is legislatively enacted (by the federal government on Baby Does, for instance) may incorporate values (e.g., that "everything possible" must be done for handicapped infants with life-threatening conditions or that "only the very best is good enough") that conflict with the values incorporated into a particular physician's practice (e.g., "quality of life" assessments, which in certain cases may imply that a particular infant should be allowed to die, since medical regimens would only prolong dying). Similarly, court-ordered medical treatment for minors may run contrary to the religious beliefs of the minor's parents.

Another crucial source of moral conflict stems from therapeutic experience itself. What is presented to the healer (through observations, talk, tests, physical exam) are symptoms—various bodily and personal displays (swellings, disfigurements, discolorations; complaints, groans, and other linguistic and quasi-linguistic phenomena; attitudes, beliefs). None of these is self-interpreting. Not everything observed or said is to be noted or, if noted, given equal weight; nor does any set of such data come ready-marked with a single interpretation to be used in trying to make sense of what is observed, much less for trying to help. Rather, the symptoms are open to various interpretations, not all of which could possibly be true in a given case.

How one interprets any set of symptoms, including which data may be ignored (if any) and which attended to, will have clear ramifications for the patient, both for his or her present and the possible or preferable futures. Since the point of medicine is to help patients and since helping is tied into the way in which one interprets symptoms, conflicts inevitably occur. Even if some of these conflicts are not moral, many involve moral issues, such as which "right action" is eventually to be decided. There is not always agreement about what is wrong, nor, even if there is agreement about that, about what can or should be done about it. This facet of medicine, symptom interpretation, will occupy us in greater depth at a later point.

There is a third source of conflict. So far as medical care is an effort not only to interpret a patient's presenting symptoms but also to do something therapeutic about it (the "right action"), medicine is unavoidably involved in trying to determine issues of benefit and risk. Every medical situation shows this, for even in the simplest cases there is always an alternative, which is to do nothing (at the time, or at any time). Each alternative necessarily involves risks and benefits. The very point of therapy is to do something positive about the distress or affliction, that is, to alter the patient's condition, which includes risks and benefits that "not doing" will not entail (although that will obviously have its own sorts of risks, harms, and benefits). Different assessments of risks, harms, and benefits are therefore a source of actual or potential conflict.

Finally, there is a source of possible conflict in determining whose judgment of a patient's best interests is to be accepted, given weight, or even taken into account.

There are thus several significant sources of moral conflict quite independent of whether or not medical practice goes on within a culture marked by moral heterogeneity. By the same token, such conflicts may well appear at more than one level of medical practice—personal, professional, institutional, legal, governmental, or societal. For instance, what is accepted within the medical profession at a particular time (e.g., chiropractic is not legitimate medicine, while osteopathy is) may in some part be a dispute over such issues as symptom interpretation (how back pain is to be understood), as well as over what ought to be done about it (medication, physical therapy, surgery, or chiropractic manipulations, for instance). Such disputes are not innocent of moral, not to mention other philosophical, issues.

The presentation of moral quandaries or conflicts are diagrammed in Figure 4, which shows the relative variations in certainty and clarity they invariably display.

Whatever the specific source of conflict in a given case, the quandary will be exhibited along both of these continua; each will present as relatively potential or actual and as relatively vague or clear (uncertain or certain). Thus, all the sources of moral conflict should be mapped onto the diagram simultaneously. Of course, there are cases in which an accepted moral point of view in a time of moral heterogeneity (e.g., individualism) may come into conflict with the basic therapeutic theme of medicine itself; for example, a hospitalized patient under the care of a particular physician may refuse medical treatment.

Contending with these sorts of conflict is a clinical discipline that requires "going to the things themselves" of clinical practice: Moral issues are presented solely within the contexts of their actual occurrence. The actual occurrence of these complex and multiple issues, I have suggested, is primarily through moral quandaries or conflicts, and these have at least the sources indicated.

It is important to recognize that "what's going on" in a particular case

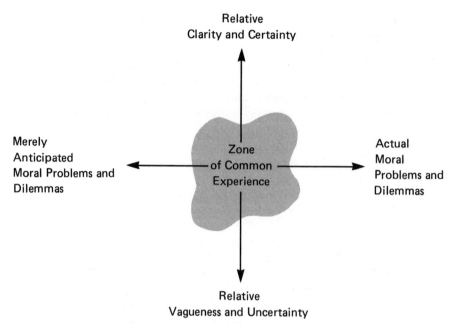

FIGURE 4.   Relative variations in moral conflicts.

can vary in still another way. For instance, it may be that the situation is one in which the best interests of a patient are known and even agreed upon by all concerned, and the question is whether those who must decide will have the courage to act accordingly or whether prevailing legal, professional, governmental or other policies or standards are such as to permit the decisions to be carried out (and, if not, what can then be done). On the other hand, there are cases in which the patient's best interests may indicate several alternative courses of action, but it is simply not clear which is preferable, and there may not even be clear ways of deciding among the alternatives. There are also situations where "what's best" for the patient cannot be determined (at the moment, or at all, perhaps) in view of ineradicable uncertainties or ambiguities (of diagnostic tests, observed data, social history).

REVIEW: CASE AND COMMENT

Although these themes cannot be fully probed at this point in the study, a case will help conceptualize them in an initial way.

> This case concerns a 16-year-old unmarried girl in her first pregnancy. After having some prenatal care in her hometown, including one ultrasound, prescribed at about 26 weeks gestation because a routine office visit showed an apparently enlarged quantity of amniotic fluid,

the girl was referred to the regional tertiary, acute-care center for evaluation and follow-up. A second ultrasound exam was performed (about two or three weeks after the first), which suggested, though with some uncertainty, that the single fetus was 28 ± 3 weeks gestation. The ultrasound also showed that the lower uterine segment and cervix appeared normal; the placenta was posterior and fundal with normal texture. Decreased amniotic fluid (oligohydramnios) was found; an equally important finding was a large cystic structure occupying the pelvis and abdomen, and a "markedly distended urinary bladder," consistent with bilateral hydronephrosis and hydro-ureter; because of obstruction, both the kidneys (hydronephrosis) and the ureter (hydro-ureter) were distended with urine, which could not be passed.

Renal parenchyma (functional elements of the kidneys) was noted to be decreased, with possible irreversible dysplasia (pathological alteration of size and shape) already begun. To the right and anterior of the distended bladder was a tubular cystic structure that was interpreted as a patent urachus (the fetal canal connecting the bladder with the median umbilical ligament was, abnormally, open). The fetal heart was located to the right of the midline (dextrocardia), and a small left plural effusion was noted. The stomach appeared to be displaced by the abdominal mass but was located in the left abdomen beneath the left hemidiaphragm.

The ultrasound of the brain showed mild ventricular dilatation, especially of the left lateral ventricle—interpreted as mild hydrocephalus, possibly progressive with unknown cause. Biparietal diameter (of the head) was noted to be enlarged for this gestational age; femur length and abdominal circumference, however, were normal. The fetus was noted to be male.

These conditions were evaluated by the multidisciplinary maternal-fetal team consisting of several obstetricians and ultrasonographers, a neonatologist, a pediatric neurologist, a hospital attorney, and an ethicist. The team found the fetus's condition to be most consistent with posterior-urethral valves with bilateral hydronephrosis and hydro-ureter. There was also thought to be either a gastrointestinal tract obstruction or possibly an abnormality in swallowing (which, if later confirmed, along with the dextrocardia, would suggest possible congenital neurological defects).

Faced with the problem of determining alternatives for this minor girl and her parents (the minor boyfriend had disclaimed further involvement), the following were considered:

1. Termination of pregnancy—regarded as not a feasible option due to (a) gestational age greater than 24 weeks, (b) consequent fetal viability, and (c) absence of threat to the life or health of the mother ("psychological health" risk being problematic under prevailing state law).

2. Amniocentesis for lung maturity studies (lung immaturity is a critical problem at this fetal gestational age) and chromosomal studies (for possible genetic defects)—regarded as possible plan in view of uncertain family history, but this option was rejected due to (a) probable low results and (b) relative risks involved with amniocentesis that outweighed the expected benefits at this gestational age.

3. Induction of labor now with either vaginal delivery or cesarean section delivery as indicated—rejected because (a) delivery at 28 weeks would most likely result in significant morbidity (and possible mortality) due to prematurity and (b) morbidity and mortality risks of cesarean section would be greater than allowing the pregnancy to continue.

4. Fetal therapeutic intervention—a ventriculoamniotic shunt could be surgically implanted *in utero* to effect drainage of accumulated fluid in the kidneys and ureters. This was regarded as not indicated for this fetus at this time due to (a) presence of multiple fetal anomalies (with increased mortality-morbidity risks, and did not fit the team's surgical protocol, which required a single anomaly), (b) risks of intra-amniotic shunting outweighed the benefits to be gained in view of the amount of viable renal parenchyma present at this time, and (c) fetal gestational age (intrauterine shunting has been most effective at less than 19 weeks gestation).

5. Weekly ultrasound studies and obstetrical reviews—this option was recommended by the team, along with full disclosure to the mother and her parents of the options and the team's reasoning and recommendations. Weekly ultrasound studies were deemed appropriate for the detection of any further renal atrophy and ventricular dilatation; weekly obstetrical reviews were seen as necessary to monitor cervical status and maternal-fetal statuses.

Concerning possible induction of labor, it was believed that attainment of 31 or 32 weeks gestation would probably result in a decision to deliver (with induction of labor if necessary) as opposed to shunting, as the risks of prematurity at this age are significantly decreased and neonatal shunting (with a live infant) would then be possible, with fewer risks than intrauterine shunting.

Several times the girl and her parents had expressed a strong desire for resolving the issue by abortion, which they believed would result in the death of the fetus. However, it was pointed out that abortion is not necessarily a destructive intervention, since labor can be induced and an alive fetus removed. According to state law, the girl's fetus at 28 ±3 weeks had to be considered viable, and the only permissible intervention was therefore termination of pregnancy and removal of the alive fetus, with subsequent neonatal care in the NICU. It was necessary to emphasize, nevertheless, that not even fetal removal was medically indicated at this time because of gestational age and the decreased risks to the fetus from removal at a later age.

Knowing that the fetus was afflicted with multiple anomalies, with severe compromise and poor prognosis, the girl and her parents regarded this recommendation as unacceptable. Expressing considerable anger and frustration, they decided heatedly to seek evaluation at a diagnostic center in another state, rather than continue the pregnancy for even three or four more weeks.

The team, too, felt strongly that their recommendation, even though well reasoned and the only one legally permissible, was probably inappropriate for the girl. Why, it was frequently asked, should we force this young girl to continue her pregnancy, especially now that she and her parents know full well that the fetus is massively damaged and not likely to survive even if it is eventually born alive?

As reported by Kramer (1983) and Blane et al. (1983), prenatal ultrasonography is noninvasive and can now safely permit the accurate diagnosis of many congenital anomalies, including those that afflicted this fetus. Identification of "up to 90 per cent of the kidneys by 17–20 weeks gestation and 95 per cent by 22 weeks" is common (Kramer, p. 375). If unrelieved, hydronephrosis may produce progressive kidney damage and eventual failure. If detected early enough, fetal surgery to drain the fluid to the amniotic cavity can benefit the fetus. But this is suggested only in cases of bilateral obstructive hydronephrosis, and prior to significant and irreversible renal damage. Since these conditions matched those of the girl's fetus, the fact that the anomalies had not been picked up early enough constituted a main problem. Considering alternatives, however, has to be weighed against the fact that "diagnostic errors of *in utero* ultrasonography can be significant" (ibid.). Thus, even with early detection, there must be repeated ultrasound studies, especially real-time ultrasound, in order to confirm these findings.

It remained uncertain why, in our case, the fetus's anomalies were undetected by the first ultrasound exam performed by the family obstetrician in his office at about 26 weeks gestation. Perhaps it was beyond his skill. While in 1984, "more than 30% of obstetricians have ultrasound equipment in their own offices" and about 34% of all pregnant women in the U.S. who use an office-based obstetrician have at least one ultrasound exam (Perone et al., 1984, p. 801), minimum standards for such exams had not yet been finally established, much less put into practice at that time. The Section on Obstetric and Gynecologic Ultrasound (SOGU) of the American Institute of Ultrasound in Medicine, however, had at the time of the case proposed minimum standards of competency, which included the minimum of information to be expected from a standard obstetric ultrasound examination (ibid., p. 802). If these recommendations are accepted generally, this minimum would include the recognition of "large pelvic masses" and "amount of amniotic fluid." While the girl's obstetrician had detected an abnormality relative to the latter, he did not detect the former.

It can also be asked why he waited until the 26th week gestation before performing the first ultrasound, since the procedure is most commonly used between weeks 7 and 13 to check cardiac activity and at around 15 to 18 weeks to check gestational age and fetal lie. Since up to 90% of the kidneys can be identified and abnormalities detected by 17–20 weeks gestation, an earlier ultrasound could have picked up this fetus's major problem in time to permit either intrauterine surgical shunting or therapeutic abortion. As it was, however, these options were precluded.

Other studies strongly suggest that the prognosis for neonatal life connected with oligohydramnios with bilateral hydronephrosis (conditions demonstrated by this fetus) is invariably almost nil. For instance, Hobbins et al. (1984) reported a five-year study of 25 fetuses with antenatal diagno-

sis of obstructive uropathy, 17 of which had bilateral obstructive hydronephrosis. Of the 17, 10 died of pulmonary hypoplasia, 3 were aborted, and
only 4 survived (all of which had serious problems). Furthermore, all 17
had oligohydramnios, a finding that best correlates with early neonatal
death. None of the fetuses that died of pulmonary hypoplasia had been
diagnosed, however, prior to 25 weeks gestation; indeed, the only ones diagnosed prior to week 24 were those that were quickly aborted.

The girl's fetus thus could only have a very poor prognosis for survival. Yet, because the abnormality was not detected until week 26, the option of abortion was foreclosed; after week 24 the fetus is regarded as viable and cannot be aborted unless there is a clear threat to the life or health
of the mother (*Roe v. Wade*, 410 U.S. 113, 1973, reaffirmed in subsequent
cases).

Clearly, the concept of viability as defined by the Supreme Court in
Roe v. Wade has been a central factor in cases involving ultrasonographic or
other antenatal diagnostic technologies. Viability, in the language of the
Court, is that point at which the fetus is "potentially able to live outside the
mother's womb, albeit with artificial aid" (*Roe v. Wade*). But the fetuses that
concern us here do not fall within that definition. While few things are perfectly certain in medicine, the most reasonable medical judgment is that the
chances for survival of such fetuses are almost nil. According to the study
reported by Hobbins, only 4 of 17 managed to survive, and each of the sur-
viving 4 faced severe problems, multiple surgeries, and compromised lives.
More to the point, every one of the 10 fetuses diagnosed after 24 weeks
died soon after delivery. Emphasis must thus be on early diagnosis if either
in utero surgery or therapeutic abortion are to be real options. Otherwise we
face the distressing alternative of forcing a woman to continue her pregnancy in the full knowledge that her fetus is afflicted with seriously compromising and possibly lethal anomalies.

It thus has to be asked whether it is at all medically coherent and morally right or fitting to require that these cases be judged in terms of the
notion of fetal viability as currently defined. We should note that it has
been judged legally correct to hold that parents and children have the right
to recover damages from wrongful birth (*Gleitman v. Cosgrove*, 227 A.2d
689 [N.J. 1967]; *Stewart v. Long Island College Hospital*, 296 N.Y.S.2d 41
[1968]). The same has been held in torts for wrongful life, when infants are
born with multiple congenital anomalies that severely compromise their
lives, if not also cause their early deaths (*Curlender v. Bio-Science Laboratories*,
165 Cal. 477 [Cal. App. 1980] [damages to both parents and child]; and
Turpin v. Sortini, 643 P.2d 954 [Cal. 1982] [damages to parents only]). Regarding these cases, Engelhardt has suggested,

> the general principle that one may be liable to both parents and their children
> for not having given adequate information that would have influenced rea-
> sonable individuals in their choices regarding contraception and abortion re-
> mains in place. (Engelhardt, 1985, p. 314.)

Given these choices, might it not also be morally (and perhaps even legally) appropriate to hold that parents should be allowed to abort regardless of the 24-week gestation ruling on viability? In a sense, the *Curlender* court seemed to intimate this. Faced with the issue of incorrect transmission of information with regard to whether a couple carried Tay-Sachs disease, and an affected child was born, the court not only awarded damages to both parents and child, but also raised the possibility that parents could be held liable for damages for continuing a pregnancy that they knew would likely result in a multiply handicapped infant (see Engelhardt, ibid.). Furthermore, the Washington State case of *Harbeson v. Parke-Davis, Inc.* (656 P.2d 483 [1983]) found that parents have the right to prevent the birth of a defective child.

None of these cases, however, utilizes the standard of viability, so presumably such parents could prevent birth only prior to the 24th gestational week (absent a threat to the life or health of the mother). Thus, in the cases like that discussed here, not even these court decisions prove very helpful.

What, then, about this notion of viability? Fost, Chudwin, and Wikler have written that every definition of it to date is either too limited or fails to recognize that it is an essentially relative notion expressive of a developmental process. There simply is no "single event in a fetus's development" at which viability occurs. Instead, viability "can refer to a variety of points . . . depending on such variables as the environment into which the fetus would hypothetically be born and the imagined duration of survival" it might have (1980, p. 12). "Environment," they argue, must include both "natural" supports (food, warmth) for some infants and "artificial" supports (ventilator, shunts) for others.

After analyzing various proposed definitions, including the Supreme Court's definition of viability as "potentially able to live outside the mother's womb, albeit with artificial aid," it is argued that any definition must include certain conditions that necessarily involve "value judgments." The latter relate specifically to the environment (intrauterine or extrauterine), the amount of neonatal survival time believed to be appropriate, and the kinds of acceptable "artificial aids." As involving "value judgments," however, such variables are said to be essentially "arbitrary" (ibid.); each is "a matter of individual preferences" or "conventions." For that reason, even though viability does have a useful role in clinical decisions, it has only "limited moral significance" in moral theory, legal decisions, and social policies (ibid., pp. 11, 12).

But that conclusion, somewhat dubious in itself, is too strong for the arguments given. The central problem with the viability criterion is not that it involves personal preferences or conventions, but rather that it has been tied to a specific gestational age. It is not viability but its limitation to any single, specific time (or, for that matter, birthweight) that is arbitrary.

The reason for this is made decisively, if also tragically, clear by cases like the one I have presented. Such a post-24-week fetus seems hardly viable; if the prognosis for such a fetus is probable death soon after delivery, then it seems legally and certainly medically and morally incoherent to regard it as viable while still a fetus simply because it is 25, 29, or even 38 weeks gestational age. (To be fair, the Supreme Court's ruling can be interpreted more flexibly as merely suggesting, based on then current medical evidence, that viability occurs at about 24–28 weeks.)

From another perspective, if there are sound reasons (medical and moral) for withholding treatments from multiply afflicted infants (Baby Does, whose lives or viability, as we saw in the last chapter, is seriously in doubt and for whom treatments are "futile" or "virtually futile"), it does not seem unreasonable to suggest that the very same reasons would be appropriate for post-24-week fetuses diagnosed as having the sorts of impairments discussed. Continuing with such pregnancies, regardless of gestational age, seems as inhumane in the one case as continuing treatments is said to be in the other.

It is thus understandable why the girl, her parents, and the medical team all felt the way they did—guilty, resentful, angry, frustrated, and trapped. Through these feelings (focused on, oriented to, and directed toward the girl and her damaged fetus) we can detect precisely the moral dilemma centered around the incoherence of viability. At the heart of it is the profound unfairness and the injustice invoked by having no choice (other than plain deceit or illicit action) but to continue this pregnancy with the full knowledge that the fetus is not only severely damaged but also highly unlikely to survive at all. If by chance it did survive, it would suffer grievous neurological and physiological compromise, which neither the girl nor, more significantly, the fetus seems to have in any way deserved. This theme will be taken up again later in this study.

THE MORAL BASIS OF MEDICINE: ANOTHER VIEW

Even though only a sketch thus far, this view of the moral dimension of medicine is at odds with a quite different view. Albert Jonsen, himself involved in medical ethics for years, believes that there is a "profound moral paradox" pervading modern medicine, a deep tension arising from the "incessant conflict of the two most basic principles of morality: self-interest and altruism" (Jonsen, 1983, p. 1532). Admitting that their status as "principles" of morality is quite debatable, Jonsen's view is nonetheless that "the institution of medicine, like my city of San Francisco, is built smack on top of its own structural rift"—a rift between altruism and self-interest (ibid.).

Medicine, he says, has two basic sources: One, the Hippocratic, delivers the self-interest theme; the other, the Judeo-Christian, provides the altruistic one. I believe this view is quite mistaken, but demonstrating this will have to be postponed until the historical character of medicine, and in particular the Hippocratic theme, have been adequately developed. It is in any case Jonsen's idea that self-interest and altruism are the basic moral principles at the foundation of medicine that seem questionable.

In the first place, self-interest is quite ambiguous. On the one hand, Jonsen defines it as "the principle that one should act so as to promote the values of personal preservation, growth, and happiness; good done for others redounds to one's own good." On the other hand, in the main part of his discussion he emphasizes that "medicine is a skill so rare that it can be sold at great price" (ibid.). Now, while the motive for the latter, as Jonsen acknowledges, is neither shameful nor dishonest, it is just as surely not the same thing as acting so as to promote the values of personal preservation, growth, and happiness. The reason is quite straightforward: While it may well be that practicing medicine for the end of achieving financial and other similar rewards can be in conflict with the altruistic end of helping other people (e.g., when these others cannot pay for one's services), the first definition is quite another matter. Indeed, self-interest in the first formulation seems inseparably part of altruism as Jonsen himself conceives it. More to the point, to conceive the moral foundation of medicine in terms of the conflict between selfish and altruistic interests may well be to misconceive it.

It is fruitful to view the opposition between self-interest and altruism in the light of MacIntyre's analysis of "social practices." In agreeing to help a patient, the physician is at the disposal of that patient's best interests and works, ideally, within a covenantal resolve to serve the patient in the best possible manner. Precisely in view of this, medicine is indeed an inherently moral enterprise. For the same reason, it is clearly a basic "internal good" of medicine as a social practice (MacIntyre, 1981, pp. 169–89).

A practice is any coherent and complex form of socially established cooperative activity through which goods internal to that form of activity are realized in the course of trying to achieve those standards of excellence that are appropriate to, and partially definitive of, that form of activity, with the result that human powers to achieve excellence, and human conceptions of the ends and goods involved, are systematically extended (ibid., p. 175).

Assuredly a practice in this specific sense, medicine has both internal and external goods, like every other social practice. The external goods are those that are only contingently attached to the practice, not constitutive of it—such as money, fame, and power. What Jonsen takes as foundational is in fact quite external. Goods internal to a practice, contrariwise, are definitive of (hence foundational to) it, because (1) they can be specified only in terms of the practice in question or by means of relevantly similar practices (and examples from both) and (2) they can be identified and recognized only "by the experience of participating in the practice in question" (ibid.). Thus, anyone lacking the relevant experiences is for that very reason not able to serve as a judge of goods internal to a practice. Finally, when goods internal to a practice are achieved, this enriches, sustains, and benefits the entire community of those engaged in the practice (quite un-like external goods), as well as those who may benefit from the work and products of the practice (in the case of medicine, patients).

Medicine is a social practice, then, incorporating definitive internal goods (expressed by its therapeutic theme and underlying moral resolve, and their situational specifications). These goods are realized (when, and to the extent they are) precisely in the course of the effort to achieve the standards of excellence within medical practice (such as clinical proficiency or intellectual competence). They cannot be realized other than by being actually engaged in clinical practice or in a relevantly similar practice.

The so-called "structural rift" Jonsen claims to have detected in his years of "doctor-watching," then, is quite mistaken so far as it is said to be the foundation of medicine. While there is surely tension, even at times conflict, between self-interest and altruism, these are surely not the basic moral principles at the heart of medicine. It is rather a conflict that arises for a variety of reasons within any socially organized practice, between goods internal and goods external to that practice. That physicians, like the rest of us, are interested in earning a living is true, not shameful nor dis-honest. But that this interest constitutes one of the "moral pinions" of med-icine as a social practice or profession is simply false.

My point can now be made with greater clarity. Medicine is an inher-ently moral enterprise precisely in view of its specific internal goods that together define its internal standards of excellence (though, of course, these must be specified in greater depth as we proceed). So far as moral issues are thus inherent to medical practice, an ethics responsive to those issues must be conceived as a clinical discipline. The issues themselves are internal to that practice; they are understandable solely within its frame-work and must be handled strictly within its specific context. This is not to deny that there are goods external to medical practice, nor that there are no moral issues associated with them. It is merely to emphasize that here we confront still another kind of moral complexity, requiring rather different sorts of considerations and attention so as to avoid serious moral and other confusions.

CHAPTER 3

"How the Hell Did I Get Here?": The Patient's Place in the Therapeutic Dyad

There is much about medicine that still needs to be more fully understood. Before going any further into that, however, it seems wise to consider more directly the other side of the therapeutic dyad: the patient and the patient's family.

A PHENOMENOLOGY OF ILLNESS: OUTLINE

It will be helpful to give a survey of this very difficult terrain first. Call to mind any encounter with a distressed, ill, or injured person (oneself or another). In the first place, any sort of affliction, trivial or grievous, effectively breaks into the usual textures of daily life with its taken-for-granted network of concerns, interests, preoccupations, activities, and involvements (Schutz, 1973; Zaner, 1981). For instance, if I break my leg, I can no longer take walking, sitting, or standing for granted in the usual ways. A person with angina faces a stairway in quite different ways than before. Even a mild case of flu requires that typical encounters with other people, for example, must now be somewhat differently managed.

Precisely because of such breaks in the daily round of life, affliction is always presented within a context of some degree of anxiety, uncertainty, frustration, suffering, and loss. The usually settled ebb and flow of life be-

53

comes unsettled (if only temporarily), and there is then the effort to settle things again. In these terms, Schutz remarks, everyday life is governed by a "pragmatic motive" (Schutz, 1973, pp. 25–58, 182–228).

In the second place, to put oneself, or to be placed by someone else, within the practice of health professionals is to become one who asks for or needs assistance and who, in this sense, appeals for help. The medical encounter is necessarily one that evokes and requires trust (whether or not, or to whatever extent, this is justified or fulfilled). The person now perforce relies on these others to do whatever it takes to permit the person to get on with his or her life. When another is trusted to help during those times when one cannot help oneself (for whatever reason), it is not only that one wants to get well or better, but is also distressed over what afflicts and inhibits and over the inability to do for oneself. Hence, having to rely on others is textured by and expressed through a complex range of wishes, wants, hopes, and fears.

In the third place, to appeal for help is to ask others to put themselves—their knowledge, time, energies, and experience—responsively at one's disposal. Thus, in addition to evoking trust and reliance, medical encounters also evoke the need for responsive care from others. From the patient's perspective, medical encounters are textured also by caregivers and their wanting "to do the right thing" for the afflicted person, whether the "right thing" is well understood or not in particular situations and however the various discussions about the course of action may be conducted and decisions arrived at. Thus, not only the patient's complex set of feelings, but also those of the caregivers texture the variety of facts presented by any medical encounter.

Fourth, except for relatively trivial situations, both being afflicted and dealing with afflicted persons invariably occur within a context of more or less uncertainty, ambiguity, and fallibility on everyone's part. Every medical situation is marked by these complex features, features that evoke sometimes quite strong emotions and volitional and valuational feelings. These reactions, too, form an inherent part of the facts of each clinical encounter.

Fifth, the caregivers in whom the patient invests unavoidable trust and reliance are almost invariably strangers. This of itself severely complicates the tasks of the helping professions, medicine in particular. Why help or care for strangers? On the other side of the dyad, why place one's trust in strangers, most especially when so much is or can be at stake and when the slightest mistake may prove to be disastrous? As Richard Titmuss emphasizes, "in the relatively affluent, acquisitive and divisive societies of the twentieth century," a "fundamental moral issue" is unavoidably posed by the sheer fact that giving and receiving, helping and being helped, trusting and caring in our times, go on among strangers (1972, p. 11). Within medicine, this trusting-caring relationship is further complicated by the fact that the nature of medicine often requires that some of the most intimate sorts of actions be performed on strangers by strangers. This aspect demands circumspect attention to the specific ways in which each individual case presents with different ranges and types of feeling, action, decision, and interaction among physicians and patients and their families.

Finally, looked at from the perspective of either physicians or patients, each clinical encounter is marked by a structural "asymmetry of power in favor of the helper" (Lenrow, 1982, p. 48). Compared to the patient, the physician is in a position of knowledge, resources, and skills, backed by considerable legal, social, and institutional legitimation. The physician or healer "professes to possess precisely what the patient lacks— the knowledge and power to heal" (Pellegrino, 1982, p. 159). The asymmetry of power in the helping relationship is marked by the "peculiarly vulnerable existential state" of the patient and the power of the professed healer(s) (ibid.). This special state of vulnerability and deprivation is, moreover, quite unique:

> The poor, the imprisoned, the lonely, and the rejected are also deprived of the full expression of their humanity, so much so, that men in these conditions may long for death to liberate them. But none save saints seeks illness as the road to liberation. In no other deprivation is the dissolution of the person so intimate that it impairs the capacity to deal with all other deprivations. The poor man can still hope for a change of fortune, the prisoner for a reprieve, the lonely for a friend. But the ill person remains impaired even when freed of these other constraints on the free exercise of his humanity. (Ibid.)

From the perspective of the patient, illness or injury forces breaks with the usual flow of daily life, places the patient within numerous unavoidable trust relationships, and obliges the patient to rely on the care of other persons who, by the nature of the case, work within the contexts of relative uncertainty, ambiguity, and fallibility. Patients are invariably strangers to those professing to be able to help and, thus, interrelate within an asymmetrical relationship of power in favor of the healers. Each of these features requires deeper study, for each uniquely textures the presence of feelings, actions, and decisions characteristic of every clinical encounter.

The complex of feelings is specifically evoked by the afflicted person and is directed to the specific patient's present condition as efforts to do something about it. Finally, these feelings are aimed at the patient's possible future(s) and in this sense are concerns about how to be most responsive to the specific person in order to enable the patient to become, to the extent possible, restored, comforted, relieved, even healed. Whatever else feelings may be, they are clearly concerns about doing what is most appropriate, that is, doing what is best, good, or just for the patient, within the constraints imposed by the patient's particular condition, biological wherewithal, values, social circumstances, and the available medical procedures (routine, investigational, experimental, or even exotic).

These feelings, therefore, are not simply overt reports by a patient about his or her, or a physician's, subjective life at the moment, that is, literal "ex-pressions"—the "pressing-outward" of what lies "inside" as purely private. As evoked by, directed to, and aimed at the specific patient in his or her present distress and possibly restored future(s), such feelings are the experiencing person's specific orientations toward the circumstances and wishes of the patient and the patient's family. In this respect, feelings are not merely subjective; to the contrary they are as objective as any scientific or other fact.

Careful attention to the complex and subtle ranges of emotive, volitional, and valuational feelings serves to focus a crucial moral question: What is it about any specific patient that evokes, directs, and aims just these specific feelings and serves to orient the discussions, decisions, and actions of others (physicians, family, nurses)? This clinical issue guides the subsequent reflections.

PATIENTS PRESENT THEMSELVES

To understand the patients' side of the dyad the best thing to do is to listen to patients (including, of course, ourselves) talk about their illnesses. Robert C. Hardy's collection (1978) of patients' reactions to their respective encounters with illness, physicians, nurses, and institutions provides an excellent selection.

> A hospital administrator in his middle 50s, who has had several bouts with cancer, reported:

> > When I stop and think about that, which I don't very often, it occurs to me that most people never get cancer. They just worry about it. . . . On the other hand, everybody who gets cancer isn't about to toddle off this mortal world, either, which is the kind of thing you have to remind yourself of if you think about it at all.
> > I don't think about it much. It's been three years since I was operated on for lymphoma in my right axilla—the polite word for armpit you know—and it's been even longer than that since I had skin cancer, I guess two years or longer. . . . But I almost never think about it. . . . Frankly, I think about it only at the three-month checkups I have at the internist's office.
> > The word cancer will strike panic in your heart. . . . The first time this happened, I wasn't even in a doctor's office. The announcement came about very casually, and I'm sure the doctor meant it to be that way, but it had the same effect: panic! (Ibid., p. 21.)

> He was having lunch with friends, including a physician he had known for some years. Just when the lunch was about over, the doctor suddenly said: " 'That's a cancer you've got on your cheek there. Why don't you come on over to the office and we'll take it off?' " (Ibid., p. 22.)

> Instead, "more than a little shocked by what the doctor said at lunch," he went directly to his internist's clinic to see the dermatologist. He was

told that two things could be done: " 'We can scrape it off or we can burn it off. I prefer excising the lesion,' " because this procedure doesn't leave as much of a scar.

> So he stuck it a few times with a local anesthetic and carved away. It didn't hurt and didn't bleed much. . . . I figured that's all there was to that. . . . and that the small procedure he had just performed would probably handle everything.
>
> Well, it didn't. What seems now like a year later . . . there it was again. In the meantime, the dermatologist had taken off to Atlanta, moved completely. . . . It was necessary to find another dermatologist and resort to . . . radiation therapy. (Ibid., p. 22.)

His second bout with cancer, although worse than the first, was still not the "bad news" of lung or rectal cancer:

> I was lucky. I had a kind of cancer I could identify, at least I knew it was there, and it was one which the doctors could do something about. This one showed up as a lump in my right armpit. But at first I didn't even know it was there.
>
> You know what saved my life? A pair of grass shears, for goodness sakes! . . . We were expecting out-of-town guests and I wanted to spruce up the place and make it look nice, so I decided I would do the edging with the hand shears [his power edger was on the fritz]. Well, it's not ordinarily all that much work, but it was this time. At first, I thought I was just out of practice or out of condition because the squeezing motion necessary to operate the shears caused my hand to get stiff and numb and painful.
>
> This pain continued up my arm and persisted for a few days after I had done the edging. . . . I was naturally curious about this . . . and began to feel around my hand and arm and it was then that I discovered the lump in my armpit. It didn't quite look or feel like the other armpit and although I had never noticed it there before, it didn't seem to be all that important. You know, you always hear about the seven danger signals of cancer and strange lumps is one of those. But when you raise your arm, there's a sort of lump instead of a hollow there anyhow. And even though I compared one side to the other side, I wasn't ready yet to admit that I was anything more than a little lopsided.
>
> As I recall, the discomfort in my hand diminished although it didn't go away altogether. The lump bothered me. Not physically, understand, as it didn't interfere with anything I was doing, but I was conscious of it. It just sat there, silent and painless, except for occasional funny feelings down my arm and in my hand. (Ibid., pp. 23–24.)

Eventually, he did go to an internist, who said:

> "Well, I don't know what that is but it will have to come out." Bingo, just like that. I think doctors are very intolerant of strange lumps. Anyhow, he sent me down the corridor to see the surgeon. The surgeon didn't know what it was either, but he came to the same conclusion. "We'll have to just snake that right on out of there, whatever it is." (Ibid., p. 24.)

Surgery was necessary. They gave him a sedative, and he was carted off to the operating room. Joking with the nurses until he went under, at about nine o'clock in the morning, he began to come to around supper time, "no pain, no strain" (ibid.). The excised lump, of course, still had to be studied by pathology. Several days later, he was informed that the lump was "malignant . . . reticulum lymphoma, grade III, and I'm not sure to this day just what that means" (ibid.).

The panic returned. He was told a course of cobalt radiation would be necessary for his upper torso; for this he would be referred to a hematologist. Hospitalization was recommended, and accepted; besides a "rest cure . . . you know . . . I had two insurance policies" that would cover the workup and procedure.

After a seven-day workup, cobalt therapy was initiated. Despite the well-known side effects of this treatment, it was finally over.

> All and all, I'm lucky. I have passed 60 percent of a five-year cure. You know, that's the way they figure cancer survival. If you survive for five years, they figure you've got a pretty good chance to keep going. I didn't suffer all that much in the process and insurance paid all the costs. . . . As I said when I started out, I hardly ever think about cancer any more. . . .
>
> Cobalt radiation is cumulative so once you've had a round, you can't have another round because it builds on itself and there's a limit to how much radiation one can tolerate. Fortunately, standing in the wings, is cancer chemotherapy. So if I have to go over this route again, the medical profession won't be completely out of therapeutic resources. (Ibid., p. 28.)

A second case presents somewhat different issues.

> A rather plump, 40-year-old woman, with black hair piled high on her head and framing her fair, very white skin, is the wife of a retired military officer and the mother of a teenage girl. She works in a downtown city government office.

> I have had a history of being heavy and, of course, gaining weight and then losing it causes loose skin. I had very often thought, "Wouldn't it be nice to take a knife and cut off the fat, you know, and get rid of it." Through the years they finally have improved upon this method of removing fat from your stomach.
>
> I had gone with this girlfriend to see a plastic surgeon and I asked him about it: were they doing this kind of surgery, was it perfected and would a person find it advantageous to have it done? He said that in the last seven years they felt they had improved on this method and it would be to my advantage to have it done if it was that important to me to remove what I felt was a disfigurement. It's called an apron. (Ibid., p. 35.)

The woman described the procedure, a panniculectomy:

> What they do is cut through the . . . sometimes they do a "W" cut and pull from all four directions and take the loose skin off and it makes you have a tight abdomen again. Some women do it to get rid of old scars from other surgery and some women do it to

get rid of stretch marks from having babies or gaining weight. Myself, I did it to get rid of loose skin where I had carried weight and then lost it. The doctor said he would recommend it to me, that he thought I would feel better by it.

So I went back to see him later and he explained exactly what he was going to do. I have always wanted it so it was right quick-like. Within two weeks I had made up my mind. (Ibid.)

At the same time, she decided to have breast implants put in (she had had her breasts removed earlier). The material, she reported, had been "much improved" over the silicone used on her earlier—which had hardened and was then rejected by her body. The new material, as she understood it, "is something of a lubricant-type material," initially made as a lubricant for large drilling tools. "It's clear . . . some kind of a rubber product but it's not silicone and it's not plastic."

What was done on her stomach was satisfactory, "except the mistake that was made here [*points to left side*], and I can't say it was his fault any more than mine" (ibid., p. 36). When she awoke after surgery for three and a half hours she "hurt like the dickens [*laughs*]. . . . It was a real burning pain. I couldn't move because I was cut from about two inches behind where my arms hang down clear around to the same place on the other side. . . ." (ibid.).

She experienced respiratory problems, so a "special doctor" was brought in. He "ran some tests and he said I didn't have enough oxygen in my blood. . . . So they gave me oxygen. They brought some kind of machine in and used it two or three times" (ibid.). She also learned that 284 stitches had been used to sew up her incision, which had been covered up with thick gauze pads and ace bandages. She had difficulty keeping these in place. She didn't know what they were for anyway, she reported, and hadn't been informed either why they were in place or how to keep them in place. The result was that the left side did not heal properly, because the bandages kept slipping out of place. She was then told that the procedure would have to be done all over.

Her doctor "had me come in the back door [*laughs*], and I had a feeling that he didn't want anybody to see me. . . . My family was really worried about me, said I looked terrible" (ibid., pp. 37–38). This visit was also when she learned just how important the bandages were, something she hadn't realized before. In fact, she became very aggravated: " 'You have made me lose one week of healing by not telling me this. You're the doctor. I'm the patient and I don't know what it takes to get me well. You have the knowledge and you should have told me that' " (ibid., p. 38).

Now, the importance of keeping the bandages very secure was clear: to prevent post-surgical build-up of body fluids. Now doing it correctly, she reported her suspicions about who actually did the procedure:

I'm almost sure, although I can't swear to it because I don't have any proof, that the assistant who is studying under the doctor did my left side. I'm sure he is a very fine breast surgeon . . . but I think this stomach deal is something very new. . . . But it was funny because my right-side incision was real rough and it stuck out, looked like it was puckered, and my left side was just laid down so smooth and had real fine stitching. One day I was teasing this younger doctor . . . "Who sewed up this right side?" And he said, "Dr. John did." And then I said, "Well, who sewed up this side? The same person didn't sew up both sides." He said, "I did this side." I said, "Boy, this right side really looks a mess. It really looks ugly." And the assistant said, "Well, he takes a rougher stitch than me." The left side looked good but, of course, that's the side that turned out bad. (Ibid.)

It was so bad that Dr. John wanted to do it over. Then, she reflected:

But you know, after they put you out, you have to trust these people, the physicians, like you do God. You're all in their hands, and if they don't take care of you, who's going to? It's God and them. It is really a responsibility and I think a doctor should have a little more dedication to the patient. I took him at his word because I know his reputation, being a very fine surgeon. I trusted him not to let an inexperienced person mess up my life. I have lost one month at work. I like to have lost my job because of the time I was off and now I am going to have to go back into the hospital. (Ibid., p. 40.)

While in the hospital, she had problems with hyperventilation. When a specialist was called in, he "came in and stood at the foot of my bed and told me who he was. He said, 'You don't have enough oxygen in your blood.' And I said, 'I don't?' And he said, 'No.' Then he pulls out his card and he said, 'If you ever need a doctor, call me.' And he turned around and walked out" (ibid., p. 41).

At another point, a nurse was sent to draw some blood. She was quite nervous, never having done it before. She poked around without finding the vein. Clearly upset, the woman told the nurse she'd better find the right vein and get it over with, and while telling her this, noticed "a guy standing behind her, a young man. Of course, by then, I was quite touchy. And I asked, 'Well, who is he?' And they said, 'He's applying for a job.' And I said, 'The hell he is! This man doesn't even know me and he's standing in my room. Get him out of here.' You expect the nurses," she went on in some anger, "in a hospital to see you nude, but this man walked off the street to apply for a job. I sure didn't care for him experimenting with me if he didn't have any experience. He left, but I thought I had my right of privacy in that room, you know" (ibid.).

One time, during one of her visits to the surgeon, she met another lady who had decided to have the same operation:

I couldn't tell that she was needing it as bad as she was wanting it, so I said, "There's more to it than meets the eye. Unless you can talk to someone who's had it done." "Well, I don't know anybody," she said. I said to her, "Let me tell you one thing. Be ready to give up one month of your life and have people wait on you. And keep those ace bandages very tight. From the moment they put them on you, do not ever take them off for at least three weeks." I explained to her why.

A week or so later, I seen her in there again and she was sittin' there just so perky and I said, "How are you doing?" She said, "Fine. I'm going back to work next week." And I thought, "Oh, God!" Because I'm still going in and being pumped every day and still had the darned ace bandages on 'cause he had to put a tube in to help drain it. I was getting pretty aggravated with it all. She said, "I really appreciate you telling me about those ace bandages. You know, they didn't tell me a darn thing."

I felt sure they wouldn't. I don't think they do it on purpose. I just think they take their job so for granted that they do a good job but they fail to inform a person. They don't realize we are ignorant as to what we are paying for.

The other day the doctor said to me, "Really, you don't look that bad." And I said to him, "If I wore a girdle, I didn't look that bad before I come to see you, and for $2,000, you're supposed to make me look better."

The next operation is on him. (Ibid., p. 43.)

A final case will serve to highlight still other issues.

A tall, gray-haired Virginian in his middle 40s, the man is an architect with planning responsibilities, which include the supervision of design and construction of buildings on the campus of a growing state university. He is easy to be with, quiet and slow to express criticism, but highly articulate when the occasion calls for it. A major in the Army Reserve, he spends two weeks every summer as a soldier.

My sequence of events began on December 30 of last year. I remember that date because when the whole thing began to unfold, I realized that I wasn't going to go to a New Year's Eve party the following night. I found myself in the hospital instead.

That evening, December 30, I went to bed after a more or less normal evening at home and a normal evening meal. About two or 2:30 in the morning, I woke up with a very acute pain in my side, not only an acute pain but the feeling that there was a large, more or less solid mass in my right side above the belt line. . . . My initial reaction was "I'm having an attack of appendicitis again." But I had had my appendix removed when I was 15 years old. The attack then, which led to the diagnosis of acute appendicitis, was of similar intensity of pain and slightly similar location in the body.

This time, below the rib cage, there was a very hard knot or lump. It was almost as though I had swallowed my fist. It was the size of a baseball or a small orange and it was very easy to put my hand on it. I tried to assume various positions in bed, or standing up, or walking around, or walking around bent over to relieve the intense pain. I finally found that by lying in bed on my left side and sort of suspending this hard mass in the space of the body cavity, I was as comfortable as I could get. . . .

Finally, when morning came, my wife awakened and began to ask what was going on. I said, "Well, I'm in very acute pain." I'd had a bowel movement but I had not thrown up. I'd sort of thought the intensity of the pain might lead to vomiting . . . I've had things of that kind once or twice. (Ibid., pp. 244–45.)

After his night of acute pain, he checked in at the local hospital. Heavily sedated, "just kind of out of it," he was given "some kind of pill that apparently tends to centralize in the gall bladder . . . [which] made me very ill." Some lab work was done, and he was visited by a surgeon, who seemed to convey the idea that the decision to have surgery had already been made and he was there to get the job done. My initial question to him was 'Is there any other alternative?' His response was one of surprise or being caught off guard. . . . He left the scene, apparently having decided that my family physician and I should come to a further conclusion before his continued interest would be warranted.

I have a natural reservation about surgery but my real posture as a patient was one of not having information. I was being called on to make a decision at a time when, first of all, I had no awareness of what the lab reports would show, if anything. My reservation personally was that, although my physician had indicated that my problem was a gall bladder problem, I was not sure that he had very much confirming evidence in terms of the x-rays and the lab work, since neither were available or at least had not been reported to me at that time. . . . I had no data base. Very little information, a lot of supposition. (Ibid., p. 246.)

About the nurses, though, he had "very good feelings," especially with "their ability to deal with members of my family and with me and their response, the care with which they seemed to operate and the sensitivity with which they dealt with me as a patient. They dealt with me more as a person than a patient" (ibid., p. 247).

After several hospitalizations, he gave a kind of "post mortem" of two strong impressions. First, "I was treated very well as a patient by the people in the hospital," even regarding his firm refusal of surgery.

The other thing that struck me, though, was that the community hospital was an unknown quantity when I was admitted there and I have good feelings about the way the hospital is administered and the way the people who work in it care. (Ibid., pp. 247–48.)

Eventually, he was able to control his problem with diet and medication and was quite comfortable with his decision to refuse surgery:

Maybe I've avoided what will turn out to be inevitable. But at no time in this whole thing have I been told by anyone that there was a confirmation of the fact that my gall bladder was really not functioning. There were some short periods of time that it wasn't functioning reasonably, but the five tests done to ascertain gall bladder function, two of them taken when I was in an acute sort of condition, both indicated there was some sort of problem but three of them taken later indicated that my gall bladder was functioning in a reasonable way. Business as usual. (Ibid., p. 249.)

"WHAT'S WRONG WITH ME?"
"DO YOU REALLY CARE?"

As Hardy remarks in an unpublished reflection on his collection of patient stories, there are two clear themes running throughout. First, sick people want to know what's wrong with them; second, they want to know that the people taking care of them really care. This is not to say that all patients make it a rule to find out what's going on or whether their physicians or nurses really do care for them. What the patient stories in Hardy's collection make pretty obvious is that many patients have compelling difficulties in their efforts to find out what is going on with them.

Possibly some patients fear being regarded as too pushy; others may be apprehensive about appearing insulting to physicians and nurses. Some, like the architect, are more insistent. In any event, hospitals are rarely places that encourage persistent questions from patients. They are busy places, with a busy staff dealing with serious and preoccupying situations. A patient's questions interrupt nurses and physicians in their daily rounds, especially in their care for other patients. The questions may then appear selfish, and the patient does not want to appear presumptuous or self-centered—in a hospital no more than elsewhere.

Furthermore, patients are not often in a good position to question those who take care of and have control over them. They often cannot evaluate what is being done to them or why it's being done, nor can they judge whether treatments or procedures are appropriate or effective or whether there were alternatives that might have been better. Open and direct communication, difficult enough in hospitals anyway, can be further compromised. Some patients do not know how to talk to medical professionals (especially when they look so busy and serious); others may not want to do so (at a particular time, or at all); and some are content simply to act out the sick role they believe they are expected, and perhaps even encouraged, to perform by hospital personnel and staffs. There is here, like elsewhere in society, a premium placed on the "good patient," who is compliant, cooperative, and quiet.

Although the architect was insistent on having the results of tests at hand before he would consider surgery, other patients are not that way at all. The mother of a partially sighted child stated, for instance, that if you have a good mind,

> you want your doctor to understand that. . . . But people are too timid around doctors. . . . They have become super-human because of the way people treat them. Until you've been around doctors as friends you don't realize that they have fears, too. But . . . they sense how timid you are and that makes them more overpowering. They've got an edge on you. . . . Somehow if doctors would just sense how much hold they have over a person's feelings. (Hardy, 1978, pp. 89, 92–93.)

A judge who had come down with diabetes pointedly remarked that "if you can't communicate and you can't understand your disease, then you don't have any confidence in the medical help you are getting. The better the doctor explains to you, the better position you're in to abide by what he wants you to do" (ibid., p. 236). However, he went on,

> there are lots of feelings that are hard to put into words, especially if you've never had the feeling before. I had to explain things to my doctor which were a brand new experience to me, and I had nothing to compare it to. So if you

can't communicate back and forth, and explain to him what's bothering you, how can he help you? (Ibid.)

Reading these stories or listening to patients talk about their experiences with illness, one is constantly struck by just how much people of all sorts know about sometimes quite rare afflictions (such as Lesch-Nyhan syndrome, Bang's syndrome, plantar warts, or omphaloceles), as well as about the complex medical or surgical procedures to deal with their conditions (panniculectomy, stapedectomy, lymphangiogram, ultrasound). Just as remarkable, patients are frequently fascinated and intrigued by the wild growths, bumps, gurgles, spasms, and jerks their bodies display, as well as by the procedures and tests they go through in efforts to diagnose and treat them. They often report how "interesting" it was to be prepared for surgery, have an angiogram, be treated in an intensive care unit, or radiated at just the right spot for cancer.

As Hardy came to know well, patients want to know. Robert S. Mendelsohn, in his introduction to Hardy's book, was so impressed with this finding that he was moved to emphasize: "A remarkable finding of these interviews is the consistently profound base of information patients manifest about their condition" (ibid., pp. vii–viii). Patients also show genuine appreciation of the dilemmas, successes, failures, and mistakes of clinical practice—regardless of whether they are then moved to forgiveness (which is quite frequent), apology (also quite frequent), or condemnation (surprisingly infrequent in Hardy's collection).

Moreover, patients often succeed in finding out information despite the reluctance of physicians and nurses to inform them and discuss their cases in depth. Not only is this very often the case; it seems clear that to be a patient is to be constantly on the alert for any "news" about themselves, present and future.

At times, this alertness can result in misfortune. One patient with emphysema and pneumonia, for instance, was told "very little" about his problems. He recalled, though, how acutely alert he became, constantly trying to learn about his condition (perhaps even interpreting incorrectly what he thought he heard, or interpreting the wrong things, or interpreting the right things in the wrong ways). "I got provoked with my doctor," he reported. "He was talking with a resident physician who makes rounds with him, a young doctor, and I heard him tell that doctor I've got only 16 percent and he didn't see how I could do as well as I did. . . . Well, it makes me mad and I was very depressed" (ibid., p. 53). He thought that maybe he was wrong to be feeling so good! But then he thought that maybe he would "show" that doctor! Earlier, while he was in the ICU, "I don't guess the doctors knew I could hear them, but I heard them talking and they were going to do a tracheotomy. . . . I was in there three weeks and, oh, it was just like being in a cell" (ibid., p. 49).

Patients also want to know that those who are taking care of them really care. Whatever else the phrase may mean, for patients medicine is indeed "an inherently moral enterprise" (Cassell), and they are often acutely alert to any sign suggesting that their caregivers really do, or do not, care. This is evident from their dismay, humiliation, and anger at not being told about their conditions (the architect) or how to manage their injuries (the woman with the apron); they sense that they are not being respected and, thus, not cared for. It is also evident in their praise and gratitude when they have been treated with respect (the architect about his nurses, the administrator about his physicians).

Another patient reported losing confidence in her family physician because he simply had not kept current about new developments, which created additional problems for her (ibid., p. 285). The hospital administrator, on the other hand, had only praise for his physicians, radiologists, and surgeons; he had the sense they really did care about him while they took care of him. A truck driver, to strike a different chord, became quite irritated by never being allowed to say anything to the doctor who treated him in the office, as well as by the rush and lack of time:

> You go to the doctor's office and you sit for about an hour past your appointment and then you get up and go sit in the examinin' room or the shot room for another 15 or 20 minutes. . . . This irritates me. In the old days, I believe that people entered the doctor profession out of compassion and caring for other people. But not one person in ten believes that they do today. They enter . . . for the money. (Ibid., p. 186.)

Clearly, illness and affliction are the occasions for at times profound emotion, passion, and other feelings. But there is often great difficulty expressing these feelings in the right way, at the right time, or to the right people.

TEARS IN THE FABRIC OF DAILY LIFE

The routines of daily life (edging the grass, talking with friends, looking in the mirror before going out shopping, getting a drink of water) can become destabilized and interrupted—either suddenly or gradually. These changes sometimes may seem ordinary (having to strain to read a street sign), at times puzzling (having weight loss even when exercising and eating properly), at other times dramatic (awakening from sleep with acute abdominal pain). The familiar may then seem quite strange—an apparently innocuous lump becomes the occasion for panic.

A variety of taken-for-granted recipes for conduct (Schutz, 1973, pp. 105–10), assimilated through socialization for managing the unsettling of routine life, may be brought into play: using the grass shears with the other hand, squinting to see the street sign better, shifting one's body to ease the abdominal pain. Interpretations of what's wrong may be entertained: It "must be a viral infection" or "it might be a violent attack of food poisoning"; not seeing the street sign "prompted me to see an ophthalmologist"; not knowing what the ace bandages were for, "I thought it was to keep the drain tubes in place."

Sometimes, such recipes and everyday typifications are all that is needed for settling the unsettled routines, if only temporarily. At times, and for some people, simply ignoring the disturbing event may seem all that's needed, and this may even become a matter of habit. It happens, too, that other people may know about us better than we know ourselves. The judge with diabetes, for instance, learned from his wife that she "really knew he was ill long before he did. . . . You can tell," she reported, "by looking. It's like taking one of your children to the pediatrician and saying. 'He doesn't look right to me,' and he didn't. I knew he was ill" (Hardy, 1978, p. 238).

Just how unsettled the routines of the everyday must be before a person seeks the help of others will obviously differ with each individual. It will vary, too, depending upon the specific circumstances, illnesses or injuries, habits, and life-styles of each person. Whatever the illness or injury, afflictions are experiences in which the person's own daily embodied capacities fail or are somehow compromised, in which the everyday routines of life are disrupted and thereby call attention to themselves.

Indeed, one measure of the severity of an illness is whether a person's ordinary concerns can be continued, require modification in order to be continued, or are obliterated by the illness (see Rawlinson, 1982). It has been made wonderfully lucid by Schutz (1973) that the veritable mark of everyday life is what he terms its "taken-for-grantedness." By way of culturally and socially inculcated typifications, we learn in the usual course of affairs simply and habitually to take hosts of things for granted, as going to be more or less as they have proven to be in the past, at least for all practical purposes. Only if something does not conform to our typified expectations are we at all alerted to it specifically, called on to take notice of it, and then to do something about it. Our attention is then typically directed to settling only what has become unsettled in order to proceed with whatever occupies us at the time—getting the grass trimmed, seeing the street sign, easing a shoulder pain, or seeing the tops of the legs for the first time. Should we be obliged to change a habit (using eyeglasses or crutches) or alter our lives more substantially (losing a leg, becoming blind), we even then more or less grow used to it, and our respective stocks of taken-for-granted habits and knowledge remain governed by the pragmatic motive of daily life.

Illness and impairment have a unique way of cutting into that fabric, and the person's life may sometimes become radically altered—temporarily, as with a case of the flu, or for longer times, as with diabetes. Whichever it may be, the person's embodying organism, especially that part or member that has been affected, becomes "front-and-center," often dominating the person's awareness (the "apron," the "lack of energy," the "pounding heart," the "acute belly-ache"), or at least hovering constantly, if silently, in the background of experience (the lump in the administrator's armpit that "just sat there, silent and painless, except for occasional funny feelings down my arm and in my hand"). In short, the afflicted person is no longer able to take for granted some of what he or she had hitherto been taking for granted, to whatever extent it may be and for however long it may go on. The woman with flu can no longer be up and about in the same ways; the man with end-stage kidney disease must now maintain a rigorous dietary regimen and undergo regular dialysis. Now, daily things must be done differently, or they may even have to be done for the person by some-one or something else.

Illness or injury constricts the ordinary course of life (bodily activities, objects experienced or handled, even the usual flow of time and shape of space). Ordinary actions—reaching out, going toward, embracing, listening to, looking at—become compromised and altered. The usual ways of ex-pecting, hoping, greeting, and promising become confounded to some ex-tent. As Rawlinson remarks, "The future, either short-term or long-range, takes on a brittle quality. One finds one's plans disrupted and possibilities withheld" (1982, p. 75), or, it may be that these have to be put on hold for however long it takes. Illness and injury are losses of vital abilities and ener-gies that, in the more dramatic cases, may signify the end of all time, the closure of all space, the wipe-out of the world—death.

The various ways in which the fabric of the everyday is split—the con-traction and restriction of ordinary experience, time, and space—are al-most never deliberately sought out. Illness, rather, befalls the person, un-asked for and most often disquieting (see Zaner, 1982, pp. 51–58). It "never constitutes a value in itself which one might appropriately cultivate. One falls ill, and the insistence, intransigence, and opacity of the body in illness signifies the limits of one's ability to direct one's own history" (Rawlinson, 1982, p. 76). To be sure, there are people who more or less unconsciously seek to become ill (see Ford, 1983; Meropole, Ford, and Zaner, 1985) in order to get attention or to punish themselves. Such cases are not exceptional. Many of these patients have been described as having borderline personalities (Nadelson, 1979), antisocial personality disorders, Munchausen's syndrome (Carrodus et al., 1971; Nadelson, 1979; Stein-beck, 1967), malingering (Agle et al., 1970), or other problems (Meropole, Ford, and Zaner, 1985). In short, they may be best understood as exhib-iting "a destructive will, an ill will in fact," as Rawlinson suggests (1982, p. 76). Such cases do not, therefore, suggest a need to alter our understand-ing of illness or injury as befalling or as accidents to a person.

To experience affliction in its various forms is to find oneself critically and uniquely singled out as vulnerable. Our bodily abilities compromised, our personal activities confounded (not being able to choose, for instance, those with whom to associate), our need to be preoccupied with the pains and suffering that befall us—in short, illness affects our own vital sense of ourselves, to one degree or another.

For the most part, our sundry ailments, cuts, abrasions, breaks, and sicknesses pass away, become healed, or are eventually cleared up. At their passing we are often left with a sense of relief, sometimes quite profound, of no longer having the pain or distress. With relief, there often passes away, too, the sense of being vulnerable and the associated feelings of urgency and apprehension. Even so, the experience of affliction is marked by a relative loss of personal control over bodily activities, feelings, and actions. Like it or not, the fever of influenza is simply there to be somehow contended with; the hands cannot grip the shears properly without pain; the belly hurts no matter how one shifts about. Hence, the more a person believes, or likes to believe, that he or she is in charge of things, the more illness represents a veritable assault on that person's vital, everyday integrity—in the end, on what defines the person's humanity. As the French physician Leriche emphasized about physical pain:

> Always purposeless, it impoverishes man. The most enlightened mind becomes a poor wretch because of it, thrown back on himself, preoccupied with his affliction, selfishly indifferent to everything and everybody, obsessed by the fear that the pains will return.
>
> Oh, I know that people can forget their ills and that certain heroic souls manage to dominate their suffering and not show it. I do not disregard what exalted religious and philosophic ideals are capable of.
>
> But such an attitude is exceptional, and is only achieved in moments of heroism. Not everyone has a soul of fire; in the reality of human life, even for the great mystics, *the struggle against pain is usurious.* (In Rawlinson, 1982, p. 76.)

The patient who comes to a professed healer for help is not merely in the office, the clinic, the hospital, or the emergency room because of a wound, a fever, or a lump. To be sure, there are such presenting characteristics or symptoms, but there is with each case, more exactly and fully, a complex of presenting data of the sorts indicated, and these are always presented within the context of breaks and tears in the fabric of the person's ongoing typified routines of daily life. The fact is, too, that these are presented through, and deeply textured by, feelings of apprehensiveness and anxiety, frustration and relief, fear and hope, anger and gratitude, innocence and guilt—even if these feelings are muted, silent, or suggested only in indirect ways by the patient.

What are often taken to be the presenting symptoms, thus, always have their specific contexts within which they appear to the physician and which cannot be separated from them (a point to which we shall return in our historical explorations of medicine). In more familiar terms, the wound, the lump, or the fever is strictly the specific person's wound, lump, or fever and is deeply textured by that person's own biographical situation, with its specific sorts of routines, taken-for-granted beliefs, values, habits, and life-style. What a wound, a fever, or a lump may mean to the person who has it, whose embodying organism has become compromised by it, is inseparable from the physical impairment and thus is crucial for knowing how to contend with the impairment therapeutically.

Precisely in view of the subtle and indirect ways in which this meaning is presented—as being muted, or silenced, or buried within more prominently displayed feelings—getting at this underlying context of "what's wrong" requires a kind of diagnostics or hermeneutics of daily life. Just what this requires of us in the practical settings of clinical work will become clearer after the context of being ill and providing care has been more fully laid out.

UNAVOIDABLE TRUST

As illness impairs the integral sense of body and person, so too it alters the ordinary relationships with others and the surrounding world of things and events. Impaired in some way or other in the ability to do for himself or herself, the afflicted person unavoidably enters a complex network of trust relationships—most obviously, the unavoidable trust in others to do whatever is best and less obviously, but equally significant, the ineluctable reliance the patient must have in medications, procedures, regimens, equipment, and the like.

The woman with the apron, as was noted, stated with considerable dismay: "you have to trust these people, the physicians, like you do God. You're all in their hands. . . . I trusted him not to let an inexperienced person mess up my life." But, initially, of course, she had to trust not only her physician, but a host of others as well—nurses, lab technicians, researchers, administrators, manufacturers, and others. She also had to trust a great many things—the rubbery stuff injected into her breasts, the bandages, the anesthesias, and the surgical equipment. In addition, she had to trust that these things were appropriately sterilized and designed for use for her specific problems and condition. Also, once she agreed to have the surgery performed, she had to rely on the effectiveness of the surgical procedures and methods, the personnel involved, the way in which she was sewed up (differently on the two sides, as it turned out), and the way in which she was bandaged (and didn't fully understand, as it also turned out).

Clinical settings are deeply textured by such multiple forms of trust and reliance. Up until the point at which the problems became obvious to this woman, she was quite submissive, dependent, obedient, and cooperative. She believed, as do most patients, that it is essential to maintain a cooperative relationship, even though in her case it got her into real difficulties. Although many patients may realize in advance that such difficulties can happen, people are surprisingly haphazard in the way they select their doctors and in the way they stick with them even after bad experiences.

The hospital administrator, when he was made to realize that his skin lesion was cancerous, simply went to the clinic where his internist had his office and asked for a dermatologist. Later, he took the word of the clinic and went unquestioningly to the specialist it recommended. A couple seeking a fertility test reported that "just by asking around, we got onto another doctor" (Hardy, 1978, p. 105); apparently they were willing to trust the word of those to whom the question was asked. Another patient, told that she should consult a gynecologist, said, "I worked in OB at the hospital as a unit clerk and know some of the specialists but I really can't tell you why I settled on Dr. Smith" (ibid., p. 108). She sought a gynecologist for no minor matter, either: She wanted to be sterilized. In fact, she stayed with Dr. Smith even though he subsequently performed a laparoscopy (apparently only because the hospital had just acquired the equipment, and he thought he would try it out by checking his earlier surgery on the woman). She developed kidney disease (a risk about which she had not been informed, and she even reported that she would rather have run the risk of pregnancy than that of kidney disease), and, to top it off, she got pregnant anyway (ibid., pp. 109–10)! She sued Dr. Smith, but only after he then had the audacity to charge her for the botched surgery, which he had said he would not do.

Surprisingly perhaps, this woman, like many patients, was able to understand that physicians are human, make mistakes, and only at times are guilty of negligence. What is important for these patients, it seems, is less the mistake than the willingness or unwillingness of the physician to own up to the mistake and be ready to make amends in some reasonable way (ibid., p. 114). Though vulnerable, compromised, and compliant, many patients nonetheless seem uncommonly able to understand and forgive. At the same time, to establish trust they not unreasonably expect physicians and nurses to show their own humanity, not only in their mistakes but in their subsequent conduct as well.

A patient with lung cancer emphasized: "When the doctor told me I had this tumor, frankly, it alarmed me, but he did it in such a way that it left me with a feeling of confidence. He was outright and open about it" (ibid., p. 9). The judge with diabetes similarly emphasized, "if you can't communicate and you can't understand your disease, then you don't have confidence in the medical help you are getting" (ibid., p. 236). He then addressed the need for communication: "A lot of confidence and respect for doctors is lost because of lack of communication. Doctors are human. They can make mistakes even though some of 'em don't think so" (ibid., p. 237).

At times, the unavoidable trust in people has happy results. The person is healed, comforted, or at least made to feel confident in the caregivers. The point is only that the afflicted person undergoes critical alteration of his ordinary relations with others, precisely insofar as illness or injury debilitates, isolates, perhaps even humiliates. He can no longer do for himself and is now "at the mercy of others to regulate, manipulate, investigate, and, perhaps, restore those failing capacities" (Rawlinson, op. cit., p. 76). Affliction thus invariably involves some degree of "surrender of one's autonomy and integrity" for the purpose of restoring failed capacities (ibid., p. 77).

THE EXPERIENCE OF BEING CARED FOR

Just as medical encounters place patients in positions of unavoidable trust, they also evoke the need for responsive care from those in whom trust is invested. Eric Cassell has rightly remarked that patients not only experience pain but suffering as well. These must not be confused, and both must be the focus of the physician's concern (Cassell, 1982). He reports an illustrative case of a 25-year-old sculptress with metastatic disease of the breast who was treated by competent, caring physicians using the most advanced techniques and therapies. The treatments, as well as the disease, were sources of both pain and suffering. Her future took on a brittle quality (Rawlinson), uncertain and promoting fear, but the sculptress could obtain little information from her physicians. She had no idea that her irradiated breast would become so disfigured, or that she would become hirsute, obese, and devoid of libido. Because of the tumor in the supraclavicular fossa, she lost strength in the hand and arm she used in sculpting. She then grew increasingly depressed. When she fractured her femur, treatment was delayed while her physicians openly disagreed about placing pins in her hip.

With each medical response to her disease or associated problems (side effects), she would become hopeful again, only to be confronted with another problem. When a new course of chemotherapy was initiated, for instance, she felt the acute dilemma of being torn between a desire to live and work and the familiar fear of allowing hope again, when, as so often happened before, it only exposed her to misery if the treatment failed. There were also the inevitable side effects to contend with—nausea, vomiting, and hair loss. The future thus became fearsome, auguring increased pain and disability, not heralding recovery or comforting remission.

Distinct from the pain, or rather texturing it, were thus several forms of acute suffering: over how she appeared to others, especially her friends; about her sense of her own disfigured body; over her inability to understand the source of her pain; over what the future would bring; ultimately over death. Cassell notes three important things here: First, her suffering was not confined to physical symptoms; second, she suffered from both the disease and the treatments; and third, one could not anticipate, but rather had to ask, what she would herself describe as suffering (ibid., pp. 639–40).

The unhappy fact is that she was not asked. Reflecting on this and other cases, Cassell argues for three critical points. The first, that "suffering is experienced by persons," is intended to make it clear that, on the one hand, it is inappropriate to treat sickness as something that happens solely to the person's body; ignorance of the many facets of personhood actively contributes to a patient's suffering. The second point, taken from Cassell's own clinical experience, concerns the intensely personal quality of suffering: Representing a threat of impending disaster, it "can be defined as the state of severe distress associated with events that threaten the intactness of the person" (ibid., p. 640). The third point follows naturally. It is not possible to know without appropriate discussion what might be the sources of suffering, and suffering can occur in relation to any aspect of the person's life (social, personal, bodily, religious).

Noting that although pain and suffering are closely identified in the medical literature, Cassell emphasizes that they are nonetheless "phenomenologically distinct" (ibid., p. 641). Indeed, some types of pain—for example, childbirth—can be quite severe yet be experienced as rewarding. There are also pains that even though severe are not experienced as a source of suffering, because the patient knows what the pain is, what its sources are, and when it is known to be controllable. Cassell thus concludes:

> In summary, people in pain frequently report suffering from the pain when they feel out of control, when the pain is overwhelming, when the source of the pain is unknown, when the meaning of the pain is dire, or when the pain is chronic.
>
> In all these situations, persons perceive pain as a threat to their continued existence—not merely to their lives, but to their integrity as persons. That this is the relation of pain to suffering is strongly suggested by the fact that suffering can be relieved, in the presence of continued pain, by making the source of the pain known, changing its meaning, and demonstrating that it can be controlled and that an end is in sight. (Ibid.)

Besides this relationship between pain and suffering, Cassell insists that the sources of suffering can be quite different from the pain, its sources, or whether it is or is not controllable. Thus, a person can suffer over lost capacities, over compromises to personal traits or abilities, over alterations to what a person takes to be significant body parts or members, over disruptions to family life and associate bonds, and over constrictions to the person's future (short-term or long-range).

> With this in mind, we can also realize how much someone devoid of physical pain, even devoid of "symptoms," may suffer. People suffer from what they have lost of themselves in relation to the world of objects, events, and relationships. We realize, too, that although medical care can reduce the impact of sickness, inattentive care can increase the disruption caused by illness. (Ibid.)

Cassell's patient obviously illustrates this range of suffering. She had become housebound and bedbound, her face was disfigured by the steroids, she became masculinized by the treatment, and she lost most of her hair. She was also deeply apprehensive about the pain—from the disease and from the treatments—which was apparently not discussed very fully with her by her physicians. Fearful of the seemingly inevitable pain, apprehensive about the future, lamenting her loss of sculpting capacity, wanting to hope but afraid of more disappointments—practically every characteristic Cassell suggests as defining suffering were vivid realities for her.

A good many of Hardy's cases also illustrate the distinctions Cassell finds. One man, a barber, went to a family physician thinking he had prostate difficulties. Taking the recommended drugs, prescribed even though the tests showed nothing, he obtained no relief. The pain became so intense in his upper leg and buttocks that "it became a mental trauma" (Hardy, p. 170). Back to the doctor he went, and this time he was diagnosed as having hemorrhoids and was prescribed treatments for them. He again complied, and again had no relief from the increasingly severe pains. He got an infected toe from clipping his nail and went in to the same doctor with complaints of pains in his foot, only to be told that he had to lose a good deal of weight. That, too, did no good for his pain, and he began to have difficulties walking, standing, and even sitting.

A "prominent bone doctor" and a friend came into his barbershop one day, and in the course of telling the doctor about the pains, the barber was told to go to an orthopedic specialist. "By this time, my mental state was just wrecked, not knowing what it was or if it was a bone infection or whatever" (ibid., p. 172). A friend recommended a podiatrist, but "I didn't even know what a podiatrist was. I just wanted somebody to look at my foot" (ibid.).

As things turned out, it was determined that he had experienced a fallen arch. The podiatrist succeeded in giving him his very first, and immediate, relief. At one point, moreover,

> as he was examining me, he asked: "Do you ever have pain up in your crotch?" I said, "Do you mean pain like prostate trouble, or somethin'?" And he said, "Yeah, I would imagine that you have experienced a lot of difficulty in your upper leg because of this. You've got all of the upper muscles of your legs really in a bind there. I don't see how you've been able to do long distance walking or prolonged standing." And I said, "You wouldn't believe what I've spent for drugs and examinations in the last two years over this pain in the upper part of my left leg." (Ibid.)

From the beginning, "I had no idea I had a foot problem because when your rear end hurts you don't think of your foot" (ibid., p. 170).

This man went through two years of severe pain, treatments, diagnoses, and considerable suffering (a "wrecked mental state," "trauma"), complicated by the frustration of not knowing what was causing the severe pain. He reported at the end of his story: "The G.P. is still my good friend but I'm changing doctors. You know, after a while he hated to see me comin'. He wanted to give me the sugar pills they give the little old ladies because there was nothing wrong as far as he could find" (ibid., p. 173).

Patients want to know what's wrong with them, what their chances are, and what's going to be done for them. They also want to know that those who are taking care of them really care, a clear part of which is that those who take care of them keep themselves current and clinically competent. However kindly and concerned physicians may be, patients understandably want them to be competent, up-to-date, caring, and intelligent. But competency, for patients, is by no means equivalent to technical proficiency (though it surely includes that). As this patient makes very clear, competency is often centered around the relief of suffering—one of the main sources of which is not knowing the sources of pain, its reasons, and thus its meaning for the patient. Cassell remarks at the conclusion of his essay:

> The paradox with which this paper began—that suffering is often caused by the treatment of the sick—no longer seems so puzzling. How could it be otherwise, when medicine has concerned itself so little with the nature and causes of suffering? [It] is not a failure of good intentions. None are more concerned about pain or loss of function than physicians. Instead, it is a failure of knowledge and understanding. We lack knowledge, because . . . we have artificially circumscribed our task in caring for the sick. (Cassell, 1982, p. 644.)

By not disclosing, adequately or at all, what's gone wrong with a patient's body, by treating a patient's complaints as if sugar pills were the appropriate response, by not keeping up on medical developments (in short, not being or remaining competent in the fullest sense), the physician—from the viewpoint of the patient—has effectively *abandoned* the patient. The patient is left having to guess at what's wrong and often settling for haphazard interpretations of sometimes only recondite signs of afflictions, discomforts, and pains.

The patient has little choice but to trust those who take care of him or her, and this of itself evokes a correlative need to be genuinely cared for. Patients generally understand rather well the need to establish good relationships with nurses and physicians, where this invariably means that patients' unavoidable trust will be warranted and they will be cared for in their suffering as well as in their pain. However well intentioned a provider might be, the care provided is seen by patients as good and caring primarily as a function of accurate, adequate, and understandable information being promptly, sensitively, and continuously given, so that they may better understand "what's wrong" and "what's being done about it." Patients are capable of understanding their care in these general terms (even though this may in some cases take time and considerable patience in finding appropriate language for communication). Failure to communicate to patients is to abandon them even more than their illnesses have already effectively done—adding, if you will, insult to injury in a most literal manner.

SOUNDINGS AT UNCERTAIN LEVELS

Illness provokes attention, the patient's no less than the professed healer's. Both want to know "what's gone wrong" and how best to contend with it. Indeed, a whole cluster of questions is provoked when one becomes a patient: What is wrong? Is it serious? What does it mean for me, now and for the future? Is it curable, and if so by what means? What are the risks of treating it one way or another, or not at all? What will it cost? What ought to be done?

When a person becomes a patient and goes to a professed healer for help, this cluster of questions reduces to three main ones: What has gone wrong? What can be done about it? What, among the things that can be done, should be done (see Pellegrino, 1979a, p. 174)? Although a patient wants to know with certainty, so as to be able to reckon with his or her affairs and to know what to do about them (including what to do and think about oneself), at every point of the encounter with professed healers there is room for uncertainty, doubt, ambiguity, and error. To be a patient is to find oneself having to deal with the quandaries of uncertainty and with the consequently vital issue of personal risk (by far the most significant sense of "risk").

The architect who suffered the severe gall bladder attack highlights the personal dilemma often faced by patients going through the diagnostic component of clinical evaluation. After the lab work was done, he found himself visited by a surgeon who, intentionally or not, conveyed the "idea that the decision to have surgery had already been made and he was there to get the job done." The surgeon was caught "off guard" when asked about alternatives and quickly departed. As the architect pointed out, his reservation stemmed primarily from having "very little information, a lot of supposition," and from the fact that, so far as he himself knew, the results of the lab work had yet to be reported, at least to him. As things turned out, these results were quite unclear anyway:

> My body functions were such that my body did not concentrate the dye material, or whatever it is that reveals the configuration of the gall bladder. The absence of the gall bladder dye tended to cast in doubt whether or not that was the central problem. I'm a little hazy on that point now but the lab work tended to show that the gall bladder, which had been malfunctioning the night before was, on a second test, functioning more or less normally. (Hardy, 1978, p. 246.)

At no time during his hospitalization or afterward was he "told by anyone that there was a confirmation of the fact that my gall bladder was really not functioning"—except for the short periods when he had the attacks (ibid., p. 249). Despite the readiness of his physician and the surgeon to proceed with the surgery, the architect's point seems well taken. No clear-cut decision, especially for something as risky as surgery, could be reached on the basis of these tests or the diagnosis.

In another case, a physician experiencing muscular weakness while still a medical student, was found on examination at the time to have no normal reflexes. Largely ignored at the time, it finally led him to consult a G.P. friend of his. Nothing was found, and he was sent to a neurologist. "He didn't think too much of it but he did get an electromyogram, an EMG, which he felt showed old polio; in other words, a burned out, inactive process. And that was the end of that" (ibid., p. 275). Convinced that the process was not inactive but quite progressive and getting worse, over the next few years he consulted more neurologists, had more EMGs done, and matters still were inconclusive. No one had yet mentioned the possibility of muscular dystrophy.

Only after a good deal of specialized study on his own did it finally occur to him, some years later when he was very much weaker, that he might have "limb-girdle muscular dystrophy." A neurologist he then consulted honestly did not know whether he had the disease. With the problem dragging on now for over six years and diagnostic judgments remaining equivocal, it was finally established that he did indeed have muscular dystrophy, and he was then able to manage in his own practice and life. He remarked, however, that even though neurology "is an inexact diagnostic science," muscle disease should have been obvious (ibid., p. 178).

In response to Hardy's question about how a lay person would experience this sort of disease process, the physician emphatically agreed on how deeply troubling it would have to be for someone who did not know much about medicine and the workings of the body. Even while this and similar diseases are difficult to diagnose—correct diagnosis may take years, not months, much less days—the failure to take seriously what he as a patient was telling his physicians gave him profound emotional difficulties. "It is one thing to say 'Don't worry about it' when you haven't got it and quite another thing to not worry about it when you have got it" (ibid., p. 279).

The patient may be unsure about what has happened and even at times doubt his or her ability as an observer of his or her own bodily condition. Others (family, friends, physicians) may also come to doubt what a patient reports. For one thing, the diabetic judge remarked, "There are lots of feelings that are hard to put into words, especially if you've never had the feeling before . . . [or] had nothing to compare it to." There are real difficulties, too, in putting our feelings into words when the common language and the social settings of everyday usage do not readily provide for such talk.

But even if a sound communicative relationship has been established, certain diseases are intrinsically difficult to diagnose. While they may have symptoms very much like other ailments, clinical diagnosis can only approximate the ideal degree of certainty. Assuring patients may be somewhat problematic on occasion. As Pellegrino points out, the diagnostic phase of clinical judgment "most closely fits the scientific paradigm and under ideal conditions can yield a diagnostic conclusion with a high degree of certitude" (Pellegrino, 1979a, pp. 174–75). Even this, however, is a matter of probability.

> The conditions for such certitude must be stringent. . . . The input data of signs and symptoms must be reliably observed, standardized and specified; the classificatory patterns must be equally reliably determined; the probabilities of different combinations of signs and symptoms must be derived from sufficient numbers and combinations of sets and subsets of signs and symptoms; laboratory and other ancillary data must be sensitive, accurate, specific and precise. The rules of deductive or probabilistic logic must be followed rigorously.
> In addition, a highly specific and sharply discriminating test is required—like a biopsy, fiber endoscopy, angiography, or an enzymatic or immunological determination. (Ibid., p. 175.)

As happened in the case of the physician with muscular dystrophy, diagnostic tests (muscle biopsy, EMG) are not always reliable, definitive, or appropriately interpretable. In any event, these rigorous conditions are "only rarely satisfied in clinical reality" (ibid.). Data are frequently unstandardized and poorly quantified; tests vary widely in sensitivity, specificity, and accuracy. It is thus always difficult to assign a precise numerical value to every key point in the diagnostic decision tree.

In the end, the "process of differential diagnosis is really most akin to the process of classical dialectic" (ibid., p. 176). Each stage is in effect a "claim"; each claim is introduced or considered on the strength of available evidence or warrants and evaluated in the light of that; each of these, moreover, is set over against other alternatives and assessed in respect of their relative strengths. On that basis, a "clinical conclusion" is reached, but this is always open to subsequent re-evaluation, for instance, in the light of subsequent developments with the disease and the effectiveness of treatments. "This is more akin to arguing a case in court than it is to proving a scientific hypothesis. The whole effort is to make one diagnosis sufficiently more cogent than the others so that it becomes a defensible basis for decisive action" (Ibid.).

The *diagnostic* phase of clinical judgment is surely the most rigorous. But even here, there are degrees and types of uncertainty and ambiguity. This is even more apparent in the second, or *therapeutic*, stage of clinical judgment, to determine what can be done.

It is true that therapeutic decisions can be relatively easy when there is a specific, highly effective treatment available for a particular disease (penicillin for pneumococcal pneumonia, for instance). Still, "genuinely scientific information is scanty," there are many "pitfalls" in therapeutic trials, and even randomized clinical trials can raise serious questions. At times, physicians may utilize "therapeutic maneuvers which are not *radical*—i.e. they do not eradicate the causal agent or the offending process" (ibid., p. 178). In other cases, they are faced with questions of whether to recommend complex, expensive, essentially palliative procedures that have unpleasant and, at times, dangerous side effects (chemotherapy, for instance). Even when scientific data on effectiveness and toxicity are available, the questions are different: "Is the discomfort worthwhile for this patient? Is length of life more important to him or her than its quality?" (Ibid., p. 179.)

The final stage of clinical judgment seeks to determine, among the available alternatives, what *should* be done, which Pellegrino terms the "prudential" question concerning the "right action." Here, that different order of questions becomes predominant, and the medically or scientifically (or even logically) correct thing to do may not be at all what should be done:

> When it comes to making the *right* decision—the *judicious* one for this patient—the categories of *must not, must, should* and *may* can all shift, depending upon a myriad of factors in the patient's life situation and his/her notion of what he/she deems worthwhile. . . . For one person, a lipoma, acne or sebaceous cyst is something to be ignored; for another, it is a horrid blemish, so emotionally disabling that it demands removal. For this person, *may* becomes *must*. For an elderly man or woman chemotherapy of disseminated cancer may mean a few months more of life, less pleasantly lived. For this patient, a *should* or *may* becomes a *must not*. (Ibid., p. 180.)

The reasoning at this last stage is *dialectical* (weighing alternative courses of action to determine which is the best for this specific patient), *ethical* (attempting to settle upon the right action for this patient), and *rhetorical* (the artful persuasion by both patient and physician about which action is the right one). None of the stages of clinical evaluation (diagnosis, therapy, prudential) is free from relative uncertainty any more than from possible error, but the third stage is most exposed to these.

For the patient, it is not the niceties and refinements of medical methods that are significant, nor are the uncertainties and ambiguities quite the same. Wanting to know "what's wrong" and "what can be done about it" have less the sense of probabilities than "being-at-a-loss," adrift, and distraught without being able to "take-one's-bearings" or to know how to reckon with things. Experiencing illness as a kind of "bad luck," "misfortune," or "throw of the dice," the ill person seeks to know in order to get on with his or her life. The right action is the one that sets things right enough to allow the person to know what to hold by, believe in, or reckon with (see Ortega y Gasset, 1957).

As Cassell remarks, "while probabilities may be crucial to directing the diagnostic thinking of a physician, probabilities are often not as necessary in making a diagnosis as what the sick person *says*" (Cassell, 1979, p. 201).

But this, he observes, opens what for physicians may be little short of a real can of worms—that is, the subjective, which is frequently seen as the least reliable source of data, especially when the person is debilitated, in the throes of pain, and thereby is often seen as unable to be coherent, much less make decisions. Indeed, those aspects of subjectivity that have received the most attention in medicine—what Cassell calls the "sociologic person" and the "unconscious"—do not concern the specific sick person as *this* individual.

Social variables of disease have played an important role in medical understanding and treatment: for example, the incidence of tuberculosis among children living in ghettos as opposed to those living in suburbs. Such variables, however, do not tell us about *this* specific patient; they rather contain information about the statistical probabilities of the *class* of such patients. Similarly, the "way the unconscious domain of the subjective is most often used in medical practice excludes the subject" (ibid., p. 202). By definition, the patient is not supposed to know the (i.e., his own) unconscious; it is not within the patient's control, and thus not even the patient's words can be taken as trustworthy guides to it. Rather, "we, the physicians, take it that we know better than the patient what are the unconscious determinants of his symptoms or his disease (ibid.).

These statistical considerations are at best "uncharitable." Even more, "to dismiss the importance of the patient's understanding is to dismiss him as subject" (ibid., pp. 202–03). After all, every patient experiences his or her own bodily condition in a variety of ways—pain, discomfort, swellings, hurts, or soreness. Every patient also interprets the experience (i.e., gives *meaning* to it, however vague it may be from the physician's point of view and whether or not it is based on accurate information). Precisely because of this difference between experience and interpretation of experience, however, "the doctor can insert himself between the patient as experiencer and the patient as assigner of understandings" (ibid., p. 204).

Classically in medicine this substitution is done as a matter of course, by entertaining diagnostic hypotheses other than the sense or meaning the patient gives to his or her own pain or other bodily experience. Cassell argues that this classic picture proves to be inadequate; it holds out promises of clarity, certainty, or confidence that often cannot be made good. For that matter, even the physician's clinical judgments are at root also uncertain.

As will become clear, this is a point of some significance for our study and requires some reflection even at this stage. This substitution of the physician's interpretation for that of the patient is problematic, primarily because in so doing, vital things about the patient may then be missed. In particular, a physician risks missing how a specific person "interacts with basic pathological mechanisms to produce the illness that is *this* person with *this* disease," about which the person is "virtually the only source of information" (ibid.). The critical second and third stages of clinical judgment can thus be compromised.

The classic view typically regards the patient's own experiences and interpretations as obstructive rather than inherent or helpful to the diagnostic process. Careful historical study shows that this dispute reaches back into medicine's earliest roots, continuing through each of its historical periods to one of the more decisive periods for our times, that from Descartes through Bichat (which will be the focus for a later part of our study).

Even for this classic viewpoint, a patient's own experiences and self-understanding are often critical both for compliance with prescribed courses of action and for the course of the disease itself. For instance, the clinical expression of the major diseases today, such as hypertension, arteriosclerotic heart disease, diabetes, degenerative bone disease, perhaps even cancer,

> depend on the individuating characteristics of the patient. Further, in marked contradistinction to the infectious diseases or the surgical diseases, the patient is the primary agent of his own treatment. That is to say, the patient must change his life style or behavior and comply with often complicated treatment requirements. (Ibid.)

Furthermore, the subsequent course of a disease may be affected by the afflicted person's interpretation of it. A patient with rheumatic heart disease, for instance, told that an operation might be required within two years, may live in constant and continuing dread of the surgery, thereby possibly altering the course of the disease itself. Another patient, told that the medication now being taken is designed to forestall an acute episode that might occur some years in the future, may live with his heart condition without any sense of impending doom (ibid., p. 207), and this attitude may affect the way medication is taken, and thereby the disease process itself.

If the physician pays attention only to the objective data, "he will hear only about disease and will miss the person." If the physician listens only to what a patient tells him, "he will miss the disease." To pay attention to both of these and know nothing about the interaction between diseases and persons "is to miss everything" (ibid., p. 214). The trick is to attend to both while having knowledge of disease and knowledge of persons and thus "to make *use* of the subjective (rather than just to live it in the everyday)" (ibid.). Thus, the physician must learn to distinguish between what is observed and how it is to be interpreted, and to do the very same with and for his patients.

WHO IS MY STRANGER?

To become ill and be hospitalized is to enter into forbidding and oftentimes alien environs. The patient is surrounded by persons (patients, hospital personnel, doctors, nurses, orderlies, dietitians, social workers, medical specialists, and other affiliated personnel) who are invariably not personally known by the patient. Some of these persons may know each other and what each is doing at any given time, but these persons are not typically disposed to convey this knowledge to patients. Only a select few of these other persons are legitimated within the hospital to tell a patient anything about his or her condition, and even these legitimated communicators (primary physicians, primary care nurses, perhaps a few others who have the express permission of the primary physician) do not always try to convey "what's going on" to the patient. Even if they do try, they do not always succeed. Even so, as we've seen, patients are on the alert to varying degrees for information and understanding about themselves. Patients are thus regularly on the lookout for indications, hints, suggestions, clues, and signs by which to interpret themselves, their pains and discomforts, and their prospects.

Hospitals can be a real culture shock. They are sociologically and architecturally designed more to enhance this foreignness than to ameliorate it. The strangeness is enhanced even more: Patients are stripped of familiar things (clothes, possessions), however necessary this may be for medical purposes, and made to put on anonymous and accessible gowns. They must disclose the intimate details of personal and bodily life to whomever is assigned to care for them, and they must expose their bodies in the most intimate and humiliating postures for strangers to poke and prod, swab and stick, palpate and feel. To be a patient takes remarkable patience! It is hardly surprising that many patients seem somewhat unnormal—to themselves as well as to others—beyond what their illnesses may have brought about by disrupting the routines of daily life. The debilitating effects of illness or injury are thus deepened, even if not deliberately.

Illness itself is alienating. A young man with ulcerative colitis, for instance, stated that the "ileostomy is hardly any hassle at all, once I got used to it, but it's just the emotional part, losing a part of your body which you have had all your life" (Hardy, p. 337). Another patient, scheduled for cardiac bypass surgery, expressed his "only fear" was being anesthetized. While "confident" in his surgeon, he noted:

> I was very fearful of the anesthetic. I voiced this with the surgeon ahead of time. I asked who the anesthesiologist would be. . . . I didn't like the idea of being put to sleep by someone I'd never seen. . . . I kept waiting and waiting for the anesthesiologist to come and see me. He didn't come the night before the operation but I slept well anyway and the next morning, I was still wondering where the anesthesiologist was. The boy came up and prepped me for the operation, they gave me the pre-op shot and started down to the operating room with me and I thought, "Gee, where is that guy? I'm not going into that operating room until I've seen him." But I was also thinking, "I don't have a whole lot of choice, strapped down on this stretcher and all." (Ibid., pp. 225–26.)

Finally, he appeared, all "suited up, his mask up and all" (ibid.), just as the patient was being wheeled into surgery.

On the other hand, certain everyday actions may be rigorously prohibited in hospitals, but their prohibition may not be understood by patients. One, for instance, had been put into a room next to an elderly woman with intestinal problems and developed a kind of friendship with her. Later, the elderly woman was moved to another room, "and I was quite concerned for her." As each of them had viewed their hospitalizations, neither had been treated particularly well:

> She had told me several times, "They're killing us both." And I kinda believed her. So I went down to her room to check on her. She'd been operated on in the meantime and I wanted to see how she was getting along. I wheeled down there and had just gotten in the room when this head nurse came in and grabbed my wheelchair and flew me out into the hall and back to my room. "You know you're not supposed to be in there." Well, I was crying and mortified and couldn't understand why they'd treat me like that. Then this girl came in and I said, "What's wrong with me? Why can't I go down there?" She said, "Don't you know what you have?" "Oh, my God, what do I have?" And she said, "you have staph infection." . . . I didn't know anything about staph infection. (Ibid., p. 163.)

Communication about the disease, as the diabetic judge emphasized, is critically important; otherwise "you don't have any confidence in the medical help you're getting."

Disease can also be strange and present peculiar problems. A young fireman, for example, suffering from renal disease, was both amazed and bemused by what he had begun to experience in himself:

> A funny thing about a kidney patient. Every one of them craves something. I craved gasoline. I would do anything in the world to get gasoline, to sniff it. I finally got off it, thank God. I talked to several other kidney patients up there at the VA Hospital and people craved rocks. They would actually eat pebbles. Mine happened at the filling station. We were sitting there, filling up with gas, and all of sudden, I had to have that gas, had to have it on a Kleenex to sniff. There was one guy up there who had to have this blanket over his head or he wouldn't go, couldn't go. It was unbelievable to me. I didn't know what was going on. (Ibid., p. 145.)

On the other hand, the strange can at times be made somewhat more comfortable and familiar and can be more readily reckoned with if the patient's confidence is established, restored, or maintained. As a heart attack victim reported, "we were like a team, and this was a campaign. I was a member of the team. I was the cause of all the trouble, but I was also a member of the team. We were holding hands" (ibid., p. 209). A cancer patient reported feeling very confident because his physician was "outright and open" (ibid., p. 9).

When the sense of strangeness is enhanced by lack of information, patients can feel even more compromised. Hearing a fellow patient complain that her doctors did not "tell me a darn thing," the woman with the "apron" stressed that "I felt sure they wouldn't. . . . I just think they take their job so for granted that they do a good job but they fail to inform a person." The mother of an asthmatic boy said: "Doctors do not tell you all of the things to look for. It could be that they don't have time but then there's something terribly wrong with our society. They should have time. . . ." (ibid., p. 60).

In a society in which relationships among strangers predominate and being a neighbor has become rare, communication tends to be designed more for temporary ease of social passage and commerce than for intimate disclosures. Being sick and hospitalized in environs that are strange and being in pain and not fully understanding why or what the immediate future will bring—with pain and anxiety demanding and capturing attention—the patient faces strangers who propose and then proceed to carry out a variety of intimate intrusions into his or her body and personal life. A coronary patient reported how "you really grasp at the things which are encouraging and anything that intimates you've got something wrong with you, you grab onto that, too, so you have two hands full of straws" (ibid., p. 40).

Whenever a person finds himself in a strange place, there is the quite natural effort to "find your way," to look for familiar landmarks. This is made all the more acute by being sick, distressed, or injured. It is important for the patient to know and to understand, even though this need to know may be expressed well or poorly in ambiguous and tentative ways, in a copious flow of words or through silences and furtive looks. Sociologically, the patient is a special kind of "stranger" in Alfred Schutz's sense (see Schutz, 1964, pp. 91–105).

Nor should it be surprising that patients will at times take the most otherwise innocuous and apparently unrelated gestures, words, objects, and circumstances as imbued with deep and sometimes foreboding significance. Not being responsive to a patient's full condition as a stranger, then, can at times mean that the patient is effectively abandoned. Nondisclosure or inadequate relating of pertinent information about a person's condition and future, even not engaging in simple everyday talk, abandons the patient to having to guess at what's going on, even to make haphazard interpretations of recondite signs only poorly, if at all, understood.

At the same time, the patient wants and needs to know that those who are taking care really do care, a major index of which is common discourse. "Talk" is a fundamental affirmation of the person. In Cassell's terms, a patient's concern is not merely for relief of pain, but for relief of suffering. What is suggested from patients themselves is that responsive care is closely tied to everyday talk that is open, accurate, adequate, and understandable. The diabetic judge hit it squarely: "if you can't communicate and you can't understand your disease, then you don't have any confidence in the medical help you're getting." Without confidence, there is no basis for trust, and lack of trust signifies that an essential part of the therapeutic dyad is threatened or missing, thus that therapy itself may have become seriously compromised. The judge concluded:

> Doctors are human. They can make mistakes even though some of 'em don't think so. If you can go to your doctor and say, "I don't think you did this right," and he can say, "Well, gosh, I believe you're right. Let's fix it," from the legal standpoint, I think you'd probably have a lot less malpractice suits. (Hardy, 1979, p. 237.)

In the somewhat different terms of the mother of the child with congenital cataracts, "you love to run into a doctor who is not condescending. If you believe your mind is good, too, you want your doctor to understand that" (ibid., p. 89).

A knowledgeable patient is not only more likely to benefit from what health professionals can offer, but is also more likely to be appropriately cooperative. What has long been known about patients on hemodialysis—that active participation in their own treatment improves their chances of success (see Zaner, 1982)—is no less true of patients in general. Especially in a time of predominantly stranger-to-stranger relationships, it seems imperative to remind ourselves that "them is us": Our own experience as patients may be the most important source of understanding and responsive care for others who are ill.

To be a patient is to find yourself in a deeply ironic predicament. The most intimate actions of touching, feeling, talking, and probing, which typically promise or attest to personal intimacies, now go on between strangers, and thus they have a very different significance in the relation between helper and person helped.

POWER AND VULNERABILITY

It has already been noted that many patients have compelling difficulties in their efforts to find out what is going on with them. It has to be recognized that patients are not often in a good position to question those who take care of and have control over them. Patients are usually not able to evaluate what is being done to them, nor judge whether treatments are appropriate or not, are done competently or not, or are working or not. Open and direct communication, difficult enough in hospital settings among strangers in any case, is further complicated by illness—by the way specific ailments diminish a person's alertness—as well as by a person's own particular temperament, habits, and attitudes. Some patients do not know how to talk to people in authority (of any sort); others may not want to do so (at one time, or at all); and some simply play out the "sick role."

But this is still only a glimpse at the basic asymmetry of power in the relationship between healers and patients. The mother of the partially sighted girl remarked that

> in the doctor-patient relationship, they sense how timid you are and that makes them more overpowering. They've got the edge on you. . . . Somehow, if doctors could just sense how much hold they have over a person's feelings. Of course, some, a few, stay human and touchable. (Hardy, p. 92.)

The lady with the panniculectomy poignantly stated, "You're all in their hands, and if they don't care for you, who's going to?" (Ibid., p. 40.)

There can be severe difficulties in asking for help from persons who are and are known to be "overpowering" and "in charge." Patients know the importance of having a sound relationship with doctors. But that is deeply complicated by the relation's characteristic asymmetry of power, so poignantly revealed in the woman's concern about having to trust "these people" when they "put you out," or in the cardiac bypass patient's anxiety over being anesthetized.

This asymmetry is both understandable and unavoidable. Especially in situations in which their vulnerability is most prominent, patients are, as the woman remarks, "all in their hands." In the plaintive words of the cardiac bypass patient, " 'I'm not going into that operating room until I've seen him.' But I was also thinking, 'I don't have a whole lot of choice, strapped down on this stretcher and all.' " The mother of the partially sighted girl put it directly: "They've got the edge on you."

> Unless the person wishes to ignore his illness, or to rely wholly on his own healing powers, he must seek the help of another. The ill person is condemned to a relationship of inequality with the professed healer, for the healer professes to possess precisely what the patient lacks—the knowledge and power to heal. (Pellegrino, 1982, p. 159.)

We are compromised and diminished by illness, specifically in the ability to care or decide for oneself, much less to heal oneself. "The ill person . . . may not even be free to reject medicine when he is the victim of overwhelming trauma, pain, shock, or coma" (ibid.).

Quite independently of the otherwise important issue of physician authority (see Agich, 1982), this asymmetry of power is constitutive of the helping relationship. Physicians are specially knowledgeable (by way of special forms of education, training, and licensure) in the ways of the body. They have access to resources (people, technologies, equipment, instruments, institutions, funding) that are socially and legally legitimated (even obligated in certain ways and in certain situations). As Peter Lenrow noted, "compared to the person needing help, the would-be helper is in a better position to take initiative and mobilize needed resources (e.g., allies, information, skills, protection, or opportunities to demonstrate competence)" (Lenrow, 1982, p. 48).

This, as it may be termed, epistemic and therapeutic power is strongly enhanced by its formal institutionalization, social legitimation, and legal authorization. As should now be amply clear, this inequality of power is intensified by the afflicted person's distress or illness, and even more by the fact that the patient is ineluctably one who appeals, primarily to strangers, for help. The patient is a petitioner whose appeal is precisely an endorsement of the very phenomenon that constitutes the inequality—the ability (power) to heal, comfort, or restore. In Pellegrino's words, "in no other deprivation is the dissolution of the person so intimate that it impairs the capacity to deal with all other deprivations" (1982, p. 159).

THE HELPING RELATION AS PROMISE

Illness or injury is an accidental, unasked-for disruption in the routine flow of life and renders the person uniquely vulnerable, placing him or her within a complex network of unavoidable trust relationships. It is disruptive of a person's usual ways of interrelating with other people, making the ill person unusually reliant on others who, by the nature of the case, work within contexts characterized as relatively uncertain, ambiguous, and fallible. These others, invariably strangers working within settings mostly unfamiliar to the afflicted person, are, on the other hand, persons possessing, or at least professing to possess, the power to know "what's wrong," "how to deal with it," and "what then to expect." At the same time, to become sick or injured is to want and seek to know, to understand vitally, precisely to the extent that we do not (or, perhaps, cannot) know "what's happening," "what's wrong," and "what can be done about it." At times we desperately need to know that those strangers really do know what they profess to know, really can do what they profess to be able to do, and really do care for us while taking care of us.

To be a patient thus seems unavoidably to be centered about oneself. While this is surely a commonplace observation, this peculiarity nevertheless harbors some interesting and less obvious depths. A patient afflicted with end-stage kidney disease and now on home dialysis reflected at one point:

> Yet sometimes when I'm feeling fine, and the machine is running perfectly, and I've enjoyed my dinner, and the music is good and the book I'm reading is interesting, and our cat is purring around my feet, and Leslie [his wife] is smiling at me, a thought suddenly runs through my head: "How the hell did I get here?" (Foster, 1976, p. 6.)

Illness is remarkable and disturbing, for unlike most things in a person's life it uniquely singles out the person as "this" individual person. The bodily pain, the exacting dietary regimen, the profound dependence on "that damned machine" for his very life, the anxiety over future prospects, the forced reordering of personal and family life, the way the disease preoccupies, the riveting focus of pain and strange new feelings only barely known, if at all—all these sharply and poignantly bring the person face to face with himself, his own human frailty and fragile hold on things, his very life and therefore death. In other words, "How the hell did *I* get here?"

In some part, this has its source in what becomes forcefully prominent in illness, though more usually in grievous illness. Each of us is afflicted in basic ways as regards what constitutes our humanity. More basically, it marks out each of us as able to die: In the midst of life, robust or otherwise, illness, suffering, loss, grief, make death *present*. In the familiarity of daily life, the awesomeness of the radically strange suddenly appears. Illness befalls us and, especially when it is serious, is experienced as a rudimentary threat, as having a felt poignancy and fearful keenness that ineluctably carries over into the practice of medicine itself (see Hauerwas, 1982, p. 92). It, too, is deeply marked by this existential reality.

To be confronted with what the person is, was, and ever hoped to be, with his or her own finality, is not mere self-centeredness. It is rather a unique singling out of the individual as the person he or she is through telling glimpses of loss and death. Wanting to know and wanting to be cared for are thus human appeals through which the patient seeks recognition, affirmation, and appreciation of just this singular, singled-out person. To want to be cared for, in this deeply personal sense, is to want fundamentally to be this self in the eyes of those who take care of the person within the wholly unique, individual context of his or her own vulnerable condition. Similarly, trust is a deeply personal wanting to know and to be with the nurses, physicians, and others, just as those persons they are, in their very caring for the trusting person.

In these terms, the therapeutic dyad (caring and trusting) is a profoundly moral phenomenon. The promise of the relationship is not only that the sick person may recover or be comforted. It promises the recovery of ourselves as the persons we are, patients as well as those who take care of them. To be sure, the promise may not be fulfilled, for various reasons. But even dying can provide the occasion for this recovery of selves. Illness may be the mask that death sometimes wears, giving only brief and compelling glimpses of chilling nothingness; hence illness may be experienced as deeply dreaded or feared or perhaps may be embraced with grace. Here, the physician and nurse may take on their most significant task, as Cassell observes: to give patients "in this final stage of life the same kind of control that can be taught in earlier stages of living" (1976, p. 203).

All this suggests that the therapeutic relationship is more akin to an educational process than might have been thought hitherto, as Hauerwas has also recognized (1982, p. 92). The dying person is dependent on caring others now perhaps even more acutely than those whose afflictions may promise recovery (or at least stabilization), and the relationship between the dying patient and the caregivers is no less based on trust. "Both inner resources and trust in others are required because the enemy is fear" (Cassell, 1976, p. 204). What people fear most, it seems, is loss of control—over their bodies, their abilities to do, ultimately over themselves. Hence, illness bodes the loss of self. And here, Cassell wisely remarks,

> Those who die well and in control have something to teach the living about the body and about living. They show us that it is possible to come to peace with the body, both to be controlled by its limitations and to control it to a far greater extent than unlearned existence would suggest. They teach us that control is not denial or repression. That which we deny or repress about ourselves or within ourselves controls us by the very fact of our constant need to deny rather than to come to terms. Control implies acceptance of limitations plus an awareness that the limitations provide room for the continued exercise of self, even into death. The beauty and potential of growth lie not only in intellectual transcendence and the formation of transcendent emotional bonds, but also in the possibility of dynamic unity with the body. In that state the fear of death, an essentially backward look, becomes unimportant. (Ibid., p. 228.)

Commenting on these words, Hauerwas observes that medicine "is therefore a learned profession because it literally learns from patients the skills necessary for acceptance of the possibilities and limits of the body" (Hauerwas, 1982, p. 93). As a tradition based in the moral resolve to be at the disposal of afflicted persons, medicine incorporates historically cultivated skills for caring for, comforting, restoring, and at times even curing those who are ill or injured. It is also a profession, Hauerwas suggests, "because it has learned how to teach and initiate new agents into that tradition and how to govern the practice of their skills" (ibid.).

Medicine is therefore surely a moral enterprise at root. But the same is true as regards the patient's relationship to the healer. The therapeutic dyad establishes people as bound together in common humanity, in community, offering the promise of the mutual enablement of their common lives.

"TELLING" ILLNESS: GRATITUDE AND LUCK

The dyad harbors still more, something which comes through vividly in the words of that 42-year-old coronary bypass patient:

> I wouldn't take anything for this total experience, wouldn't trade it with anyone. This will sound stupid, I'm sure, but it was one of the best things that happened to me in my whole life, having the heart attack, having the angiogram and having the bypass. . . . It brought back what I would consider for myself, not necessarily for others, a new system of values. Many things which I had been overlooking for years now have a great deal of meaning for me. Life itself has more meaning for me, each day, each breath. Things which I had taken for granted for so many years are important. . . . It really doesn't

matter whether a job gets done, or you're late or you're on time because if you don't take each breath, who cares? You're always one breath or one heart beat away from extinction. (Hardy, 1978, p. 229.)

Earlier, when he was first brought into the ER by his wife, he was told that he had had a heart attack. He then reported that after he was sent to the cardiac intensive care unit and the pain had finally begun to ease a bit,

> this was in a way a religious experience, too. I don't mean by that there was any feeling of, or seeing anything or hallucinating, or voices speaking. But you do have a feeling of closeness to your Maker because you are laying there, looking straight up. There's nothing you can do. It's too late for any great deeds that are going to help you at all. The only thing goes through your mind is "Forgive me for whatever I've done before." You're sort of released, you let go and let your Maker have His way. There's nothing much to worry about. It's not a frightening experience. . . . There's just no need for fright. It's useless. You just feel a waste to be frightened. Before then I was frightened that I wouldn't make it to the hospital. It was such a relief upon arriving before I was completely gone and was finally in the hands of others. (Ibid.)

Another patient, suffering from a myocardial infarction, also had bypass surgery. He reported that his "experience in recovery was a very profound one, and at the risk of sounding a little starry-eyed, I just have to tell you about it" (ibid., p. 208). During this period, prior to the change in plasma management, he was not doing at all well. Around midnight, still using a lot of blood, and with the head nurse in recovery beside him,

> I perceived that this just wasn't going all that well, so I asked this woman, "Nancy, is this going to work out?" I wasn't afraid but I was alert to my condition. And she took me by the hand and said, "We're going to work it out." She was such a tremendous, vibrant person that I knew that that was going to happen. I know how corny this must sound but it was a moving experience and I'll never forget it.
> . . . We were like a team and this was a campaign. . . . I was the cause of all the trouble but I was also a member of the team. We were holding hands. (Ibid., p. 209.)

There is a kind of relief, as the one patient noted, at being "in the hands of others" before "I was completely gone." There is as well a kind of relief when pain abates, or even when it is better understood and its sources known. Some patients, indeed, are able to forget or ignore their pain and severe debilitation and are able to live with their condition.

Two things seem crucial here. First, these patients have been able to blend the otherwise counter-attitudes of compliance and collaboration. Patients with severe heart disease, cancer, end-stage renal disease, and other serious illnesses become uniquely reliant (on machines, substances, procedures, technicians, physicians, nurses, administrators, manufacturers, and still other things and people). At the same time, they exhibit a kind of gratitude, which textures their experiences quite as much as, if not more than, the diminishment and even humiliation that illness often includes. "I am deeply grateful," a patient with end-stage renal disease (ESRD) reported, "that I am offered two possible methods of survival [i.e., transplantation and dialysis]" (Coene, 1978, p. 7). After the hospital administrator had the cobalt treatment, he felt moved to gratitude: "Fortunately, standing in the wings, is cancer chemotherapy. So if I have to go over this route again, the medical profession won't be completely out of therapeutic resources."

Second, such patients' lives are deeply marked by a sense of their good fortune, when they are lucky enough to have supportive, responsible, and responsive families, friends, employers, physicians, and nurses in whom they can trust. Another patient, Lee Foster, observed:

> On home dialysis I have been able to pursue my career as well as most of my outside interests with only slightly less vigor than I would have under other circumstances. This achievement has been a direct result of the determined effort my wife and I have made to pursue as normal a lifestyle as possible. We have reorganized our personal schedules around dialysis, designed our daily menu around its dietary restrictions, and organized our household with dialysis as a primary thread. Most important, the supportiveness of my wife has been . . . essential in my success. (Foster, 1976, p. 7.)

Successful treatment for such diseases, to be sure, "requires a strength of character and determination" from everyone (Coene, 1978, p. 7).

The sense of gratitude, moreover, extends even further. The first cardiac patient cited above, for instance, concluded his story:

> I've always been a little bit distrustful of the word "luck". I know that if you work 12 hours a day, seven days a week, you tend to get lucky. But I think in this case, boy, I've been lucky in a lot of ways. One, the fact that I got into a vigorous exercise program and was given a warning. . . . Two, I was lucky I was in shape anatomically to be able to stand up to surgery. In other words, I wasn't sick when I went in. I was healthy. . . . And three, I was lucky to be in this city where they have the kind of talent and facility I needed when my Type A behavior caught up with me. (Hardy, 1978, p. 212.)

This patient's relief and gratitude for his "total experience," for his having acquired "new values" and a renewed sense of what is really "important," show a clear moral dimension. Like other patients, who may or may not express gratitude in such direct ways, he is most eager to talk about his experience, to share it with other people.

People tend to be quite eager to share—in the form of warnings, concerns, or elation—what they have learned through the experience of illness, whatever the experience may have been. The sick person presents as in need of caring help; the very helplessness and the (perhaps only implicit) appeal for help can be the occasion for awakening a moral sense in others. Similarly, the aftermath of grievous illness is often marked by gratitude. (It will be necessary to return to these issues later.)

The gratitude is not merely a warm feeling of goodwill toward some benefactor (for instance, the physician or one's spouse), though this is surely a part of it. It is more basically a knowledge, an intimate realization of what the cardiac patient calls "the total experience": the fear, pain, uncertainty, confusion, as well as the multiple forms of relief and comforting. Being in possession of this knowledge clearly carries moral significance not often detected or socially (and linguistically) encouraged.

This comes through with wonderful directness in these patients' stories. Thus, the first bypass patient, though eager to tell his story, is yet painfully aware that "this will sound stupid, I'm sure." The second one, too, while believing that he has had a profound, even religious experience, nonetheless knows that though he runs the "risk of sounding a little starry-eyed, I just have to tell you about it." Coupled with the need to tell others, thus, is at the same time a strong sense that telling the truth about how one actually feels is somehow improper, awkward, even embarrassing. *While* "it was a moving experience and I'll never forget it," *yet* "I know how corny this must sound."

As illness is a kind of misfortune that befalls the person, so in a way is the good fortune of being in the hands of competent, well-equipped others or the luck of being in the right city (not to mention the good fortune of recovery) something that also (and fortunately) befalls the person. As others have responded to the need for help, so does recovery seem to carry its own kind of responsibility, as we will later see in greater depth—expressed, if nowhere else, in the very eagerness of patients to talk about their experiences and be of help to others similarly afflicted.

This need not be only from the perspectives of those who chance to recover or have the happy experience of successful surgeries. Thus, the woman with the apron, whose condition seemed worse after the cosmetic surgery, eagerly responded to another woman, a complete stranger, contemplating the same operation. Indeed, patients frequently feel great concern for other patients, even while they are themselves still in the throes of their own ailments—as in the case of the woman with a staph infection who got herself tossed out of her new friend's room. Patients, moreover, have a strong sense of the moral nature of these encounters.

The experience of illness is thus a complex and compelling moral experience. At the same time, the relationship of the professed healer to patients is also a complex moral phenomenon. An ethics responsive to the realities of clinical practice must therefore be capable of discerning and dealing with whatever specific moral issues are presented in each particular case, and to do so strictly within the contexts of their actual occurrence.

It remains, of course, for us to focus more carefully on these complex moral phenomena, on the therapeutic dyad, so as to understand more deeply and accurately both what it is and how ethical deliberation can become clinically responsive. To prepare for this, a somewhat extended (and perhaps amateurish) exploration into medicine's fascinating history seems to me necessary. This is the burden of the next two chapters.

CHAPTER 4

Patient Discourse and Medicine's History

THE COMPLEXITY OF THE FIELD

Considering the domain of what Pellegrino calls "professed healers," it was seen, brings one immediately into a specifiably complex field of work. Every healer brings to the clinical encounter a specific biographical situation (Schutz, 1973), including a range of personal and professional values. Every healer also practices within a context including other healers and support personnel in the same or other health professions. Each clinical encounter goes on within the context of some more or less complex institutional arrangement (unit, department, clinic, hospital) and is textured by an array of local, state, regional, and federal regulations and codes, as well as by cultural and historical values and expectations. Each of these levels includes personal, professional, political, economic, and social rules (written and unwritten) and other formal and informal ways of acting that (more or less) govern permissible and impermissible types of conduct for professed healers. Each level, finally, bears directly and indirectly on "what's going on" in each specific case. Significant moral issues can and do arise at each level.

A similar complexity is found on the side of patients. Every person has a particular biographical situation and a nexus of family, friends, and associates. Every person resides in some particular community, belongs to specific sorts of formal and informal groups (often including religious groups, with their own nexus of values and is (most often) a member of the same culture as the healers and providers. Not only are each of these levels frequently, if at times only indirectly, presented within the clinical encounter, but significant moral issues can and do arise from each of them, thereby texturing the clinical encounter in important ways.

An ethics that is to be responsive to the clinical encounter thus faces a complex duality. On the one hand, clinical medicine is premised on conscientious, competent, and scrupulous care for distressed or damaged persons. This has been termed the "therapeutic dyad." It was suggested that on both sides of this dyad a responsible and responsive ethics faces inherent moral phenomena. There is the concern for healing, restoring, or merely comforting, which, as was noted, rests on a fundamental moral resolve at the heart of the therapeutic theme. On the other hand, distressed or damaged persons are in their very conditions presentations of compelling moral demands and appeals. The underlying motif of clinical medicine, its therapeutic experience, is the resolve to help persons whose conditions, to one degree or another, make it difficult or perhaps impossible for them to help themselves.

This moral resolve within therapeutic experience, furthermore, requires physicians and others to be responsive to the specific and special problems and lives of each individual patient. Because of this, that resolve must be specified appropriately for each individual patient's circumstances and particular condition, available medical procedures, and prevailing professional, institutional, and societal norms and expectations. The right action for an individual patient, in Pellegrino's terms, is a decision for which "the categories of *must not, must, should,* and *may* can all shift, depending upon a myriad of factors in the patient's life situation and his/her notion of what he/she deems worthwhile" (1979a, p. 180). To factor into this decision the personal, social, political, psychological, and other characteristics of the patient and the patient's family may well force modification, or even cancellation, of the scientifically and medically indicated action.

An ethics responsive to the clinical encounter has to submit each individual case to a differential moral interpretation that takes into account the dual complexity intrinsic to it. Guiding this special type of moral inquiry is the necessary recognition of the moral resolve underpinning the therapeutic experience, as well as the moral appeal defining human affliction. Clinical medicine's resolve to care for distressed people is thus tied to the afflicted person's trust, which is inherent to receiving such care. That tie is a moral covenant focused on the present condition of the patient and his family and aimed at the range of possible and preferable futures for them.

This covenant can of course be affected, even compromised, by several factors. The deeply seated moral heterogeneity characteristic of our culture can generate conflicts at every level of the clinical encounter—personal, intra- and interprofessional, institutional, governmental, cultural. The covenant is also affected by those conflicts intrinsic to each patient—personal, familial, consociational, communal, religious, or cultural. Apart from the moral heterogeneity, every clinical encounter is in substantial part defined by the therapeutic experience itself; that is, the effort by the professed healer to make sense of (to interpret) his or her experience with a specific patient. Conflicts can arise both as regards determining what is wrong with the patient (symptom interpretation), and as regards attempting to do something about it in terms of the patient's best interests (determining the "right action" for this patient). Both of these determinations can and do often show degrees of clarity and uncertainty, distinctness and ambiguity, correctness and fallibility.

If the one side of the dyad, clinical medicine, shows certain sorts of goods internal to its practice (MacIntyre), the other side, patients-families, also shows certain internal characteristics. The experience of being ill or injured suggests a specifiable complexity, most often presented through impassioned feeling. Illness breaks the usual flow of daily life and, to one or another degree, impoverishes the person, diminishes alertness, and compromises the person in various ways. When such a person presents to a professed healer, he or she thus enters into a complex of unavoidable trust relationships, reliant on the care of others who work within contexts of relative uncertainty, ambiguity, and fallibility. These others are for the most part strangers, who have the power or ability to "do" to and for the patient and family what the patient and the patient's family can neither "do" nor, very often, "know." The interrelationship of care and trust is asymmetrical with power on the side of the professed healer, backed by institutional and social legitimations enhancing the power even further.

MEDICINE'S TWO SIDES: A HISTORICAL IRONY

The ethicist seeking to be appropriately responsive to the clinical encounters within which moral issues are found, faces a necessarily complex dyad, a sort of intricate text that requires interpretation. Certain aspects of this text, of course, seem more readily understandable than others. It seems clear that human affliction (whether due to injury, disease, or the terrible marks of genetic, congenital, or social circumstance) presents a number of moral issues—troubling or relatively minor, dramatically clear or puzzling, as the case may be. Not only does the afflicted person appeal to others for their concern and care, but in a way this person's very afflicted condition solicits notice and provokes a special alertness—to be cared for and treated, restored and comforted. Depending on the gravity of the condition(s), such a person is unable to "do" for himself, to whatever degree, and at the same time seeks to be able to "do" again, to become well (healed, hale, healthy or whole) again, so far as possible.

It may be similarly accepted that there are various modes of response to these appeals: casual and informal advice from family or friends, guidelines from public media, and the more vigorously organized and socially legitimated form of the sophisticated clinical medicine of our times. These also present a spectrum of moral issues. That illness debilitates us, marks us out uniquely in our human vulnerability, and thus solicits attention and concern, seems clear enough. And, that the various forms of response to such appeals may also present problems, also seems obvious. Still, even these textual features may harbor unsuspected dimensions, and it will become necessary to probe them more deeply in order to secure some facets at least of a responsive and accountable ethics.

Even a casual notice of other facets of this complicated text, however, is enough to suggest some real puzzles. For instance, what can it possibly mean for a person, diminished and compromised in multiple ways, to trust other persons who are not only complete strangers but who also have a unique kind of power over that person? For that matter, what can "care," in that commonly coupled set of words, "health care," possible mean when those for whom such care is to be given are complete strangers (and, at times, rather offensive ones at that—such as the "gomer" so well known in ERs)? How can decisions about sometimes quite serious afflictions be reached (decisions which are frequently definitive and sometimes irreversible) when the basis for making them is so often uncertain and ambiguous and when decision makers are so markedly fallible? At just such times, we understandably want to be most confident, certain, clear, and correct. Yet, occasions of illness or injury are invariably marked by uncertainty, ambiguity, multiplicity, and fallibility (recall, for instance, the use of office-based ultrasound for prenatal diagnosis), which make the right action for a patient deeply unsure.

Our reflections thus far have suggested a number of sources of moral issues inherent to the enterprise of medicine. Even so, the analysis, underscoring the therapeutic dyad and proceeding from it, has been critically partial in a key way. In one sense, that can be appreciated when we note certain repeated, although not particularly clear, criticisms of medical practice. One criticism is that the typical, indeed "classic" (Cassell, 1979, pp. 204–05) understanding of medicine today is deficient because it excludes the "patient as person" and focuses instead merely on the body (or even more, merely on the disease entity or organ system affected) for diagnostic and therapeutic purposes. Medicine, it was repeatedly asserted in the late 1960s and throughout the 1970s, seems invariably to dehumanize patients, partly because of its sometimes strident bureaucratization, partly because of its sophisticated technologies, and partly because of its primary concern with illness, crisis, and curing (not with health, prevention, and caring). Despite the presence of what has been identified as the therapeutic dyad at the heart of medicine and medicine's underlying moral resolve to be at the disposal of afflicted persons, many people both within and outside medicine were led to become deeply concerned that its fundamental *raison d'être* (helping afflicted persons) was being obscured and even compromised.

Such a development is not without its historical irony. The very things that have so distinguished medicine in this century seem to have brought about the most profound and complex moral dilemmas. Just insofar as these are the very issues that initially motivated physicians and medical educators to turn to persons in the humanities (those with presumable knowledge of moral issues), anyone concerned to develop an ethics responsive to the actual practices of clinical medicine must be responsive to such issues.

On the one side, then, we have medicine as a historically oriented human practice that is at root a moral enterprise. On the other, medicine in its daily, routine practice, as well as in its more exotic, sophisticated and technological moments, seems productive of the very moral issues that have so deeply troubled our society. What lies at the root of this peculiarity?

THE TEXT OF THE CLINICAL CONTEXT

There is a curious anomaly within the most routine, daily clinical encounters between physicians and patients, that is, in the most commonplace *talk* between them. Patients talk to physicians; physicians talk with patients. It is, obviously, talk with a purpose: The patient is concerned to know what's gone wrong (what's causing the pain, for instance), what can be done about it, and what the future holds—in short, what *should* be done in order to help the patient as much as possible to become restored. The physician is also concerned to know what's wrong, what can and should be done about it, how best to say what he or she knows (or comes to know) to the patient, and what's in store for the short-term and long-range future.

As Cassell points out, though, people vary considerably in their respective abilities "to report details about the time and place (including place on the body) of experiences" (ibid., p. 206). Some patients may remember with relative exactness just when and what happened, how they felt and now feel, and just where (on or in their bodies) the pain or discomfort or funny feelings are localized. Others are far more hazy about such details. People who are not feeling good or who have experienced some trauma not only have their respective experiences but they also interpret them as, for instance, "terrible," "useless," "hopeless," "amusing," "distressing," "a nuisance," "dirty," or "smelly." They may also connect what they have experienced with the experiences of family members, friends, acquaintances, or even strangers. Pain and stiffness in an arm, thus, may be taken as similar to what an older acquaintance experienced, and the person may then go on to interpret this as "arthritis, like Charlie's got." Beyond this, of course, especially in view of the public prominence of health- and sickness-related information, many people may use technical or quasi-technical terms for their interpretations of pains, swellings, bumps, and twitches: "I had a virus last week"; "my duodenal ulcer is acting up"; "my son's lymph glands were swollen."

For the physician, even though such talk in general initiates the encounter with a patient, it is, beyond a certain point, typically neither helpful nor especially suggestive for the clinical-diagnostic task at hand. Rather, the physician has the task of providing a medical (and scientific) interpretation of the reported experiences, so as to suggest possible therapeutic measures for helping the patient with the problems that brought him or her to the physician in the first place. This is able to be done, as Cassell emphasizes, just because a patient's "report of experience is not the experience itself" (ibid., p. 204), but rather one among many possible interpretations of the experience (which include the memories and sensations of the original experience). There is always room for different interpretations, better interpretations, and re-interpretations. In different terms, whatever a patient may believe about what he or she experiences, "the doctor can insert himself between the patient as experiencer and the patient as assigner of understandings" (ibid.). The doctor not only can do this, but this is precisely what is done in classical clinical procedure—the physician offers (to himself, possibly to the patient) another interpretation (or hypothesis).

However ample or poor a patient's talk about his or her experience may be, then, much of this talk fails to capture the physician's primary interest, even if the physician continues to listen to a patient with respectful attention. The patient's talk is of interest, not as a possible, sound interpretation of the patient's bodily condition, on a par with the physician's (even if it be only hypothetical), but rather as an initial *locational index*. That is, the talk is of medical interest so far as it expresses where in or on the body the patient's experiences are located. In this sense, the full communicative intent of the patient's talk is from the outset altered, narrowed down to its spatial directions. What a patient wants to "tell" is the suffering as well as the pain, the fear as well as the hurt, the ordeal as well as the aches. What is "heard" is not the suffering but where the pain is, not what an ordeal or burden illness is but where it hurts or aches.

William Donnelly's "casual survey" (1986, p. 81) of doctors' conversational usages provides numerous illustrations of this linguistic displacement of the patient. At the root of the "sorry state" of the physician's language for and about the people in their care, he observed, is "the unexamined assumption that the scientific way of knowing is the only way of knowing anything germane to the doctor's tasks" (ibid.), whether the talk occurs on morning report, grand rounds, or even at the bedside. Paying attention not to the technical scientific languages of medicine but to the rather more humdrum house staff slang, shoptalk and other daily conversations among physicians, one finds a richly textured and relatively unexplored source of information about medical practice.

There are the usual quaint, but quite telling, slang expressions for certain patients: "gomer" or "crock" for a difficult patient or "circling the drain" for patients who are terminal and whom one may well wish to "turf" to another service before they "box" (i.e., die). More significant, Donnelly notes, however, is what he terms "clinical vernacular" (ibid., pp. 83ff.), which includes both colloquialisms and the precise terms of medicine and biomedicine. What students and residents quickly learn is that nobody, attendings most especially, wants to read lengthy histories, however revealing and even literate they may be for understanding the person. Indeed, the patient rapidly disappears into a "case," whose observed "complaints" become presenting symptoms, commonly rendered into convenient, computer-friendly shorthand (such as dyspnea, preeclampsia, hypoxic).

Frequently, of course, information about a patient's personal circumstances are important for medical management decisions, but are commonly mentioned in ways (e.g., as psychosocial problems) that hardly encourage their being taken with the same weight as medical data. "Words that pathologize human situations seem much more popular than plain language for the human experience of illness" (ibid., p. 86). Thus, instead of hearing that a patient is courageous or cowardly, happy or discouraged, one more often hears words like apathy, denial, depressive, or anxious. In any event, Donnelly suggests, physicians too often know little about the life or circumstances of patients, with results ranging from the trivial to the tragic. The presence of patients in medical discussions tends to be mostly irrelevant anyway, as it is the disease that counts far more than, if not to the exclusion of, the human experience of illness.

At the root of the slang, the shoptalk, and clinical vernacular relating to patients, Donnelly argues, is the simple fact that "much, if not all, of what is distinctively human about human beings is irrevocably outside the dominant belief system of Western medicine" (ibid.). (It is worth noting, incidentally, that Donnelly's own words betray the power of that tradition: "Belief system" is quite as much a form of medicalized lingo as "problem list" or "noncompliant.") The dominance of the biomedical model, the functioning of which effectively strips the patient's communicative intent to a spatial index, reaches right down into everyday doctor talk about (and often in the face of) patients.

The physician is concerned with arriving at a sound clinical judgment regarding the patient's condition, to make sense of what are, in medical terms, presenting symptoms. On that basis, the physician seeks to arrive at a diagnosis that carries with it or implies certain accepted diagnostic categories and therapeutic indications, whose point will restore or heal, comfort or perhaps cure, the patient. Thus, if a patient reports to a physician, "I have really been hurting, so much I can't get up mornings and get the kids off to school; I guess it's bronchitis," such information is meaningful in diagnostic terms solely insofar as it functions to direct the physician's attention to those bodily experiences (i.e., presenting symptoms) to which the patient applies the term "bronchitis." The physician can no more automatically accept whatever the patient may mean by this term than he or she can accept any other of the terms patients are wont to use in conveying "what's gone wrong." What certain experiences may mean to a patient, then, must be systematically set aside, bracketed, or taken into consideration solely as an index to what the physician treats as symptoms suggestive of one or another diagnosis. What a physician says (to himself or even to the patient) may or (most often) may not conform to a particular patient's view of things, expectations, or even ideas of what it is reasonable to believe about his or her body and future prospects.

Cassell believes that there are good reasons to think that this accepted view of clinical procedure is "inadequate"—"deficient because it excludes the person from the diagnosis" (1979, p. 205). Even so, he is clearly aware that his view is an exception to the widely accepted classic view. His argument will concern us in more detail at a later point; for now, it is important to be as clear as possible about the common view. For this, Pellegrino's lucid analysis of clinical judgment will best serve our purposes—sensitive as it is both to the requirements of medical and scientific procedures and to the needs of particular patients.

THE STAGES OF CLINICAL JUDGMENT

As Pellegrino notes, the nature of clinical judgment has been the topic of considerable discussion and dispute in recent years. He contends, though, that much of the dispute can be bypassed "if two significant features which have been neglected are sufficiently taken into account" (1979a, p. 170). In particular, he emphasizes the specific practical goal, the right action for a specific patient, which "must modulate each step leading to it," which casts a "value screen" over the whole process. Secondly, he argues that there is no single explanation or logical method that encompasses the different sorts of reasoning modes and evidences inherent to clinical work (ibid.).

The entire process of clinical judgment may be thought of as a series of steps, the sum total of which is oriented toward that practical end, with the individual steps demanding different types of reasonings, methods, and evidences. This process as a whole is designed to reach a justifiable and quite particular course of action: the right action for a specific patient. The process must therefore take into account the patient's particular existential situation and physical condition at the time the decisions must be made. Each step along the way toward the decision(s), however, is unavoidably "shot through with uncertainties, some eradicable, some not" (ibid.). What is therefore sought in the process is the optimization of these uncertainties and possible sources of error. Because the latter vary for each patient, however, the methods, reasonings, and associated evidences needed to achieve that optimization must also vary.

In short, clinical judgment is ineradicably individual, and while the clinician surely seeks to determine the truth of the patient's condition, "prudent and judicious action . . . is the end to which the whole [process] is directed" (ibid., p. 171). Pellegrino thus argues that medicine is justified basically when it is truly focused on the needs of the patient.

These considerations lead him to the schema already mentioned in our last chapter. It includes three basic components, each of which responds to one of the three "*generic* questions" (ibid., p. 174): (1) the diagnostic (in response to, What can be wrong?); (2) the therapeutic (in response to, What can be done?); and (3) the prudential, or the search for the right action for a specific patient (in response to, What should be done?). Each of these components should be clearly in mind for our subsequent reflections.

The Diagnostic

We have already discussed the diagnostic component, so a summary will suffice here. Diagnosis aims at establishing the most accurate "classificatory patterns," given the signs and symptoms presented by a particular patient. It proceeds in the closest approximation to the scientific paradigm and, ideally, yields the diagnostic conclusion having the highest degree of certainty, with the error rate approaching zero (ibid., p. 175). For that kind of certainty to be realized, the conditions must be the most stringent possible and must be adhered to most closely.

Even so, Pellegrino emphasizes, such "rigorous conditions are only rarely satisfied in clinical reality" (ibid.), with compromises on such ideal certainty entering in at every point: observations of signs and symptoms; reliability of classificatory patterns of diseases; standardization of "bedside data"; variation in laboratory tests regarding sensitivity, specificity, reliability, and accuracy. Accordingly, the point of differential diagnosis is "the selection of some diagnosis as more probable, or more justifying of an action than others" (ibid., p. 176).

Furthermore, the kinds of reasoning required to optimize some specific action for a patient, even at this first stage of clinical judgment, will vary, depending mainly upon whether some recourse to further observation or testing is still available, or whether, for understanding the pathophysiology of specific presenting symptoms, a relatively definite and applicable classificatory schema is at hand.

For some purposes, probability statements about statistically significant populations may be appropriate. These are, however, "weakest in their description of the actual state of any individual in that population" (ibid.), and thus accurate diagnosis will require a different mode of reasoning. Nor is it the case that adding to the empirical data will always change the diagnostic picture. It could as easily compound the sources of error or serve only to obscure how matters stand with a particular individual. "At some point, every diagnosis must proceed without further recourse to empirical input," and, when this stage is reached, the reasoning process is more like arguing a case in court than attempting to prove a scientific hypothesis or assessing probabilities.

Finally, when it is recalled that this stage of clinical judgment is, after all, in the service of reaching the "right action" for a specific patient, in the light of the patient's particular condition and situation at the time when a decision must be made, still further modifications of the kinds of diagnostic reasoning become apparent.

The Therapeutic

Within limits, the therapeutic stage can also approximate a kind of certainty. If there is a verified, or verifiable, basis for knowing the course of a disease, its modification by some medical or surgical procedure, and precise data on the effectiveness and toxicity of drugs, a kind of closure on therapeutic action can be reached with at times compelling certainty. As Pellegrino points out, the use of penicillin for pneumococcal pneumonia, vitamin B_{12} for pernicious anemia, and abdominal surgery for a ruptured peptic ulcer are instances of procedures that provide such a basis.

Nevertheless, Pellegrino emphasizes that genuinely scientific data in therapeutics are far more "scanty" than in diagnostic work for reaching a clinical judgment about effective and safe therapies. In addition, the kinds of questions a clinician faces in attempting to determine what can be done for a patient are often of a different order. Although therapies may be available, they often are complex, expensive, and not radical—that is, do not eradicate the causal agent or the offending process. In such cases, the physician is forced to ask whether the side effects are worthwhile for the patient, given the patient's particular situation. In other words, the therapeutic stage of clinical judgment—what *can* be done?—most often shades into the final stage—what *should* be done?

The Prudential

Determining what should be done for a patient, Pellegrino insists, "involves the counterposition of . . . what the physician *thinks* is good, and what the patient will accept as good" (ibid., p. 180). To be sure, making the right decision for a particular patient will often mean that the decisional categories (must not, must, should, may) can shift, as was already pointed out, as a function of the patient's situation and values. However, when there is relative certainty about what is wrong with a patient (diagnosis) and what can be done about it (therapeutics), the prudential dimension can be rather more straightforward and settled in advance. For example, an acute abdomen, a stab wound in the chest, severe blood loss, bacterial endocarditis, and other diagnoses present few if any choices (unless, of course, the patient is clearly competent and elects to refuse therapy).

Pellegrino's point is that the kind of reasoning appropriate at the prudential stage of clinical judgment differs from those at the first two stages. He also wishes to stress, if I understand him correctly, that it is at this third stage that a patient's talk, narrowed to what I've termed its locational index during diagnosis (and often, at the therapeutic stage), is most appropriately given due consideration. Here, what is personally believed by a patient could well "modify, or even nullify, the scientifically cogent or logically consistent answers to the questions of what can be wrong? and what can be done?" (Ibid., p. 181.) Indeed, at this point, where the definitive decisions must be reached (the goal of the whole clinical process), "scientific modes of reasoning and scientific reasons are least pertinent, and indeed must be submitted to drastic revision in consideration of the patient's value choices" (ibid.).

DEFICIENCY OF THE RECEIVED VIEW

Pellegrino's schema seems deeply appreciative of what patients have to say about themselves and their situations. Even so, if we wonder about the formal status of patient's talk for medicine, it seems clear that even Pellegrino must consider the patient's full discourse (along with its communicative intent) as relevant only at the final stage of clinical judgment. Prior to that (for diagnosis and therapeutics) a patient's discourse about his or her bodily condition, suffering, and hardship functions solely as a locational index for the physician. In this respect, Pellegrino's sensitive analysis of clinical judgment seems in keeping with what Cassell calls the classic clinical approach.

To be sure, for Pellegrino the "end" of the whole process—the "right" or "judicious" action for a specific patient—governs diagnostic and therapeutic work. Even so, it is not so much what a patient says about his or her own experiences that is important for the physician, as it is what the physician must keep in mind about the stages of clinical judgment and its "ordained end." A patient's talk is not a pertinent component of the evidences, nor is reflection on it part of the clinical reasoning required for the physician's diagnostic or therapeutic deliberations. It is the locational index of the patient's discourse that is significant; or, in Pellegrino and Thomasma's later terms, diagnosis "must create a dialogue with this [patient's] body to ascertain the nature of the disease" (1981, p. 113). In these terms, medicine is fundamentally a clinical interaction that works in, with, and through the body (ibid., chap. 3), and a patient's talk is significant solely to the extent that through it the physician is able to initiate that "dialogue" with the patient's body. In other words, the locational index alone has clinical significance. The patient's full discourse becomes pertinent only when the patient is able to say no to the physician's judgment.

As I understand him, it is Cassell's point that just this approach is "deficient," primarily because the individual patient is invariably left out. Operating with "classificatory patterns" of disease categories and their typical symptoms already at hand and at the focus of attention, the physician following the classic approach "will emerge knowing little about the person who has the disease" (1979, p. 205). What is different about different patients, which may well be the decisive thing to know, is typically regarded as "*obstructions* to the diagnostic process rather than as an inherent part" of it (ibid.). Focused on classificatory patterns and categories rather than on the specific individual patient, the doctor risks not understanding the particular interactions between *this* patient and the basic pathologic mechanisms that constitute just *this* person with just *this* disease. Thus, the doctor risks finding out only what he or she already knows and missing precisely what the individual patient actually presents for diagnosis and therapy.

Donnelly also emphasizes that the traditional understanding of medical practice contains serious errors, stemming from the emphasis on natural science and its modes of thinking in medical education and clinical training. All things considered, he believes, "the biomedical model is a way of looking at disease and was never intended as a model for the practice of medicine" (1986, p. 90). Like Cassell (and Pellegrino, at least on this point), he believes that medicine has to be reformed from the bottom up, from a student's premedical days to those of actual clinical practice.

Cassell does seem to agree with physicians such as Pellegrino regarding infectious diseases or some conditions requiring surgery, for which something like the classic paradigm may well serve the patient best. He insists, however, that the clinical expression of the primary diseases of our time (arteriosclerotic heart disease, hypertension, diabetes, degenerative joint disease, and possibly the malignancies) "depend on the individuating characteristics of the patient" (1979, p. 205). Here, in contrast to the infectious or surgical diseases, "the patient is the primary agent of his own treatment" (ibid.). To effect treatment, the patient must "do something," must alter his or her life-style or behavior in order to comply with often complicated treatments.

Just because of such changes in disease patterns and the preponderance of chronic diseases (including many of the malignancies, now increasingly regarded as chronic, not acute, conditions), it has become ever clearer, Cassell argues, that the patient's admittedly subjective understanding of his or her own bodily condition must become an integral part of diagnosis and therapy. Where Pellegrino's argument seems to exclude the patient's full discourse and to focus only on its locational index, then, Cassell argues that this full discourse can be crucial at those very stages—especially as regards the major diseases of our time (Cassell, 1985).

In the remaining pages of his significant essay and in his current research, not to mention practice, Cassell seeks to find ways by which to incorporate the patient's full discourse into clinical judgment. In this, as should by now be clear, he departs in a significant way from the classic paradigm. At a later point, his argument will prove to be one of the keys for conceiving the fundamental features of an ethics responsive to clinical medicine. For now, however, another set of issues must concern us, to enable an understanding of what it is about medical practice that makes it an inherently moral enterprise and thus to prepare for such an ethics.

THE DISPLACEMENT OF THE PATIENT

We have had to recognize a curious anomaly right at the center of the most commonplace encounters between physicians and patients. The talk between them seems oddly out of joint, for while much is said by both, the patient's talk seems structurally dislodged from its context, its communicative intent set aside or narrowed to its locational directives. However sensitive and concerned physicians may be, they are by training and self-understanding of their professional role geared toward the symptoms presented by the patient's body. Whether sympathetic or not with a patient's plight, the physician's dialogue is far more with the body than with the person. In this sense, whatever a patient's experience of his or her own body may be, however this may be told, the telling has significance solely as a sort of directional guide to the patient's malfunctioning or discomforting body parts.

At the root of this displacement of the patient's discourse within the clinical encounter, is, we may now say, a *displacement* of the patient's lived relationship to his or her own body in all its intimacy and everydayness and at the same time a *replacement* of it by the physician's diagnostic relationship to that body, now conceived as an objective and scientific body for clinical understanding and treatment.

To appreciate this, it is enough to note that a patient's talk is not only, as Cassell remarks, an interpretation of the patient's own experience. It is also, and more fundamentally, an expression revealing (to some extent) what and who that person is. What a patient says, for instance, about a weakened leg (that it is perhaps "useless") not only reveals that certain bodily experiences are being undergone but also expresses the patient's own understanding of it, what it means, or how the patient stands with respect to it (that the person cannot, say, go hiking). It is an expression of its value for the patient, as well as how it is understood in relation to other people and to the individual's personal scale of values. "The pattern of valuings of a person is a basic constituent of that person" (Cassell, 1979, p. 209), and just this pattern is an expression of who and what we are to ourselves.

To talk to a physician, thus, is not only to provide locational indexes to hurts, aches, and the like, but also to disclose oneself, to whatever degree it may be. For a physician to displace such talk with clinical-diagnostic and scientific interpretations, then, is to do far more than merely describe the same experiences differently. It is, in truth, to invite and even encourage the patient to adopt the physician's interpretation, that is, to view himself or herself in the way the physician does, and in this respect to ignore or mute those experiences and focus instead on that interpretation.

For that matter, precisely because the physician takes the medical view of things as the correct one, clinical discourse necessarily tells the patient that his or her own view of "what's wrong" is *not* the correct one or at least is not wholly accurate. The physician's displacement of the patient's talk and replacement of it with the physician's talk, therefore, is at the same time directive (it tells the patient how matters should be viewed) and censorious (it tells the patient that other views, the patient's included, are wrong, uninformed, or inaccurate).

Nor is this the end of the matter. Patients, as we have discussed in some detail earlier, have had their lives disrupted. They are vulnerable and enmeshed in unavoidable trust relationships with others who are, while strangers, nonetheless socially powerful and legitimated brokers of interpretations and work within socially powerful and legitimated institutions providing significant sources of support for these interpretations. A physician's talk, then, is not merely an example of one among several alternative ways of talking (about bodies or diseases). It comes heavily laden with real social power and authority. In different terms, it is no accident that the principal source of our current social understanding and self-understanding of our own bodies has been and continues to be clinical and research medicine—not only as regards how experiences are to be properly interpreted, but also what these experiences really are.

Another issue is equally unavoidable: What is it that patients, and the rest of us while we are not patients, are invited and powerfully encouraged (directively and censoriously) to think about when our usual, everyday understandings of our aches and pains are replaced by the clinical-diagnostic terms of medicine? What is "the human body" within this framework? If a patient's everyday understanding of and discourse about himself and his own body stands in need of being displaced and replaced—at least within clinical encounters—what precisely is inaccurate or wrong with that everyday view of things, including one's own body? Furthermore, if a patient's self-understanding of his own ailment is wrong, inaccurate, or incomplete, yet is an expression of what and who that person is (that person's scale of values), then not only is that patient's understanding of his own body in need of displacement, but so it would appear is his understanding of self wrong, inaccurate, or inadequate and in need of replacement. Thus, it becomes necessary to ask: What is the "self" or "person" for modern medicine?

CARTESIAN DUALISM

Many critics of modern medicine argue that the root of this set of difficult issues is what is frequently identified as the "Cartesian dualism." For instance, Cassell traces medicine's classic clinical approach to this source, insisting that it is this mind-body dichotomy that is the basis for medicine's failure to distinguish between pain and suffering and, thence, to ignore the latter or identify it with pain. One result of giving the immaterial, noncorporeal sphere over to the church and the physical world to science was that the body became the domain of medicine. Since the person was regarded as outside that physical and bodily sphere, the only remaining place for the person was the mind. As the mind was increasingly problematic (not identifiable in objective terms), its status and value also diminished for science—and with that, so, too, the person. Suffering, then, was regarded as merely subjective and thus not "real," or it became identified with bodily pain and thus was medicine's exclusive domain. However, Cassell concludes, not only is this approach misleading and distorting, since it "depersonalizes the sick patient, but it is itself a source of suffering (Cassell, 1982, p. 640).

Ivan Illich, too, points his critical finger at Descartes, not only for supposedly divorcing mind and body (conceiving the body along the way merely as a mechanism) but also for thereby placing "a new distance, not only between the soul and body, but also between the patient's complaint and the physician's eye" (1976, p. 156; also pp. 146–47). Howard Brody also traces medicine's failure to "embrace the whole person" to the "outrage" committed by the Cartesian dualism of mind and body (1980, p. 135).

However, if critics of medicine, many of whom are physicians, lay the basic blame on Cartesian dualism as the foundation for medicine's conceptual structure and clinical approaches to patients, defenders of medicine often, if also curiously, embrace precisely that very dualism.

For example, the well-known brain researcher Wilder Penfield came to endorse dualism at the end of his distinguished career. He contended that it is not possible to "explain the mind on the basis of the neuronal action within the brain"; he maintained that the mind develops quite independently in the course of a person's life. Likening the brain to a computer, which needs to be programmed and operated "by an agency capable of independent understanding," he saw himself forced to the conclusion that human life is a composite of two basic elements, mind and body (Penfield, 1975, p. 80).

Noting the impossibility of developing a neurophysiological theory that could explain "how a diversity of brain events comes to be synthesized" into a unitary conscious experience, Sir John Eccles came to posit a "self-conscious mind" as "a *self-subsistent entity*" that "reads" the brain and integrates its diversity, while yet being different in kind from it (1979, pp. 226, 227). Although it might be too strong to identify either Penfield or Eccles as strict Cartesians, it is surely true that their views retain the basic categories of the Cartesian dualism—practically without conceptual modification. What is modified is only the neurophysiological understanding, which, although considerably advanced beyond what Descartes knew, retains the same basic conception of matter or body.

The same is true of others in contemporary medicine. For instance, the neurosurgeon Samuel H. Greenblat, noting that every brain specialist invariably makes key philosophical assumptions (among them the Cartesian dualism), emphasizes that when "pushed against the wall, most of us will readily admit that we are stumped by the Cartesian problem. But when given a little elbow room," he frankly admits, "we ignore the problem" (1976, p. 243), a stance which is quite common nowadays in medicine.

Medicine today is "a fusion of the neo-Hippocratic spirit with a new, mature Cartesian conviction that human illness can be described in physico-chemical and quantified terms" (Pellegrino, 1974, p. 11). Whether taken as a reason for dismay or delight, whether denounced or embraced, it seems that Descartes's monumental work stands at the origin of much of the current self-understanding of medicine.

For the critics, Cassell's claim seems definitive. The failure of medicine to concern itself with the person, and more specifically with the nature and causes of suffering as distinct from pain, "is not a failure of good intentions," but rather of "knowledge and understanding." Working from within "a dichotomy contrived within a historical context far from our own," that is, Descartes's, contemporary medicine has in effect "artificially circumscribed" its care for sick people (Cassell, 1982, p. 644).

For those who embrace dualism, it may well be what Eccles calls the *reductio ad absurdum* inherent to all versions of "materialism," along with the demand to endorse the accomplishments of medicine and biomedicine over the past century, that lies behind the acceptance of both a material body and an immaterial mind (see Eccles, 1979, pp. 212–15). In any case, however particular physicians or scientists may stand on the issue of dualism, it evidently provides the fundamental framework within which theoretical and practical-moral discussions go on in our times. As the eminent scholar Hans Jonas demonstrated brilliantly, dualism, specifically the so-called "Cartesian" variety, is "so far the most momentous phase in the history of thought" (Jonas, 1966, p. 16). It is "the vehicle of the movement which carried the mind of man from the vitalistic monism of early times to the materialistic monism of our own" (ibid., p. 12).

Our reflections on the therapeutic dyad, and especially on the anomalies presented by the commonplace discourse between patient and physician, therefore lead directly into a historical theme. Apparently, if we read these physicians and scholars correctly, many of the most basic moral and philosophical issues presented by modern medicine arise from and in response to that dualism. What is not clear in all this, however, on the one hand, is precisely what is to be understood by the Cartesian dualism and, on the other, just which moral issues arise from the historical practices and theories of medicine because of that dualism. To gain better understanding of these issues, in our search for an ethics responsive to clinical medicine, it thus becomes necessary to delve into that history.

THE CARTESIAN PUZZLE

What exactly is the "Cartesian problem" supposed to be? The one that Dr. Greenblat confesses so "stumps" the neurologist when "pushed to the wall," but that such specialists would just as soon "ignore"?

Stuart Spicker and H. Tristram Engelhardt put it this way in their introduction to the volume of essays devoted to the philosophical dimensions of the neurosciences:

> As it became apparent that the nervous system is not simply another organ system of the body, but is *in some sense* the embodiment of mind, neurophysiology was caught up with the question of how the ways we talk about mind should bear on how we talk about the nervous system. *In some sense*, one experiences and lives in and through one's nervous system, especially the neocortex of the brain, so that such experience can be said to be a function of the nervous system. The problem has been to specify [this] sense. (1976, pp. 2–3.)

The classical formulation of this issue, it is usually claimed, was Descartes's metaphysical dualism. Providing an account of man that allowed the body to be treated by itself as a machine or mechanism and the mind or soul to act independently of the brain, Descartes nevertheless believed that mind and body interact. This interaction, Descartes says at one point, occurs through a single part of the brain, the pineal gland (there are texts in which Descartes seems to contend that it occurs throughout the entire body, or at least the nervous system). In his *Treatise on Man*, Descartes sought to treat the "body-machine" as if there were no soul in it, and in the opening pages of that work says that "when God will later join a rational soul to this machine . . . He will place its chief seat in the brain." (1973, pp. 406–07).

The problem here, it is said, is that Descartes could give no more than a bald assertion of this supposed "interaction" and could not demonstrate it. For instance, when he was challenged by Princess Elizabeth in her letter of May 16, 1643, to explain "how the soul of man (since it is but a thinking substance) can determine the spirits of the body to produce voluntary actions" (Descartes, 1976, p. 106), he replied in part:

> It does not seem to me that the human mind is capable of conceiving very distinctly, and at the same time, both the distinction between the soul and the body, and also their union; because to do so it is necessary to conceive them as one thing alone, and at the same time to conceive them as two, which is self-contradictory. (Ibid., p. 114.)

The reason behind this has to do with the metaphysical idea of "substance": that is, anything that exists in and for itself and requires nothing else either *to be* or *to be conceived*. Mind and body are "substances" in this sense; neither requires the other to be or to be conceived; each can exist "in itself" independently of the other. They are thus governed by the principle of non-selfcontradiction—to exist, everything is either "mind" or "body," and nothing is both. Yet—and this is the classic puzzle—Descartes also insists that although thus radically distinct and different, mind and body are, in the case of human beings (and, of course, Descartes himself!), "united intimately."

The puzzle, in simplest terms, is this: If mind and body are "substances," how can we understand even the most trivial act of moving one's arm? Or, as Eccles put it, how can an act of will (which is "in the mind") set in motion a sequence of neuronal events leading to the discharge of "pyramidal cells" in the motor cortex, thereby activating the neuronal pathways that lead to muscle contraction (Eccles, 1979, p. 214)?

If these two substances are in truth radically different and separate, then there simply is no way for the one to set the other in motion. When it comes to moral life, furthermore, the issue is exacerbated. Since moral affairs belong to the mind, or at least cannot reasonably be placed within the realm of matter, then what goes on at the level of the body simply has no bearing whatever on the mind, and vice versa.

Therefore, if medicine has to do solely with the body, then it is totally innocent of values and need not be concerned in the least with such moral issues. Just this, of course, seems to have been what happened historically in medicine for the next two-and-a-half centuries, as we will shortly see. Regarding the anomalies of patient-physician talk, this, too, bears no relationship to medicine if this kind of dualism really is at the foundation of medicine's conceptual and practical structures.

The issue here is certainly no matter of mere idle philosophic gossip. Descartes apparently bequeaths to posterity, but especially to medicine and biomedicine, not just a "problem" to be someday, somehow "solved," but rather, so it would appear, a momentous, and probably indecipherable, riddle that reaches right into the heart of medical theory and clinical practice.

This kind of discussion, which has gone on continuously in our times and earlier, has its quite peculiar side. There is, apparently, a "dichotomy contrived within a historical context far from our own" (Cassell), but yet seems to be a constant presence in our own times. It is said to be an "absurd" dichotomy (Eccles), yet at the same time unavoidable (Eccles, Penfield). While Greenblat would at times prefer simply to "ignore" it, he yet proposes that it needs to be analyzed historically and philosophically. We seem to have here little more than a piece of cognitive pathology. Yet all things considered, it seems impossible to deny that some things (rocks, atoms, trees, bodies) are indeed material, and that other things (dreaming, thinking, liking) are indeed mental, and that the one is not the other.

Perhaps the best way to proceed is to plunge directly in Descartes's own works, his books and letters, and see for ourselves in just what ways, if any, he really was a dualist. If there is a cognitive pathology here, not only is it necessary to trace out its etiology, but even to perform a kind of radical epistemodectomy.

There is a quite odd passage in an August 1641 letter Descartes wrote to Hyperaspistes:

> We know by experience that our minds are so clearly joined to our bodies as to be almost always acted upon by them; and though in an adult and healthy body the mind enjoys some liberty to think of other things than those prescribed by the senses, we know that there is not the same liberty in those who are sick. (1967, p. 361.)

This is a most curious thing for Descartes, the rational, metaphysical dualist, to say: that our "minds" are "joined" to our "bodies," that we "know" this "so clearly" from "experience," and so on. On the face of it, one can only wonder at the apparent contradiction here, one that Descartes himself emphasized in his letter to Princess Elizabeth. Obviously, unless it is proposed that Descartes had taken leave of his wits (but whether in the one or in the other letter is hardly obvious) or was having his little joke, something is askew here. Some rather careful exploration is needed. Since Descartes mentions "those who are sick" in the passage, it might be interesting to probe into this reference. We know that he practiced both anatomy and physiology; we also know that he sometimes engaged in some clinical consultations on behalf of patients. Let's look into the latter first, and then take up the former.

DESCARTES AS MEDICAL CONSULTANT

In a fragment of a 1646 letter, apparently addressed to Boswell, a case of nosebleeding is discussed. One should avoid the use of vinegar, mustard, wine, and saffron, as well as strong emotions. If these measures proved unhelpful, then the patient should be bled. Bloodletting should be performed from the left foot if bleeding occurs from both nostrils or only from the left. But if there is bleeding only from the right nostril, bloodletting should be performed from the right foot in a quantity of one or two spoonfuls, and should be repeated after a few hours if nosebleeding continues.

The author of this long-distance consultation was Descartes, who had no apparent reluctance to give his medical advice on a number of occasions, often in the same long-distance manner (see Lindeboom, 1978). When he learned that his friend Claude Clerselier was suffering from epileptic attacks, he wrote to Mersenne that this disease was neither lethal nor incurable. He concurred with Clerselier's Paris physicians that the patient should indeed be bled at the beginning of the illness. He advised caution, however, about heavy bloodletting (which was the practice at the time in Paris) and warned against continuing the procedure as it could weaken the brain without curing the illness. He believed that since the illness had begun with a kind of gouty attack in the foot, an incision to the bone should be made there.

Earlier, in 1630, when Descartes learned that Father Mersenne was suffering from erysipelas (Descartes, 1963, p. 235)—redness and swelling of the skin and subcutaneous tissues—he urged Mersenne to hang on until Descartes himself could discover the medicine for which he was then searching and which, he was convinced, would be based "on infallible demonstrations" (ibid.). On another occasion, Descartes and Cornelius van Hogelande, a Dutch physician and Descartes's close friend, were jointly consulted about and then examined the niece of Huygens. She suffered from curvature either of the long bones or of the spine, and it was recommended by them that surgery be performed (Lindeboom, p. 29).

The case of Princess Elizabeth is perhaps better known. On learning in the spring of 1645 that she had been suffering for several weeks from a fever, Descartes promptly wrote her that, although he was not a physician (see Descartes, 1967, p. 127; Lindeboom, p. 36), he thought that the cause of most such fevers was sadness of the soul—a condition that could be helped, he believed, not merely by various remedies and mineral waters but mainly by philosophy. The only way to cure it, he said, is by "diverting our imagination and our senses as much as possible and in using only our understanding in considering the enemies, who are within us and with whom we live." These "enemies" were presumably thought to be the suffering of her father over having lost his throne as King of Bohemia and the exigencies of the family living, well beyond their means, in exile in Holland (Descartes, 1973, pp. 564–68; Lindeboom, pp. 91–92). It seems indeed that Descartes was so utterly convinced of the continuous daily interaction and union of the mind and body that he felt it necessary to recommend an early kind of psychotherapy, even in the case of Elizabeth's apparently quite somatic fever (see Riese, 1966, pp. 237–44).

At first sight, such consultations (much less what is recommended) may appear to us as little more than the idle musings of a dabbler and med-dler, one having little knowledge of or respect for medicine. It is of course well known, in this connection, that Descartes did indeed have a rather low opinion of the medicine of his time (see 1931, Vol. 1, p. 120). When the student Burman interviewed him in April 1648, for instance, Descartes in-sisted that a person over the age of 30 "should have no need of a physician, but should be his own doctor" (Lindeboom, p. 95). Borrowing a maxim from Tiberius Caesar, Descartes thought that by that age, a person should have had sufficient experience and knowledge of what is injurious and use-ful to his own health. Echoing the ancient Hippocratic work *Epidemics VI* that "nature [*physis*], without instruction or knowledge, does what is neces-sary," and that "natures [*physies*] are the physicians of diseases" (see Majno, 1975, p. 200; Coulter, Vol. 1, 1975, pp. 10–33, 68–88), Descartes informed Burman that the prolongation of human life—which he regarded as the real goal of medicine and science (see Descartes, 1963, pp. 799–801)—could best be accomplished by listening to the voice of nature and by living as do the animals: eating and drinking what and only as much as pleases us. Better this, he advised, than to take the revolting medicines physicians pre-scribe!

Still, for all the quaintness of his prescriptions (especially that historic bane of medical pharmacopoeia, bloodletting [Majno, pp. 365, 419, 420]) and despite his low opinion of medicine at his time, Descartes was much admired by physicians for his medical advice. Beyond this, Descartes was certainly no slouch in his ideas. As he pointed out to Mersenne, he had spent eleven years of study in anatomy and physiology (Descartes, 1967, p. 127). Although he admitted that he didn't really know yet how to cure a fever, he firmly believed that if properly cultivated in a rigorous and scientific manner, medicine constitutes the essential goal of all knowledge (see Descartes, 1931, Vol. 1, p. 120).

DESCARTES'S ANATOMY AND PHYSIOLOGY

Early in his life Descartes had trained himself in physiology and anatomy by dissecting a variety of animals, including fish. He had also, as he told Mersenne, "considered not only what Vesalius and others have written on anatomy, but also many more particular things than what they wrote about." This concern, he noted, "has occupied me for eleven years, and I believe that there is hardly any physician who has observed these things as precisely as have I" (Descartes, 1967, p. 127). Descartes was clearly aware of the "contradictions and controversies" that would in all likelihood ensue from the publication of his medical writings, however, and thus resolved not to have them published during his lifetime. He not only wanted to avoid losing valuable time for his own inquiries by having to engage in such controversies, but he was very much aware of the disputes that had already beset Galileo (Descartes, 1963, pp. 492–93; 1931, Vol. 1, p. 122). He did, however, want very much to help others in the pursuit of what he regarded as the "essential knowledge," that is, medicine, and thus engaged in copious letterwriting with physicians and others.

In his splendid study of blood transfusion, Richard Titmuss notes that the first attempt at transfusion may have been performed in 1490 on Pope Innocent VIII, who lay dying, apparently of old age. It was proposed to rejuvenate him by putting the blood of three healthy young boys into his body (blood for rejuvenation was long included in the medical pharmacopoeia). "There appears to be some question as to whether this blood was given intravenously or as a drink but there is no doubt about the result. The boys died, the Pope died, and the doctor fled the country" (Titmuss, 1972, p. 17n). In any case, there was almost certainly no intent to inject the blood into the circulation; it was not until 1616 that William Harvey discovered that the blood circulates throughout the whole body.

Titmuss points out that as "news of Harvey's work spread in Europe, there followed a wave of transfusion experiments"; the first transfusion, from animal to man, occurred in 1665 (ibid.). Still, Harvey's claim was by no means readily accepted, even by experienced physicians and scientists. It was hotly contested and denied by prominent physicians in Holland, Belgium, France, and elsewhere (Lindeboom, pp. 18–19, 72), and it was not until 1818 that the first successful human-to-human transfusion took place (Titmuss, p. 17).

Descartes was one of the first champions and defenders of Harvey and expressly credited him with "having broken the ice in this matter" and recognized him as "the first to teach" how arterial blood enters the veins (through, as Descartes put it, the "many little tubes," i.e., capillaries) and thence returns to the heart (Descartes, 1931, Vol. 1, p. 112). This was in 1638, but apparently Descartes had come to his own view somewhat earlier, as he goes on in the same place to say that "I had explained all these matters in some detail in the Treatise which I formerly intended to publish" (ibid., p. 115). Here he is referring to the *Treatise on Man*, which was one part of the longer work on man and world completed between 1629 and 1632 but withheld because of the condemnation of Galileo (see Lindeboom, p. 53).

Descartes agreed with Harvey's demonstration of blood circulation. Apparently, he had examined the matter himself and found what he took to be "a manifest proof of the circulation of the blood," as he wrote to the physician Plemp on February 15, 1638 (see Lindeboom, p. 117; Descartes, 1967, pp. 21–24). Still, he was unconvinced by Harvey's idea that the heart is a pump with two valves. Rather, he thought he had "infallible proof" that the heart is a sort of expansion device. Blood enters drop by drop into the right and left ventricles and is immediately rarefied by a "fire without flame" (*feu sans lumiere*) (1931, Vol. 1, p. 109); through this ebullition, the blood is expanded, thereby giving it its velocity. In this, as in many others of his physiological ideas, Descartes simply followed the old Galenic doctrines, regarding (incorrectly) the diastolic and not the systolic (and correct) phase as the most active part of cardiac movement. Harvey, it turned out, was correct.

Be that as it may, Descartes went to great lengths to convince his physician friends, especially Plemp, that this view of heart action, as well as Harvey's view on circulation, was correct. So strongly did he feel about the matter and about his other work in medicine, physiology, anatomy, and physics more generally, that he wrote in a letter to Mersenne (Feb. 9, 1639) that if these works should prove to be false, "the rest of my philosophy would be worthless" (1967, p. 125).

What deserves our notice in these writings is not so much their clear shortcomings and failings—Descartes remained, in the end, an amateur in anatomy and physiology—but rather the central importance Descartes gave to medicine, both clinical and scientific. For it is precisely with this in mind that the entire question of dualism must be judged—and with that, the issues that preoccupy us in these reflections about an ethics responsive to clinical and scientific medicine.

DUALISM REVISITED

If one approaches matters from within the framework of Descartes's metaphysics of substance and ignores these medical writings, the familiar dilemma seems to reemerge: Metaphysically, one cannot conceive both the union and the separateness of mind and body. To understand the body and at the same time to avoid self-contradiction, one must treat the body as if there were no soul within it—as Descartes in fact did in his *Treatise on Man*. On the other hand, to understand the mind, it is similarly necessary to consider it independently of the body. And this Descartes did, for the most part, in his classic *Meditations*. Thus, the old enigma crops up: Although man is said to be a unique and intimate union of two radically different substances, this very idea itself is completely unthinkable (i.e., metaphysically).

In Descartes's medical and related writings, including his discussions of medical topics in his famous *Discourse on Method* and *Meditations*, however, matters are fundamentally different. Thus, in the latter text, Descartes insisted that

> nature also teaches me by these sensations of pain, hunger, thirst, etc., that I am not only lodged in my body as a pilot in a vessel, but that I am very closely united to it, and so to speak so intermingled with it that I seem to compose with it one whole. (Descartes, 1931, Vol. 1, p. 192; see also p. 118.)

The "nature" mentioned here is expressly distinguished from what

Descartes terms "the light of nature"—the rationality at work in constructing the metaphysics, among other things. Indeed, using "nature" in the first sense to indicate "those things given by God to me as a being composed of mind and body" (ibid., p. 193), Descartes contends that it is this "nature" that "truly teaches me to flee from the things which cause the sensation of pain, and seek after the things which communicate to me the sentiment of pleasure and so forth" (ibid.). These "perceptions of sense" have, he says, "been placed within me by nature merely for the purpose of signifying to my mind what things are beneficial or hurtful to the composite whole of which it forms a part, and [are] up to that point sufficiently clear and distinct" (ibid., p. 194).

In the letter to Hyperaspistes cited earlier, Descartes states that it is through experience that we "know so clearly" the intimate union of mind and body. For instance, we see that sick persons are so utterly focused on their aches and pains that they lose the liberty they experience while they are healthy. Furthermore, in the very same letter to Elizabeth in which he points out the self-contradiction in attempting to think metaphysically about both union and separateness, Descartes unhesitatingly urges the Princess to look to her own concrete, daily experience as the proper way to think about these matters:

> The metaphysical thoughts that exercise the pure understanding serve to render the notion of the soul more familiar to us; and the study of mathematics, which principally exercises the imagination in considering figures and movements, accustoms us to form very distinct notions of body; and finally, it is by *availing oneself only of life and ordinary conversations*, and by *abstaining* from meditating [i.e., metaphysics] and studying things that exercise the imagination [i.e., mathematics], that one learns to conceive the union of soul and the body. (Descartes, 1973, p. 45; *also* 1976, pp. 113–14.) (Emphasis supplied.)

Similarly, when asked by Burman how the soul could affect the body "when their natures are completely different," Descartes replies, "This is very difficult to explain; but here our experience is sufficient, since it is so clear on this point that it just cannot be gainsaid. This is evident in the case of the feelings and so on" (1976, p. 28).

Now, lest it be thought that Descartes is either begging the question with Burman or merely mollifying the good princess, we need but refer again to the letter to Elizabeth. Immediately after the passage cited above, he emphasizes to her, "I almost fear that your Highness may think I am not speaking seriously here; but that would be contrary to the respect I owe her" (1973, p. 45).

In plain terms, then, the fabulous dualism seems if anything merely a product of metaphysical thinking. But even that would be to misunderstand Descartes, since, properly speaking, even within the metaphysics (and similarly the mathematics) there simply is no dualism. The former, he insists, "render the notion of the soul more familiar to us," while the latter serves merely to make that of the "body" more distinct. To attempt to think a dualism within the context of either is in fact to try to think the strictly unthinkable: a self-contradiction.

But neither can there be a dualism of mind and body in any other respect for within daily life and "ordinary conversation," there is only the "composite whole." However "difficult" it is to "explain" (as Descartes says to Burman), the truth is that "experience is sufficient," indeed "so clear" that it cannot be "gainsaid." Attending carefully to Descartes's own words, in both published texts and letters, no dualism of the sort so often attributed to him can be found, and this, surely, is quite enough reason to reconsider the entire issue of the supposed dualism.

In fact, the appeal to daily life, ordinary conversation, and the experiences of pain, hunger, thirst, and pleasure (i.e., feelings) suggests that Descartes fully understood the force of his own words. It is necessary to add, however, that these sources were especially brought home to him through his various medical involvements. Here, indeed, he was nothing if not utterly candid and clear. His central and life-long aim was to devote "all my life to the investigation of a knowledge which is so essential" (1931, Vol. 1, p. 120)—that is, to medicine. He sought a knowledge of the causes and remedies of the "infinitude of maladies both of body and mind, and even also possibly of the infirmities of age" (ibid.). Even more, he explicitly sought, along with Bacon, what he terms a kind of "practical philosophy" (what we might term both science and technology) through which we can "render ourselves, as it were, the masters and possessors of nature" (ibid., p. 119). This he found desirable not merely for the many goods that would emerge, but "principally because it brings about the preservation of health, which is without doubt the chief blessing and the foundation of all other blessings in this life" (ibid., p. 120). The same point was made in a letter to the Marquis of Newcastle (October 1645): "The preservation of health has always been the principal aim of my studies, and I don't doubt in any way that there have been the means for acquiring a good deal of knowledge concerning medicine which have thus far been ignored" (1967, p. 624).

These medical and related writings clearly not only demonstrate that for Descartes there simply is no dualism, but they also show that for him there is, strictly, *only* the union of soul and body. They also show that this union cannot be comprehended by metaphysics or mathematics; these are, in fact, said to be obstacles to understanding the unity of human life.

When we look into these matters, then, the very thing that is commonly asserted nowadays to be the foundation for contemporary medicine and the moral issues presented by it—the Cartesian dualism—turns out to be absent in the work of its supposed author. As its absence in Descartes's work surely motivates a study to find out what Descartes in fact contended, so too it strongly motivates a study to find out the sources of that fabulous and mistaken notion in the history of medicine.

THE BODY-MACHINE ANALOGY

In a closely argued study of the "mastery of nature" theme in Descartes, Richard Kennington also points to the same thing. The "composite whole" of mind and body, he contends, is neither a "compound of two substances, nor is it a substance itself." Indeed, the composite whole has no "metaphysical unity, nor any unity known by clear and distinct ideas"—that is, within metaphysics or mathematics—"but only the experienced unity conferred on it by the sensation of pain and pleasure, especially pain" (Kennington, 1978, p. 217). While one can question whether this unity is "conferred" by sensations—a claim which I think is obviously mistaken—Kennington's main point is still very well taken. There is not only a theoretical incompatibility in the substance doctrine. The fact is Kennington argues, the conception of substance is defined in such a way that an account of pleasure, pain, and the passions is excluded (ibid., p. 218).

The reason for this, Kennington maintains, lies in the two senses of "nature" already mentioned above, which become especially clear in the case of sick persons. For instance, in the Sixth Meditation, Descartes refers to the case of a patient with dropsy, which he contrasts to his own analogy comparing the body to a machine (such as a clock):

> This is but a purely verbal characterization [*une simple dénomination*] depending entirely on my thought, which compares a sick man and a badly constructed clock with the idea I have of a healthy man and a well-made clock, and it is hence extrinsic to things to which it is applied. (Descartes, 1931, Vol. 1, p. 195.)

But not even this analogy ("sick man" and "badly constructed clock") will do:

> In regard to the composite whole, that is to say, to the mind or soul united to this body [of the dropsical patient], it is not a purely verbal predicate [*une pure dénomination*], but a real error of nature, for it to have thirst when drinking would be hurtful to it. (Ibid., pp. 195–96.)

Thus, when considering the "composite whole"—which we know only from our experiences and discourse in daily life and clinical encounters with sick persons—such analogies are in fact inappropriate and inaccurate. As Kennington puts it, within a mathematical science of nature, "a body sick or a body healthy equally exhibit the laws of nature," but from the standpoint of human life, that is, the "union," a body that is sick is "naturally defective and bad" (Kennington, p. 218).

"Nature" in the one sense (mathematical science of nature) permits such "purely verbal characterizations" (such as clock or other mechanism). But in regard to "nature" in the second sense (when considering the dropsical patient and his experiences or the "composite whole" in its daily life), such characterizations completely fail.

Precisely in view of this, Lindeboom points out, Descartes's anatomy and physiology (which are among the "sciences of 'nature' ") make use of what must be understood as strictly "convenient fictions" (see Descartes, 1963, p. 379, n. l) or "comparisons": The body, for such sciences, is like a "machine" (ibid.) or "clock," as the *Meditations* say (1931, Vol. 1, p. 195; see also Lindeboom, pp. 60–61). But, it must be emphasized, such sciences know nothing of the "real error of nature," which results in defects of the dropsical patient's body.

At the end of the *Meditations*, then, there is not a dualism but a triad: (1) what belongs to the mind considered "in itself"; (2) what belongs to the body, and to body in general ("nature" in the scientific sense), considered "in itself"; and (3) what belongs to the mind-body composite (which involves "nature" in the other sense). In these terms, the "nature" in (2) is fundamentally different from that in (3), for in the latter "nature" is understood to name "something truly found in things and is therefore not without some truth" (1931, Vol. 1, p. 195), as contrasted to "nature" in the former sense, which permits a "fictional comparison" to a clock or other mechanism.

While anatomy and physiology thus treat the human body as a "machine," this is strictly a convenient analogy, one which has no "truth in the nature of things." In everyday life and clinical encounters—in which such feelings as pain and pleasure are met—by contrast, one has to do with "the composite whole" (mind-body, not mind and body), and this is known only "by experience," daily life and ordinary conversation. While for the sciences of nature there is no difference between sick or healthy bodies (both exhibit the same laws of nature), for daily life and clinical medicine there is all the difference (for the whole itself is affected). The sciences of nature, then, know nothing about the life of feeling ("pleasure, pain, and so forth," as Descartes said to Burman); clinical medicine and daily life, on the other hand, know nothing about the machines that the sciences are obliged to use as metaphors.

There are, unhappily, times when Descartes forgets himself, as Lindeboom points out (1978, p. 59), and talks more literally of the "bodily machine." Yet, in the paragraph preceeding the above-cited passage in his *Passions of the Soul* (1931, Vol. 1, p. 333), the fact that this is just an analogy is made perfectly clear:

> we may judge that the body of a living man differs from that of a dead man just as does a watch or other automaton (i.e., a machine that moves of itself), when it is wound up and contains in itself the corporeal principle of those movements for which it is designed along with all that is requisite for its action, from the same watch or other machine when it is broken and when the principle of its movement ceases to act. (Ibid.)

In the *Meditations* it is quite expressly stated that such comparisons are strictly "extrinsic" characterizations that depend "entirely on my thought" and not at all "real" or literal truths (1931, Vol. 1, p. 195).

One may, of course, use such "fictions" or "extrinsic" analogies. Descartes uses them in his anatomy and physiology, for instance, for in this way their basic concepts can be readily assimilated to the mathematical laws of physics and mechanics. However, as he "quite seriously" tells Elizabeth, neither metaphysics nor mathematics (nor, therefore, the sciences of nature) can comprehend the union of soul and body. It is therefore quite obvious, as Kennington observes, that Descartes was "not guilty of the charge, often made, of universal mathematicism [i.e., *mathesis universalis*], of 'the geometric prejudice,' or of the inflexible demand for clear and distinct ideas [as in the metaphysics]. This mathematicism is only regional" (1978, p. 212). Mathematics is relevant to the human body only so far as the body is susceptible of being considered heuristically as "mechanism," and then this is only "extrinsic," a "manner of speaking" (*une pure dénomination*).

How much Descartes was aware of the dangers of such "comparisons" is not clear. It is, however, quite clear that post-Cartesian physicians and philosophers rapidly took these "purely verbal characterizations" quite literally. For instance, Thomas Boyle (1627–91) came to view the human body as a "machine—an 'engine'—and that part of the soul related directly to the machine, the sensitive soul, [is] under mechanical rule" (King, 1978, p. 31). Like Descartes, Boyle relied on analogies between man-made machines (clocks and other automatons) and the human body, but Boyle simply begged the question about the justification for this and was even much less aware of the issue than was Descartes.

Friedrich Hoffman (1660–1742), a self-avowed Cartesian (ibid., pp. 34–39), regarded all living bodies as machines or automatons, and though like Descartes he finds God a necessary postulate to account for mind or soul, he regarded the "animal spirits" in the brain and nerves as nothing but fine matter endowed with some mechanical powers. On the other hand, other physicians found the Cartesian postulate of mind unacceptable, even unintelligible. Thus, La Mettrie (1709–51) was already talking about the "old and unintelligible" doctrine of substantial forms in Cartesian thought. It became increasingly accepted that the proper study for medicine is the human body, and by the early 19th century this idea had finally triumphed, aided especially, as we shall see later, by the anatomical works of Morgagni and Bichat, which connected anatomy and pathology and thereby revolutionized subsequent medical thinking and practice. Indeed, as L. D. Rather emphasizes, these works, especially that of Bichat, "to a very great degree succeeded in wiping out recollection of the attention traditionally accorded to mind-body relationships" (Rather, 1965, p. 15).

So far as the so-called "Cartesian dualism" is concerned, then, this turns out to be almost pure fable, a concoction of subsequent history.

Descartes seems to have known quite clearly what he was doing—and it most assuredly was not what has been attributed to him by subsequent physicians or philosophers. The mind and body form a "composite whole" within daily life and clinical situations, and it is there alone that they can be properly apprehended—whether through ordinary discourse, experience, feelings, or clinical encounters. Descartes also seems to have recognized that medicine, in its clinical encounters with diseased, injured, or crippled patients, knows this "union" just as intimately—through patients' pain, pleasure, and narrowed focus on their own bodies. Therefore, even if one could speak of a dualism in Descartes's works, it is by no means the fabled mind-body dichotomy of the textbooks or that to which current physicians, philosophers, and biomedical scientists refer. Indeed, not even the metaphysics can support that dualism: There being no question there of a union of substances, as that is a strict self-contradiction, there cannot be any dualism. Nor can there be a dualism within daily life or clinical medicine. Here, the "composite whole" or "union" alone is manifestly presented and concretely lived. The issue that has so plagued subsequent medicine, science, and philosophy, therefore, is quite specious.

THE LIVING BODY, THE DEAD CADAVER: THE "SUBTLE HOAX"

Still, there is a real puzzle in these works. Kennington, for instance, argues that there is an unresolved "conflict" that Descartes "made no effort whatever to unify" and that eventually led to the abandonment of the metaphysics of substance. This conflict, he says, is between "the scientific concept of nature which is neutral to good and bad, and the human experience of sickness which is bad by nature" (1978, p. 218).

Kennington leaves the matter with this opposition. I think, however, that the issue must be pressed, especially in view of the immense significance given to the (quite specious) Cartesian dualism today. How is it that the human body is uniquely capable of being characterized as both intrinsically ("intimately") "unioned" with mind and yet is also a sort of "in itself," analogous to a "clock"? Even more, Kennington curiously ignores the fact that for Descartes medicine is not only scientific but also clinical. We must therefore also ask, What accounts for the two medical ways of talking about the human body?

Although we have found the traditional kind of dualism quite specious, there nevertheless seems to be a dualism of a sort here, and it centers in the human body—the dual way of talking about it, specifically within medical contexts. While *clinical* medicine knows the "composite whole" (for example, of the dropsical patient), *scientific* medicine must make do with mere "verbal predicates" or "fictions." We have already noted that there are times when Descartes forgets himself and talks in apparently literal terms of "*notre machine terrestre.*" Still, for the most part he assiduously avoided that trap. Indeed, it is interesting in this connection to note that the Dutch physician Niels Stenson (1638–86), who embraced and then abandoned Cartesianism, nevertheless felt compelled to come to Descartes's defense against his avowed followers. In his famous *Discours sur l'anatomie du cerveau* (1665), Stenson carefully noted that the machine model is merely that, a heuristic and convenient device not to be taken literally (see Lindeboom, pp. 60–61).

It is in any case the careful Descartes who provokes that peculiar question about the two ways of conceiving the human body. There are, in fact, two questions for us. First, what legitimates (if anything) viewing the normal body as being like a "well-constructed clock" and the sick body as being like a "badly-constructed clock"? Second, why should any analogies or fictions, heuristic or otherwise, be regarded as necessary in the first place?

In other words, if there is a "Cartesian problem" it is surely not what is alleged—the "mind-body dichotomy." The problem is rather that Descartes makes no effort to justify the specific analogy he uses ("mechanism") nor the place of analogy more generally; nor, for that matter, does he give any justification for using any analogy at all.

The question is significant, for after all Descartes makes no bones about the point that the only way to know the composite whole or union (indeed, to know it "so clearly") is by daily life, ordinary conversation, or feelings of embodied life (pain, pleasure)—and, as I have argued, by the experience of, and clinical encounter with, disease, injury, or handicap (i.e., clinical medicine). It is perfectly legitimate to wonder, therefore, why one should take mechanistic analogies as the mode of discourse for scientific medicine (and even, in a way, for clinical medicine). Why, indeed, not the reverse? Why any analogies in the first place? We need to consider these issues more carefully.

In the first place, I can offer only a kind of speculative hunch. For this, we have to take seriously Descartes's own work and considerable pride in his anatomical and physiological studies. He engaged in this for eleven years, claimed to have surpassed even the great Vesalius, and even claimed to be more knowledgeable than most physicians of his time. He was also instrumental in persuading a number of physicians of the correctness of Harvey's discovery of blood circulation and took issue with Harvey's idea of heart action. Indeed, he came to his position on Harvey's work from his own anatomical and physiological studies—a not inconsiderable accomplishment for one who remained a plain amateur in the field.

As he related to the physician Plemp, it was through vivisecting animals and fishes and the surgical ligation of the ruptured veins in the leg of an injured man (see Lindeboom, op. cit., appendix II, pp. 104–22, esp. pp. 111–17) that he was led to the conviction that Harvey was correct on circulation (but wrong on heart action). He recognized that anatomical dissection of cadavers was no help, though, since it is only in the living that one finds blood circulation, hence "life," and only in clinical medicine and surgery (and animal vivisection) that one can actually see and study the "composite whole" (as injured or sick). But in just such encounters, one cannot find any source for "clock" or other mechanistic analogies.

My speculation concerns cadaverial anatomy and postmortem dissections, for it is in dealing with corpses and cadavers that a hauntingly odd thing about the human body forcefully appears. Whatever the early anatomists may have been seeking to see, as one of the earliest reports states, "with our own eyes" (ca. 1292, see Singer, 1925, p. 73), whether the soul or its former lodging place, what is insistently found by them is simply more body, and all of it quite dead. The body is vacated; the soul fled to some elsewhere.

Though the earlier anatomists seemed to take the corpse as still somehow manifesting the departed soul (as a sort of spectral presence), by the time of the great Vesalius (*De Fabrica* was published in 1543) and certainly that of Descartes, the corpse is seen as merely an empty husk. It is now at most "ex-animate" matter, if you will, now definitively of a piece with physical nature in the most obvious way. Indeed, the conception of "nature" as mere extension (in Descartes's famous term, *res extensa*), defined in mechanistic ways, may well owe something of its historical origins precisely to the work of cadaverial anatomy. Here, there most definitely is no soul, nor any clear former dwelling place for it, search though so many of them earnestly did to find at least the latter.

It is with the cadaver, then—the no longer ensouled body—that this body is now able to be "considered" as a kind of "in itself," as if there were no soul tied to it. More than that, it is in fact definitively disclosed and experienced precisely as that in these dissections. Here, the "as if" is quite literal; here, mind and body are quite decisively separated, with the body now openly available not only for dissection but also for being "known" in an entirely new way, profoundly different from that of ordinary life. Now it can be imaged and analogized as a mechanism like the rest of nature. Moreover, as cadaver, the human body is an actual part of nature more generally and perforce can be conceived in the same ways: If nature is a "mechanism" then so is the body-as-cadaver! It thus becomes clear that the decisive event is human death, whether death is conceived as the final departure of the soul or, as Descartes says in his *Passions of the Soul*, is thought to occur "because some one of the principal parts of the body decays" (1931, Vol. 1, p. 333). At death, the body is disclosed, or left, as "in itself."

It thus becomes plain that the fundamental Cartesian problem concerns the relation between the living body and the dead cadaver. For, if the latter can be understood as "like a broken watch" or other automaton (ibid.), then it may well have seemed to Descartes that the former could as well, at least for heuristic purposes. The condition for the possibility of considering the body as if there were no soul yet joined by God to it, I am suggesting, might well have been the concrete encounter and experience with the cadaver in anatomical or postmortem dissections.

To take the living body, even for heuristic purposes, as "like" a mechanism, of course, would require as well that the living body be regarded all along as already mechanistic (at least, in all relevant respects)—that is, that the dead human body, the cadaver, function as the truth of the living human body. Only when the body is dead, can one know what the human body really is. In turn, this requires that the idea of mechanism was already at hand and conceptually available for Descartes—and taken as the truth of nature itself, as indeed seems precisely to have been the case, even though Descartes apparently offered "the first mechanical explanation of the world as a whole" (Lindeboom, p. 55; see also Dijksterhuis, 1964).

Just this view, moreover, seems to be at the basis of Jonas's intriguing contrast between classical times and our own. In the former, Jonas says, the corpse is the "primal exhibition" of "dead" matter and thus the limit of understanding not to be accepted at face value. By contrast, today it is the living organism that is the limit of understanding, gradually "unmasked as a *ludibrium materiae*, a subtle hoax of matter" (Jonas, 1966, p. 12). It is only when the body is a corpse that it seems fully intelligible, for then it loses its "puzzling and unorthodox behavior of aliveness" and reverts to being merely a body among other bodies where "matter" serves as the principle of comprehensibility. The fundamental direction of modern scientific thought on life as a physical fact is in this sense to efface the "boundaries between life and death." Today, in different terms, "our thinking . . . is under the ontological dominance of death," and all modern theories of life must be understood against this background of deadness, "from which each single life must coax or bully its lease, only to be swallowed up by it in the end" (ibid., p. 15). Underlying our own views of life and death is precisely the Cartesian view, especially that of matter as dead (see also Koyré, 1958).

THE ODDITY OF ORDINARY LIFE

As the living body becomes likened to the cadaver (as a mechanism), so does clinical medicine come to be judged and conceived in terms of scientific medicine and the sciences of nature; that is, the truth of disease is found in anatomy and physiology (and, later, in pathophysiology). With this step, moreover, something very much like a dualism does indeed get introduced—not between mind and body, however, but rather within the body itself, between bodily life and death.

Furthermore, as that idea develops and medicine becomes increasingly focused on the body as "in itself," a kind of magical materialism emerges. The body alone counts for the understanding of human life (as Jonas says, the "understanding" of human life as a physical fact"), and it is the body understood in the Cartesian manner—in other words, the cadaver. Death, in the form of the cadaver, is the principle of life, in the form of the living organism that is intimately united to the mind or person in daily life (in pain and pleasure, the life of feeling and passion). Soul or mind, however, remains an insistent, if also unaccountable, presence—not a "mechanism," not a mere extended quantity, not able to undergo transformation from life to death in the manner of the human body. In life, nevertheless, it is what is "intimately united" with the living body, and in death is no longer present.

Oddly, what is not followed out, by Descartes no more than most others after him, is Descartes's remarkable insight: to learn to think of nature, and biological nature especially, on the model of the living body of the composite whole encountered in daily life and clinical settings. Indeed, not until the early decades of our own century has there been any serious effort among biologists to study the specifically human in other than quantitative and reductivist terms. Such scientists as Adolph Portmann (1954, Jacob von Uexküll (1953, 1956), and others (see Grene, 1974) have attempted to follow out precisely what is implicit in Descartes's advice to Princess Elizabeth. As came to be recognized, not only does clinical medicine perforce have to deal directly with the living composite whole—the actual living person—but so in a crucial sense does physiology. After all, the signal medical discovery of Descartes's times, the circulation of the blood, seems directly evident only in the case of the living body, never the cadaver.

This leads me to the second question. I asked, Why should Descartes have thought that any analogies or "fictions," heuristic or not, were necessary in scientific or clinical discourse? In other words, what reason is there for taking the live human body as susceptible of mechanistic analogues? The answer may be suggested in Descartes's anatomical work; the apparently clearest instance of a body definitively separated from anything mental or "soulish" is the cadaver.

But then we have to wonder, Why the specific clock analogue? After all, however impressed Descartes seems to have been with such mechanisms (see Lindeboom, p. 58), the clock seems no more like a corpse than vice versa and is of no use whatever in proving, for instance, the circulation of the blood. At this point, all that could be surmised was that Descartes was simply in the unquestioning hold of the idea of mechanism, like so many of his contemporaries (see Mumford, 1970, pp. 28–76). What is at work here is the cunning legerdemain of plain presupposition. Perhaps, though, there really was no other way out for Descartes.

Here, I can again offer only a speculation. If there was any issue of a way out at all (and I don't mean to suggest that there was something like a choice), it would have to have been among the major components of

Descartes's thought more generally: the metaphysics, the mathematics (and, of course, science), or daily life or ordinary conversation. Obviously, when we take him seriously, only the last "knows" the "composite whole" or "intimate union" characteristic of the living person embodied by his or her own living organism. The metaphysics and mathematics, after all, prove to be plain "obstacles" to knowing this whole or union. Hence, if one wants to know the latter, much less to treat patients, there would seem to be no choice, no other way out, except to turn directly to ordinary life and discourse and study them for their own sake. But this could only be a positive embarrassment, an epistemic nightmare, so far as genuine knowledge is concerned—especially for Descartes, but also for much of subsequent medicine and philosophy.

Since ancient times—when Parmenides taught that the realm of sensible life is the "way of seeming" and illusion, when Herakleitos intoned that common people are "always incapable of understanding the *logos*," and when Plato relegated the sphere of the everyday (the "sensible") to decidedly second-class citizenship in the domain of True Being—the ordinary or everyday has been regularly regarded as precisely what must be left behind at all costs when it comes to the serious business of knowledge. Unreliable, shifting, deceptive, ambiguous, and vulgar—the everyday is the most capricious and suspicious of all!

Yet, Descartes says over and again, only within the ordinary can the union be truly experienced and known (so far as it can be known). At the same time, it seems the most suspicious of any domain. Descartes maintains, after all, that it is the first region to fall under his famous methodical doubt, which leads directly into the metaphysics of substance. From that perspective, of course, Descartes is quick to remind us, the union cannot be apprehended at all! Yet again, in the Sixth Meditation, the union gets reintroduced, primarily through the case of the patient suffering from dropsy. At just this vital point, be it noted, it is nature in the other, nonmechanistic sense that proves central—and with it, the sphere not only of ordinary discourse and daily life, but also of clinical medicine, becomes central. The question might thus be asked, Why is it that methodical doubt should have any effect at all on the daily or the clinical experience of intimate union? After all, if this union really is so "intimate," one would think that such doubt could gain no purchase whatever on it.

I suppose, in the end, that this also had to be ruled out. Although Descartes played at it, often at long distance, clinical medicine was simply beyond him. He had to admit to Mersenne in 1639, for instance, that despite his eleven years of study, he still did not understand even simple fevers or how to cure them (even though, six years later, he prescribed a rigorous course of intellectual study for Princess Elizabeth as a cure for her somatic fever). Perhaps his prescription for Princess Elizabeth was an early form of psychotherapy. However, Descartes did not pursue this prospect.

Neither everyday life, ordinary conversation, nor clinical practice, then, seem capable of supporting the considerable burden of scientific, medical, and other forms of knowledge. Moreover, the plain fact about clinical medicine is that only since very recent times has it actually been effective in combating disease, and this, it is said, is primarily due to the fruits of that significant marriage of medicine to the biological sciences, foretold by Bacon (and even Descartes) and consummated mainly since the late 19th century.

THE POST-CARTESIAN CONTEXT

We still, of course, face that curious anomaly nestled within the commonplace of talk within the clinical encounter. To grapple effectively with the host of current moral issues within clinical medicine it is still imperative for us to understand that peculiarity—to search elsewhere for it.

We have found that the Cartesian inheritance is quite different from what it has commonly been portrayed to be. What remains as the genuine Cartesian problem, it turns out, is not at all the separation of mind and body, but, to the contrary, their experienced union—not the metaphysics, but rather the "knowledge" gained from daily life, ordinary conversation, feeling, and clinical encounters. Whether or not it is possible, or even instructive, to consider the body "as if" it were sort of "in itself" from some point of view or other, it is clearly not possible to do so within daily life or clinical medicine. Similarly, while it may be that scientific discourse finds analogies or metaphors useful, these are inaccurate, not useful, and possibly even quite damaging within daily life and clinical medicine.

Even so, what quickly happened after Descartes is instructive: The merely heuristic, scientific language became understood quite literally, medicine came to see its main and eventually even exclusive object as the body ("in itself"), and the sphere of daily life, ordinary conversation, and feeling continued to be regarded as subjective, capricious obstacles to be overcome in the effort to gain genuine knowledge.

Post-Cartesian history is of course not as simple as that. Many physicians remained deeply convinced that medical practice required astute attention precisely to what Descartes termed "ordinary conversation" and the "life of feeling." Thus, the French physician Cabanis declared in 1795:

> Woe to the medical man who has not learned to read the human heart as well as to recognize the febrile state! . . . How can he restore calm to the disturbed spirit, to the mind consumed by persistent melancholy if he ignores those organic lesions which such moral disorders can cause and the functional disorders with which they are connected? (In Rather, 1965, p. 10.)

The German physician Jerome Gaub (1705–80), whose essays on psychosomatic medicine were widely known during his own lifetime (and are translated by Rather [ibid.]), wrote that while the physician "in his thoughts" can "abstract body from mind and consider it separately in order to be less confused in the marshalling of his ideas," yet

> in the actual practice of his art, where he deals with man as he is [i.e., in daily life], should he devote all his efforts to the body, and take no account of the mind, his curative efforts will pretty often be less than happy and his purpose either wholly missed or part of what pertains to it neglected. (Ibid., p. 70.)

Gaub's concern was that physical illness may well lie "in the mind," while on the other hand "the body frequently both begets mental illnesses and heals its offspring" (ibid.).

In short, the difficulty found within the Cartesian corpus, however puzzling it surely is, is found throughout medicine more generally after Descartes, especially in the relations between the medical theorist and the practicing, clinical physician. As Rather notes,

> The latter is aware that he treats neither minds nor bodies in isolation. He treats people whom he takes to be more or less like himself. And he knows that the way these people feel about themselves, their physician, their treatment, and their immediate human environment may have important effects on their bodily ailments. The practicing physician soon finds that he cannot behave like the philosopher and ignore the world of "lived" experience in favor of a theoretical construct. His patients are unwilling to permit this, and insofar as he is a genuine therapist he will be disinclined to do so. (Ibid., p. 9.)

Rather also notes that the "strain of psychosomatic practice" that runs through Western medicine is by no means the mainstream. Indeed, it has often been "overshadowed by the growth and power of medical theories placing exclusive weight on corporeal phenomena" (ibid.). Still, medicine, historically and currently, is filled with tales of astute clinicians "whose finger is on the pulse of a person rather than on that of a physiological machine" (ibid., p. 10), that is, physicians whose practical relationships with patients are deeply informed by what Descartes had already emphasized about the union of body and mind in ordinary life. Unfortunately, not only most medical theorists, but even those practicing physicians when they from time to time come to think theoretically, find themselves before a "physiological machine" and those other abstractions that separate mind from body. In these contexts, moreover, talk of souls (minds or persons) and "intimate union" seem strictly out of place.

THE ELUSIVE EVERYDAY: A HISTORICAL THEME

The Cartesian enigma remains. So far as knowledge is concerned, there seems no way to include daily life and ordinary conversation, and clinical medicine quickly becomes conceived most often on the model of science, however odd a science it admittedly must then be. And this is exactly the issue with which we must contend if we would hope to make sense of those anomalies in the everyday talk between physicians and patients and of the human body.

During the past several decades, this enigma in talk has reemerged, usually within discussions about the "patient as person." While this theme has been around some time before Paul Ramsey made it popular, as was noted earlier, its point is worth noting in this context. Scientific medicine, especially under the often dramatic impact of newly developing diagnostic and therapeutic technologies and the increasing bureaucratization within the well-known medical centers of our times, began to trouble many physicians. According to them, medicine seems invariably to "dehumanize" patients. The specialization of medicine accompanying these developments led physicians to be more attentive to specific disease-entities and organ systems, it was felt, than to the people suffering from them.

Indeed, Cassell has emphasized that that very focus has led to patients not being listened to and their suffering being regularly confused with the very different phenomenon of pain (Cassell, 1976 [1985])—that is, to what we termed the narrowing of patient talk to its locational index. While we have been staying within earlier historical epochs thus far, Paul Starr's lucid study of American medicine, although it does not address the issue directly, does suggest that more recent trends incorporate this enigma (Starr, 1982).

One of the landmarks in the development of medical policy in this century was the formation in 1926 of the privately funded Committee on Costs of Medical Care (CCMC). Earlier, Starr suggests, it might well have been called Committee on Costs of Illness, indicating thereby a key shift in medicine's self-understanding and emphasis from patients-as-persons to disease-entities. An independent body of some fifteen economists, physicians, and public health specialists, the CCMC focused just on medicine. It issued some 27 reports during its 5-year existence, "providing the most detailed information yet assembled on medical care in America" (ibid., p. 262). It embodied a strong commitment to improved medical care, especially for more effective organization. Yet, however admirable it surely was, the CCMC embodied "unacknowledged and perhaps unconscious" prejudices, especially on the need for more medical care, and with that, on medical power.

In one influential report for the CCMC, Roger I. Lee, Lewis Jones, and Barbara Jones asserted that medical care is not an economic but a medical issue. They assumed that individual physicians could and should set standards for medical care, allocation of scarce resources, and the like. The need for medical care, they argued, must be defined strictly in terms of the physical conditions of sick people and on the capacity of medical science to deal with them. "The ordinary layman," they wrote, "lacks the knowledge to define his own medical needs." Rather, patients must rely solely on "the expert opinion of medical practitioners and public health authority" (ibid., p. 263).

As if to underscore their understanding that medical needs should be defined by the cultural authority of medical professionals, the authors went on to assert that such a "technical definition" was valid only in a society like America, which believes in "the efficacy of scientific medicine" for promoting health. Americans, they asserted, "value health and have accepted the science and art of medicine as the proper instrument for its advancement" (ibid.).

As Starr remarks, "Nowhere in the report was there any mention of the risk that the medical profession might exercise monopoly power" through this conception (ibid., p. 264). Nor, for that matter, did these authors see any apparent need to defend the view that ordinary laypersons lack the knowledge to respond to, much less to define, their own medical (or, rather, illness) needs. These, and not merely medical care, were relegated unquestioningly to medicine. The enigma at the heart of physician-patient discourse has now become an automatic presupposition buried within the self-understanding of the medical profession.

Although the issues of social policy and medical authority are obviously important and fascinating topics, the work of the CCMC makes prominent another issue more directly of concern here—a view of ordinary life and people as incapable of understanding, much less of attending to, so-called "medical needs" as well as "medical care."

As Foucault suggests (1973), this view is a fundamentally historical phenomenon deeply marking the understanding of clinical practice and medicine more generally. In order to understand it properly—always in pursuit of that enigma at once in Descartes's works and in everyday talk between physician and patient—it is necessary to give at least some emphasis to medicine's own basic goals: knowing disease and healing it.

Lester King points out that at the beginning of the 19th century these twin goals underwent a fundamental change, as a function of basic changes in pathological anatomy, changes that the Spanish physician P. Lain-Entralgo identifies as a veritable "Copernican revolution" in medicine (1963). King emphasizes that early in the 19th century there occurred a definite change in direction, thanks to which it is appropriate to "speak of a new stage, which I call the period of clinico-pathological correlation" (King, 1978, p. 30). While the number of autopsies greatly increased in this period, what is significant is not the increase but rather the "new total approach" of which the autopsy was only a part (ibid.).

Attributing this change to the spirit of innovation that prevailed in Paris after the French Revolution, King also mentions the plain fact of physicians being able to follow-up on large numbers of patients, both through their clinical courses and then through postmortem examinations. But King does not seem much concerned with the conceptual and moral issues underlying this historic shift, issues that we will turn to in the next chapter.

CHAPTER 5

Themes from Medicine's History: Interpretive Reconsiderations

The appearance on the current public scene of so much discussion of ethics and morals within, and occasioned by, medical research and practice has been a source of both puzzlement and dismay to many physicians. Some, as was seen, have responded in a quite positive way, welcoming the help as well as the criticism of persons from nonmedical fields, especially ethics. Others, perhaps the majority, maintain either a skeptical attitude or react with disdain. On the other side, medicine's critics continue to hammer away in public contexts and professional forums, seeking to promote a keener appreciation of medicine's problems and the presumable need for greater public policy controls on them (as, for example, embodied in the Baby Doe amendment).

In a clear way, such discussions signal a cluster of centering issues that, perhaps because of their very heat and frequent passion, only rarely get posed plainly. If medical research and clinical practice occasion serious social and moral issues, it may well be due to a widely shared, if still only faint, sense that medicine itself—as a social practice, a profession, and a positive cultural value—has begun to appear perplexing. Its results at times seen to be equivocal; its practitioners, to many people, not always trustworthy. Things seem to have gotten out of hand or threaten to do so.

Medicine as a phenomenon in our culture seems to pose as many, if not more, problems than it resolves, and it seems increasingly in need of careful critique. What once could be, and was, taken for granted quite generally—for instance, that the doctor knows best and is therefore the real decision maker for ill people—is no longer so readily able to be taken for granted, both within and outside medicine.

Also being questioned is the idea that there are persons in our culture, such as philosophers, theologians, and ministers, whose special training and presumed expertise are believed uniquely to equip them to be primarily responsible for dealing with the serious moral and religious issues occasioned by medical situations. Such persons' words, however, are often only bewildering, their values diverse and at times divisive, and their judgments irresolute and without what Gabriel Marcel once called "a bit on the real" (*une mosure du réel*). When it comes to moral issues, the ideas of these professionals also seem sorely in need of careful critique.

Along with all this, social life in our times frequently appears so heterogenous, diverse, and complex—especially as regards the central issues of illness, health, life, death, and moral conduct—as to threaten resentment, violence, and even social anomie. People, patients and their families in particular, often seem desperately in need of firm, sure, univocal values, facts, and goals; but most often they find only uncertainty, ambiguity, and equivocation. In the absence of an ethics of uncertainty, this situation encourages the growth of mass movements, each by the nature of the case claiming exclusive access to "the truth." It creates the social conditions within which people are more and more inclined to become "true believers"—unthinking, unwitting adherents to whatever ideal, cause, or movement chances along.

It is, Eric Hoffer long ago observed, "the certitude of his infallible doctrine that renders the true believer impervious to the uncertainties, surprises and the unpleasant realities of the world around him"(Hoffer, 1958, p. 76). Hoffer continued, "the effectiveness of a doctrine should not be judged by its profundity, sublimity or the validity of the truths it embodies, but by how thoroughly it insulates the individual from his self and the world as it is" (ibid.).

In a time when certainty and simplicity, within a nexus of commonly shared communal values and ends, seem absent, people yet face the harrowing decisions of life, loss, compromise, and death. When what is deeply felt to be needed, certainty, is yet known to be missing, violence, anomie, and fanaticism are not far behind. Everyone must at some point then find himself or herself wondering about conflicting claims of right and wrong, rival duties and obligations, irreversible decisions made on the basis of not altogether reliable data, soaring costs and scarce resources, overuse of medicine and medical overkill, and criminal and civil liabilities arising from seemingly humane (and even at times unavoidable) decisions when the powers of disease outstrip the powers to cure or even partially to restore. Careful critique seems a profound need here, too.

To be responsive to such issues, it was necessary to probe, if only very modestly, some of the themes in the complex history of medicine. My idea has been that such a perspective could help to focus some of these issues and might uncover in this labyrinth some paths helpful for grappling with the unavoidable demands of value conflicts in our times.

HUMAN ANATOMY: A FIRST LOOK

It is well known that anatomical inquiry in its earliest stages was primarily conceived as a study, a search for knowledge of the human body. Indeed, it was not until the mid-18th century that it began to be pursued in earnest for the purpose of pathological understanding which could, even potentially, point the way to possible therapeutic concerns. Morgagni, whose *De Sedibus et Causis Morborum* was published in 1761, was the first to correlate observations made at autopsy with the clinical symptoms reported, often by the patient, prior to death. Before this time, although abundant autopsy reports were published, such data were recorded quite uncritically and "offered," King notes, "little correlation between clinical and anatomical findings" (1978, p. 194). However, Morgagni's work changed that radically, and the road to the "clinico-pathological correlation" was entered.

The example King provides from Morgagni's work is illustrative. It was reported that a 59-year-old woman had been "seized with an apoplexy," with her right limbs and the eyelid of her right eye absent of feeling and motion. She had no difficulty swallowing fluids, however. After her death, Morgagni and his students looked for damage on the left side of her brain, for according to the then-recent observations by Valsalva suggesting contralateral localization, an organic injury to the left part of the brain would show up in organic losses on the right side of the body. Dissection showed, indeed, "on the external side of the left thalamus" an area that "was very soft, and liquified, and was found to be mixt with a certain bloody fluid . . . so that nothing but a disagreeable smell was wanting to make us pronounce it absolutely rotten." Regarding it as an abscess, Morgagni declared, "You see this doctrine confirmed, that the injury of the brain is found in the hemisphere which is opposite to the paralytic side of the body" (ibid.).

As King then indicates, Morgagni took the autopsy as "explaining" the clinical symptoms observed earlier. Representing an "organic lesion," as opposed to a functional or even hysterical disorder, Morgagni took the lesion as an abscess definitely localized in a specific part of the brain. In this way, he succeeded in correlating data from one sphere, clinical observation, with data from another, anatomical description. The connection he drew was not a scheme of pathogenesis, nor did he indicate the progressive steps that led to the disease. His, as King terms it, "existential" rather than "causal" explanation fully satisfied his audience's curiosity (ibid.).

At the time, however, Morgagni's work seemed to have little impact on medicine more broadly. Disease, Foucault points out, was understood at the time as little more than a clustering of symptoms (most often as reported by patients themselves) characterized by a certain history (again, as reported by patients) and not considered as localized within a specific organ or body part. With changes in the clinical settings of medicine—what Foucault analyzes as the "birth of the clinic" (1973)—correlations between clinical symptoms and anatomical findings, and especially the localization phenomenon, could be better received.

Of particular significance was the emergence of the idea of internal bodily "lesions," which the physician Xavier Bichat located with greater refinement within the different components of the bodily organs, such as connective tissues, serous and mucous membranes, muscles, and bones. "The notion of constituent tissues," King observes, "allowed more precise correlations," and thus diseases "could be referred not to disorders of entire organs but to specific components of those organs. Histology thus provided a 'deeper' level for explaining disease" (King, 1978, p. 195). Of equal significance, as we will later come to appreciate, is this emphasis on the bodily interior as the place to search for the locus of disease and, thus, as the object for medical attention.

With the development of the clinics, more exact and continuous observations of bodily symptoms displayed by patients became possible. Autopsies on these patients were more readily available. Thus, the correlation of the two observations became even more sensible, especially with Bichat's refining of localization from entire organs to tissual components of organs ("lesions"). Bichat thought of tissues as simple surfaces without further interior (not unlike the "simple ideas" favored by many philosophers of the time).

Two shifts are noticeable. First, taking tissues as the "simple ideas" of human anatomy and as open for direct visual observation at autopsy, Bichat no longer had any need to understand diseases as historical. Patient reports of their feelings, aches, and pains became irrelevant. Anatomical inspection of tissual surfaces for disruptions or discontinuities was sufficient for a medical judgment about the locus of a disease. Thus, Foucault emphasizes, with Bichat visual-anatomical looking (the "*surface gaze*") became the hallmark of medical truth (1973, p. 129). Clinical inspection of symptoms and patient reports of feelings gave way to anatomo-clinical perception focused on tissual abnormalities ("lesions").

In the second place, therefore, whereas prior to this time a symptom (especially as reported by the patient) was a sign of something "feeling bad" and thus of something's having gone wrong with the mind or the body (of some pathology), with Bichat the concept of symptom changed radically. Diseases are not the same as their symptoms. Rather, the locus of disease became the tissual lesion, the observed damage or discontinuity seen on the tissual surface. Hence, the correlation of common symptoms and disease gave way to the lesion itself, and the diagnosis of disease became definitively separated from the patient's experience of his or her own body and feelings.

Bichat could thus emphasize to the readers of his *Anatomie Generale* (1801) with considerable enthusiasm that

> for twenty years, from morning to night you have taken notes at patients' bedsides on affectations of the heart, the lungs, and the gastric viscera, and all is confusion for you in the symptoms which, refusing to yield up their meaning, offer you a succession of incoherent phenomena. Open up a few corpses: you will dissipate at once the darkness that [clinical] observation could not dissipate. (In Foucault, p. 146.)

With this step—completing what Lain-Entralgo terms the "Copernican turn of the clinical-pathological lesion"—Bichat could not only effectively ignore a patient's discourse; in truth, the clinical-anatomical correlation made that a justifiable necessity. "What's wrong" with a patient is measured by the clinician, even though a definitive diagnosis could not perforce be given until autopsy.

L. J. Rather points out that despite the long tradition in medicine that sought to give legitimate recognition of the mutual influence in diseases of mind and body, the triumph in the 19th century of a medicine centered strictly on the body as an object of scientific study, combined with the new cellular, pathological anatomy, effectively erased all traces of the traditional emphasis on mind-body relationships (Rather, 1965, p. 15).

In Sullivan's words, "the eye began to replace the word as the privileged vehicle of medical truth," and thus disease could "be defined now independently of patient awareness as a purely natural phenomenon of the biological body" (1983, p. 4). Now for the first time, indeed, it became possible for medicine to offer what was seen as the genuinely scientific explanation of what is strictly individual; anatomical experience at correlating tissual lesions with formerly observed (and recorded) clinical symptoms permitted increasingly controlled inferences from the latter to the former. And, with this, clinical observation itself became increasingly a matter of "autopsy-in-advance," with observations becoming anticipations of what actual autopsy would eventually find.

With anatomically informed clinical observations becoming front and center for medicine, replacing discourse with the visual gaze, the stage was clearly set for that anomaly in physician-patient talk which set my historical inquiry in motion.

BETWEEN DESCARTES AND BICHAT

A close analysis of the works of Descartes and those immediately after him shows that what Foucault terms "the medical gaze" was already in the making. Specifically, although the kind of dualism evident in Bichat's anatomy—between the outer body (symptoms) and the inner body (tissual lesions)—tended to wipe out, as Rather says, "recollection of the attention traditionally accorded to mind-body relationships," it nonetheless echoes the actual dualism found in Descartes's writings, especially those relating to medicine. As has been underscored repeatedly, the so-called "mind-body dichotomy" is far more a product of subsequent, alleged Cartesians than Descartes's own work. Instead, it is the duality within the human body that, if anything, can be labeled a dualism. As living, the body is experienced as intimately unioned with the mind or soul; as dead, it is definitively separated and is then (as corpse) of a piece with nature more generally. That dualism, such as it is, underlies what was also found in Descartes's works: the dual modes of discourse about the human body—the "ordinary" as opposed to the "metaphysical"; the "clinical" as opposed to the "scientific" and "mathematical"; and "nature" as inherently good or bad, as opposed to "nature" as mechanistic and indifferent to values.

The fundamental difference between Bichat and Descartes, then, concerns the significance of talk or ordinary conversations with patients. For Descartes, as we saw, it is only within ordinary conversation that the intimate union or composite whole is at all experienced and able to be known (whatever that knowledge may turn out to be). Although one must be somewhat speculative here, it is credible to postulate that for Descartes such ordinary conversation had to function centrally in the clinical practice of physicians. The physician was obliged to ask patients, "How do you feel?" Only through such common discourse, it seems, could the practicing physician get a handle on what's wrong, that is, on what is experienced and reported by patients, and consequently set about to do something about their ailments.

For medicine after Bichat, on the other hand, such discourse was interpreted as a totally irrelevant source of confusion and an obstacle to effective clinical diagnosis. The question now, if questions addressed to patients were even necessary, became, "Where does it hurt?" Thus, while Descartes still had to rely on analogies and "purely verbal characterizations" for scientific discourse and explanation, by the time of Bichat medicine was almost completely focused on the anatomically disclosed cadaver. Scientific discourse had thus already become interpreted as literal description based on direct visual-pathological observation of tissual lesions—although, it must be added, their interpretation in mechanistic terms is by no means an obvious or necessarily correct usage.

As was already emphasized, it would be a serious mistake to think that the history from Descartes to Bichat is a thematically unbroken line. Many physicians tried mightily to preserve what they (mistakenly) believed to be Descartes's central insight—the mind-body dualism (see King, 1978). Living shortly before Bichat, Gaub had developed a quite sophisticated psychosomatics in his lectures on *De regimine mentis* (1747, 1763), in which he attempted to recognize the effect of the mind on the body and vice versa. Clearly familiar with and influenced by Descartes's medical and other writings (Rather, 1965, pp. 14, 40, 57–59, *passim*), Gaub was convinced that notions such as mind and body in isolation from each other were mere "abstractions" and that the physician's duty was to care for the "whole man" (ibid., p. 70). He was quite aware that, as he put it, a physician who undertakes to deal with the mind in its relation to the body may well be "wielding his scythe in a stranger's field," for that "properly belongs to the philosopher" (ibid., p. 73). Nevertheless, he maintained that if someone raised this objection to him,

> I would have him know that it should be regarded as care of the body rather than of the mind, although indeed such that the mind, too, is helped by the same exertions when the body's parts are altered under the guidance of the physician. For this reason I have called [medicine] the management of the mind by means of the body. (Ibid., pp. 73–74.)

Gaub saw himself as following Descartes's emphasis on medicine as the goal of knowledge and health as the goal of medicine (ibid., p. 70) and even contended, not unlike Descartes, that "mind and body are always watchfully in touch, and at every moment one is being acted on by the other" (ibid., p. 77). As a physician, though, he was committed to the "management of the mind by means of the body," being convinced that the mind was controlled by the body to "even a greater extent than body by mind" (ibid., p. 51).

Discussing the kind of psychosomatics that Gaub represents, Rather cites Lain-Entralgo's distinction between two different meanings that psychosomatic medicine can have for us today. It can mean either "an elaboration and attempted union of the more or less traditional psychological and somatic trends in Western medicine" or, on the other hand, "a view of disease in which the sick man is first and foremost a free person" (ibid., p. 16) to be treated as a whole. Rather contends that Gaub's work must be placed in the first, not the second, category, for in his work "we can see a bias, characteristic of Western medicine and especially evident today, toward the transformation of moral into physiological problems" (ibid.). This characteristic bias of Western medicine, Rather argues, is derived from ancient Greek medicine, which is "radically naturalistic" and overemphasizes the role of the body while slighting that of the person (ibid., p. 15).

There is, however, good reason to wonder whether this judgment about Greek medicine is just, or altogether accurate. There is, to be sure, a prominent tradition in ancient Greek medicine that seems very much like that Rather suggested. Nonetheless, this is not the only tradition in Greek medicine, nor is it the most interesting one for my primary purposes at this stage of the study.

We have thus far seen that the typical bypassing of the patient's full communicative intent, to focus merely on its locational index, has historical roots at least partially in Descartes's writings—but not in a supposed dualism of mind and body. A careful analysis of Descartes' work shows a keen, if still largely unaccountable, appreciation of that communicative dimension of "ordinary conversation." It has also been pointed out that one of the thematic concerns buried within the Cartesian corpus—cadaverial anatomy—became increasingly buried in subsequent medicine, leading eventually to the works of Morgagni and Bichat. Bichat makes a clear break with Descartes's concern with the "everyday." Picking up on and expanding the thematic focus on anatomy, Bichat effects a veritable revolution in medical understanding and clinical practice. However, this dual interest—bypassing the patient's words in favor of the clinician's anatomically informed visual observations, and locating disease in the tissual lesion—may well have a deeper historical root than thus far suggested, for that dual interest does not of itself simply and suddenly appear on the historical scene like some mythic Athena from the head of Zeus.

CONFLICT OF INTERPRETATION
IN ANCIENT MEDICINE

Before entering this complex terrain, a caveat is called for. I cannot claim to be a medical historian, most especially regarding ancient Greek medicine. The following may then be little more than the musings of a rank amateur, completely reliant on the works and translations of others. Studying and learning from the latter can be instructive, nevertheless, and that is all I propose to do here, in pursuit of the themes that the history of medicine itself provokes us to pursue.

There is an important clue in these ancient texts: a universality of human concern about wounds, diseases, and dysfunctionings of bodily abilities, as well as about proper functioning, health, and balance. This concern is clearly suggested in Majno's splendid study, *The Healing Hand* (1975), devoted to wounds and human responses to wounds in the ancient world generally. On the one hand, there is the experience or encounter with damaged human beings; on the other, there is the effort to treat, correct, or heal by providing therapeutic measures for their wounds or other damage.

Experience, specifically that of the would-be healer, is basic and has two sides: experience of the afflictions and experience gained from attempts to do something about them. As the medical historian Harrison

Coulter says, "Medical thought thus grows out of, and is governed by, therapeutic experience. Therapeutic theories in all their variety are attempts to make sense out of the healer's experience with the patient" (Coulter, Vol. I, 1975, p. viii). However the experience may be obtained—through observation, listening, or the use of instruments—none of this information is self-interpreting. Its meaning or significance, for purposes of knowledge (the epistemic) or treatment (the therapeutic), is not written on the face of the data. Neither symptoms, words about aches and pains, nor results of measuring devices provide the healer (ancient or contemporary) with more than a complex, variable "text" requiring interpretation. And, no single interpretation is uniformly, invariably at hand for interpreting the data.

There thus arises a historical conflict of interpretations which lies at the center of medicine. It is a conflict that is itself generated by the fundamental experience governing medicine and has deeply marked medical history. At least two major alternatives are apparent: (1) to emphasize the paramount significance of what is actually observed for its own sake (the *phainomenon*), with treatment based on that alone; or (2) to seek another order of data, one taken to be different from but determinative for the observed realm, with treatment being guided by whatever assumption(s) is (are) made about the nature of this other, at times quite metaphysical, order of reality.

It is important to emphasize that these alternatives are not merely two different but relatively innocuous ways of interpreting data obtained through therapeutic experiences. Instead, they are deeply antagonistic, rival ways of understanding what is experienced. They are frequently found in the same period of medical history, sometimes even in the same physician's writings, and are found in one of the most particular, intimate, and practical of encounters between two persons—the healer and the patient.

These alternatives first become apparent in the Hippocratic corpus itself and are usually associated with the empirics and the dogmatics (or rationalists, as they are sometimes called). The conflict between them extends to every category of medical knowledge and therapeutic experience, including interpretation of symptoms, the relations between theory and practice, the understanding of the place of patients, the meaning of disease, the kinds of disease, the role of the physician, and the kinds of therapies.

The dogmatist takes symptoms as the direct, causal effects of "proximate causes." When the causes are morbid, the symptoms will also be morbid. Medical treatment must aim at this proximate cause, hence is to be based on pathology—that is, the thesis that the body's interior (which is not normally "visible") is abnormal, and this as a causal consequence of the operation of truly invisible "humors" (that other order of reality determinative for the observed realm).

The empiric is precisely the opposite. Symptoms are taken just as they present themselves for observation (and memory), are held to be corrective signs of the body's own restorative powers (*physies*), and are thus taken to be positive and beneficial, not morbid, phenomena. Therapy is a matter of helping the body in its natural fight against the forces of disease. Therefore, everything presented by, and observed about, a patient must be taken into account and interpreted, in order for the art (*techne* = medicine) to be effective and appropriately supportive of the body's own powers.

For the dogmatist, *diagnosis* is central: the effort to distinguish or reason to the proximate causes of external symptoms observed at the present moment. For the empiric, *semiosis* is central: to understand, deliberate about, or interpret the meaning of bodily and personal signs, including the past as well as the present. The dogmatist seeks to intervene actively into the disease process (hence, into the patient's body), to counteract the symptoms by canceling out the proximate causes (and underlying humoral imbalances). The empiric puts himself at the service of the body's *physis* (i.e., curative and restorative powers), for "the *physies* are the physicians of diseases" (*Epidemics*, section VI in ibid., p. 241).

Because this conflict of interpretations is so significant for medicine's subsequent history, and especially for the themes that preoccupy this study, it is necessary to dwell somewhat on it. Another caveat seems in order at this point, however. Few if any individual physicians are or have been pure dogmatics or pure empirics. Moreover, these very terms can be misleading—especially if one thinks of their historical richness and diversity of usage in subsequent times. Rather than taking them, as, for instance, Coulter tends to do, as having pretty much the significance they acquired in the 18th century, they may more properly be taken as designating what Schutz terms "ideal types" (Schutz, 1967) or, perhaps better, what Suzanne Langer once termed "techniques" or "generative ideas."

Langer noted that every historical period has its own specific sort of preoccupation. Its problems are peculiar to it, "not for obvious practical reasons—political or social—but for deeper reasons of intellectual growth" (1942, p. 1). Viewing any historical period, one can see certain groupings of ideas, evident "not by subject-matter, but by a subtler common factor which may be called their 'technique.' It is the mode of handling problems, rather than what they are about, that assigns them to an age" (ibid.). It is therefore an age's particular curiosity that should be sought in trying to understand it. The "technique" or "treatment" of a problem, Langer suggests, concerns the way in which questions are asked, for this determines and limits possible answers that can be given. These are natural dispositions of thinking, implicit ways that are for the most part, in Schutz's term, simply taken for granted, followed without being explicitly avowed. Making up a person's basic outlook, "they are deeper than facts he may note or propositions he may moot" (ibid.). In a sense, a question is already a proposition; it sets out the framework of possible responses. Thus, the intellectual treatment of any subject "is determined by the nature of our questions, and only carried out in the answers" (ibid.).

Terming these "techniques" the "generative ideas" constitutive of an historical period or epoch, Langer suggests that "every society meets a new idea with its own concepts, its own tacit, fundamental way of seeing things; that is to say, *with its own questions, its peculiar curiosity* . . . [which] one may call . . . *generative ideas* in the history of thought" (ibid., pp. 3–4). What I want to try and characterize are the alternative "techniques," "generative ideas," or rudimentary curiosities already present within ancient Greek medicine as a way of getting at the conflict of interpretations that has deeply marked the history of medicine. My suggestion will be that it is precisely this conflict that becomes more obvious during and after the Cartesian period, especially in the evident (even if only implicit) dispute between Descartes and Bichat. It is this conflict, too, that will help us gain firmer purchase on the prominent moral issues in our own times, specifically those arising from the various anomalies found in the common conversations between physician and patient.

THE FIRST CLUE: INTERPRETATION OF SYMPTOMS

At the heart of the matter is what may well be the central problematic facing a healer at any period of medical history: the dual problem of symptoms and their appropriate interpretation. A patient presents with certain complaints, aches, discomforts, distress. How are these to be understood? What are they, and what is to be done about them? Is what the healer sees enough to inform him about what is wrong with the patient? Are the patient's words enough, or even relevant, to the healer's task?

What is to be understood by symptom? Among the many observed features of a patient, which are properly designated as symptoms, and which are not (and may thus be ignored)? What kinds of symptoms are there, and how should they be understood? At the heart of medicine, and present from the outset of its recorded history (and doubtless its prehistory as well), is this therapeutic experience, and at its base is the problem of symptoms and their interpretation. Somewhat more detail and direction can be given here, for there are epistemological, metaphysical, and moral dimensions to the issue.

Epistemologically, the problem concerns how symptoms are to be interpreted. They may be taken as signs of inner bodily events or parts that are themselves invisible (though possibly able to be made visible). They may also be taken as signs of invisible forces (attraction or repulsion, e.g.) or entities (deities, e.g.), which are not in principle able to become visible. Examples are the infamous humors, whose mixtures or improper mixtures (termed "*dyscrasias*" in the dogmatic tradition) must be treated first as a condition for the disappearance of outer symptoms. Alternatively, symptoms may be understood as referring to a patient's past experiences and living conditions and as suggestive of the body's own efforts to correct itself (after, for instance, a bout of improper eating or drinking). They may be taken as causal effects of inner bodily entities or events (and possibly still deeper layers of causality) or as results of morbid influences (dietary or environmental) or just plain bad living—or, perhaps a combination of these.

However understood, additional and unavoidable epistemological problems crop up. Which of the bodily displays are actually symptoms: The red swelling on the leg? The patient's groans and complaints? The patient's inability to walk? The patient's fears or hopes? The inner bodily humors? Since a patient presents a complex set of signs, the healer must either admit everything as a symptom or select only some. If selection is done, then presumably some criterion must be appealed to, so as to ensure that the proper selection has been made. This raises the additional issue concerning the determination of the proper criterion.

Furthermore, even if what shall count as relevant symptoms is settled, there may be correct and incorrect ways of interpreting the symptoms, and thus it is essential to know which is which and how the difference between them is to be established. It then becomes important to know what to make of possible errors: Are they due to ineptitude, to the fact that then-current practice is not sufficiently developed, or to something else? Are errors due to the wrong interpretation of symptoms, or the use of the wrong criteria for selection? What is medical error, and what sorts of error are there?

Unavoidably, too, metaphysical issues also crop up concerning the status of symptoms. For instance, if there are different kinds of symptoms, does this difference suggest different orders of reality—for instance, physical, biological, conceptual, spiritual, cultural? Where in such a schema should health and disease be located? My *body* may be injured, yet (as we say) *I* hurt: What is the status of this difference in language? Does it indicate that health and disease are matters pertaining only to the "I," or should they be restricted to "my body"? For that matter, if it is the latter, still further issues arise. The body, after all (as even the ancients knew well), consists of different parts—organs, muscles, skin, fluids, bones. Are these various parts ultimately different, or are they the same? Are all bodies the same, or are the apparent differences significant? For instance, are human bodies different in kind from merely physical things like rocks? That is, is nature ultimately itself dual in character: biological (animate) and physical (inanimate)? Or is nature multiple, including many different kinds of things?

There are also serious ethical implications to the issue of symptom interpretation. When a patient presents as injured, for instance, what should be the focus of the healer's attention—the body, the injury, or the person? What should be treated, who should determine the treatment (its scope and duration), and according to whose instruction or wishes should it be done? Moreover, why should anyone, healers included, attend to an injured person in the first place? Should the healer perhaps care only for those who ask for help or only for those who can afford the healer's attention? If a healer does undertake to care for some patient, what are his or her obligations and responsibilities? Does the fact that a person is injured, diseased, or otherwise distressed itself constitute grounds for special obligations and responsibilities? To what should the healer be responsive, and for what should the healer be responsible? Learning about a patient's symptoms and modes of life gives the physician considerable power over the person: What should be done about this? Is what a healer learns to be kept secret from others, disclosed to others, or disclosed only on certain conditions and only to certain others?

Clearly, what one takes to be symptoms, how they are interpreted, what one then does about them, and how one treats critical information about patients, are all significant issues impacted within the therapeutic experience at the heart of medicine (ancient and modern). In ancient Greek medicine, all of these themes eventually become expressed and handled, although in rival, conflicting ways. In this rivalry lie several more clues for our inquiry.

THE DOGMATIC DOCTRINE

Within the dogmatic tradition there is evidence of a consistent pattern of interpetation. The hallmark may well be, Coulter argues, "the conviction that therapeutics is based on pathology and that before proceeding to treatment the physician must ascertain the patient's pathological state" (Coulter, Vol. I, p. 217). The main thesis is that underlying all complaints and external bodily symptoms is a "proximate cause," itself "invisible," which "indicates" an improper mixture of "humors." Thus, the Hippocratic text *Nature of Man* asserts:

> The body of man has in itself blood, phlegm, yellow bile, and black bile; these make up the nature [*physis*] of his body, and through these he feels pain or enjoys health. Now he enjoys the most perfect health when these elements are duly proportioned to one another in respect of compounding, *dynamis*, and bulk, and when they are perfectly mingled. Pain is felt when one of these elements is in defect or excess, or is isolated in the body without being compounded with all the others. For when an element is isolated and stands by itself, not only must the place which it left become diseased, but the place where it stands in a flood must, because of the excess, cause pain and distress. . . . If, on the other hand, it be to an inward part that there takes place the emptying, the shifting and the separation from other elements, the man certainly must . . . suffer from a double pain, one in the place left, and another in the place flooded. (Chap. IV, in ibid., pp. 51–52.)

The four humors (blood, phlegm, yellow bile, and black bile) are thus the key to the organism's functioning in sickness and health. Disease is the excess, mislocation, or deficiency of one or more of the humors. The humors are located not only within different areas of the body (as stated in *Regimen in Health*) but are also correlated to the different seasons (see ibid., pp. 61–65). On the whole, health is said to be the correct location and mixture of humors. *Dyscrasia* inhibits or perverts the body's natural functioning. This dysfunctioning is not itself the disease, but the consequence of the disease. Thus, disease consists of (1) the imbalanced humors, (2) the dyscrasia (or, proximate cause), (3) the damage thereby done to the specific bodily function, and (4) the overt (external) symptoms.

There is, then, a crucial stress on knowledge as the principal focus and basis of medicine. As is stated in the text *Regimen, I:*

> He who aspires to treat correctly of human regimen must first acquire knowledge and discernment of the *physis* of man in general—knowledge of its primary constituents and discernment of the components by which it is controlled. For if [the physician] be ignorant of the primary constitution, he will be unable to gain knowledge of their effects; if he be ignorant of the controlling thing in the body, he will not be capable of administering to a patient suitable treatment. (Chap. II, in ibid., p. 61.)

This knowledge, furthermore, is primarily a knowledge of causes, for, as the text *Breaths* states: "Knowledge of the cause [*aition*] of a disease will enable one to administer to the body what things are advantageous" (chap. I, in ibid., p. 63). Such knowledge, however, is not itself mainly a matter of experience. Those who practice the art (*techne*) of medicine must proceed differently from the common run of people, who "trust eyes rather than mind, though these are not competent to judge even things that are seen" (Regimen, I, in ibid., p. 61). Although common people "do not understand how to observe the invisible through the visible" (chap. XI, in ibid., p. 63), healers must learn to do just that, and in this sense observation and experience are subordinated to medical reasoning, knowledge, or theory.

This approach is clear in the dogmatics' understanding of symptoms and their interpretation, which leads into the central medical task of diagnosis. Symptoms engage the healer's attention first; his task, however, is to take these symptoms and read them as suggestive of the underlying *dyscrasia* causing the external symptoms of disordered functioning. Thus, not all overt bodily, or personal, expressions are to be noted (indeed, to do so, it was believed, would be to invite confusion owing to the sheer morass of signs presented). Furthermore, many symptoms are not useful for the healer's purposes, and thus the healer must learn to distinguish among them. This he does by means of reasoning (*logos*) in advance of actually meeting any patient. The physician knows to begin with that a given symptom is connected to a particular internal pathological alteration. This connection is a signative relationship: Symptoms are thought to be "indicative signs," that is, visible indications of underlying proximate causes and humors, which are themselves invisible and which, therefore, can be discovered only through reasoning.

A hard pulse, for instance, indicates a dry heat; a slow pulse indicates a cold heart. Hot blood and much yellow and black bile indicate a hot liver; fickleness of opinion indicates a hot brain. If external symptoms are thus indicative signs pointing to underlying proximate causes, they are on the other hand direct causal consequences of such dyscrasias; the former point to the latter because, ultimately, they are caused by them. But these symptoms do not of themselves describe the internal pathological conditions; the healer thus requires additional knowledge in order to detect and know the relationship between symptoms and diseases. That knowledge is not supplied by experience. Proximate causes are not available to experience, but only to theory, of which the healer is already in possession: knowledge *a priori*.

Such knowledge, however, is not possible as regards individual instances. As Aristotle, who became seminally important for the dogmatics, stated, "The physician does not prescribe what is healthy for a single eye, but for all eyes, or for a determinate species of eye" (*Posterior Analytics*, 97b, 27–28). "None of the arts [*techne*] theorize about individual cases. Medicine, for instance, does not theorize about what will help to cure Socrates or Callias, but only about what will help to cure any or all of a given class of patients; this alone is its business. Individual cases are so infinitely varied that no systematic knowledge of them is possible" (*Rhetorics*, 1356b, 29–32). (It might be noted here that in light of this traditionally fundamental thesis, Bichat's accomplishment may be truly revolutionary. His tissual pathological anatomy may have enabled medicine for the first time to theorize about individual cases by connecting clinical symptoms with later anatomical observations. We will return to this later).

For the dogmatic, therefore, only those symptoms that indicate the kind or class of proximate cause are the crucial ones. The class is the thing, not the individual patient, who, therefore, becomes subordinated to the class (or, at least, to the species). The healer thus needed a way of classifying the kinds of proximate causes, in other words, a logical classification of diseases. Thereby, it became possible to organize, select, and focus on only some of the presenting symptoms (indicative signs) and to ignore, justifiably it seemed, the infinitely variable list of other individuating signs. This classification, which listed the finite number of proximate causes (diseases), was not a matter of experience but was conceived as *a priori*. It permitted a formal connecting of symptoms with proximate causes and directed the healer's therapeutic interests—which concerned not the symptoms but rather the invisible proximate causes within the body, and ultimately the humors.

The dogmatic healer must attend to those presenting symptoms that are indicative signs connecting the outer symptoms to the invisible, proximate causes and humoral imbalances, thereby revealing the disease locus and classification. With this classification in hand, the healer can then proceed to develop the various theorems that constitute the medical doctrine. The reasoning that permits this development was termed "analogy" (*analogismos*)—"defined as reasoning from the evident [i.e., observable by the senses] to an understanding of the non-evident [i.e., open only to reasoning]" (Coulter, Vol. I, p. 229). Thus, matters that cannot be perceived by the senses can still be known in this signative manner. Difficult breathing, trembling, and fever, for example, indicate an afflicted heart; the nature of an afflicted stomach can be determined by the quality of the humor vomited; skin pores can be inferred from the appearance of sweat; seeing people die of heart wounds can indicate that heart wounds are fatal.

> When encountering a new diseased state these physicians first attempted to deduce the cause from an examination of the symptoms; if unsuccessful, they reasoned from diseases with similar symptoms to the conclusion that the causes were also similar. Then, using the syllogism, they transferred the previously known treatment to the new case (Ibid., p. 230.)

The basis for correct interpretation of the body's indicative signs, as well as for the classification of diseases, was sound knowledge of the normally functioning organism. Hence, dogmatic medicine not only gave major emphasis to pathology but also provided important motivation for the development of anatomy through both dissection and vivisection. Armed with that growing body of knowledge, plus that provided by the classification of diseases (indicative signs, proximate causes, humoral imbalances), the dogmatic healer could then turn to therapy.

The primary therapeutic indication was to be taken from the underlying cause of disease. Since disease is either an excess, mislocation, or deficiency of one or more humors, therapy must proceed by correcting, that is, by actively intervening against that cause. Treatment is a matter of opposing the indicatively signified proximate cause and thereby the humoral imbalance. Therapeutics is governed by the principle of opposition, or contraries, and includes either quantitative or qualitative measures, or a combination of the two. The qualitative treatment involves directly opposing or neutralizing a humor, for instance, opposing hot to cold or wet to dry. The quantitative procedure involves evacuating a humor from the body, for instance, inducing vomiting through the use of purgatives.

Thus, to the dogmatic physician medicine was essentially a body of logical knowledge about the functioning organism and its nature in sickness and in health. As the Roman physician Celsus expressed it: "They, then, who profess Rational [i.e., dogmatic] medicine propound as prerequisites, first, a knowledge of the hidden causes of diseases, next, of evident causes, next, of the actions of the *Natura* [*physis*], and, lastly, of the internal parts" (*De Medicina, Prooemium*, 13, cited in ibid., p. 227).

THE EMPIRIC TRADITION

Running directly contrary to every part of the dogmatic conception, the hallmark of the empiric approach is the idea that it is the body's own sustaining powers [*physies*] that are the chief weapon for combating disease. "The *physies* of all are untaught" (*Nutriment*, chap. XXXIX, in ibid., p. 240). "The *physies* are the physicians of diseases" (*Epidemics*, VI, chap. V, in ibid., p. 241). "Even where the resources of art are applied, the *Natura* [*physis*] can do the most," and "with the *Natura* in opposition, the art of medicine avails noting" (Celsus, *De Medicina*, II, in ibid., pp. 241–42).

Such assertions imply the renunciation of the core of dogmatic theory and practice—proximate causes, humors, indicative signs, and classification of diseases. To learn about the *physis* of the body, for the empiric, it is essential to examine and interrogate each individual patient with great care and, thus, to learn how this particular patient's condition emerges from his own specific life circumstances and in what ways his particular, unique bodily *physies* are acting and reacting in response to this condition. Where the dogmatic healer spoke of the need for diagnosis (connecting observed signs to inner, invisible proximate causes), the empiric healer spoke of the need to practice semeiosis—the judicious interpretation and weighing of all presenting symptoms specific to each individual patient. For the empiric, only what is itself visible or able to become visible is admissible into medicine. Therefore, there simply are no signs that could supply knowledge of internal and invisible bodily conditions, much less of direct causal connections to so-called "humors." Rather, the empiric espoused the idea that the human body is governed by its own *physis*, with the physician conceived as their servant, and that *physis* (although there is some ambiguity over the precise meaning of the term) is basically a matter of body heat (coction: *pepsis*) and transformation-distribution of food within the body (digestion: *anadosis*).

Thus, the empirics also denied the possibility of grouping patients into classes or species through the logical determination of proximate causes. There are no diseases apart from the persons suffering from them. Each patient is unique in himself and presents a unique set of symptoms for interpretation and treatment. Accordingly, the empirics denied as well the dogmatic doctrine of indicative signs.

For the empiric, the only signs are the commemorative variety: connections between two affairs, both of which are experiential (one in the past and now recollected, the other in the present reminding one of what was formerly experienced). For instance, a scab signifies a former wound. The empirics admitted that some of these signs seemed common to many individuals (the *communia*), whereas others were peculiar to the individual alone (the *propria*). For example, in wintertime, many different people experience an excess of phlegm, but each reacts differently to the climate.

The *propria* are by far the most significant for medicine, however. The empirics believed that it was the individual's own peculiar temperament (*idiosyncrasia*) that was most significant for therapeutic purposes. For even while there are general, typically similar modes of bodily response by the body's *physies* to external influences, each individual's response is different and unique. What certain substances or weather conditions will do will differ from individual to individual. Since, moreover, it is the whole purpose of medicine to help those who are afflicted (and only secondarily to gain knowledge), the empiric healer was committed to working with and within the almost infinite variety of symptoms presented uniquely in each individual case. Everything else was secondary to therapeutics, including social position, payment for services, even knowledge (including knowledge of the body, as in anatomy).

Still, it would be a mistake to think that the empiric promoted a kind of cultivated ignorance of human anatomy. To the contrary, not only were some empirics among the most renowned surgeons of antiquity, but the founder of later empiricism in medicine, Herophilos, was also one of the first to initiate and develop anatomy, along with the dogmatic Erasistratus. (Both practiced in Alexandria in the third century B.C.) More to the empiric's point, it was maintained that, however useful it is to learn the positions and relations among the body's organs and parts, such knowledge does not yield therapeutic directions. For practicing healers, as the empirics saw themselves, sufficient knowledge of anatomy can be obtained from observations of the wounded or during surgery, as well as through dissections. What the practitioner requires, far more than such knowledge, is an understanding of how to deal therapeutically with each unique individual. For that, what is important is not diagnosis but rather *semeiosis*—interpretation of the symptoms of the actually living patient for the purpose of providing practical help to that person (i.e., therapeutics).

For that purpose, sensory experience and memory are primary—that is, the observation and recollection of visible affairs. It was argued that the dogmatic doctrine of indicative signs promoted, and did not resolve, disputes among healers. Moreover, that doctrine was designed not for the treatment of unique, different individuals but for the treatment of classes of individuals; hence, it ignores precisely what the empiric believed must be the focus of the healer's art—the idiosyncrasy of the individual patient.

Empiric therapeutics was designed specifically to support and serve the body's own natural curative powers. Thus, the organism was viewed as a whole, as integral with the person and his own specific life circumstances (locale, diet, past). Symptoms were taken as quite positive phenomena— signs of the body's own natural struggle against what has affected it. Everything about a patient must therefore be considered medically relevant, and considerations are dropped only if suggested by subsequent experience with the patient. Life-style, locale, habits, and diets, as well as inflammations or swellings and vomiting or sneezing, are symptoms requiring empiric interpretation (*semeiosis*) and treatment.

The aim of therapy being to support the body's own struggles, the empirics contended that symptoms were to be intensified and not, as with the dogmatics, opposed. The body of an afflicted person, that is, was taken as reacting to morbid influences (environmental, dietary); to help that person required that these reactions be supported, added to, if possible. Thus, the empiric therapeutics was based on the principle of similars, not contraries.

Both the dogmatics and the empirics recognized that the number of diseases, as well as their bodily symptoms, were endless and variable. The central question both faced was how to contend with this variety. For the empiric, experience was basic. That, however, required some sort of order or classification, and later, Hellenistic, empiricism shows at least the beginnings of such an effort.

The Hellenistic empiricists (as contrasted with both the earlier empirics and Hellenistic skeptics, as we will see) distinguished between "experience" (*empeiria, experientia*) and the single, unique "encounter" or "experiment" (*peira, experimentum*). Both involve the reception of sensory information and its memorial accumulation. While *peira* designates the single experience of a particular patient, *empeiria* designates the accumulation of such single experiences. Medical experience, or what might be called the empiric fund of knowledge (*empeiria*), is the sum of all the encounters (*peira*) of all medical practitioners. Since the empiric was concerned to experience each individual patient as regards what distinguishes him from other patients, yet to record as well the similarities among patients, this accumulated fund of empiric knowledge is basically a matter of history. Medical theory thus turns out to be medical history, and this is the record of actual encounters (including the talk, the observed bodily symptoms, and the forms of attempted relief).

This fund of empiric knowledge, furthermore, was developed into a method having three main parts. Medical experience involved (1) some actual perception of actual events with some particular patient (*autopsia, per se inspectio*); (2) a recorded account of such events, that is, of past events (*istoria, historia*); and (3) an attempt to move from "like" to "like" or reasoning on the basis of cumulative similarities (*omion metabasis, transitio similis*).

Developed into a quite sophisticated method for acquiring that empirical fund of knowledge from experience, the method's third element, the passage among similars, is perhaps most interesting. Here, the Hellenistic empiricist was able to respond in detail to the need for expanding medical knowledge and therapeutics. In effect, this was the empiricist's answer to the dogmatic's use of the syllogism. By its means the empiricist hoped to be able to move from what had already been discovered to what had not yet been discovered. Thus, remedies effective in one part of the body might be used in another part; one effective in one disease might be used for a similar disease; or one medication might be substituted for another where similiar effects had been previously observed. Always restricted to what is observed by means of sensory perception, this part of the method was understood as not providing altogether reliable guidelines. It yielded only a "possible judgment" and had to be tested by trial and error.

Influenced by certain philosophical empiricists and skeptics (Pyrrho, Carneades, Aenesidemos, Timon), these medical empiricists developed a rather sophisticated method enabling them to distinguish among four grades of reliability—clearly a serious need if their doctrine were to succeed. The highest grade consisted of those events that occurred with regularity and without contrary instances; the second grade, those events with only a few negative instances; the third, those with approximately fifty percent probability of occurrence; and the final one, those that occurred only rarely, with negative instances prevailing (see ibid., pp. 270–71). Following the skeptics, the empiricist physicians also allowed for events that occurred without any apparent order.

The major device enabling the empiric to differentiate among these grades of reliability was the "expert experiment" (*tribike peira, trivica experientia*). Reliable knowledge concerned only those events that recurred with the greatest regularity; what was needed, then, was a way of duplicating events at will, so as to test some hypothesis. Able to be derived only by a truly experienced and expert physician, knowledge from this method was thought to be "as reliable as if it had been obtained from events occurring many times" (in Coulter, Vol. 1, p. 270). Its origin was Carneades's notion of a "closely scrutinized judgment," just as the grades of reliability derived from his analysis of the different forms of probable judgments (probablism) (see Schutz, 1970).

The empiricists were not opposed to reason, but only to the dogmatics' appeal to *a priori* or syllogistic reasoning in medicine. What was required was to identify the form of reason at work in, and an inherent part of, their own three-part method. They recognized that there is a kind of reasoning present in the move from *peira* to *empeiria*, as it is present in the cumulation of these into *istoria* and in the movement among similars. So, too, was some form of reasoning present in the theory of reliability of judgments and in what could be gleaned from "crucial experiments."

To distinguish this form of reasoning from what the dogmatics termed *analogismos*—connecting the "visible," or evident, with the "invisible," or nonevident, or more accurately, the attempt to think about what is not evident to the senses by means of *a priori* syllogistics—the empiricists, and even the earlier empirics, termed the mode of reasoning they had adopted *epilogismos*. Here, the effort is to reason within and about the perceptually evident things of experience with the aim of providing therapies designed to enhance the good inherent in things and support the bodily *physies* in their struggles against what inhibits or diminishes them. *Epilogismos* is spoken of in the early texts as a kind of "weighing of evident things," a mode of thought rooted in sense perceptual life that yields results acceptable to everyone, but especially to healers and patients (in Coulter, Vol. 1, pp. 271–72).

Later empiricists, including Herakleides and Menodotos (ibid., p. 272), expressly connected *epilogismos* to the specific elements of the method. The reasoning at each stage was a form of probablism, proceeding with an awareness that therapeutic experience could supply only probables, never the kind of reliability that the dogmatics sought through the use of the syllogism.

THE DESCARTES-BICHAT DIFFERENCE REVISITED

As has been stressed throughout, any effort to understand the ethical issues within medical practice must grapple with, and sustain attention to, medicine itself. This led us to the basis of medicine, the therapeutic experience—the professed, would-be healer's experience of someone who is wounded, ill, or otherwise distressed; and the subsequent efforts to provide aid, cure, or merely comfort for the person.

This experience does not of itself, it was also noted, include or necessitate any single meaning of symptoms, that to which the would-be healer must attend as guides to "what's wrong" and "what can and should be done about it." What counts as a symptom must rather be a matter of interpretation, and our brief historical excursus disclosed that what is presented to a healer's experience by an afflicted person is open to different, indeed rival interpretations. A patient manifests numerous bodily displays or features (swellings, lumps, sores, coloration); perhaps alterations in bodily abilities (walking, thinking, seeing, grasping); grimaces, groans, and other quasi-linguistic and linguistic expressions; and a certain personal history, set of attitudes, and values.

To which of these perceptually experienced and elicited features, alterations, expressions, and other data should the would-be healer pay attention? Which, if any, should be given priority, and which, if any, can safely be ignored? Bichat, whose tissual patho-anatomy is one pillar of current medical practice and theory, had an unequivocal answer: Listening to what patients tell you, or observing their bodies and conducts, even for twenty years, only promotes confusion. But, "open a few corpses" and all will be revealed. As it was expressed over a century later by the Committee on Costs of Medical Care, "only the expert opinion of medical practitioners and public health authority" can truly define a person's medical needs, much less the appropriate sort of medical care. Ordinary, nonmedical people came to be regarded as incapable of defining, much less managing, their own lives, at least so far as these relate to illness and medicine.

Although, in Lain-Entralgo's terms, Bichat's work effects a "Copernican revolution" in medicine by establishing scientific correlations between clinically observed bodily symptoms and the pathologic lesion (discovered and confirmed only at death, at autopsy), that way of interpreting disease has much deeper historical roots. For even though prior physicians, such as Jerome Gaub, had sought to include the person (the "patient as person"), as well as the patient's body, within the sphere of proper medical concern, their conception of medicine was fundamentally somatic and, in this respect, within the dogmatic tradition. Gaub, no less than Bichat or most physicians in our times, believed that the physician's basic relationship was with the body, and not with the person as a free agent nor even with the body-person totality. The "medical management of the mind by means of the body," in Gaub's terms, which is rooted in the belief that the body controls the mind far more than the reverse, is a later expression of the dogmatic tradition (as we'll see in greater detail in the next chapter). It is also an earlier expression of Pellegrino's term for clinical diagnosis: a "dialogue" with the patient's body "to ascertain the nature of the disease."

Some physicians in the post-Cartesian period (Boyle, Hoffmann) thought it necessary to address both person (mind) and body, because, so they believed, Descartes's works had demonstrated that this was necessary. Others (La Mettrie), although flatly denying reality to the mind while affirming the truth merely of matter, still were not only reacting to Descartes (thus presupposing that framework) but conceived matter very much as had Descartes. Yet, with Descartes himself the issue turned out to be far from so obvious. The by-now familiar litany about the Cartesian dualism is not what it has been put out to be. Rather, with Descartes we encounter an almost perfect case in point of what Coulter terms the "divided legacy" within medicine and medical history. So far as Descartes says, for instance, that no one over the age of 30 should have any need of a physician, but should by then be capable of taking care of himself; or suggests that some bodily conditions (e.g., fevers) may best be treated by focusing on the person and the condition of his or her mind (e.g., Princess Elizabeth); or says that it is only within ordinary life, including the practice of clinical medicine, that one confronts the actually embodied, whole person (the "composite whole" known only within daily life and feeling); or insists that the dropsical patient's body is clinically different from a healthy body— Descartes's words clearly pick up on the ancient Greek empiric and skeptical traditions in medicine.

But when Descartes writes as an anatomist or physiologist, saying that the body is a "mechanism" (the "clock" metaphor); or that the body, like the rest of material nature, is little more than spatial extension and utterly unlike mind; or that the body of the dropsical patient is scientifically no different from the healthy body, so far as mechanical physics is concerned—Descartes clearly exhibits the prominent traits of the classical Greek dogmatic medical tradition.

In medical terms, the impressive anomaly within Cartesian thought, in short, is that it paradoxically attempts to endorse both the empiric and the dogmatic ideas and conceptual frameworks ("generative ideas"). The basic difference, then, between Descartes and Bichat is that Bichat expressly departs from the tenets and framework of empiric medicine; his critical attitude toward ordinary discourse with and observation of patients betrays the same criticism against the empirics that was espoused by the dogmatics.

Thus, with physicians like Bichat (and even Gaub), the central themes of ancient dogmatic medicine are decisively renovated—albeit now within the context of wholly new insights from anatomy, physiology, and biological science more generally. Central to Bichat's "Copernican revolution," however, is also the rejection of the time-honored dogmatic concept of the humors as the invisibles knowable solely by syllogistic logic. What to the ancient Greek eye was definitely invisible—the bodily insides, especially the body's sundry tissues—has now become exquisitely visible, if only at death, by means of autopsy.

Hence, Bichat's tissual pathology and notion of "lesion" are direct descendants of the Alexandrian dogmatic school's beginnings of human anatomical dissection and vivisection. But Bichat's discovery—which picks up on Morgagni's first efforts to correlate clinical findings with autopsy findings—harbors still greater significance. By successfully correlating past-observed clinical symptoms with the pathological lesion disclosed at autopsy, the beginnings of a scientific approach to the individual patient seems to have been won. With that, the traditional dogmatic assumption that only classes of individuals, but specifically not individuals themselves, seems to have been surmounted, and the central argument of the ancient empirics decisively answered by being incorporated into the new scientific medicine. What had long escaped the dogmatic (now perhaps more properly termed "rationalist") medical tradition—the uniquely individual characteristics of each patient—is now able apparently to be pinned down at autopsy. Precisely what the empirics had argued could not be therapeutically directive—anatomy, dissection, autopsy—is now apparently shown to be false.

What remained to be done after Bichat was only the labor of fulfillment, the key to which (as Foucault showed) was the development of the clinic: the placement of increasing numbers of patients together in the same locale, thus permitting regularized recording of clinical symptoms and the causal correlation of these (often by the same physician) with autopsy findings of pathological lesions. The truth of disease thus became the anatomist's and pathologist's eye (what is visible) at autopsy, a step that seemed clearly to have secured the older Cartesian advocacy of a mechanistic idea of the body. And, to the residual empiric distrust of dissection (and vivisection)—that it can never ensnare the actual body in its aliveness, with which the healer must work—the subsequent developments, and especially the most recent innovations in diagnostic and radiological technologies and techniques, seem if anything the final closure to the empiric's quarrelsome opposition to dogmatic medicine.

These reflections, however, move us ahead of our historical probing. What has been suggested—the fundamental significance of the human body, especially in the light of anatomical dissection—still needs to be explored. We do this in the next chapter, and thereby prepare the way for reentry into the moral issues within clinical medicine that our times have found so common and so troubling.

CHAPTER 6

The Anatomist's Conceit, the Body's Cunning

The empiric's continual insistence that the living body must always escape the anatomist's "gaze" (and whose sense of reason cannot therefore be the same as the practicing physician's) seems to have been answered. That critique seems refuted, if not through the correlation of clinical symptoms with autopsy findings, then surely through subsequent developments in diagnostic and radiological techniques. The ability, for example, to image (by X-ray, ultrasound, computed tomography, nuclear magnetic resonance, positron emission scans, and other, especially "real-time," devices) the patient's organic structures and functions and to maintain close correlations between these and the patient's clinically observed condition, thus making the invisible remarkably visible, surely puts the empiric argument finally to rest. Bichat's words—talking with patients yields little more than "confusion" and "incoherent phenomena" whereas opening "a few corpses" quickly dissipates the "darkness"—then ring in clarion tones.

Even the empiric's emphasis on the probabilistic viewpoint in clinical work has become an intimate part of medicine after Bichat. Indeed, as Pellegrino has repeatedly suggested, even the ancient empiric's strongly worded call for discourse with patients, for developing an empiric fund of clinical knowlege and a profound sense of patient and professional history, has been incorporated into scientific medicine. As Pellegrino ingeniously argues, even that centerpiece of empiric medicine, clinical judgment on be-half of each specific patient (i.e., *epilogismos*) is infused with both scientific and value components, in its being uniquely governed by a fundamentally practical, moral end—the right action for a specific patient. Even the most scientific components of clinical judgments, the diagnostic and therapeutic, not only include a diversity of modes of reasoning but are specifically or-dained to that end. "What is wrong?" and "What can be done about it?" must be modulated by "What should be done?" The seminal achievement of medicine in our times thus seems to be unmistakable; the "divided leg-acy" so deeply marking medicine's history seems divided no more. Medi-cine today, Pellegrino has maintained, is "a fusion of the neo-Hippocratic [i.e., empiric] spirit with a new, matured Cartesian [i.e., dogmatic or ration-alist] conviction that human illness can be described in physicochemical and quantified terms" (Pellegrino, 1974, p. 11). The question is whether that "fusion" is in principle even possible or coherent.

REDUCTIVISM AND DUALISM IN CURRENT MEDICINE

Some physicians and scientists today pick up solely on the reductivism in the second part of Pellegrino's claim. Nobel Laureate Macfarlane Burnet states unhesitatingly that during the past 50 years medicine has completely changed its basic understanding of disease, injury, and handicap, which are now believed to be scientifically preventable or treatable. All that remains to be dealt with clinically is "almost wholly dependent on the genetic consti-tution of the individual and his or her response to the social environment" (Burnet, 1978, p. 2). It is likely, indeed, Burnet continues, that everything about human behavior is determined at the genetic level, including "war and evil, pain and disease, aging and death" (ibid.). In plain terms, even the sphere of moral values must be conceived in genetic terms. Hence, there simply is no other reality than the genetic (i.e., strictly biological) and, ulti-mately, physical order.

Burnet's notion that moral issues such as war and evil may be resolv-able only by reference to this genetic determinism is not an uncommon view these days. For instance, psychologist Kenneth B. Clark, deeply con-cerned with the crisis presented by the "pathos of power" in our times, notes the "mocking fact that the human brain can provide intellectual and moral rationalizations for a nonadaptive, ultimately destructive use of so-cial power" (Clark, 1973, p. 93). Believing this threat to be "ultimate" and "urgent," he postulates the critical need for psychological and social sci-ences capable of "precision, predictability, and moral control"—an ap-proach he believes to be "essential to the survival of man" (ibid., p. 94). To answer this "ultimate moral question," Clark argues that the psychological and social sciences have to be utilized to control the "animalistic, barbaric, and primitive propensities in man" (ibid.). The available evidence, he believes, shows that precise psychotechnological interventions "geared toward strengthening man's moral and positive human characteristics" can be obtained and implemented "within a few years" (ibid., p. 95).

Such interventions have become possible mainly thanks to research in neurophysiological, biochemical, psychopharmacological, and psychological areas. Through them, Clark believes it possible and necessary to "stabilize and make dominant the moral and ethical propensities of man and subordinate, if not eliminate, his negative and primitive behavioral tendencies" (ibid., p. 95). In order to test such interventions scientifically, however, he asserts that "the pretest subjects would have to be human beings," the implications of which "are clear": "there would be moral and rational justification for the use of compulsive criminals as pretest subjects in seeking precise forms of intervention and moral control of human behavior" (ibid., p. 96). He then calls on "power-controlling leaders" to legitimate and make use of the earliest perfected forms of psychotechnological, biochemical intervention, urging along the way that they must be used "affirmatively, wisely, and with compassion," and on a "sound scientific, factual base" (ibid., pp. 97, 98).

While such views are not uncommon, even if not spoken as directly, other physicians and researchers are unwilling to adopt that extreme. They rather opt for a more modest point of view. While endorsing the determinist-reductivist claim about the body, behavior, and disease, they seek to affirm the independent existence of the mind. Such views were already mentioned in some detail earlier, and obliged us to investigate their supposed origins in Descartes's work. They deserve some repetition here, however.

Wilder Penfield, we noted, states (in an intriguing convergence with the ideas of the early 18th-century physician Jerome Gaub) that the brain, taken to be a computer, "must be programmed and operated by an agency capable of independent understanding." Identifying this as "mind," Penfield is thus "forced to choose the proposition that our being is to be explained on the basis of two fundamental elements" (Penfield, 1975, p. 80). Putting this in medical terms, we could say, following Pellegrino, that the physician is called on to become an adept clinical observer (presumably on such occasions dealing with mind or person), and *at the same time* to interpret and explain the clinical and other findings in physicochemical and quantified terms.

Or, in historical terms, it appears that the Cartesianism of contemporary medicine lies in its attempt to "fuse" precisely what Descartes himself knew to be quite impossible—to think of mind and body as both unioned and separate. To postulate this, Descartes told Princess Elizabeth, "it is necessary to conceive them as one thing alone, and at the same time to conceive them as two, which is self-contradictory" (1976, p. 114). Although, we now know well that such a dualism is by no means an invention of Descartes, it is nevertheless an intimate part of contemporary medical understanding. In still earlier historical terms, the idea seems to be that medicine must at the same time be both empiric (the neo-Hippocratic spirit) and dogmatic (somatic and quantitative), a proposal that, as we will see later in this chapter, is equally problematic.

Yet, there can be no reckoning with medicine, especially as regards the moral issues occasioned within its practice, without taking into account its prevailing tendency to explain human affliction and behavior either in straightforward reductivist terms or in the dualistic way of clinically observing persons and scientifically explaining what is observed and diagnostically disclosed in strictly somatic and quantitative terms, without reference to persons. In either framework, the reductivist-materialist (Burnet, Clark) or the dualist (Penfield, Pellegrino), there is a common view of the human body; but in the latter, there is also a view of the human mind and, presumably, of the interrelationships between the body and mind.

Both views, we have been urging, are historical constructions, artifacts that present distinctive problems of their own. The human body is understood as a strictly biological affair, innocent of values, personal or social; the body is to be understood and explained as far as possible without reference to persons, souls, psyches, spirits, minds, social life, and values. Indeed, even so-called "mental disturbances" or "mental illnesses," so far as they are regarded as medically treatable, are understood as having biological or chemical causes or even as being themselves ultimately physical. To the extent that mental afflictions, or problems deriving from personal or social sources, do not seem amenable to such an approach, one confronts a curious fact about medicine—the dilemma of not knowing just how to proceed, except perhaps by referrals to psychiatry, clinical psychology, or social work (which are often as not equally dualistic or reductivistic in style). If all else fails, there may be referrals to clergy and even, more recently, to ethicists. Medicine seems focused on the various bodily systems, organs, structures, and functions. Where mind or person are regarded as at all pertinent, Gaub's basic point comes into play: The physician's task is the "management of the mind by means of the body," for the body controls the mind (if, and so far as, it exists at all) far more than the reverse.

THE ANOMALY OF GALLOWS HUMOR

In just these terms, however, a number of curious things continually crop up, veritable anomalies that demand our notice. One has been thematic for a long time in this study—the commonplace talk between physician and patient. There are others that now need attention. Paul Ramsey, for instance, has made the following observation in another connection:

> In the second year anatomy course, medical students clothe with "gallows humor" their encounter with the cadaver which once was a human being alive. That defense is not to be despised; nor does it necessarily indicate socialization in shallowness. . . . [W]hen dealing with the remains of the long since dead, there is a special tension involved . . . when performing investigatory medical actions involving the face, the hands, and the genitalia. This thing-in-the-world that was once a man alive we still encounter as once a communicating being, not quite as an object of research or instruction. Face and hands, yes; but why the genitalia? Those reactions must seem incongruous to a resolutely biologizing age. For a beginning of an explanation, one might take up the expression "carnal knowlege" . . . and behind that go to the expression *"carnal conversation,"* an old legal term for adultery, and back of both to the Biblical word "know." . . . Here we have an entire anthropology impacted in a word, not a squeamish euphemism. In short, in those reactions of medical students can be discerned a sensed relic of the human being bodily experiencing and communicating, and the body itself uniquely speaking. (Ramsey, 1974, p. 59.)

Wishing to evoke the "felt difference between life and death," Ramsey emphasized that this difference makes itself known even in the case of the cadaver, the "long since dead," and thus to pick up on our earlier point, not even here do we find the limiting case of a "medical object" without the presence, in some sense, of a person. To be sure, the incommensurable contrast between life and death seems met most dramatically with the newly dead: If the cadaver on the dissection cart provokes gallows humor, the mangled body lying on the ER stretcher awakens dread and awe. Both, however, suggest the almost haunting presence of once-living flesh— of bodily gestures, attitudes, glances, movements—that a "resolutely biologizing age" may too easily and too readily ignore or suppress as "merely subjective."

Although Ramsey's own view of the "body itself uniquely speaking" merely reasserts the very dualism he otherwise seeks to dispel (see Zaner, 1981, chap. 2), the gallows humor he notes suggests that there really is "an entire anthropology" or theory of human being impacted at the heart of it, the implications of which seem to me to differ from what Ramsey has in mind. Beyond this, though, Ramsey's statement also indicates that the cadaver is precisely an "object of research and instruction" in contemporary medicine, that is, the "once-aliveness" of the cadaver is profoundly suppressed and yet, perhaps for that very reason, invariably crops up as gallows humor only. Of course, it is perfectly obvious that medical students and practicing physicians should and do learn from anatomical dissections, just as investigators learn from research utilizing dissections. However, the obviousness of this should itself give us pause. How does it happen that the live human body can be explained, if it can, by means of the dead human body?

THE SOMA AND THE CORPSE

Although there is that "special tension" when performing investigatory medical actions on the face, hands, and genitalia, it is by such actions that the live body seems to become finally intelligible to us. The "what's wrong?" of diagnosis seems answerable, in the final analysis, by the eventual determination of "what *was* wrong" through autopsy.

As we saw in the last chapter, moreover, this mode of reasoning is in striking contrast to that of classical times. For the latter, as Jonas pointed out, the corpse was the "primal exhibition of 'dead' matter," functioning as the limit of all understanding and as the basic thing needing understanding. For modern medicine, again following Jonas's indications, the "living, feeling, striving organism has taken over this role and is being unmasked as a *ludibrium materiae*," that most subtle hoax of matter. For, it is only when the living body is dead, has become a corpse, that it seems plainly intelligible, it is then able to be assimilated to the general laws of nature and thereby finally comprehended. This, Jonas argues, is the basic direction of all modern thought concerning death as a "physical fact," and, in that respect, "our thinking today is under the ontological dominance of death" (Jonas, 1966, pp. 12, 15).

In Jonas's terms, then, it is life that constitutes for modern times the fundamental "limit of all understanding and therefore the first thing not to be accepted at face-value" (ibid.). Or, in slightly different terms, it is life that poses the most puzzling enigmas for us, and in this Jonas is in agreement with the great Spanish thinker José Ortega y Gasset (see 1957).

But Jonas's analysis is not without flaws. If, in his terms, for classical times death was the great incomprehensible and life what was closest to hand, for modern times, he implies, it is precisely the opposite. Conversely, in modern times life is but a "subtle hoax of matter," and we are thereby under the ontological dominance of matter, hence death. But, contrary to the implication that death is thereby not only understood but, with matter, provides the canon of all comprehensibility, death, not to mention dying, seems just as incomprehensible for us as life and living.

Jonas's argument trades on an ironic and quite subtle equivocation at its crucial point: The deadness of a cadaver and that of material stuff are hardly the same thing. Or, more precisely, while the "direction of thought on life as a physical fact" seems to require that they be identical—the cadaverial body now a piece of physical matter like any other, as Descartes had tried to argue (albeit only "in a manner of speaking")—it is precisely the gallows humor, much less the shock and even stark enigma of death in our times, that reminds us that things are quite otherwise. That some forms of matter, if you will, can "die" is quite as much a *"ludibrium materiae"* as that they can be "alive." Matter in the strictest sense is neither *de*-animate nor *ex*-animate; it neither feels nor desires nor strives, neither lives nor dies. What is thus intriguing about Jonas's argument is the profound irony in his equivocation on death: the deadness of the corpse, while it by all theoretical reckonings ought to be the same as that of material particles, yet is not the same. The one is not the other; dead matter does not as such evoke humor, much less gallows humor, whereas the corpse does.

There are several suggestive things about this ironic equivocation, however. Modern medicine has increasingly become a crisis-oriented, acute-care discipline or (in some sense) science, as is evident not only from the stereotypical portrayals in the media but equally from the emphasis in medical education (see, e.g., LeBaron, 1981). Its central focus (evident in the modes and quantity of funding, the stress on scientifically understood clinical encounters, or the continuing and considerable pressures for developments of still more potent technologies and therapeutic measures) is disease, illness, injury, or affliction. Despite the fact that most of the time physicians spend with patients concerns mundane complaints, gripes, and routine ailments rather than actual crises, medicine's principal public and socially encouraged image is of a discipline on the critical, cutting edge of life and death, warring constantly and valiantly against an aggressive, impersonal, implacable enemy (e.g., cancer).

Such images come quickly to mind and need not be repeated here. Suffice it to say that the humdrum, the prosaic, and the routine have little place either in medical education or in much of the acquired self-understanding of physicians. What socially attracts our notice is not the family physician, but the sharp-witted wags of "M.A.S.H.," whose buffoonery and jokes serve only to make the keen and special crisis skills of physicians that much more evident and valuable. The prominence of combative and military images and metaphors (whether in such television scenarios, or in Siegler's sharp criticism that medical humanists have merely the "counterfeit courage of the non-combatant") is clear enough, as are the moral values they naturally evoke—bravery, perseverance, valor, and superb skill in the face of at times overwhelming odds and intractable enemies, that is, the brute and radically nonpersonal entities of disease.

Such images have their place and source in that subtle hoax of matter—both alive and dead. Just as life, by Jonas's account, is puzzling and unorthodox in such a scheme, so must death be profoundly enigmatic. It then seems manageable only when ultimately modeled as disease and therefore something to be (and able to be) tamed, domesticated, and eventually conquered like any other disease (the "enemy"). In somewhat less dramatic terms, modern medicine seeks to make death the unsurprising consequence of human genetics, the result of "genetic errors in somatic cells," as Burnet put it (1978, p. 75). Not only that, however, for Burnet continues to "suspect that our reactions to the actualities of dying are determined by the genes we were born with to the same degree as any other aspect of our behavior" (ibid., p. 98).

Thus do we attempt to make our own mortality a matter for medicine, like so much else in our individual and collective lives—rendered (so far as possible) apparently familiar by being placed alongside other "enemies" to be combatted and, we hope, conquered by medicine. Death, like diseases, is reduced to "genetic errors," as if by that (probably quite magical) means we could then coherently postulate that, if it be due to "errors," death, like genetic diseases, is then subject to something like correction. Hence, death could be accommodated to materiality (conceived along Cartesian lines as "mechanism") and thus be finally explicable by reduction to the same kind of supposedly familiar physical universe as the rest of nature.

But, so these images run, if death, then so, too, should life be similarly accountable, and the metaphors come full circle. Life itself gets imaged as a constant struggle for survival against disease no more nor less than against what Clark regards as "nonadaptive" and "destructive" uses of human intelligence. By such means does medicine come to be seen as serving the now-familiar and supposedly natural functions of evolution. If, in these terms, morality controls our adaptation, then medical science—aided by psychotechnology, biochemistry, and other fields—must control our morality through psychopharmacological interventions (a quaint, if effective, euphemism for drugs).

Indeed, thanks to the remarkable developments in genetics, it is increasingly commonplace to find it asserted, as in the writings of Nobel Laureate Sir John Eccles, that "planned genetic manipulation" has replaced the natural biological processes and that now nature (including human nature) can itself be "enslaved for man's purposes" by deliberately changing it through genetic engineering. In this way, Eccles believes, man, physical nature, and the social environment "can be more useful for exploitation" (Eccles, 1979, p. 120).

To witness the workings of such metaphors—aside from the question of their truth—is to be forced to notice the fulfillment of Bacon's combative usages. Knowledge and power, as he asserted, become wedded in the struggle to conquer man's otherwise endemically vulnerable and helpless natural condition. Modern theories of life, including those of medicine, while they comprehend neither life nor death, have yet become major forces for understanding the nature of body and mind and thereby for altering human social and individual life. To the precise extent that medicine's exercise of power (as Bacon already envisaged, Descartes sought, Auguste Comte preached, and the 20th century has begun to realize concretely) is successful in combating afflictions, as it surely has in many ways, it has understandably acquired immense social prominence and prestige. Medicine is one of the major remaining sources of taken-for-granted social authority in our times.

THE HISTORICAL THEMATIC

We must not lose sight of several crucial things. First, and in a way paramount, gallows humor and its underlying consort, the subtle hoax of matter, mark out both life and death as deeply enigmatic even while they are said to be the main themes of medicine and biomedical science. A second phenomenon is medicine's accepted view of human reality, a view both historical and constructed—a historical artifact. Third, medicine has historically become, especially during the last century, a human enterprise of immense power and authority.

In an age like our own, which has witnessed the flight of the gods, of transcendence and norms, and of elders (tradition), medicine—the discipline apparently most directly attentive to life, death, affliction, guilt, and failure—has come to assume remarkable decisional governance over the basic conditions of human life. But medicine, girded with the armor of biomedical science, is not without its distinctive and possibly endemic dilemmas, which are themselves also historical in character.

H. Tristram Engelhardt, Jr., has pointed out that "medicine is the most revolutionary of human technologies. It does not sculpt statues or paint paintings: it restructures man and man's life." Indeed, he continues, "medicine is not merely a science, not merely a technology," but, more pointedly, "is the art of remaking man, not in the image of nature, but in his own image; medicine operates with an implicit idea of what man *should* be" (1973, p. 445). As such, medicine is essentially a historical, ongoing human enterprise; at the same time, it is essentially moral, working with and within a spectrum of values concerning "what man *should* be."

Medical research, for instance, has made it possible for the personal and social aspects of sexuality to be separated from the reproductive aspect. Consequently, human life has been decisively altered, with changes occurring in family structure, child rearing, educational structure and policy, and population planning. New issues have been generated, such as the rights of fetuses and the rights of certain persons (e.g., the mentally retarded) to reproduce or not. Indeed, technological and biomedical prowess makes it currently plausible not only to develop and practice genetic control of future generations (to take our own evolution in hand, as Eccles has said), not only to develop and practice behavior control over individuals and even on entire populations (through psychopharmacological and behavior-modification interventions), but also to subject our own mortality to medical control (taking death as a kind of genetic disease or result of genetic errors).

Such frankly awesome control, of course, forces medicine itself to change. It also implies the power to alter, for better or worse and perhaps irrevocably, our very capacity to reckon with and understand the medical interventions that change us. Thereby, our ability to know that we have been, for instance, biochemically altered may itself be compromised, and thus, too, our most intimate kind of self-relationship altered. Medicine's power implies the potential fracturing of the self's relationship to itself and to its own body, by intervening between the self and its body, even between the self and its own self-awareness. This power thus has the capacity to cancel out all awareness of its ever having been used in the first place.

It is, as Jonas has argued, the drastically enhanced scale of technological interventions into nature, society, and the lives of individuals that forcibly reveals their critical vulnerability in a unique, historically new way— "unsuspected before it began to show itself in damage already done," such as in the air we breathe or the water we drink (1974, p. 9). In this respect, he emphasizes what he terms the inherently "utopian" drift of modern technology:

> Technological power has turned what used and ought to be tentative, perhaps enlightening, plays of speculative reason into competing blueprints for projects, and in choosing between them we have to choose between extremes of remote effects. . . . Living now constantly in the shadow of unwanted, built-in, automatic utopianism, we are constantly confronted with issues whose positive choice requires supreme wisdom—an impossible situation for man in general, because he does not possess that wisdom, and in particular for contemporary man, who denies the very existence of its object: viz., objective value and truth. We need wisdom most when we believe in it least. (Ibid., p. 18.)

Jonas argues that the very conditions for what even Clark saw as necessary—wisdom at both the individual and societal levels—are lacking: Human beings in general do not possess wisdom, and in our times they do not even believe in its very possibility.

Medicine's focus is human life, individual and collective. In our culture, however, its focus is especially on human afflictions and disruptions in personal and social life. Medicine's design, of course, is not merely to treat; rather, as Engelhardt points out, it "remakes" human life and is thereby itself remade. It is therefore an essentially historical enterprise, both as regards its therapeutic theme and its alteration of those who are treated.

That historicity, however, did not emerge merely in the 20th century, even though the impetus provided by biomedical science and its associated technologies surely gives it unique prominence today. We have already laid out several of the main historical themes leading to medicine as we now know it, giving particular notice to the Cartesian tradition as it led to, but remained distinct from, that of Bichat. These historical relationships, we saw, pointed to certain ancient themes in medicine, especially the conflict of interpretations evident in the empiric and dogmatic traditions. It has become increasingly obvious, however, that there is another theme here, centering in the human body and its anatomical dissection. It is now time to probe that theme more carefully to disclose the historical nexus that leads to the ways in which the therapeutic and alterative themes become such intimate parts of medicine as we now understand it.

THE POSTMORTEM IN MEDIEVAL MEDICINE

The beginnings of dissection in Western Europe date to the latter part of the 13th century. Dissection, in the form of the postmortem examination, had already become comparatively common at the University of Bologna by the end of that century, and poses something of a mystery when one considers how little else seems to have been developed in the sciences at that time.

As Charles Singer has indicated, dissection was not at first practiced as a pursuit of knowledge, not even medical knowledge. The medical faculty at Bologna was in existence as early as 1156, but the university was mainly known as the seat of legal learning in Europe. The medical faculty was part of the law faculty and did not become even relatively independent of it until the beginning of the 14th century. Indeed, dissection was practiced mainly in the form of postmortems: examining the human corpse as part of the process of gathering evidence for legal purposes. Only later did it develop as anatomy for the purpose of gaining knowlege (Singer, 1925, pp. 69–71).

The first open reference to postmortem examinations, it seems, dates from 1286. A pestilence raged in Italy that year, and a chronicle by Salimbene of Parma (1221–90), written in 1288, reports that a physician from Cremona opened a corpse to see if he could find the cause of the disease; he apparently opened only the thorax, to glance at the heart. The first formal account of definite postmortem examination dates to 1302. A certain Assolino died at Bologna under suspicious circumstances. Poison was suspected; the judicial inquiry that was held ordered a postmortem, which was conducted by two physicians and three surgeons. Their report concludes with the words: "we have assured ourselves of the condition by the evidence of our own senses and by the anatomization of the parts" (ibid., p. 73).

Dissection of the human corpse for the purpose of anatomical study began to be pursued at about the same time, or immediately afterward. Of particular interest in this movement is Mondino de' Luzzi (or, Mundinus, ca. 1270–1326), whose *Anothomia*, written in 1316, was the principal anatomy text for the next two centuries. Like that of others before and many after him, much of Mondino's understanding is based on Avicenna, who, for the most part, simply records and repeats Galen. Unlike his successors (until Vesalius), however, Mondino himself did the dissecting (and did not rely on a menial *demonstrator*, who was directed by an *ostensor*, who was in turn directed by the professor) (ibid., p. 76).

Mondino's description of the organs is rudimentary at best and often totally inaccurate. The stomach is described as spherical, the liver is said to have five lobes (and to be the seat of yellow bile, one of the "humors"), and black bile is said to be secreted through what are in fact nonexistent channels into the cardiac end of the stomach. Such notions were all derived from Galen, even though the corpse lay right before the dissector. Nonetheless, as J.H. van den Berg points out (1978), this first cutting into the human corpse for the purpose of knowing harbors immense significance.

Mondino's text did not include any drawings. His disciple, Vigevano, however, published an anatomical treatise in 1345 that included a number of illustrations. Of particular interest is one depicting the actual dissection. It shows Vigevano next to an upright cadaver, which he has begun to open with a knife. As van den Berg notes:

> One would expect Vigevano to look at the knife. But he does not. He looks at the closed eyes of the dead man. He has a relationship with the corpse, with the man of that corpse, with this deceased fellow-human being. He puts his left hand in an affectionate, intimate manner around the dead man's body. (van den Berg, 1978, p. 124.)

Two centuries later, in 1543, Andreas Vesalius published his seminal work *De Fabrica de Corporis Humani*—the first definitive break with Galen's anatomy and a dramatically more sophisticated text than any hitherto. In one famous drawing, Vesalius, the anatomist, looks out at the viewer while holding an arm that is cut open to display a number of details; it is as if Vesalius is inviting his readers to look at, to *look into*, the dissected body part. If one believes that in life the soul inhabits the body, the anatomist is in effect showing the viewer here that all that one can find when looking into the dead body is more body, never the soul.

We are here confronted not so much with a corpse as with an anatomical preparation. Depicted in this famous drawing is not a full corpse, but a thing, an anonymous arm, splayed and separated from the full body, not to say from the former person of that body. Other line drawings, themselves quite remarkable, are only anatomical pantomimes of the formerly living body. The wonderfully executed, detailed drawings of cadavers in full musculature, full skeletal, full vascular, and other postures are caricatures of partialized cadavers in at times almost choreographed stances, themselves in equal mimicry of life.

MIND AND BODY AS HISTORICAL ARTIFACTS

Comparing Vigevano's and Vesalius's drawings, separated by 200 years, van den Berg argues that they hold a lesson, for in their contrast we see "that man has been alienated from his own body . . . that man has changed, has become two, has been divided into two parts: body and soul" (ibid., p. 127). This occurred, it might be added, more than 75 years before Descartes's metaphysics and mechanics, which were constructed, as we saw, on the premise of the separability of the two (even though Descartes never himself endorsed that dualism).

Moreover, dating from this period a kind of elemental distress affecting the mind or soul becomes evident. Scarcely a century after Descartes, for instance, this internal schism of human life shows up explicitly and is for the first time given a name, "the English malady," or neurosis, by the Scottish physician George Cheyne (1773). Indeed, during Descartes's own time, Harvey (1628) had declared not merely that the heart is a hollow muscle but is in fact a mechanical pump. Still, even he continued the long tradition of regarding the heart as the seat of certain distinctive human characteristics: "In quantity the heart of man is large, wherefore timid, wherefore courage from a common intelligence" (Harvey, 1961, p. 175).

Even with such vestiges of earlier beliefs, however, it is the mechanical action of the heart and the heart as the source of bodily heat that figure most prominently in Harvey's anatomical work. By this time, that is, the heart is already coming to be regarded merely as a mechanical device and no longer as the seat of human faith, emotion, or feeling (even if the common tongue continues such expressions even today). Synchronically with Harvey's work, such ideas were continued not only in the common tongue but in theological contexts as well. Thus, for instance, Jean Eudes inaugurated the Order of the Sacred Heart at about this time, and Blaise Pascal, one of the eminent scientists and mathematicians of the time, probed in his writings for the "logic of the heart"—that is, of "feeling," especially for that by which we know and "hear" God.

By the 1780s, Mesmer had discovered among some of his patients what he termed a "magnetic sleep," resulting from what he thought was his own magnetic power (mesmerism). Puysegur (1784) discovered the same ability, calling it "spontaneous somnabulism." In 1786, Jean Paul Richter had talked about the *Doppelgänger*, and shortly afterward it was described by Ludwig Tieck (1791). By the end of the 18th century, the human soul, van den Berg remarks, had "turned into a double existence . . . split in two" (1978, p. 128).

In the next century, Kierkegaard wrote in his singular way about the despair affecting subjectivity (inwardness: through which God is known). By the end of the 19th century, Freud's attention was drawn to hypnotism, but even more to the internal divisions of the psyche on which he placed characteristic stress—especially the prevalence of the unconscious and its governance by that rudimentary and wholly impersonal neuter, the id (*das Es*). The human self or subject had effectively become a fundamentally pathological entity, affected by its own impersonal and tumultuous desires and passions (the id), which are able to become explicit only in recondite, indirect, and symbolic ways. The truth of self is essentially hidden to the self. By the end of the 1940s this psychic neuroticism became conceived, by Rogers and Sullivan, for instance, as an interpersonal, and no longer merely an intraphysic, phenomenon. Normal human social life had thus itself become pathological, and crisis normalized.

Van den Berg argues that this history (a history of "anthropathology") is synchronously matched within other crucial cultural events: in painting, for instance, with the emancipation of the landscape (and the disappearance of the human subject from the landscape); in theology, with the desacralization of the cosmos (the "flight of the gods"); and in industrialization, whose first use of the flying shuttle came in the same year that Cheyne described the English malady. His claim is that we witness "a steadily growing separation of man and the universe," synchronically with the separation of mind and body; precisely here begins the "pathology of the human subject" (ibid., p. 134).

What Jonas calls the *ludibrium materiae*, which I have argued must be extended to include death as well as life, may well begin to make its appearance, not with the so-called Cartesian bifurcation nor with the emergence of physics and astronomy shortly before that time, but with the earlier medical-anatomical intrusions into the human cadaver. At the very least, the cultural and intellectual soil for those later developments was already richly prepared by the history of anatomy dating from the late 13th century. For what begins to occur, it seems, from the time of Mondino to that of Vesalius, is the withdrawal of the vivid presence of the soul of the now-dead person. In addition, the appearance of the corpse changes from the still-lively presence of the now-departed soul (Mondino, Vigevano) to an entity or anatomical preparation now taken merely as a piece of material nature more generally (Vesalius, Descartes).

How it occurred that the physician-now-turned-anatomist would thereupon feel able and free to dissect the once-living and now-still flesh of the other—how soma becomes cadaver and thus available for dissection, then to become merely an anatomical preparation—I do not rightly know. It was preceded by postmortems, apparently called for by legal considerations or perhaps curiosity about deaths occurring during plagues. But from there to the anatomical study of the human corpse seems a substantial leap.

In any event, once this occurred, we begin to note the "relicization" of the human corpse, which, although dead, retains its human character and evokes, like a relic, the vestiges of human fellow-feeling (with Vigevano's eyes still looking into the dead man's eyes, as if still asking permission and forgiveness for the dissection). Thereafter, however, there rapidly develops a critical disappearance of, and turning away from, the humanness of the body (now a mere cadaver, with Vesalius).

The "subtle hoax of matter," especially in its deeply ironic form, is most prominent precisely with this cadaver, this "thing-in-the-world". It is this phenomenon that prepares the way for the later versions of dualism (including that body dualism we noted with Descartes, and later versions such as the mind-body dualism espoused by Boyle, Hoffmann, or Gaub). It is also this thing-in-the-world, it would seem, that actually lies behind the Cartesian idea that the material body, and material nature, can be conceived as "in itself," as "pure matter," and then as strictly quantitative (i.e., *res extensa*): which is neither *de*-animate nor *ex*-animate, as is the human corpse, but is rather *in*animate. Matter, in the sense of the modern sciences, thus seems modeled less on ancient atomistic doctrines and far more on what is now definitively seen and actually experienced in full concreteness as a cadaver. What is now experienced as vacated of life (i.e., exanimate) prepares the way for what is taken as totally unalive (i.e., inanimate). Yet, it is this entity that remains, even for contemporary medical students, a relic of a once-alive and communicating person. The relicization of the human corpse remains despite its unaccountability in theoretical or epistemic terms.

THE CORPSE AND THE SOUL

The centering phenomenon is, again, the human body: as embodying (in life) and as vacated (in death). Even patients suffering from paresis in a limb, we might note, undergo a marked attitudinal change toward the now-unfeeling limb. We might, in fact, learn a good deal about that subtle hoax from this experience, so as to help sharpen our historical probing.

The physician Herbert Plügge, notes, for instance, that a dead limb takes on an aspect of "objective thinglikeness, such as an importunate heaviness, burden, weight," an essentially strange and wooden thing, "like plaster of paris, in any event as largely space-filling and hence not altogether as a part of ourselves" (Plügge, in Spicker, 1970, p. 296).

Even while alive and embodying a person, certain body members can assume the characteristic of "thinglikeness," and, as Kurt Goldstein discovered when studying brain-injured patients, they then no longer have that "look" and "life" of aliveness (see Goldstein, 1947) and are no longer experienced by the embodied person as "mine." These body parts no longer actuate the person's wishes, desires, or strivings; they are more akin to the limbs of a corpse than of an embodying organism. In such moments (whether in paresis of a limb or even when a limb "falls asleep"), the person's own embodying body is experienced as a kind of alien presence, as strange and dead—"mine" yet "not mine" (see Zaner, 1981, chap. 3). These dead or numbed limbs then seem to have very much the sense of nature; the *de*animated assumes the character of a kind of *in*animate. It may well have been this complex, inner duality of the embodying organism (while alive), as well as the body disclosed as definitively dead (as corpse) and incorporated into 17th- and 18th-century medicine and anatomy, thus, that prepared the way for the nature of modern science more generally.

To be sure, there are numerous other events that went into this subtle and complex historical separation of mind and body. Still, it seems clear that those first anatomical dissections are critical milestones in this history. With the anatomical opening up of the human body, the fateful path for conceiving material nature as sheer, quantitative, and unfeeling stuff in measurable motion has been opened up as well. But at the same time, that elusive lift of the alive, embodied person, that insubstantial and fugitive soul, becomes ever more unsure, despite Descartes's keen insight into its moments of clear presentation (in daily life, in clinical encounters). After being divided out of its own body and its environs (both of which became conceived as material and quantitative), soul and, with it, life become a kind of subterfuge of mere matter whose only habitat had to be that plainly uncompelling metaphysical substance, the *res cogitans*, striving through clever logic and its own strictly internal "ideas" to reach beyond itself to the world and even to its own body. As with Descartes's famous arguments or those in later empiricism, however, such efforts to contact the real world directly, to reach what is other than itself, could succeed only problematically, if at all.

With the stripping away of the otherwise obvious opulence of animate life from nature, now conceived as merely materially extended particles in motion defineable by mathematical formulae, and with the relegation of the wealth of human experience to the strictly subjective and essentially private regions of the mind (beauty, and all other qualities, are "in the eye of the beholder"), there begins the historical process leading eventually to modern-day relativism or nihilism, or what van den Berg identifies as the "pathology of the human subject":

> We would never be talking about mental health if we had not already for some hundred years been suffering from a general and in some ways gentle disease that encompasses our world. The first, most important symptom that there is something wrong with our *mental health* lies in the word "mental." Yes, if we are asked to live *mentally*, that is, as a *soul*, in a strange anatomical body, in a strange chemical-physical world, nobody can expect us to live in good health. (1978, p. 135.)

The gallows humor noted by Ramsey, so prominent in gross anatomy labs, as well as the special tension subtly felt by physicians, instructors, and researchers, thus assume a deeper significance. The humor is profoundly reflexive. It is an ironic play whose setting is the dissecting room and its carts; whose supporting cast, bedecked with cutting tools and clothed in gowns, are the budding dissectors; and whose central characters and theme are the cadavers, only barely, theoretically distinct from the carts that bear them (both, after all, are only material nature).

But in that bare difference is precisely the reflexive irony: As a relic of a man once alive and communicating, the corpse is a haunting presence of that once-alive man as he was or might have been in actual, living relationships to us and is therefore a haunting presence of the anatomist to himself—a faint but telling reminder of intimacies now foreclosed, fellow-feelings now forbidden, impossible, or irrelevant. Even so, for all the subtle reminders within every action on or to the corpse, that difference has become a historically bare difference. That body, that corpse, is now definitively disclosed merely as a complex of organs, tissues, systems, mechanisms. Thereby does the gallows humor have its bite: That former life, once with us, is now no longer and, theory tells us, was really never there in any quantitative, measurable way anyway, yet it compellingly does remind us of that formerly alive, once-communicating person.

The view (expressed by Pellegrino and evident in Burnet and Penfield and in modern medicine more generally) that this medicine is a fusion of the Hippocratic empiric tradition and the neo-Cartesian conviction that disease, and bodies more generally, can be explained in physicochemical and quantitative terms clearly harbors numerous dilemmas and enigmas. For if it is correct, there simply is no way to understand or account for that peculiar gallows humor, the special tension, the haunting reminders of persons once alive and communicating with us.

The question, again, is whether this concept of fusion is even a coherent one, or whether the supposed fusion is in fact something quite different, namely, the subordinating of the empiric approach to the governance of the dogmatic, quantitative one. Can the dogmatic tradition allow for the central empiric theses? Can life be conceived within an "ontology of death" (matter), to use Jonas's terms?

To get at these most difficult issues, some further grounds must be set out. After that, it will finally become possible to address the central issues that initiated this study in the first place.

THE EMPIRIC-DOGMATIC DISPUTE REVISITED

Recalling the phenomenon of therapeutic experience, it was noted that what is to count as a symptom is subject to conflicting interpretations. As we saw, while the early Hippocratic empiric insisted on basing medical judgment on experience (and memory) and never prejudging a patient's condition, the early dogmatic insisted that a certain kind of advance, indeed *a priori*, knowledge was necessary for proper diagnosis and treatment.

By Hellenistic times, however, it seems clear that both of these types of healers dealt with patients from within a certain predisposition: Both were predisposed in a certain way to consider what is presented by that patient. Both have a certain idea beforehand of "what's wrong," and this idea is present from the very first moment of the encounter.

The issue between them therefore came to concern not whether there is a kind of knowledge in advance of the encounter, but rather what sort of advance knowledge each respectively claimed to possess. The empiricist no less than the dogmatic, that is, came to lay considerable stress on knowledge. The empiricist's criticism of the dogmatic's supposedly *a priori* knowledge (of proximate causes, humors, and logical classification of diseases) is thus no longer couched in the contrary claim to have no advance knowledge at all of disease. For the Hellenistic empiricist also knows beforehand. He knows what has been done before by himself (through his own *empeiria*) and by other healers (through medical *istoria*). A fund of empiric knowledge is thus at hand for this healer. He possesses multiple healer-histories in the light of which each unique patient is encountered, interpreted, and eventually treated.

If that complex set of healer-histories informs the Hellenistic empiricist of the need to be cautious and tentative, to take everything into consideration as he deals with each individual patient, it is nonetheless true that this precautionary and probabilistic attitude is based on prior (i.e., historical) knowledge. Such knowledge, of course, does not include what the dogmatic healer specifically claimed; it does, however, permit the empiricist to move from the single *peira* to *empeiria*, thence to *isotoria*, the whole of which permits reasoning from or on the basis of similars (*omoion metabasis*). Thus, the empiric tradition, as it evolved into Hellenistic empiricism, came to lay considerable stress on what is common or similar among different patients, which was learned, of course, on the basis of past experience. In this, however, empiricism came ever closer to the basic tenets of dogmatic medicine.

The dogmatic physician believed that reasoning on the basis of the common or similar involved analogical reasoning (*analogismos*), and this remained significantly different from the empiricist's reasoning on the basis of historically recorded similarities. The dogmatic sought to connect observed symptoms with unobserved (and unobservable) inner bodily pathologies (and, beneath them, the humors). Thinking and reasoning about those invisibles (the nonevident) was the whole point of *analogismos* and permitted the dogmatic physician to engage the central medical task of diagnosis.

The dogmatic's claim was not merely that prior knowledge was to be had, but genuinely *a priori* knowledge of these invisibles. By possessing such knowledge, a logical, *a priori* classification of diseases could be developed and at hand for diagnosis and therapy. Thanks to the classification, the dogmatic healer could claim that only certain bodily features or alterations could and should be considered by the physician. Therefore, the centerpiece of empiricist medicine—weighing and considering everything presented in the light of healer-histories and ongoing discourse with and observations of a patient (*epilogismos*)—was completely unnecessary and even absurd for the dogmatic. Rather, the latter's task was seen to be set out *a priori*. Knowing already the finite number of diseases along with their associated bodily symptoms and knowing already that diseases are internal (invisible) organic pathologies caused by improperly mixed or mislocated humors, the dogmatic had to figure out (to "reason analogically") the proper causal chain of events always presented by a certain class of diseases. The dogmatic called this reasoned linking of specific symptoms to a class of causal disorders diagnosis, and it proceeded on the basis of the *a priori* linkage set out by the classificatory patterns known by *analogismos* (along with syllogistic logic).

Both empiricists and dogmatics in Hellenistic times urged the need for healers to reason by way of similars. They differed over the sources and kinds of reasoning and the place of experience in it. The dogmatic sought diagnosis, the connecting of internal disorders with outer symptoms on the body, known *a priori* to be caused by those inner disorders. The empiricist, by contrast, saw his task as the interpretation of everything presented by a patient in the effort to connect that patient's own unique past to the present cluster of symptoms in the light of the multiple healer-histories already at hand for the healer.

If nothing else, this deep conflict about the sources and kinds of knowledge and the relationships between them and experience seems so fundamental as to cast doubt on later attempts to blend, harmonize, or "fuse" them. Pellegrino's and others' belief that contemporary medicine is a fusion of these traditions (to be sure, as modified by the rich, subsequent history of medicine, and especially by the Cartesian framework), then, must pose a serious problem. Is such a fusion even coherent? Can a "new, matured Cartesian conviction" that human illness can be described and explained in physicochemical and quantified terms in truth be fused with the "neo-Hippocratic spirit" of empiricist medicine? Or, alternately, is the medical materialism of a La Mettrie or of later physicians (Burnet, e.g.) or the medical dualism of a Gaub or of later physicians (Penfield, e.g.) at all even coherent for medicine?

THE THERAPEUTIC DYAD RECONSIDERED

However central it is, therapeutic experience is but one facet of the healer-patient relationship. Underlying it is the therapeutic dyad. In somewhat different terms, what the healer in fact observes includes not only a variety of bodily symptoms—however these may be interpreted—but more significantly pertains to a specific person embodied by that distressed or damaged body with all its particular features, body attitudes and alterations, and disorders. Moreover, the distress or damage is itself experienced by that embodied person in the first place; not only is it experienced, but at the same time it is interpreted by that person.

When such a person presents to a would-be healer, then, the healer's experience is necessarily complex: The healer experiences a complex, already-interpreted experience (the patient's). In this respect, "what is observed" by the healer is indeed self-interpreted; the patient presents an interpretation of himself to the healer, specifically of his own bodily experiences and of their meaning for him.

As was noted in our review of patients, a patient may well present with a quite sophisicated interpretation (as in the case of the physician afflicted with limb-girdle muscular dystrophy) or be capable of only minimal interpretation (e.g., through grimaces, flinching, groans). The limiting case might be thought to be a completely comatose patient, although the fact of complete failure to respond (e.g., to deep pain) is not without its own specific force for the healer's experience. For even with the comatose, what the healer observes is still an embodied person, and failure to respond here has a significance quite different from the failure to respond, say, of an inanimate thing. On the other hand, if the limiting case of self-interpretation is thought to be a corpse, this, we have already seen, does not ring at all true; for even here, there is an entire anthropology impacted in such experiences.

It seems perfectly obvious that what the healer observes is in almost all cases an embodied person who both experiences and interprets his own distress, illness, or damage and, in one way or another, does this both for himself and for the healer. Indeed, in continuous interaction with the healer, patients both experience and interpret themselves in this complex manner, and both patient and physician continuously respond to and interpret their respective shared interpretations.

The issue, then, at the heart of therapeutic experience concerns what the healer is to make of the patient's complex self-experience and self-interpretation. Or, in somewhat less complicated terms, what is the healer to include in his observational field? What, among all that is in fact observed, is to be included, given weight, or ruled out? Does not every healer abstract from the observational field, by focusing on or selecting only certain of its features? The dogmatic physician was apparently more conspicuous in restricting the symptoms to only those bodily signs known (or thought to be known) *a priori* to be causally connected to invisible disorders. But the Hellenistic empiricist was also obliged to isolate abstractively, albeit far less so than the dogmatic, to those symptoms known from prior experiences (either *empeiria* or *istoria*) to be like those presented and relevant in the past.

What seems to have divided these two traditions, then, is less the practice of such abstractive focus than the principle governing it. In virtue of what is the observational field to be narrowed, and to what is it then to be narrowed? What cannot be excluded from the field of observed symptoms on pains of missing what must not be missed for the healer to do his job? What is the status accorded to the field itself?

To return to the therapeutic dyad, we can ask whether it is possible for any would-be healer in principle to ignore, exclude, or otherwise eliminate the patient's experience and self-interpretation of his or her own distress. Whatever the healer may think about a patient's self-interpretation (or even a patient's competency to interpret), whether or not the healer may substitute another interpretation for it and even whether or not therapy is developed on the basis of the one or the other interpretation, the fact is that the healer cannot avoid taking a stand on principle concerning the status of the patient's own experiences and self-interpretations of them. If the latter is regarded as intrinsic to the observational field, as part of what the healer must contend with in his ministrations, as it appears the empiric believed, it then follows that this healer's tasks (both of interpretation and of therapy) are specifically complex. The healer perforce has to interpret both the patient's experiences (including what is displayed bodily) and the patient's own interpretation or understanding of the experiences (including patient reports of experiences and what these *mean* to him). If on the other hand the patient's experiences and their meaning for him are not thought to be integral to the healer's observational field, as was apparently believed by the dogmatic, it then follows that these can be safely (indeed necessarily) eliminated from the field as irrelevant to the healer's work.

In the case of the empiric, medical interpretation is second order; it includes an interpretation of (patient) interpretations. To the dogmatic, it signifies only a first-order act of interpretation, interpreting what are taken to be non–self-interpreting symptoms. For the first, patients are fundamental and integral to the physician's work, and there is the explicit recognition and affirmation of the necessarily dyadic character of that work. In the dogmatic's case, there is a denial of the dyad (even if such denial must first be based somehow on a recognition of it), and the bodily disorders are taken as fundamental.

The question posed by Pellegrino's (and others') claim about contemporary medicine—the very possibility of a fusion between the Hippocratic spirit and the Cartesian conviction about illness as physicochemical and quantitative—thus becomes more acute.

A REVIEW OF THE TERRAIN

Our historical excursus has thus far treated ancient Greek empiric medicine as if it exhibited a thematic unity. This is not, however, precisely true, and it is of some significance for this study to dwell some on this tradition, especially in light of the later, Hellenistic developments of empiricism. A review of how we got to this point may be helpful.

Recalling one of the questions that prompted this excursus in the first place—the anomalies within the discourse between physician and patient—we went in search of the historical roots of that relationship. Our inquiry took us into an examination of Descartes, frequently charged with being the *bête noir* and source for the current crisis in medicine. Our probing, however, showed that far from promulgating the sort of mind-body dualism so often attributed to him, Descartes's own keen sense of scientific and clinical medicine in part led him to reject precisely that sort of dualism. The dualism is far more due to the work of post-Cartesian physicians—Boyle, Hoffmann, Gaub, and others—than it ever was to that of Descartes himself.

On the other hand, Descartes's own inquiries into anatomy, physiology, and medicine did result in a kind of duality, one that has plagued medicine from its beginnings in ancient Greece and has played a significant role in medicine since Descartes. This duality has to do with the human body itself: that, when alive, it is intimately united with the mind (which is known distinctly in both ordinary life and in clinical practice), and that, when dead, it is, or seems to be, of a piece with material nature. The deanimated body comes to be conceived as inanimate matter (only to reappear in concrete experience as a special tension and even gallows humor). In his efforts to comprehend both, however, Descartes landed himself in a paradox, in effect attempting to advocate the central tenets of both the dogmatic and the empiric traditions in medicine.

Further historical probing led, on the one hand, to those ancient traditions, in an effort to gain better understanding of the sense of the therapeutic experience and the rival, competing alternatives to which it is intrinsically open. On the other hand, we were led to the seminal work of Morgagni and Bichat, as a result of which the empiric tradition seems finally closed and the dogmatic paradigm apparently succeeds in absorbing the empiric.

This conclusion, however, left both anomalies unaccountable: that pertaining to the everyday discourse between physician and patient and that pertaining to the human body as alive and as corpse. Further historical inquiry thus seems necessary in order to contend with the issue within the claim that modern medicine is a fusion of the "neo-Hippocratic spirit" and the "neo-Cartesian conviction." Is this even a coherent notion? To pursue this issue, it was necessary first to go back over the empiric tradition, in the course of which several interesting things came to light.

First, the dogmatic's epistemological criticism of the empiric led the latter to an equally epistemological criticism of the dogmatic view. The result of this seems to have been that later, Hellenistic empiricism became equally fastened onto questions of knowledge, with the aims of therapy taking something of a back seat. Both the dogmatic and the empiricist, thus, encounter the patient with advance knowledge: in the one case, it is historical knowledge; in the other, it is logical, *a priori* knowledge.

Secondly, as was just underscored, when the place of the patient is questioned, the two traditions still seem fundamentally at odds. Whereas the empiricist seeks to include the patient (especially the patient's experience and interpretations of it), the dogmatic finds this irrelevant. Hence, a medicine that builds on, endorses, or otherwise includes the dogmatic paradigm as its foundation seems unavoidably unable to incorporate the main points of empiricist medicine. If the patient cannot, nevertheless, be ignored—the therapeutic dyad is a genuine dyad—such a medicine must find itself facing severe anomalies and unsolvable issues. Just this situation may well be in good part what has occurred in contemporary medicine.

Further reflections on medicine's historical origins, however, show that the empiric tradition itself is not unitary. The problem now is to dwell somewhat on this in order to lay out a more adequate basis for our subsequent reflections on the demands of an ethics that would be responsive to clinical medicine. To be thus responsive requires that clinical medicine itself be properly understood, and that this medicine itself be an internally coherent practice.

CHAPTER 7

Skepticism in Medicine

The splendid classicist and medical historian Ludwig Edelstein has brilliantly shown that the empiricist school of medicine actually originated only in Hellenistic times, while what he terms "Hippocratic empiricism" has much older roots and a quite different historical continuance (1967, pp. 195–97). Moreover, the doctrines of the former turn out to be at odds with the latter's tenets in several crucial ways. As these divergences are important for the present study, it is necessary now to understand them far better than we have thus far.

HELLENISTIC AND HIPPOCRATIC EMPIRICISM

In Hippocratic empiricism, the empiric physician is enjoined to rely on experience alone, since only what can be observed and proven by it can be considered true and appropriate for the physician's central task of therapy. Experience was held to require "the observation of every effect of every single factor on every individual" (e.g., in what he eats, drinks, and does), since only the unique can be truly apprehended. It is therefore not possible, it was believed, to "decide what should be done in the future from one's experience of the past" (ibid., p. 196).

At issue here is the physician's experiences of the past, for it is the physician's task to determine how the individual behaves in eating, drinking, and acting. The reference to "experience of the past" seems to be concerned with "the recurrent," not anything "permanent," and thus there is a question whether there is any objective or generally valid standard for practice or knowledge (see Deichgräber, in Edelstein, ibid., p. 196, n. 5). So far as the physician sought to draw conclusions or suggestions for treatment "in the future" from his own "experience of the past," that is, to base treatment on "the recurrent," the Hippocratic empiric says this is not possible.

The Hippocratic empiric fastened strictly onto the "unique occurrence" presented with each patient. Nevertheless, Edelstein convincingly shows, in disagreement with Deichgräber, this empiric did indeed have a kind of standard: "the individual reaction of the patient," which can be ascertained in each case even though "it is not something permanent or recurrent, but something unique" (ibid.).

It is just on this point that the Hellenistic empiricist school departed from Hippocratic empiricism. For the former, Edelstein contends, experience is interpreted quite differently, for since "the unique occurrence lies outside scientific knowledge," it is only the observation and recording of the recurrent that is significant for medicine. Here, as we noted in the last chapter, the focus is on similars and reasoning about them. Only in this way, these empiricists contended, is even probable knowledge possible (ibid.).

As was already pointed out earlier, both the dogmatic and the empiricist schools are therefore distinct from the Hippocratic empiric tradition. Unlike the latter, they both in essence agreed that similarities among recurrent occurrences were to be given priority in medicine and that the physician has, as we said, knowledge in advance of every encounter with an individual patient. This prior knowledge is given priority over therapy since therapy is for them impossible without such knowledge. They differed from one another as regards the source of these similarities, and the epistemic status accorded to that prior knowledge. The later empiricists contended that experience, sensory observation, was the source of similarities, whereas the dogmatic school believed it was logical reasoning; the empiricist's prior knowledge was historical and merely probable, whereas the dogmatics thought they had *a priori* knowledge of disease. The Hippocratic empiric denied each of these points; his historical successors were thus neither dogmatics nor empiricists.

Where the dogmatic physician argued for the necessary existence of "the invisible" causes of diseases (humors), the empiricist flatly denied that the invisible was knowable (there being no possible sensory experience of it). The point of the dispute, clearly, was a philosophical one concerning knowledge (ibid., pp. 198–201): the one contending that the invisible necessarily existed and was knowable *a priori*, the other that since it could not be known by sensory observation it could not exist.

In this respect, Edelstein notes, Sextus Empiricus's criticism of both these schools was entirely correct when he pointed out that even the empiricist's "negative judgment is no less dogmatic than the positive doctrines of the Dogmatic schools" (ibid., p. 193). It is just this "dogmatic" characteristic of both that constitutes the second fundamental divergence of Hellenistic empiricism from the earlier Hippocratic empiric tradition. The latter was staunchly opposed to any rigid tenets, negative or positive. The empiric was willing, indeed, to accept only what appeared to him at the moment (i.e., as *phainomenon*). He arrived at this basically skeptical attitude, however, not from considerations about the nature of knowledge but from his own medical experience, which, he believed, since it deals with unique, individual patients, permits no universal, probable, or typical judgments of any sort. The empiric held that he could "rely only on the experience he gains at this moment and from this individual, because the sole criterion is how the patient feels whom he happens to be treating" (ibid., p. 199).

Thus, the Hippocratic empiric did not deny the existence of the invisible nor even that the invisible could be known. He rather regarded the entire discussion about the hidden as having no medical significance, whatever its philosophical status. He could thus readily admit that the hidden might exist and even that knowledge of it was at least possible hypothetically. His point was merely that this was all entirely useless to him and to his treatment of patients.

For both of these reasons, then, Edelstein concludes that (1) the Hippocratic empiric "has the same medical approach as Sextus," that is, of later, Hellenistic skepticism (ibid., p. 200) and (2) it is in the later methodist school of medicine that the early empiric tradition is continued, not in the school of Hellenistic empiricism.

What is significant in all this is that the Hippocratic physician was a skeptic by reason of his own medical experiences. There can be nothing certain or rigid in medicine, just because the sphere of medical action, that is, human life, is intrinsically variable; "anything can mean anything, because in health and disease nothing is steadfast" (ibid., p. 200). What works with one patient might not work with another, or even with the same patient on different occasions. This variability and conversion of everything into its opposite, Edelstein emphasizes, are "the consequence of the nature of the human body" and human life itself, which "is constantly changing" (ibid., p. 201). To cure a patient, therefore, one has no choice but to be cautiously attentive to everything about him, trying various remedies and carefully noting their effect over time. The physician's art "consists in knowing how much each body can tolerate . . . but what in the present circumstances constitutes a remedy can only be recognized in each individual case" (ibid.).

The Hippocratic empiric physician is therefore a kind of relativist, but not because of any convictions about human knowledge. He is not first an epistemological skeptic or relativist and then, on that basis, a practical one. Rather, he is a skeptic and a relativist because of the nature of the art, medical practice, which is strictly determined by the nature of its actual objects—the human body and the embodied person in sickness and health. These are inerradicably unique and individual, "constantly changing," and variable; therefore, the art must be attentive to the unique and individual and thus itself be changing and variable.

The fact that this skeptical physician trusts only his experience, which never yields firm, recurrent results nor gives generalizations about things, is a strict consequence of what he understood as his central task and mission—the treatment of individual patients. "The skeptical empiricism of the classical physician is discovered in medical practice itself and is derived solely therefrom," Edelstein emphasizes (ibid., p. 201). Perhaps, then, this medical skepticism might more accurately be described as contextual or phenomenological, and its mode of understanding *circumstantial*; this physician insisted on keeping strictly to the *phainomena* and what they demanded of the physician, within the specific set of circumstances or contexts in which each patient was actually encountered.

As Edelstein acutely observes: "This classical empiricism is medicine's own creation and, it seems to me, its original contribution." Indeed, he points out, "if the Greeks have a dislike for the individual and a preference for the typical, the counter-balance is provided by medicine, not by geography, history, or another science" (ibid., p. 201, n. 18). The later, Hellenistic empiricism, like dogmatism, was both derivative of respective philosophical schools and thus, unlike methodism, not in the least original.

MEDICAL METHODISM

The classical Hippocratic physician, however, faced a singular difficulty. Emphasizing the "constantly changing" nature of the human body and of man and thus the necessarily individualized, circumstantial approach to therapeutic experience, he seemed to have "no criterion in medicine except the patient's subjective experience" (ibid., p. 189). The "medical standard," as Edelstein interprets it, was "the individual reaction of the patient" (ibid., p. 198, n. 5). But this seems hardly trustworthy, precisely because the "patient's subjective experience" itself is so variable and unique to each patient.

Perhaps for that very reason, and following the Greek philosophical penchant for the general over the individual, subsequent physicians turned to the former in search of a more reliable guide: either in logical reason (the dogmatic school) or in the observed recurrences and similarities of experience (the empiricist school). What then began to develop was the peculiarly Greek, and indeed Western European, preoccupation with knowledge (*episteme*), as distinct from what was called mere everyday opinion (*doxa*).

As we have noted, both subsequent empiricism and dogmatism come to the same conclusion. Having prior knowledge before patient encounters is not only a formal necessity of medicine, but is in fact actually possessed, either as historical and probable, or as *a priori* and certain. With that preoccupation, furthermore, at least these prominent traditions in medicine at once came to distrust the every day (*doxa*) and at the same time came directly under the sway of philosophy. Allegiances in medicine were largely determined by philosophical convictions deriving from one or another philosophical doctrine, and medical arguments tended increasingly to be philosophical disputes (ibid. pp. 349–66).

Hellenic empiricism, thus, was based primarily on the works of academicians, such as Kleitomachos and Carneades, who asserted the ultimate unknowability of all things. The empiricist maintained that what is invisible is unknowable. The edifice of medicine and its central concept of experience were constructed according to the categories of academic philosophy, and the tenets of the dogmatics refuted philosophically "by confronting opinion with opposing opinion and by exposing vicious circles, by demonstrating *regressus ad infinitum*, or by pointing out the absurdity of assertions" (ibid., p. 200). The dogmatics, on the basis of the philosophical works of the Aristotelians, Epicureans, Stoics, and others, claimed to the contrary that logic is the principal element of true knowledge (including medical knowledge). They allotted but limited significance to experience and sought to refute empiricism philosophically by "denying that anything at all can be observed [in experience] repeatedly in exactly the same way." Thus they argued against the very idea that experience alone can yield knowledge (ibid., p. 188).

Such philosophical disputes concerning how it is possible to acquire knowledge (including, of course, knowledge of patients and of diseases) ended up presenting a fundamental difficulty for the physician. If the physician is obliged to know and treat unique individuals, and each one is different, how is he to know what he should do in the single case? Both the dogmatists and empiricists attempted to account for individual conditions in general terms, which presupposes "that individuals are uniform as individuals," and thus that "general knowledge" of them is possible (ibid.).

However, as had been taught in earlier Hippocratic medicine, only a medicine devoted to the very uniqueness of each individual patient could be legitimate, for otherwise the very point of medicine—therapy for each individual patient—would be undermined. This, however, required renouncing all generalities, typicalities, or universals in medical practice.

Neither empiricists nor dogmatists seemed able to accommodate that central Hippocratic premise, yet both continued to interpret the Hippocratic texts and to rely on their authority. Just those writings, however, presented the central and apparently unsolvable difficulty: the absolute uniqueness of each patient, which requires equally unique treatments. The attempt to find a medical standard that is both faithful to this premise and conforms to the apparent requirements of knowledge—which apparently concerns the generalizable—seems therefore to land medicine in an acute dilemma arising from the nature of medicine itself.

Just as there arose a philosophical attempt to navigate between the Scylla of empiricism and the Charybdis of dogmatism, in the form of Aenesidemean skepticism, a reaction against both occurred in medicine, based mainly on the effort to retain the original Hippocratic skeptical empiricism by picking up on the skeptic's approach: methodism. Dogmatic philosophy came to fruition in the dogmatic schools of medicine; in the empiricist medical tradition, academic skepticism flowered. Methodism, on the other hand, exploited Aenesidemean skepticism. The name itself indicates the skeptical stance: "treatment consists of following the path prescribed by the phenomena" (ibid., p. 187). The methodist stands at the end of a long line of development from the ancient Hippocratic empirics, but his conduct as a physician remained pretty much the same. What is different, Edelstein argues, is that this conduct "is determined by a different law," a different rationale (ibid.).

What is that "different law" or "rationale," and how does it permit surmounting the dilemma at the heart of the dogmatic and empiricist dispute?

THE SKEPTIC'S CIRCUMSTANTIAL UNDERSTANDING

The skeptical component of the Hippocratic tradition has already been noted. Medical practice, or the therapeutic experience, is determined throughout by its objects, unique afflicted human beings embodied by equally unique bodies with their own peculiar *physies*. Since therapeutic experience shows that each person is wholly unique, medical practice has no choice but to attempt to be responsive to each patient individually. We have termed this the circumstantiality, or context-dependency, of medical practice. We also suggested that it might be termed phenomenological, so far as it insists, in Edelstein's terms, on staying focused on the *phainomena* of therapeutic experience.

This circumstantiality is precisely what the later skeptics, especially Aenesidemos, picked up on in their critique of preceding thought. The skeptic "declares that the phenomena are the only true things; that they exist is not disputed" (ibid., p. 186). About everything else, the skeptic withholds judgment (what was termed *epoche*); "he does not claim that the hidden is unknowable, but he has as yet no knowledge of it and it does not concern him" (ibid.). Similarly, the Hellenic methodist concerned himself solely with *phainomena*, with what appears, strictly as it appears, within therapeutic experience. Philosophical disputes did not concern him; only what his own therapeutic experience itself demanded drew his attention.

About the dogmatic postulate of the invisible, the methodist simply said, there being no apparent sign of it within the *phainomena*, it can be of no consequence to the physician. So far as the empiricist denies the very possibility of a hidden realm or that knowledge of it is totally impossible, the skeptic replied that that sort of negative claim is as dogmatic as any which the dogmatist makes, and no more defensible or indefensible than any other similar postulate or claim not grounded in *phainomena* of therapeutic experience. Indeed, so far as any such postulate departs from the *phainomena*, it must invariably ignore the uniqueness of the individual patient and is therefore ultimately damaging not only to patients but also to the art.

The dogmatist and the empiricist are thus both hoisted on the same petard: While attempting to take different individuals as such into account (i.e., as *phainomena*), they yet suppose that individuals must be treated as alike; they presuppose that individual patients are uniform or typical, and thus in fact that individuals are not individuals at all! Since, for the dogmatists and the empiricists, treatment follows knowledge (whether historical or *a priori*), it, too, becomes focused on the general, the typical, or the universal. What initiates and underlies therapeutic experience, indeed its very point, is accordingly precisely what is then lost: the individual as *phainomenon*.

How does the medical skeptic, the methodist, handle this decisive issue? Edelstein's analysis shows, first, that these physicians were acutely aware of this very problem. Second, by basing themselves in part on the ancient Hippocratic insights and in part on skeptical philosophy, a way out of the dilemma is suggested. For, "in Skepticism there was the same rejection of all general principles, the same limitation to the here and now, as in Hippocratic empiricism" (ibid., p. 189). Indeed, as Sextus Empiricus pointed out, even though the empiricist school based itself on certain of the skeptics, it was not genuinely skeptical at all. The only school with which the true skeptic physician could align himself, Sextus argued, was the methodist, because the methodists alone, in Edelstein's terms, "refrained from judging" whether about the reality or non-reality of the invisible. Instead, "they limited themselves to the phenomena, and in the manner of the Skeptics they learned from the phenomena whatever seemed useful" (ibid., p. 197). That is, the physician allowed himself to be guided by the conditions actually observed with each patient.

The rationale for the methodist's skeptical approach, like the "different law" within philosophical skepticism, is to be found in the phenomena themselves—that is, in the afflicted person's own body and experiences (and, of course, self-interpretation of these). The "law" that governs treatment, then, is derived from the afflictions, experiences, and self-understanding of the patient himself. In acting on this, however, Edelstein emphasizes, the skeptical healer was not subtly appealing to a "principle" derived either from his own experience or from his intellect and then applied to his patient. Rather, "each case suggested to the physician a suitable individual treatment. The physician went solely by the patient he was treating" (ibid., p. 189). This at once satisfied the demands for a rationale of treatment and transformed medicine into the Hippocratic empiric's mode.

There is but one difference, then, between the Hippocratic empiric and the methodist. The Hippocratic found treatment difficult "because of the necessarily individualized character of knowledge and treatment, which allowed no criterion except the patient's subjective experience." The methodist, however, readily said that nothing was easier than treatment; "in raising to a principle the Skeptics' law that necessity resides in the afflictions of the body" (i.e., the *phainomena*), the physician was freed from that merely subjective criterion (ibid.).

As I understand the matter, although Edelstein does not remark on the point, the key difference between the methodist and the empiricist concerns what "experience" is respectively taken to designate. For the latter, it refers to the empiricist physician's own experiences (past and present) of a patient; for the methodist, to the contrary, it refers to the phenomena, that is, to the patient's own bodily experiences and self-interpretations, as apprehended by the physician.

The true skeptic and Hippocratic physician maintain that the physician must be quite literally at the service of each individual patient and his afflicted body (with its unique *physies*), that is, of the *phainomena* themselves of therapeutic experience and dyad. The fundamental discipline of medicine thus requires the physician to be strictly responsive to what the patient himself, as *phainomenon*, discloses to the physician and to what his afflicted body, also as *phainomenon*, directs the physician to do therapeutically.

THE HISTORICAL IRONY OF THE HUMAN CORPSE

We need to pause again here, to review the terrain sketched out, and notice several interesting themes that have emerged.

Since the beginning, in the late 13th century, of dissection of the human body, there has been a growing interest in and increasing sophistication about the human body's anatomy. At the same time, there also developed the idea that knowledge of human anatomy is essential to the physician: One cannot hope to relieve pain, cure disease, or heal wounds, unless one knows not only the body's inner parts but also the causal connections among them. At the heart of this is the idea that there is an essential connection between anatomical knowledge of the dead human body and the clinical practice of medicine working with the live human body.

By Descartes's time, almost a century after Vesalius's great work, not only was that idea already firmly rooted in medicine, but, with Harvey's seminal discoveries, anatomy had begun to shift from an interest in structure and spatial location of body parts and members to an emphasis on their function and effective interrelations. It becomes less a matter of where the heart, for instance, is found or what its internal structures look like, and more one of how it works in relation to other body organs and parts.

Even so, as we saw, Descartes remained divided in his convictions, at a most critical point. Considering the case of the dropsical patient, Descartes insisted that for this patient, this composite whole, "to have thirst when drinking would be hurtful" is "not a purely verbal predicate [*une pure dénomination*], but a real error of nature" (1931, vol. I, pp. 195–96). When this patient's body is considered "in itself," however, it is neither more nor less than any other material thing; dropsical or not, injured or not, both it and other physical things are defined and governed by the laws of mechanical nature and are thus neither good nor evil. The "real error of nature" concerns this patient's body solely as an essential, integral component of the composite whole, the embodied person. If we ask about the difference between these two uses of "nature," Descartes responds that the one (as in "laws of nature") is merely "a manner of speaking," a "purely verbal predicate," or simply a figure of speech (although he gives no rationale either for the specific "figure" he uses, nor for the use of such heuristic devices more generally). The other usage (as in "real error of nature"), however, is taken quite literally; the patient in this sense will be really, actually harmed by additional fluid intake, and this is no mere figure of speech but a "real error of nature."

How does Descartes (or anyone else, for that matter) know this critical difference? Again, Descartes's response is unmistakable and direct: The human body is able to be conceived as one among other physical bodies only when considerd "in" or "by itself"—that is, only if we succeed in conceptually abstracting it from its essential place as part of the composite whole. In different terms, the "real error of nature" is encountered only within the everyday, ordinary contexts of daily life, which is as well the context of clinical medicine (dealing with feelings such as pain that also present the composite whole).

What is this difference all about, finally? Descartes again seems unequivocal. So far as "nature" in the scientific sense is concerned, the body of the dropsical patient is defined like any other physical thing. That is, *this* body is precisely the *corpse.* We encounter the real dropsical patient, however, not as a corpse but as a living, feeling, striving, communicating person—an alive and embodied person in distress and pain. The difference, then, is quite literally that between human life and death.

The issues, here, however, are still more complex. On the one hand, this difference is one with historical roots; on the other, it harbors, we saw, profound consequences for subsequent medical thinking and practice. Let us take up the former point after reviewing what we have learned about the latter.

It seems clear that only shortly after Descartes's death (February 11, 1650), physicians and others were already ignoring, or were simply unaware of, that very difference and its implications both for understanding Descartes himself and for medicine. Not only was Descartes's usage of "nature" as a "figure of speech" already being obscured, as Niels Stenson felt compelled to point out in 1665, but a veritable mind-body dualism (of supposedly Cartesian origins) was being introduced (and advocated or rejected) as if it were Descartes's position.

However, the body in these later works was not the living, feeling, striving part of the integral whole with mind, which Descartes urged was encountered in ordinary life, through pain and other feelings, and therefore in clinical medicine. Rather, as is especially clear in Hoffmann, the body in that sense is quite absent and is instead taken to be a *machine* put together so as to produce motion, which "is the cause of all bodily changes [and] . . . the basis of life and health" (*Medicina rationalis systematica*, I, cited in King, 1963, p. 163). Indeed, departing even further from Descartes, Hoffmann assumes that not only the body but "life and death are mechanically conditioned and depend only on mechanical and physical causes which act by necessary laws" (ibid., p. 164). Even so, Hoffmann still attempted to embrace what he understood to be the Cartesian dualism (King, 1978, pp. 121, 153, 203–07). His conception of body, however, is precisely what Descartes has insisted could in no way be conceived as the living embodiment of the mind (soul, person).

It is clear, too, that even the more frankly medical dualists, such as Jerome Gaub, in plowing the early grounds for a psychosomatic medicine, were working not with the Cartesian sense of the living body of the composite whole or "nature" in the sense which necessitates qualifiers such as "good" and "bad" but rather with an essentially mechanistic idea of the human body—that is, with the *corpse* as the basic image of bodily *life*—and thus with what Descartes regarded as quite absurd and impossible!

With Morgagni, these themes shift ever more. With anatomy increasingly shifting from structure and location to function and interrelationships, it was thought possible to connect bodily symptoms displayed in life with organic disorders found at death, with autopsy. Similarly, Bichat's refinements—and especially his introduction of the concept of pathological-tissual lesion—continue that shift and seem to have succeeded in finally placing medicine on firm, scientific footage. Even so, the basic sense of the human body remains unchanged from what Descartes had meant in his "figure of speech" as distinct from the lively, embodying organism united with the soul. The Hippocratic heritage, urging the need for cautious, thorough observation and the progressive building up of an empiric fund of knowledge about patients, their self-interpretations, and therapeutic medications, seems nevertheless able to be married to a rigorous, dogmatically inspired science of medicine based in, and reduceable to, quantitative terms (as Pellegrino has claimed).

If a physician still wished to be concerned with the mind (i.e., with patients as "persons"), the fundamental insight of Gaub (and others following him) seemed the only legitimate one. Since the body is taken to exercise far greater influence on the mind than the reverse, this gave apparent legitimacy to the idea than a patient's concrete experiences (of pain, suffering, anxiety) could best be managed by means of interventions into the patient's body. Thus, if the mind (soul, person) is taken to be at all real, in whatever way, it is still believed that the body is knowable more readily and in more exact terms; and it is this which seems the legitimation of medicine's increasingly exclusive focus on the body. The mechanistically conceived body, the body as corpse, becomes the proper object of medicine. Thus, even if the mind exists, it is the proper object of medicine *only* via this body. The "medical management of the mind by means of the body" (Gaub) becomes a veritable principle of subsequent medicine.

Whether subsequent researchers and physicians endorse a monistic materialism or some sort of dualism, then, the body remains the principal object of medicine and continues to be understood in physicochemical and quantitative terms. The body remains very much what Descartes had indicated, as a "figure of speech," in his physics and mathematics; and it is precisely *this* body that is *never* encountered in daily life, any more than is the body as part of the composite whole encountered or comprehensible in those physicochemical and quantitative terms. Indeed, as Descartes emphasized to Princess Elizabeth, metaphysics and physics-mathematics are positive obstacles to the apprehension of the living body of the composite whole: The dropsical patient is incomprehensible within both of them.

In exactly the same way, where mind (self, person) is admitted in later medicine (e.g., by Penfield), it is a mind that has already been abstracted from its own embodying organism and taken as a mere "in itself," which is, like Descartes's metaphysical concept, not encountered in daily life or in clinical practice—just as the body in such dualisms has already been abstracted from the mind embodied by it in ordinary experience. Gaub's and others' efforts to construct a psychosomatic medicine, therefore, are built on essentially incoherent abstractions—a body that is *de*animate (corpse) and a mind that is *dis*embodied (a pure idea). It is little wonder that neurosurgeons like Samuel Greenblat in our time come to lament how the mind seems at once so "ungetaroundable," yet so unaccountable—something they would just as soon ignore if only they could!

It then becomes possible to pick up on the still-unnoticed historical irony buried beneath these themes and continued underneath Hans Jonas's otherwise lucid insights. In classical times, Jonas argued, it was the corpse that was the "limit of all understanding." This "primal exhibition of 'dead' matter constituted," especially for the early medieval anatomists, as we saw, a fundamental enigma. As van den Berg suggested, this is particularly clear in the early depictions of corpses in anatomy texts. On the other hand, subsequent historical tendencies suggest that, as Jonas remarks, "the living, feeling, striving organism has taken over this role," and "life" consequently becomes "a *ludibrium materiae*, a subtle hoax of matter."

Descartes is a central figure at this very point. On the one hand, there is the *alive* human body, encountered solely in ordinary life and conversation, in the life of feeling and clinical practice, and intimately unioned with the embodied person. Here, the *corpse* is precisely the centering enigma and subtle hoax: Now *de*animated, it is the "primal exhibition of 'dead' matter." On the other hand, there is the dead human body, the corpse, which in that *other* Descartes's understanding is (in principle, at least) wholly intelligible and explainable according to the laws of physical nature. Here, the alive, unioned body is the centering enigma and hoax; as embodying or animating, it is the inexplicable *par excellence*, forcefully evident (as in clinical encounters with the dropsical patient) and yet unaccountable in physical terms.

The profound irony underlying all of this centers in the corpse. Although clearly dead and apparently intelligible (thus no longer puzzling and unorthodox), it is yet not dead in the way material nature is dead and thus cannot be conceived as part of material nature. For "nature" in the latter sense is neither *de*animate nor *ex*animate (since material things as such never had soul in any sense), but rather is only *in*animate. At the very least, the move from the former to the latter is utterly obscure. The corpse is not in any sense merely *in*animate and never was; it is now, rather, *ex*animate or, as Ramsey put it, "once a man alive," "once a communicating being." And therein lies the significance of that difference that defines the basic character of Descartes's work. Just this, moreover, becomes obscured and eventually lost in subsequent medical theories, even while it is a continually compelling and ironic presence for the clinical practitioner.

THE PLACE OF GALEN

The history of both materialism and dualism in medicine is thus closely tied to that of cadaverial anatomy, especially as it developed in the late 13th century. As we have seen, it seems that these first medieval dissections were undertaken for two reasons. Salimbene's chronicle (1288) reports that a physician from Cremona opened a corpse (though only partially) during the plague of 1286, apparently to see if he could find the cause of the disease. The next account, in 1302, is of a court-ordered autopsy to determine whether a deceased man had died of poison, as suspected.

From that point on, autopsy rapidly developed into anatomical study. Mondino's influential book, the first specifically devoted to human anatomy since Galen's eleven centuries earlier, was written in 1316; his student, Vigevano, wrote the first illustrated text in 1345. Within 200 years, however, anatomy had become a quite sophisticated science, regarded as underlying and essential to medicine, as evidenced by the publication in 1543 of Vesalius's great work.

Until Vesalius, to be sure, anatomy was mainly Galenic; it simply incorporated Galen's anatomical ideas—mistakes and truths alike. Galen's influence can also be detected in another sense in those earliest autopsies, for the idea that one might find the cause of a disease or of the results of poison ingestion by opening the corpse of the dead person is a fundamentally dogmatic assumption carried over by Galen from still earlier physicians. Although Galen attempted a grand synthesis among Aristotlean, Platonic, and Hippocratic systems of thought and was convinced of the need for careful empiric knowledge and the empiric's dietetic approach, in the end it was the dogmatic framework and approach that won out and characterize his work and influence.

Thus, while Galen praised the empiricists' insistence upon observational data, he was dismayed by the evident lack of certainty in their approach, both in their theory of knowledge and in their therapeutics (Tempkin, 1973, pp. 15–17). What was needed, he thought, was a rational, logical knowledge of diseases and of the human body. This knowledge he conceived as rational deduction (following Aristotle's syllogistics). Experience, observation, and experiment were taken to be ways of demonstrating "what is logically proved. . . . It is both possible and necessary to penetrate beyond the visible, because what is visible does not account for the elements of which things are composed" (ibid., p. 16). Like the earlier dogmatics, Galen endorsed and furthered the idea of underlying humors knowable only by rational, logical reasoning and conceived as causes of externally displayed symptoms.

Yet, Galen was also convinced that the evidence of the senses must play a key role in medical knowledge, as is witnessed in his dietetics and anatomy. As assiduous in dissecting animals as in observing a decomposed body, Galen was convinced that dissection was essential to medicine. Physicians, he asserted, "must dissect and study the tissues and the organic parts, analyze all functions, and examine the elementary composition of the body" (ibid., p. 40; see also pp. 12–13).

Galen was also convinced that human behavior depends on the somatic constitution and disposition of the organs. For instance, passion he felt to be a temperament of the heart, and desire a temperament of the liver. As Tempkin points out, he tended "to consider even the rational soul as the temperament of the brain" (ibid., p. 84). People become what they are—just or unjust, friendly or filled with enmity—"because of the temperament of their bodies" (Galen, in ibid.).

Since the powers of the soul follow the bodily temperaments, indeed, the physician in his dietetics can work to elevate man more effectively than even moral training can do (ibid., p. 55). Still, Galen was ultimately unable, as he says, to follow Plato's teachings on the soul, especially as to whether it is mortal or immortal. Even more, he reports that he

> nowhere dared to state the essence of the soul. For as I noted in my book "On the Species of the Soul," I have not come upon anybody who geometrically demonstrated whether it is altogether incorporeal, or whether any [species] is corporeal, or whether it is completely everlasting, or perishable. (*De foetuum formatione* 6; in ibid., p. 87.)

Just because of this eventual conclusion, subsequent Christian physicians and theologians argued that Galen stood squarely within the dogmatist tradition of medical materialism, which sought to reduce mental phenomena to organic conditions or at least to explain them by organic conditions. Since Galen's own anatomical dissections were conducted exclusively on animals, of course, none of those studies could provide any demonstration of the soul anyway or even of its former "place of residence" in the body. This very fact, along with Galen's belief that the physicians of his day had to study the extant works of the earlier anatomists in order to understand the parts and functions of the human body, obliges us to go back to those earlier human anatomists in our search for why physicians should have ever thought that human dissection was essential for medical practice in the first place.

ANATOMY IN THE ANCIENT WORLD

Galen's conclusions about human anatomy were based mainly on indirect evidence, either on his own dissections of those animals he thought most resembled man or on the works of the Alexandrian anatomists Herophilus and Erasistratus in the third century B.C. As Edelstein shows in his lucid analysis of anatomy in antiquity (1967, pp. 247–301), "philosophical considerations provide the methodical basis for dissection and vivisection" (ibid., p. 292). Dissections and vivisections, of course, can be performed on animals and were in fact performed before the Alexandrian period. Why, however, are they "suddenly carried out on human beings in Alexandria" (ibid.). This, he insists, is the really decisive question for the history of anatomy.

An integral part of this key question concerns why physicians would dissect at all. Is there an essential connection between anatomical knowledge of the human body and practical medicine? The question is not an idle one. On the one hand, knowledge of the body, without dissection or vivisection, was not only possessed by ancient philosophers and scientists but also by poets, Homer, for instance, and, presumably, their audiences; it was even fairly common among people more generally in ancient times. On the other hand, ancient physicians also accumulated substantial knowledge of the body through observations during treatments, by chance discoveries of cadavers, and especially in their treatment of wounds (Majno, 1975, pp. 141–206, 313–94). Thus, one must ask why any additional knowledge of the human body came to be seen as necessary.

Neither dogmatics nor empirics during Hippocratic times regarded it as necessary to have the kind of thorough knowledge of the body such as might be gained in dissection in order to treat diseases, wounds, or other afflictions. Indeed, not even the early dogmatics believed it necessary. For them, after all, curing a patient meant restoring the right mixture of humors, not making a sick organ healthy again. For that reason, it was unnecessary to know about the bodily interior. If anatomical knowledge was thus a "matter of indifference" (Edelstein, p. 267), why was dissection and even vivisection suddenly carried out on human beings in Alexandria?

An initial indication, at least, can be found even among the early dogmatics. As we have seen, the invisible disorders (dyscrasias) were thought to be due to the fact that the humors move within the body. A poor or improper mixture of any humor, furthermore, is held to be causally responsible for internal organic disruptions. Accordingly, some knowledge of the body's internal parts and members seems necessary beyond what was known *a priori* about the humors and diseases. Indeed, it seems clear that it was precisely this early dogmatic claim that eventually led physicians to an increasing need to know more about the invisible causes of disease and their effects (both internal disruptions and outer symptoms). By the time of the great Alexandrian schools, as Celsus reported four centuries after, the dogmatists were maintaining that knowledge of the internal organs is absolutely essential to curing diseases (ibid., pp. 268–69), and for this reason it is during this period that the true flowering of dogmatism is found.

At the same time, the empiricist school, also a strong movement in Alexandria at the time, while opposing the domatics' methods and doctrines completely, nonetheless believed that knowledge of the human body is necessary in order to treat it. Their main criticism of vivisection and dissection was not that knowledge was unnecessary, but only "that these methods did not accomplish the desired end and that they were in addition cruel and frightful" (ibid., p. 269).

Dissection, the empiricist argued, only gives knowledge of the dead body; vivisection, on the other hand, is not only superfluous but also cruel, for since the subject dies, the physician still sees only the organs of a dead body. Since the entire point of either method is to be able to observe the internal organs of the living human body, the dogmatic methods must be rejected as total failures. The empiricists nevertheless believed that dissection could yield some interesting knowledge. They only denied its usefulness for achieving the goal of knowledge of the living body for the purposes of therapy. By the time of Galen, however, a century after Celsus, anatomical knowledge was considered "the most essential knowledge, and he who would be a good physician must be particularly well versed in it" (ibid., p. 271).

Still, the question remains, Why is it that physicians came to practice human dissection and even vivisection in the first place? For the ancient Greeks, after all, reverence for the dead was a duty that bound the living in a most rigorous way, taking the form of burial in the hope of ensuring that the dead will find rest. The repose of the dead man's body must never be disturbed; hence every care had to be taken to ensure that the sanctity of the grave was protected. These beliefs and others were derived from the older, magical views of the world, and the common people clung strongly to them. However, what is at issue here is not the beliefs of common people, but rather those of scholars and scientists, since they were the ones who came to practice dissection. The important question concerns their ideas of the body and the soul, of life and death.

The extant reports, mainly from Celsus (ca. A.D. 1), talk of dissection as if it were a matter of course. Indeed, the main opposition reported is that of empiricist physicians and was, as was indicated, for primarily medical reasons: The sense of cruelty was decidedly secondary to the medical argument that neither dissection nor vivisection succeeded in permitting observation of the living body. Apparently, then, the first anatomists had already succeeded in breaking with the network of magical, religious, and mythical beliefs that were so characteristic of early culture and probably even among common people at their time.

Edelstein argues that the answer will "be found by inquiring into the philosopher's ideas of death and of man's duties toward the dead" (ibid., p. 275), for it is in these works that one finds the first, then the definitive break with the prevailing animistic beliefs. The central idea, first expressed by the Platonic Socrates (see *The Phaedo*, 115c) and then by the mature Plato (*Laws*, 958d–959a) and by Aristotle (*De partibus animalium* I, a, 640b35–36; 641a19–21), is this: Man is not his body, but soul; therefore, the fate of the body cannot be of concern to man's true, essential being. While there are differences between Plato and Aristotle on the body, the soul, and their interrelationships, both agree that the human body is not the man himself, the corpse even less so.

The same basic idea is found as well in Epicurean philosophy, in Greek empiricism, and in stoicism. What happens to the human body after death is of no concern to the man. Thus any idea that there might still be a magic power inhabiting the corpse is lacking; man himself is not the body even while man is alive. Hence, Edelstein emphasizes, "with this all the religious and magical inhibitions which might keep people from touching the corpse fall away" (Edelstein, p. 279). Since in death the person is "completely destroyed . . . what happens to the corpse is of no consequence" (ibid.). Therefore, if no dogmatic physicians in ancient times dissected, this was, Celsus remarks, mainly because of the natural feeling of disgust that dissection evokes, not because of any religious or magical dread of the unclean or because of a fear of having disturbed the repose of the dead man's body.

Physicians in the third century b.c. could, then, have dissected; according to all credible sources, Herophilus and Erasistratus were the first to do so on human beings. They did so, first of all, because by that time it had become imperative to make the invisible visible, to gain adequate and accurate knowledge of the internal parts of the body so as to provide proper therapies for sick people. They were able to dissect, moreover, thanks to the fact that the prevalent and accepted philosophical ideas of the human body, soul, and their interrelations uniformly incorporated the belief that since the human essence is the soul, in life, the fate of the human body was of no concern to the man, especially in death.

If dissection was thus actually practiced in these schools, so was vivisection, as the same sources state many times. To be sure, it was regarded as cruel even by those who practiced it. It was done, furthermore, primarily for the same reasons as dissection. Indeed, given its purposes, it could possibly be even more justified, because of the felt need to get at the very aliveness of the living body every practicing physician faced in therapeutic experience. In fact, Celsus pointed out, while dissection affords a scrutiny of the internal organs, what is thereby seen, being dead, is insufficient; it does not accomplish what is needed by the physician. Vivisection was therefore necessary because it promised to provide that needed knowledge of man and his body while alive. The advantage of vivisection is that it studies living man, not merely the dead, and "without knowledge of the living it is not possible to treat the sick" (Celsus, in ibid., p. 286). If vivisection is regarded as a horrible cruelty (even as regards the criminals on whom it was apparently practiced), then, as we will see, another method of gaining that knowledge must be found.

In other words, Edelstein emphasizes, all discussions about the value of dissection and vivisection are "determined by definite philosophical and scientific theories about the nature of man" (ibid., p. 287), including all ideas about man's essense (the soul), immortality, death, the body, and the relations between soul and body. For Aristotle, for instance, in all descriptions and explanations of nature, the significant thing is to focus not on mere lifeless stuff (matter) but rather on the force or power which "*informs*" it and thereby determines what each thing, as well as the totality of things, ultimately is. More particularly, when discussing animate being,

Aristotle's insistent point is that we must apprehend the inner form, or *telos*, that inherently makes each thing be what it is: the acorn, for instance, which becomes an oak tree, never an orangutan or a rose. Similarly, each part of an animate creature is "in-formed" by its own in-dwelling *telos*, such that we can recognize that a hand made of iron, stone, or wood is *not* a human hand even while it "looks" like one. Aristotle thus came to the important conclusion that "precisely in the same way no part of a dead body, such I mean as its eye or its hand, is really an eye or a hand" (*On the Parts of Animals*, 641a3–5). To understand a living creature in its very aliveness, one must apprehend its form, or *telos*, not merely the matter, for the life of that creature lies in the former and not in the latter. In death, all that remains is the material shape of the body, not the soul nor the life that "in-formed" that matter; the corpse's hand or eye is not really a hand or an eye.

It is essential that medicine apprehend "man as he truly is," and that means "man as alive." Hence, too, cadaverial dissection could only be inadequate, however interesting it may be. It is mere matter, with its defining principle (life) gone. Man changes essentially at death; dissection of corpses can yield merely morphological data—important enough in themselves, for Aristotle, but inadequate for medicine's therapeutic purposes. Therefore, Edelstein emphasizes that if to know man one believes that one must look into his body, "one has to cut man open alive, just as formerly one cut up animals alive" (Edelstein, p. 290).

Since the dogmatists in Hellenistic times were under the influence of the Aristotelian school, it was precisely such reasoning that was at the root of their initiation of human dissection and vivisection. For that matter, even the empiricist opposition to those methods and doctrine show the same Aristotelian influence, just insofar as they were also intent on knowing the living subject. Their argument, although not eventually successful, was that vivisection did not accomplish the aim of capturing the living, functioning body in its aliveness; rather, vivisection itself kills, leaving a body quite as dead as in dissection.

It is in any case the history of philosophy that undergirds, influences, and makes intelligible the history of anatomy. So far as medicine endorses the necessity of anatomy, it too is made comprehensible by philosophy. And even though subsequent dogmatists gave up vivisection, they still regarded it as the most correct method for medicine.

The same seems true of Galen's distinction between two kinds of anatomy, one that studies the parts of the body and one that studies their functions (although the meaning of "function" remains imprecise, it seems to refer specifically to the liveliness of the living body itself). Still later anatomists likewise pick up on this distinction, and some even go so far as to regard vivisection as preferable (even though impossible to practice). For instance, in his *Commentaria* (1521), Carpus remarked that while "in our time anatomy is not practiced on living bodies," what physicians need to know "would be found much better in the living than in the dead." It is only the "monstrousness" of vivisection that made them "recoil from such an enterprise" (in ibid., p. 283, n. 43).

Edelstein points out, moreover, that in H. Braus's *Anatomie des Menschen*, written in 1929, the art of dissection is said to have as its "greatest disadvantage" the fact that "it can only be performed on the dead; times are past when the ancient investigator demanded, and received, living slaves as objects of his study" (ibid.).

In fact, even among the ancients, as Celsus makes clear, vivisection seems to have been possible only on slaves and criminals and was commonly excused on just those grounds. Apparently, Celsus states, these vivisection subjects were handed over—doubtless not without considerable coercion and resistance—to Herophilus and Erasistratus by the kings of Alexandria. The dogmatists did not demand many such subjects, however, as they seemed convinced that vivisections need be performed but "once for the benefit of future generations" (ibid., p. 297). Beyond these few vivisections, then, Celsus reports, everything else that "can be learnt from the living" will be found and demonstrated in "actual practice . . . in the course of treating the wounded"—to be sure, a "somewhat slower but milder way" of learning (ibid., p. 284).

Presumably, then, the practice of vivisection, as well as the opposition to it, was shaped by the admitted cruelty it involves. Even so, within the context of prevailing philosophical ideas of the essence of human being and life and the dogmatists' conviction that thorough knowledge of the living body is essential to medical practice, not only dissection but vivisection seemed necessarily to follow.

The heart of our problem is that knowledge of the living, embodied human being is of fundamental importance for the practice of medicine. The condition that at once makes these methods possible and justifies them as medical methods, are the philosophical theories of man, body, soul, the interrelations of body and soul, and thereby life and death.

It must be noted that these theories are by no means materialisms such as the Democritean atomism, for which man is strictly a material organism. Contrary to what might be expected, it was the basically dualistic theories of Plato, Aristotle, the Epicureans, and the Stoics whose diverse systems agreed on the key point: Since man is not essentially body, but soul, what happens to the body after death is of little or no consequence. What ultimately matters about human being is life (form), not body (matter); therefore, physicians must focus on life. If the main object of medicine is the body, then it is the living body that must be known. Hence, vivisection or at least dissection (the empiricist objection notwithstanding) seemed utterly necessary.

In the Alexandrian dogmatism, thus, the earlier dogmatic reliance on the method of analogy (*analogismos*) was effectively replaced by that of dissection and vivisection. What is invisible and closed to sensory observation had to be shown to be (at least potentially) visible, for only in that way could relevant knowledge be attained and effective treatment provided. This replacement of methods signifies a "decisive change in the way of looking at the human body" (ibid., p. 295). Now, this "way of looking" was focused by the future, the expected findings by the anatomist (as dissector or vivisector). In this respect, it might be noted, whatever may have been the reasons for Galen's use of animals closely resembling man instead of man himself, his anatomy clearly is at variance with that of the Alexandrian physicians. For, after all, "the motive for dissecting human cadavers is the conviction that human and animal bodies are incomparable" (ibid., p. 296) and therefore that animal dissection is simply irrelevant to human anatomy.

In these terms, too, it must be said, the significance of the reintroduction of dissection in the early 14th century, despite Galen's great influence, is that the Galenic hypothesis of the comparability of certain animal bodies and the human body is once again rejected, if only implicitly. It had once again, it seems, become necessary for physicians to dissect human cadavers in order to practice medicine correctly.

That vivisection is regarded as "monstrous" and impossible to perform, on the other hand, must be understood more in reference to the prevailing religious and cultural values than to any motive or value inherent to medicine. Indeed, as Edelstein remarks, "the elucidation of facts is not more conditioned by Christian doctrine than by any other philosophical doctrine" (ibid., p. 265). The church, in fact, functioned in precisely the same way as ancient philosophies, which provided the break from ancient prohibitions and thus prepared the way for the Alexandrian anatomists. But the practice of dissection and vivisection had additionally to be regarded by physicians as essential to medicine itself, and just this was the core conviction of those physicians in ancient times, empiricists (such as Herophilus) and dogmatists (such as Erasistratus) alike.

By the time of Mondino, the prevailing understanding of medicine was in effect a renewal of those ancient dogmatic convictions. Not only did dissection become seen as essential, but those very same beliefs strongly suggest the positive need for vivisection as well—or, failing that, the need for what can only be regarded as secondary substitutes for human vivisection, such as "actual practice" (Celsus) in treating the wounded and the sick, or, as in Descartes's time, animal vivisection (the main way, he reported, by which he came to see for himself the truth of Harvey's discovery of circulation).

In substance, then, the rationale for connecting clinically observed symptoms with findings at autopsy (the key notion behind Morgagni's and Bichat's work) was already present, if only implicitly, in the much earlier

Alexandrian period. What seems to have baffled earlier physicians was the basic limits of dissection—that only the dead body is observed—and the impossibility of conducting vivisections as a way of getting at the liveliness of the living body.

It can thus be surmised that the real significance of Morgagni's and Bichat's works is that they proposed a way of circumventing the long-felt need for vivisection. Clinical observations become, more explicitly than ever before, a kind of surrogate for vivisection, for they are made, as it were, with an eye on the eventual corpse and what dissection will then disclose. Clinical-pathological correlation comes into place as the most effective substitute for vivisection.

THE RETREAT OF LIFE (SOUL)

Post-Cartesian physicians endorsed either a materialism or, more frequently, a dualism. The latter, although different in significant ways from the dualisms of antiquity, in effect makes the same point: The true nature of man in life is soul (mind or person) and not body (or matter). What happens to the body, especially after death, can be of no consequence whatever (aside perhaps from vestigal values regarded as extraneous to medicine, which in any case slowly gave way as well).

If anything, in fact, this later dualism provides an even more persuasive legitimacy for dissection, precisely by endorsing a strictly mechanistic view of the human body. For, as the body is presumed able to be considered merely "in itself," apart from its "intimate union" with the soul, it is taken as nothing but extended matter in motion definable by mathematical, quantitative formulae. There is then no more reason not to dissect it than there would be not to dismantle a clock. Indeed, if one wishes to know the body scientifically, such dismantling or dissecting must be done in order to see how it "works."

The human body thus emerges in modern times as a mere mechanism, the furthest from anything akin to soul or to life. As Descartes knew well, this body is not at all the body that is "intimately united" with the mind in daily life. As Friedrich Hoffmann would later say, motion alone is what moves the body parts and is that which defines health and disease. Whatever there is in the way of value, quality, and life will be found solely either in physical motion (which seems patently absurd) or else solely within the mind. Both alternatives, we saw, make it necessary to abstract body and mind, respectively, from one another, and thus neither is capable of understanding or conceiving the "intimate union"—that is, the full embodied person actually encountered in ordinary life and in clinical settings. As Jonas might well have remarked, the modern efforts to define life in physical terms wind up inevitably with a *ludibrium materiae.*

This entity, the soul or mind, van den Berg observed, thus becomes historically a profound enigma, amenable neither to the methods of medicine nor science. Neither is it open in any objective way to observation, and therefore it is inevitably regarded as closed to genuine knowledge. Little wonder that Bichat would find himself so utterly "confused" by patients even after "twenty years" of talking with and observing them. Nor is it surprising that he would be so noticeably relieved by "opening up a few corpses."

There are several important landmarks in this historical development that should be mentioned. In 1440, Nicholas of Cusa, a cardinal of the church, wrote his famous treatise *De docta ignorantia*. As Alexandre Koyré has pointed out (1957, pp. 5–24), this work had already succeeded in fracturing the closed world of medieval cosmology and theology well before the work of Nicholas Copernicus. Cusa urged that since the extent of the physical universe is "indefinite" (interminate = *interminatum*), no "center" can be found. This formative idea of medieval cosmology therefore "loses its unique, determinate position" (ibid., p. 9). Consistent with this, Cusa insisted that in this physical universe there can be neither stability, precision, nor certainty; therefore, *anywhere* could as well be "center" as *anywhere else*. Indeed, Cusa relentlessly pursued this theme, concluding (with remarkably contemporary insight) that wherever the observer is at any moment, *there* is the "center"; that is, no place has privilege over any other. It will invariably be seen by any observer that he is at the "center," whether, Cusa remarks, he be on Mars, the Earth, or the Sun (ibid., pp. 16–18). Given that basic relativity, Cusa also observed that there can be no internal hierarchy in this universe. Therefore, God, Who is absolute and perfect, cannot be within the physical universe. He is, rather, "everywhere and nowhere": literally (physically) nowhere, and literally (spiritually) everywhere.

By the time of Descartes, scarcely two centuries later, the soul or mind comes to have very much the same enigmatic place within its own body. No anatomist had succeeded in locating either the soul or its former place of residence, although different "places"—the heart, the fourth ventrical of the brain, the pineal gland—were postulated.

In fact, as we have seen, Galen had already come to recognize that the Platonic idea of soul was not able to be incorporated within his own understanding of medicine (except, we saw, on condition that it be regarded as a "temperament of the body"). Clearly, this was not what Plato understood it to be, and it is just this idea that Galen concluded he could not reconcile with medical theory. Descartes himself had tried to maintain that the soul interacts with the body both in the pineal gland and throughout the body (in all the "little tubes," i.e., nerves). Since (like God, for Cusa) the soul is utterly unlike the body (Cusa: the physical universe), the soul is in effect everywhere ("mentally," in the manner of soul) and nowhere ("physically," in the manner of matter). Like God in Cusa's work, in Whom all "hierarchies" and qualities subsist spiritually, so the mind in Descartes's metaphysics and in later physicians' dualistic theories, in which all values, qualities, and hierarchies exist. Beauty and every other quality can only be "in" the mind. If there is in modern times a "flight of the gods" (i.e., decreasing reliance on transcendence as a principle for accounting for worldly or mundane things), it is matched in these terms by a kind of retreat of the soul from its own body and from the surrounding world of physical nature.

Coordinate with these developments, there is another of equal significance. Beginning with Francis Bacon, as is well known, there is a shift in the understanding of the relations between theory and practice, away from the way these were conceived in classical times (see Jonas, 1966). Hitherto, at least in philosophy and theology, *theoria* had to do with the changeless, or eternal, true reality or Being (from the Forms of Plato, to the Divine in Aquinas), whereas *praxis* designated the mutable, variable, sensory world of mere appearances. To know (*episteme*) meant to contemplate the eternal Being; to act or work (*techne*) in the sphere of *praxis* meant to bring about changes in, on, or among particular things or mere appearances (but even these changes were themselves understood as in-*forming* matter with an eternal, changeless form).

With Bacon, however, all that decisively changed. Regarding classical times as the mere boyhood of man, productive (as Bacon claims) of contentions but not of useful inventions (i.e., technology), Bacon urged that knowledge must be married to power in the specific effort to enable mankind to surmount the miseries of its natural estate (famines, plagues, epidemics). Nature is to be not so much understood, then, as mastered; or, rather, nature is known precisely by mastering it. Just this significant theme, Richard Kennington has argued, is the real motive force behind Descartes's work as well, especially in connection with his claim that medicine is the chief end of knowledge (just as health is the chief good for man) (1978, pp. 201–31).

THE IMPROVEMENT OF MAN

This leitmotiv may well be at the heart not merely of Cartesian medicine and all it later inspired, but also of medicine more generally. Although the usual characterization of the ancient Greek philosophical understanding of *theoria* and *praxis* is surely correct, ancient medicine may well be, or include, a significant exception to that.

Specifically, the crucial theme of dietetics is already understood in the earliest Hippocratic works as a means for improving human life. It is, moreover, a prominent theme in Galen's works. Oswei Tempkin emphasizes, for instance, that Galen clearly saw the potential for understanding dietetic medicine as including an inherent "moral aspect." Since it interprets most diseases as caused by errors of regimen (thus, as avoidable), health "becomes a responsibility and disease a matter for possible moral reflection" (1973, p. 40).

As we have already seen, passion, desire, and even the rational soul were regarded by Galen as temperaments of the body. Temperament depends on a person's own disposition and regimen; therefore, Tempkin emphasizes, a "wise diet, medicaments, and study can be of great help." To acknowledge the dependence of conduct on bodily temperaments is to "clear the path for using bodily factors [temperaments] to elevate man beyond the possibilities of purely moral teaching" (ibid., p. 85). In this way, dietetic medicine became for Galen the most powerful support for moral philosophy.

I am suggesting that classical medicine was not at all focused simply on the cure of disease, nor simply on the acquisition of knowledge (even though the latter, in dogmatic and empiricist doctrines, does receive priority); nor does it simply incorporate the philosophical assumptions about knowledge without further ado. It shows another, quite powerful motif: the very concrete, very particular, indeed very individual improvement of human beings by means of medically invoked regimens that are therapeutically designed and justified through "actual practice." In other words, actual changes are brought about in an individual. Though this is not the place to explore this theme, it may well be that medical knowledge, tied so closely to therapeutics, in effect constitutes a quite different epistemology from that more commonly known in the philosophical schools. However that may be, there is another aspect to this theme that is critical for us.

Even the earlier Hippocratic texts, the Hippocratic oath in particular, articulate the theme of improvement. Galen, in fact, may well have been picking up on just this feature of those ancient texts, which maintained that most illnesses are due to opulent living. If disease occurs, health is destroyed, and the body requires purification through medicine (as the sick soul needed purification through music). The patient's regimen has to be changed by dietetic prescriptions, for his own good. Underlying that theme—acting so as to benefit the patient for his own good—is the "fundamental truth: everything that is given to the body creates a certain disposition of the soul" (Edelstein, p. 25). However, the Hippocratic physician also believed that people generally do not understand that "truth," do not know that every sort of drink or food brings about a certain mental disposition, however slight the variations among different people may be. "But the physician knows this—his art primarily consists in this knowledge" (ibid.) As we will see later, the Hippocratic oath explicitly recognizes this, in its injunction that the physician protect his patient from the self-inflicted mischiefs to which we all are endemically prone from poorly chosen dietary regimens. Thus, "he must be a physician of the soul no less than of the body," and this included being alert to the moral implications of medical actions (ibid.).

From this, it is a short step to the Galenic addition: that dietetics can and must be used not only for those already in difficulty and ill, but more generally as a device to improve man beyond what is possible by mere moral instruction. This motif, it seems clear, is not far away from Bacon's later recognition that knowledge establishes a sphere of influence and control over things known simply by virtue of their being known—from which follows naturally the Baconian idea that knowledge and power must become "one."

This motif has special significance for our study, since it is medicine after all (as Descartes seems to have realized) that is concerned with sickness (plagues, epidemics) and the body (whether starving or too opulent) and thus is the human enterprise most directly concerned with and capable of such power and "mastery." It is medicine that must seek the causes of disease, deal with epidemics, and devise many of the "inventions" to improve the natural estate of mankind.

CHAPTER 8

Ethics in Ancient Medicine

It is difficult to know just how to assess clinical medicine in the light of the historical themes that it seemed necessary to probe. Perhaps it is time, then, to take stock.

We as a people have come to be especially concerned with, even obsessed by, issues that we commonly designate as moral or ethical. While this is surely not restricted to occasions of illness—indeed, the concern shows up regarding almost every facet of contemporary life—it is nevertheless true that these situations have a particular urgency for us. In a way, it is this peculiarity that prompted the present study: Why is it that illness, injury, or the circumstances of genetic or congenital damage provoke such serious moral concern and are the occasion for profound and centering feelings and apprehensions? The question crops up on both sides, that of medicine and that of patients and their families. As we've seen time and again, the question has numerous facets on both sides.

MEDICAL MORALITY AND MEDICAL POWER

Although the forceful assertion that medicine is indeed an inherently moral enterprise has been explicitly and repeatedly made by physicians themselves in more recent times, it is hardly a startling piece of news. Nor, for that matter, is it a point that became obvious to physicians only with the remarkable development and deployment of the powerful technologies of our times—even though these do, quite obviously, give a sharp edge to our moral concerns.

Our historical explorations into medicine's history show that a profound sense of the moral character of actions by professed, would-be healers is present in even the earliest recorded documents, the Hippocratic corpus. As there are rivalries regarding the alternatives for interpreting symptoms and treating patients, so are there far-reaching conflicts concerning the understanding of that moral character. In somewhat simplified terms, the basic conflict concerned whether this moral dimension of medical actions was inherent or extrinsic to them. As is especially clear within the history of anatomy (dissection and, in particular, vivisection), whereas the ancient empiric (and, later, the Hellenistic methodist or skeptic) tended toward the former understanding, the ancient dogmatic (and, later, both the Hellenistic empiricist and dogmatist) tended toward the latter.

In some part, this difference is a matter of what healers took the art itself to be—whether primarily a matter of knowledge (*episteme*) or of therapy (*therapeia*), that is, whether patients should have priority or, on the contrary, the art itself as a mode of knowledge is prior. Within this, we've had to recognize, is a complex of impacted issues, centered around just how the healer should understand the patient. For if, as was maintained consistently by the ancient empiric and later methodist, the patient is strictly the unique individual, with his or her own specific idiosyncrasies and personal biography, then the healer's encounter and the art itself must be conceived as equally unique for each patient. What counts for the healer, thus, are the differences each patient displays, since the healer's task is precisely to help (*therapeia*) each patient as *this* individual.

However, as was maintained by some early empirics, as well as by the later empiricists and dogmatists, if the patient, even though an individual, is understood as a type or kind, then the healer's encounter and the art itself must be conceived as primarily a mode of knowledge. What counts for the healer, here, are the similarities among admittedly different patients, and since what is common or similar among patients can be apprehended only by means of *episteme*, the healing relationship—a mode of therapy—must have disease as its focus. What makes the patient of medical interest, thus, is not the differences of biography or life-style but the fact that there is a disease to be treated. A disease is knowable and classifiable by logic (the dogmatics: "logical classification of disease") or at least by rationalized experience (the empiricists: "grades of probablism") in advance of the patient encounter and without regard for the individualizing characteristics of each patient.

Lest this difference in conception and approach to the patient be considered merely a quirk of ancient disputations—and irrelevant anyway, as is commonly heard nowadays, since effective treatments for diseases did not come about until very recent times—it is interesting to reflect on what provoked Eric Cassell's fascinating and important study *The Healer's Art* (1976, reissued 1985). While conducting a public health seminar on cross-cultural medicine, he reports, "it suddenly occurred to me that the central belief of our medical subculture was disease! Then it followed," he continues, "that modern concepts of disease are not 'the Truth' but simply a useful way of organizing observations of reality" (ibid., p. 15). Discovering that these ways of organizing and thinking about the many manifestations of illness that patients bring to doctors are not "the Truth," even though they have proven to be quite successful, Cassell came then to the idea that illness and disease may not be the same thing.

Not just a little stunned by this "revelation"—for it seemed to contradict everything in his, and every other physician's, intensive scientific and technological training—Cassell reflected that physicians seem so inured to looking for the cause of the disease that "the cause of illness is inevitably confused with the phenomenon of illness itself" (ibid., p. 16). This brought about the realization that the same is true of "healing" and "curing": If the sick person does indeed show both "disease" and "illness," then the "doctor must respond with two separate functions" (ibid.).

To the doctor who does not distinguish between illness and disease, helping a patient with pneumonia become better *means* curing the disease. Of course, if the doctor does not kill the bacteria or bring down the fever, "it will be bad news for the patient" (ibid.). There are other aspects of illness that may be ignored: being afraid and vulnerable, being cut off from friends and family, or being uncommonly reliant on other people (mostly strangers, as we noted). All too often, patients are left to their own devices to cope with these aspects of illness, at times when their own resources are at low ebb. Doctors are too often unaware of these aspects of illness or consider them beyond their competence (they probably were never trained to deal with them anyway) (ibid., p. 17).

Cassell's concern then focused on two things about the contemporary physician's experience. On the one hand, medicine's very success in combating the infectious diseases may have contributed to the "disappearance of healing as part of the doctor's manifest function" (ibid.). The effectiveness of cure, along with the consequently acquired public repute of medicine, has had the effect of muting the healing function by making it appear as not very important in such cases. On the other hand, the diseases with which we are most concerned today—heart disease, cancer, stroke and a few others—"offer many examples in which cure is impossible and the healing function of paramount importance" (ibid.).

Cassell's (and other physicians') insistent concern about illness and disease and curing and healing mirror precisely the ancient dispute in medicine. Indeed, the dispute is captured most poignantly in the traditionally accorded place of dietetics. As we've seen, not only the ancient empirics and later skeptics but even Galen understood disease to be primarily the result of bad living. But the interesting thing about this, for our present purposes, is not the dietetics so much as the implications it harbors for the relationship between the physician and the patient. As we noted, the ancient Hippocratic empiric's understanding of dietetics was primarily, if not exclusively, therapeutic: a corrective for the bad living that led the specific patient to have the presented illness. By the time of Galen, however, it had become quite clear that dietetics was not merely therapeutic but also meliorative; it implies not only that the results of bad living can be corrected, but more importantly that dietetics can, and for Galen must, be used before illness is even present.

There are several crucial facets to dietetics. On the one hand, there is the Galenic emphasis on dietetics as a support for moral life, far more effective indeed than mere moral encomiums or instruction. It is, in fact, the thesis that the medical use of bodily factors can "elevate man beyond the possibilities of purely moral teaching" (Tempkin, 1973, p. 85). In this respect, Galenic dietetics is an early form of almost eugenic thinking: the improvement of the human lot by medical means (see also Edelstein, p. 355–56).

On the other hand, however, it is important to note as well that so far as dietetics can be used in advance of presented illness, it is also an early form of preventive medicine. Thus, whether or not the human condition can be altered by medical means, medicine can (and should) be used to prevent the ravages of illness by means of judiciously worked out dietetic prescriptions for individuals.

The significant thing here, however, is not so much the various medical implications of dietetics—whether therapeutic, eugenic, or preventive—but rather the recognition of medical power, which necessarily underlies any of these uses. And here, even the earliest empirics must be regarded as profoundly aware of the power that the healer has over the patient. It is, indeed, in just this respect that the Hippocratic oath must be understood.

THE HIPPOCRATIC OATH AND MEDICAL MORALITY

Since its formulation in the fourth century B.C., the Hippocratic oath has been the topic of frequent interpretation and analysis. With the modern interest in historical studies, and its refined tools of historical research, these interpretations have also been somewhat controversial. The very fact that the oath has for centuries been the exemplary code of ethical self-understanding among most physicians obliges us to give it serious reflection. For this, as for other matters in ancient medicine, Ludwig Edelstein's lucid study is our best interpretive guide (1967, pp. 4–63).

Edelstein's main purposes are to establish as clearly as possible the date of the oath and to identify philosophical movement with which it is most closely allied. For it is, in Edelstein's judgment, philosophy that "influenced medicine rather than being influenced by it" (ibid., p. 350). This was so, however, not so much for the majority of physicians in the Graeco-Roman world—who remained little more than craftsmen—but very much so for a relatively small number of medical men who "aspired to overcome the narrow limits of their craft" (ibid., p. 351) and whose work set the tone and standards for subsequent medical history. Whether exploring the anatomy of the human body, seeking principles of biology and physiology, or engaging in questions of life and death, these physicians were not only deeply influenced by philosophy but "were themselves philosophers, as in Galen's opinion the true physician should be" (ibid., p. 353).

In brief, Edelstein's inquiry shows rather conclusively, it seems to me, that the Hippocratic oath was written during the fourth century B.C.; careful analysis of it shows that it is the adaptation "of Pythagorean teaching to the specific task of the physician" (ibid., p. 39). It is a document "uniformly conceived and thoroughly saturated with Pythagorean philosophy. In spirit and in letter, in form and in content, it is a Pythagorean manifesto" (ibid., p. 53).

Edelstein's argument is most persuasive, probably even conclusive. However that may be, what interests me here is his astute line-by-line analysis of the oath. As Edelstein suggests, it is divided into two parts. The first states the covenant binding the pupil of medicine to his teacher and his teacher's family—the transmission of the art more generally. The second part gives certain rules that must be observed in the treatment of patients—a short summary of medical morality. As the latter is most relevant here, I turn to it first.

The Ethical Code

The oath has two different sorts of rules, one set rather specific, the other more general.

Specific rules. The oath requires that "I will neither give a deadly drug to anybody if asked for it, nor will I make a suggestion to this effect. Similarly, I will not give to a woman an abortive remedy." (ibid., p. 6). What is striking about these prohibitions of suicide and abortion is that they were not at all common beliefs of the wider public or of most physicians. Abortion was a common practice in Greek no less than in Roman times; it was used at times "without scruple" (ibid., p. 13). The same is pretty much true of suicide, for many physicians apparently "felt no compunction" about giving poison to their patients who asked for it (ibid.).

The sick person apparently wished to be certain about whether further treatment would be of any avail; it was the physician's task to render this verdict. Hence, patients would often consult with the physician or urged their friends to do so. If treatment were judged to be of no avail, many physicians would suggest, directly or indirectly, that the patient commit suicide. Euthanasia, as a voluntary act seen to be preferable to prolonged pain and suffering, was an everyday reality in antiquity. The Hippocratic physician, however, pledges not to supply his patient with poison if asked, nor even to suggest that he take it. The oath specifically prohibits the physician from recommending or participating in suicide in such cases. The same is true of abortion; whereas it was commonplace among other physicians, the oath specifically prohibits it.

These two prohibitions are followed immediately by a vow: "In purity and holiness I will guard my life and my art" (ibid., p. 6). This pledge contains a more fundamental consideration shedding light on the prohibitions. While "purity" can be understood as a quality insisted on by a physician who is fully conscious of the obligations of the art, holiness seems quite another matter, belonging "to another realm of values and . . . indicative of standards of a different, a more elevated character" (ibid., p. 15). The fuller context of the oath makes this quite clear, for it concludes that the physician who fulfills it will be "honored with fame among all men for all time to come" and condemned if it is violated (ibid., p. 6). This "all time to come" goes far beyond the dictates of civil law, the common religion, or even the obligations stemming from the art itself.

There is here a specific philosophical conviction and its implied basis for the moral conduct of the healer who takes the oath: Pythagoreanism. "For indeed among all Greek thinkers, the Pythagoreans alone outlawed suicide and did so without qualification . . . and the same can be asserted of the rule forbidding abortion and rejecting it without qualification" (ibid., pp. 17–18). For them, suicide was regarded as a sin against god; it was a divine commandment to live, and the most severe punishment awaited those who sought release through suicide. Abortion was regarded similarly. As the embryo was viewed as an animate being from the moment of conception, so its destruction through abortion was condemned. At the heart of this "purity and holiness" was the "Pythagorean 'way of life'," which promulgated an "ascetic rigorism" regarding both life and sexual matters (ibid., pp. 19–20).

General rules. The more general part of the ethical code (which is also, Edelstein argues, Pythagorean) concerns the treatment of patients; it includes rules for treating diseases and regulating the physician's behavior toward the patient and the patient's family. Mention is made of diet (dietetics), drugs (pharmacology), and cutting (surgery). Of these, only the first two were viewed as proper for the physician.

"I will," the oath states, "apply dietetic measures for the benefit of the sick according to my ability and judgment; I will keep them from harm and injustice" (ibid., p. 6). The first vow seems obvious enough; the physician is enjoined to act solely for the benefit of his patients. The second, however, is curious, especially as it does not mention harms that others may do his patients, nor those that the physician himself might do. What is asserted is the pledge to "guard his patients against the evil which they may suffer through themselves," for it is a major thesis of the Pythagoreans that "men by nature are liable to inflict upon themselves injustice and mischief," and this is so in two respects of central concern to the physician (ibid., pp. 22–23).

In the first place, bodily appetites are understood as propensities of the soul, cravings for the presence or absence of certain things. Whether acquired or native, appetites tend to increase indefinitely. Just this presents the problem for the physician: To overload oneself with food or drink is to court unhealthiness and disease. Therefore, it is necessary "to select the nourishment of the body with great caution, to determine its quality and quantity most carefully, a supreme wisdom entrusted to the physician" (ibid., p. 24). But, in the second place, such mismanagement of diet is an acquired inclination of the soul, hence there is a moral element involved. "Unhealthy desire is uncontrolled desire," and therefore decisions must be made between those appetites that ought to be satisfied and those that ought to be disregarded, both as regards positive actions and negative ones (i.e., what must be avoided) (ibid.).

In both respects, dietetics is central. The physician must, as the oath says, use dietetic means, choosing them with his patient's benefit foremost in mind. The "true follower of Pythagorus" must always keep "one fundamental truth" in mind, that everything given to the body brings about a certain disposition of the soul. As we already saw, even though most people do not know this, except in a general way, this knowledge is what defines the art. Accordingly, the Hippocratic physician is obliged to make sure that "the soul of the sick, through a wrong diet, does not fall into 'idle, irreverent, harmful and licentious passions' " (ibid., p. 25). It is for this reason that the physician must tend to the soul as well as to the body, and in so doing he must not forget the moral implications of medical actions. The physician is entrusted with the task of keeping his patients from self-inflicted mischief and injustice.

Clearly, the same was true regarding drugs. The physician must use these solely with the patient's benefit in mind. He must keep patients from misuse and abuse of drugs, as much as from improper diets, and the mischief and injustice they would thereby bring on themselves.

Although the ban on lithotomy presents more difficulties for interpretation, Edelstein's argument is that this, too, is Pythagorean in origin. Surgery in general is not considered to be part of the physician's business, except possibly as a last resort, when neither dietary means nor drugs are effective in helping a patient regain his health. Surgery is not condemned, but the physician is not himself allowed to do it. If necessary, then, one's patient must be referred to others for surgery. Edelstein surmises that this may have arisen from the Pythagoreans' aversion to bloody sacrifices; they thought these were defilements of divinity, and perhaps by extension any spilling of blood was similarly regarded.

The oath includes two other general stipulations: about behavior toward the patient and the patient's family and the vow of silence. As for the first, the oath requires that the physician's relation to any sick person must be for one purpose only—to help that person. Hence, the physician forswears any other relationship with the patient or his family: he must refrain from all injustice, mischief, and, especially, sexual incontinence with men or women, patient or family.

Of particular significance here is the characteristic way in which the virtues of justice (*dike*) and forbearance (*sophrosyne*) are blended. For the Pythagorean physician, relationships with patients must always be governed by these virtues; they mark out the core of medical morality in the oath. While the Pythagoreans included in this both civic and political aspects (as with Plato and Aristotle), justice, blended with forbearance, was regarded as "the social virtue par excellence" (ibid., p. 36). Not only were all relations among people thought to have some kind of justice involved, but more fundamentally, Edelstein argues, acting properly required that one "differentiate according to circumstances," with speech and action variable depending on "the particular situation and the persons concerned." Thus, "from the right decision result timeliness, appropriateness, and fitness of behavior" (ibid., p. 37).

This peculiar blend of justice and forbearance, indeed, captures the core responsibilities of the physician toward his patient in daily life (although Edelstein initially states this as the "blend" of the two, he subsequently mentions only justice, which seems to me something of an oversight). In this, there is a keen sense of what is, in our phrase used earlier, circumstantially appropriate—that is, of what is just (*dike*) and what is judged to be, with forbearance, as appropriate or fitting (*sophrosyne*) as possible.

It is precisely this sense, finally, that lies behind the dictum regarding the vow of silence. The oath states: "What I may see or hear in the course of the treatment or even outside of the treatment in regard to the life of men, which on no account one must spread abroad, I will keep to myself" (ibid., p. 6). In other words, silence is a matter of moral obligation, not simply prudent precaution. At its core, we might say, is an obligation to respect the integrity of one's patients and their families: to act justly and fittingly at all times.

The Moral Covenant

The first part of the Hippocratic oath sets out, by covenant, the sacred agreement about medical education and the transmission of the art. Promising to regard his teacher as equal to his own parents, the student in effect promises to share his life with him: to support his teacher with money if he should need it and to regard his teacher's children as equals to his own brothers, teaching them the art without fee should they wish to learn it. He then obliges himself to transmit the art to no others but his own sons, those of his teacher, and anyone else who agrees to the oath.

Thus, the relationship between pupil and teacher is set down as the "closest and most sacred relationship that can be imagined between men, and . . . for no other apparent reason than that the pupil is being instructed in the art" (ibid., p. 40). In these respects, too, Edelstein contends, the oath is clearly Pythagorean. It is, then, a document manifesting an evident unity, its purpose being to lay out a program of medical morality concerned with the major facets of the art: medical instruction, transmission of the art, commitments about life and death, obligations for treating disease, and relationships to patients and their families. It is a solemn and sacred agreement in that it is not forced on anyone, but is rather accepted and pledged by an individual from his or her own free will.

HIPPOCRATIC MORALITY

Several aspects of the Hippocratic oath call for careful consideration. In the first place, as we have already emphasized, the place of dietetics is clearly central and governing here. There are two points that deserve particular attention: (1) The "one fundamental truth" is that "everything that is given to the body creates a certain disposition of the soul." Although people in general have some awareness of this "truth," the physician knows that every sort of food and drink "causes a certain mental habit." (2) Therefore, there is a "supreme wisdom entrusted to the physician," which consists not merely in knowing what is the proper diet for the body, but more fully what its impact is on the soul. The Hippocratic physician must therefore be a "physician of the soul no less than of the body," and this implies that medicine is an inherently moral enterprise.

Secondly, the oath's stipulations concerning the physician's relationship to patients and their families is governed by a specific blend of virtues: justice and forbearance or restraint. Justice was regarded as the social virtue par excellence, which is expressed in the Pythagorean doctrine that in every kind of relation with others it is possible to take "a well-timed and an ill-timed attitude" (ibid., pp. 36–37). The "just decision" is the one that is made "according to circumstances," respecting the variations of each situation and the persons involved and adjusting one's speech and actions accordingly. It is, thus, a "right decision" so far as it results in "timeliness, appropriateness, and fitness of behavior," therefore from justice blended with forbearance.

Finally, the oath sets out "the closest and most sacred relationship that can be imagined between men, and it does so for no other apparent reason than that the pupil is being instructed in the art." The practice of the art, therefore, seems to these physicians a most unique and demanding enterprise. While the virtues of justice and forbearance are inherent to every social relationship, that specific social relationship between physician and patient, and between physician and pupil, is sacred, such that the practitioner must be bound by moral covenant. Within these relationships, justice and forbearance are transformed into something more elevated and more demanding than is found in the common sorts of social relationships.

Entrusted Wisdom

Bodily appetites are propensities of the soul. Most of these, however, are acquired by people in the course of their lives. Since they tend naturally to indefinite increase and extravagance, these appetites and passions need to be watched and scrutinized closely, even severely. Extravagance and opulence are natural outcomes of the bodily appetites and result in illness and destruction of the body if left unchecked. Correcting these results requires a change in dietary regimen; Hippocratic therapeutics consisted mainly in dietetic prescriptions for sick people.

But the sick were not the only ones with whom these physicians had to be concerned. For if the bodily passions tend of themselves to become "idle, irreverent, harmful and licentious" (ibid., p. 23), "right living" requires that "from early youth on, one must learn to hold in contempt those things are 'idle and superfluous' " (ibid., pp. 23–24). Since the Hippocratic physician alone has the kind of knowledge required for "right living"—both for what does positive harm and for the avoidance of what is dangerous and unhealthy for people—he is concerned not only for the sick but also for those who are not yet sick (and who, if left to themselves, would tend to give in to their own natural and insatiable desires). "Supreme wisdom," then, consists in knowing both the positive and the negative harms (what one does and what one does not do) that result from the quantity and quality of nourishments; both the bodily passions and the mental dispositions they create; both the body and the soul.

Clearly, the physicians committed to the Hippocratic oath saw themselves as involved with other people in the most intimate ways, sometimes called upon to make decisions reaching far beyond the application of mere technical knowledge and skill. Possessing (or claiming to possess) knowledge of the detailed interactions between the soul and the body clearly implies an awareness of the potential for control that the physician has relative to his patients. This awareness is not only striking as regards the knowledge of the patient's body and soul, but more broadly in what the physician comes to know about the patient's life, past and present. For the physician not only enters the patient's sphere of immediate intimacy (body and soul), but also into that of his household and family.

The Hippocratic oath, we have to recall, is an empiric document, and in ancient empiric medicine (which, as was seen, is continued in later skeptic or methodist medicine) the healer is conceived as the servant of the bodily *physies*, and the patient's body is viewed as integral with the patient himself. The physician is not viewed as being the agent of cure; medicine is not interventionist. It is rather the body itself that is "the physician of diseases," and the physician's task is to support and encourage the bodily *physies* in their own native efforts to throw off the disease. The potential power implied by the physician's knowledge of the soul-body whole, however, is from the outset under the profound restraint of the art itself and its requirements regarding interrelationships with patients. That is, "supreme wisdom entrusted to physicians" is set within the requirements for that peculiar blend of "justice" and "forbearance" (self-control, temperance).

Nevertheless, the very fact of their mention within the oath points to the need for the physician to recognize this very potential for control and power over patients, that is, that the art itself is by its nature most potent and must be recognized and respected as such. Because of its potential power and its involvement with sick people and their families in the most intimate ways, medicine seems inherently to tempt practitioners to see themselves as superior to their patients. Again, however, for the ancient empiric healer, the very point of medicine is that it is for the sake of patients: therapy. *Precepts* observes, "Where there is love of man, there is also love of the *techne*" (chap. VI, in Coulter, vol. I, 1975, p. 282); the idea that the physician is superior to the patient is alien to the central tenets of empiric medicine and therefore to the oath. The ancient empiric (and later skeptic) saw himself as fundamentally governed by the good of the patient, as serving the patient's own needs. In this, Coulter stresses, empiric medicine "is a *method of treating* the sick organism" and therefore gaining knowledge of it. "Its function is purely curative, and . . . is oriented toward the patient" (ibid., p. 502). The art of medicine is not in the first place understood in relation to what it is for the physician, but rather for the patient.

The conception of medicine underlying and informing the oath—ancient empiric medicine—is precisely what Edelstein, as well as Coulter, acknowledge as perhaps the most difficult and problematic one. As we saw earlier, the intrinsic skepticism present already, if only implicitly, in earlier empiric medicine, has its roots in medical experience and knowledge, which include neither general laws nor certainty. Completely oriented toward the individual patient, this physician found treatment difficult "because of the necessarily individualized character of knowledge and treatment, which allowed no criterion in medicine except the patient's subjective experience" (Edelstein, 1967, p. 189).

In Coulter's terms, this view requires "the expenditure of time and intellectual effort" and demands "a degree of emotional involvement with the patient" (vol. I, 1975, p. 504). It relied strictly on sensory observations of, and continuous discourse with, patients themselves. Even though rigorously organized, such empiric knowledge was "not qualitatively different from the knowledge applied in many other spheres of activity," such as carpentry, cobbling, or shipbuilding (ibid.). "Good results in medicine were (and are still) produced by a careful eye, a willingness to work hard, and the skill developed by years of experience" (ibid.). To possess such knowledge, however, could not signify a position of superiority in relation to patients, since for these physicians any patient could come to be just as proficient, just as any layman could "compete with the physician in observing the patient's symptoms" (ibid.).

The potency of the art, clear and even tempting though it surely is, is under the governance of the empiric's central commitment to the therapeutic, to being at the service of and for the benefit of patients. However, the very presence of the oath's requirements does bode a significant issue.

As Edelstein suggests, it is the very intimacy of contacts with the patient and his family that raises an essential question: "What about the patient who is putting himself and 'his all' into the hands of the physician?" How can a patient be certain that trust in the doctor (his knowledge, skill, indeed in the man himself) is warranted (Edelstein, 1967, p. 329)? If the physician is to be entrusted with such intimacies and privacies, what must he do and be to deserve that trust? Even though the ordinary citizen could, and as Edelstein observed, often did acquire medical knowledge (Edelstein, pp. 350–51), most of course did not. Hence, the question he poses on behalf of the patient is clearly a pressing one and points again to the inherent potency of medical knowledge, as well as to the temptation for the physician to view himself as superior to the patient (witness, here, the frank claim to superiority by Galen!).

According to the text *On the Physician*, written several generations after the oath, such confidence can be evoked "only if the physician asked himself what he should be like 'in regard to the soul' " (ibid.). To merit the kind of trust required for the physician to be and do what the oath requires, thus, demands that every physician must *"know thyself"*: He must embody forbearance and self-control, regularity of habits, justness and fairness, and proper behavior.

Other Hippocratic texts prescribe gentleness, kindheartedness, and charity (especially toward those who are strangers and those in financial straits) (*On Decorum*, in ibid.). The physician is furthermore enjoined to be ready at all times to call in another physician as a consultant. In brief, as *On Decorum* states, "between wisdom and medicine there is no gulf; in fact, medicine possesses all the qualities that make for wisdom" (ibid., pp. 330–31), and in the first place this requires profound self-knowledge by the physician, along with justice and forbearance.

Such "supreme wisdom," thus, lies in the nature of the art itself and reflects on patients, the physician, and the potential power (and its potential for abuse) inherent to their relationship. At the heart of it is the thera-peutic dyad of trust and care, and precisely this is the rationale for the oath itself (in its positive injunctions as well as in its requirement of silence).

Virtues of the Art

The principal generic virtues mentioned, justice (*dike*) and forbear-ance (temperance, restraint, self-control = *sophrosyne*), are often taken as the major ingredients of wisdom (*sophia*) (for example, in *On Decorum* and *On the Physician*, the earliest "introduction" to medicine). At the least they are viewed as basic to that wisdom which comprises the art in its best and purest form—which invokes self-knowledge, holiness, and purity. In these terms, these virtues constitute the defining "good" of medicine or the "goods internal to the practice" (in MacIntyre's terms).

The oath states: "Whatever houses I may visit, I will come for the benefit of the sick, remaining free of all intentional injustice, of all mischief and in particular of sexual relations with both female and male persons, be they free or slaves" (Edelstein, p. 6).

The work *On the Physician* points out that the physician must be just in all his dealings with patients, for these are serious matters. Patients put themselves into the hands of the physician, and the physician comes into contact with women and maidens, not to mention precious possessions in the household. Thus, this text goes on to require not only justice but re-straint or self-control. The oath, however, goes quite a bit further. It not only requires the avoidance of injustice, but it also excludes mischief and enjoins continence toward men and women alike, whether they are free persons or slaves.

Indeed, the oath's blend of justice and self-restraint, as we saw, di-rectly suggests an abhorrence of violence, the equality of men and women, and, in the physician's performance of his duties, nondiscrimination be-tween social ranks (ibid., p. 35). In each of these, the blend of virtues is central. Pythagorean physicians thus held to a morality far more stringent and severe than that of other ancients. For instance, sexual relations, and especially marriage, were judged strictly in terms of justice and self-restraint. To be unfaithful to one's wife or husband was to be unjust.

For physicians, however, these virtues took on unique significance. The physician's work brings him into the most intimate sorts of contact with other people. As a citizen of the polis, he is like others obliged to com-ply with justice as a civic and political virtue. But as a physician going into the households of people to treat the sick, he is required not only to act for the benefit of the sick but also to exercise extraordinary self-restraint and fairness in regard not only of his patient but also the patient's family and possessions. He must therefore be above all an honest man. Even more, however, the physician is in possession of abilities, experience, and knowl-edge that of themselves imply real potential power over those who are sick, as well as their families.

Given all this, the physician faces the central challenge and temptation of his work: the potential for taking advantage of his patients, their families, and their possessions. Not only in his medical knowledge, nor merely in his intimate contacts with the patient's family and household, but also in what he thereby learns about them, the physician is in a unique position to take advantage of these persons when they are most vulnerable and accessible.

What is thus inherent to the blend of virtues, as they define the core morality of medical practice, is a most complex moral cognizance, one easily as difficult to embody as empiric medicine was to practice. The physician had to be honest and fair; circumspect and even-tempered; tolerant and patient; calm and composed. He also had to have a strength of mind and resolve of character so as to elicit and continue to warrant the trust that patients and their families had to have toward them. He had to be poised and moderate, yet vigorous and tenacious in helping patients overcome illness. At the same time the physician had to practice severe self-restraint regarding the multiple temptations his very art itself implies.

This blend of *dike* and *sophrosyne*, then, has to be understood within the context of medicine itself, as part of its essence or "internal good." To make the right and just decisions, the physician had to be continually responsive to each specific patient's actual condition, which differs from every other patient. Hasty judgments must therefore be avoided at all costs. Each patient must be approached and dealt with as the unique, incomparable person he is, and this requires that speech and actions vary depending upon the circumstances and people involved in each case. The appropriate, fitting, and timely decision is the right decision, which can be reached only through the judicious respect for the defining individuality of each case.

The "Sacred Art"

Reference to the art as something exalted beyond the limits of the common religion or civic law occurs in two different parts of the oath. Immediately after foreswearing giving or suggesting "a deadly drug" and the proscription of abortion, the physician taking the oath swears that "in purity and holiness I will guard my life and my art" (ibid., p. 6). At the end of the oath, this is in effect repeated when the physician acknowledges that fulfilling the oath will honor him with "fame among all men for all time to come" and that violating it will bring "the opposite." In the second place, in the covenant at the beginning of the oath, the physician is obliged to acknowledge that the relationship between pupil and teacher is the closest and most sacred that can be imagined—doing so, Edelstein emphasizes, "for no other apparent reason than that the pupil is being instructed in the art" (ibid., p. 40).

As was pointed out earlier, Edelstein's analysis is mainly devoted to establishing the origin—which he argues is Pythagorean—and the date of the oath—the fourth century B.C. In the course of this, he interprets the "purity and holiness" clause as parts of the "Pythagorean way of life" (ibid., p. 20). Similarly, the sacred relationship covenanted by the oath is understood as "characteristic of Pythagorean ethics" (ibid., p. 46) in every respect. While Edelstein's argument is doubtless correct, certain features of ancient empiric medicine suggest that there may be more to this than meets the eye.

In the society of the fifth and fourth centuries B.C., before the composition of the oath in the latter part of the fourth, medicine was a craft like any other. What was required of the medical craftsman was faithful fulfillment of the aim of his art—restoring health to the body—with all other aims, such as prestige or income, regarded as secondary. Thus, properly speaking, the classical age found morality "realized in man's private life, and preeminently in his life as a citizen. Even medicine, therefore, remained impervious to moral considerations" (ibid., p. 326) in this first stage of the development of medical morality.

The oath, however, sets out a refined and sophisticated personal ethics for the physician, "a life almost saintly and bound by the strictest rules of purity and holiness" and, with it, a "morality of the highest order is infused into medical practice" (ibid., pp. 326–27). The document is thus evidence of a movement beginning in the latter half of the fourth century and extending down to the time of Galen. It is a movement that effectively shapes the ethics of medical practice "in accordance with the various systems of philosophy" and that originates in a basic "revolution of the arts and crafts and in the transformation of the medical craft into a scientific pursuit" (ibid., p. 327).

In fact, the medical Pythagoreans insisted on conceiving the crafts, medicine in particular, as inherently moral undertakings, and the craftsmen as able to partake in virtue. This gradual revolution of the crafts and arts, Edelstein remarks, was surely aided "by the fact that virtue or morality was increasingly identified not with the objective content of human actions," but rather the inner attitude and intentions of the agent (ibid., p. 328). It was thus the proper use of things (good, bad, indifferent), not the things themselves, that became the primary criterion of morality.

How this inner attitude of the human agent, that is, the virtue realized in each craft, was to be understood, Edelstein shows, depended on which philosophical doctrine was adapted to medicine by different physicians. In general, "the morality of outward performance characteristic of the classical era" had by Galen's time become "supplemented by a morality of inner intention" (ibid., p. 335). For Galen, and the dogmatic tradition generally, this meant that the true physician had to become a philosopher, for only in that way could he face patients "not only as a master of techniques, but also as a virtuoso in moral conduct" (ibid.).

But Galen, like others in dogmatic medicine, insisted on a clear distinction between the tasks of medicine itself and the reasons or motives any particular physician may have for practicing medicine. The physician's specific job is to take care of the health of the body. Some physicians do this for glory, some for money, some to be exempt from public duties, and some for love of mankind. So far as they are able to bring health to their patients, all are properly called physician. Which particular motive is given by a physician is simply a matter of personal choice. Therefore, for Galen and the dogmatic tradition, there is no intrinsic connection between that personal choice of morality and the practice of medicine.

Within this tradition, therefore, the morality of outward performance is only "supplemented" by that of inner intention—and, so long as the former is fulfilled, the latter is quite incidental and relative to the different philosophies to which any physician adheres at his own discretion. Galen even argues that the same is true for the empiricist school, which practiced medicine, it was said, for the sake of glory or of money, in accord with the "common aim of men" (ibid., pp. 333–34). In both cases, morality is incidental rather than essential to medicine, since both schools taught that there is no single or definite virtue enjoining the physician as such, except the proper outward performance required to take care of the body.

The view of the Hippocratic oath, however, is dramatically different. It lays out a morality that is asserted to be inherent to medicine itself. The physician who swears to it is thereby enjoined to a way of life regarded as *sacred*. Whether considered in relation to patients or their families, as regards the proscription of abortion and suicide, or in relation to those to be instructed in medicine, it is the art itself that is regarded as holy and must never be compromised. Here, in other words, the morality of outward performance ("etiquette") and that of inner intention or commitment ("morality") are already seen as an inseparable unity, although it remains somewhat unclear just how this sacred inner commitment (the oath and covenant) are to be understood.

Later developments in Hellenistic empiricism and dogmatism do not particularly help to make this clear; in fact, these are radical departures from the oath's central themes. To what can one turn, then, to help elucidate this core of the Hippocratic tradition, both in its ancient formulation and in its remarkable historical continuation as the central understanding of medical morality?

Edelstein contends that the oath "assumes full significance and dignity," specifically in its unifying outward performance and inner intention as moral phenomena, only from the work of Scribonius. Writing in the early first century A.D., almost a century before Galen, Scribonius spoke of the love of humanity (*philia-anthropeia*, philanthropy) as the governing norm inherent to medicine. In *On Remedies* he wrote that the true physician must "in his heart" be "full of sympathy (*misericordiae*) and humaneness (*humanitatis*) in accordance with the will (*voluntatem*) of medicine itself" (in ibid., p. 338).

Apparently influenced by, or at least echoing, the stoic philosophy of humanism developed by Panaetius in the early second century B.C. and embedded in Cicero's *On Duties*, Scribonius regarded medicine as embodying a "will" that "promises" benevolence and competency toward all men in equal measure and without distinction. Medicine, as "the knowledge of healing, not of hurting," requires that the true physician not harm anyone, not even the state's enemies. As a soldier or good citizen, he may fight for the state by any means, but not as physician, "since medicine does not judge men by their circumstances in life, nor by their character" (in ibid., p. 338). To the contrary, medicine promises "succor in equal measure to all who implore her help" and professes "never to be injurious to anyone" (ibid.).

Sympathy and love of humanity are thus among the special obligations inherent to medicine. "The one and only standard of right conduct is enforced upon him by medicine itself, just as is the standard of adequate knowledge" (ibid., pp. 338–39). To fail to fulfill his specific moral responsibility is as damaging, or even more so, to the physician and the art as it would be to fail in knowledge. It is thus hardly by chance, Edelstein notes, that Scribonius calls medicine a profession (*professio*) and not simply an art or science. This term was used to emphasize the moral dimensions of work by those engaged in the arts and crafts. Edelstein suggests that it "approximates most closely the Christian concept of 'vocation' or 'calling,' " except that, unlike for the Christian, "for the member of an ancient profession his duties result from his own understanding of the nature of his profession" and not as something ordained by God (ibid., p. 339). Nevertheless, the ethics of professional work is no less strict, for as Scribonius says, the physician is "bound in lawful obedience to medicine" no less than the soldier is by his military oath. To violate the will and promise of medicine is to transgress this moral law and thereby disqualifies such a person as physician.

Now, while Scribonius admits that this humanism seems foreign to the oath, he nonetheless argues that it is there, if only by implication. It forbids the physician to assist in a patient's suicide and prohibits giving an abortive remedy to a woman. In this, Scribonius says, the idea of the "love of humanity" has been substantially prepared: "He who thinks it . . . a crime to injure future life still in doubt, how much more criminal must he judge it to hurt a full grown human being?" (In ibid., p. 340). These virtues are not demanded of the physician alone, for all citizens are enjoined to adhere to them as well. But these "are [his] professional virtues," just as Cicero had earlier argued that "truthfulness is the distinctive virtue of him who sits in court notwithstanding the fact that it is required of everybody" (in ibid., p. 342).

Contrary to what Albert Jonsen claims, there was indeed within ancient Greek and Hellenistic medicine a strong, clear tradition of altruism, more properly of philanthropy, as the governing norm of medicine. This tradition is directly traceable, Scribonius argues, to the Hippocratic oath and its belief that medicine is fundamentally a moral, indeed sacred, enterprise. This movement, Edelstein emphasizes, in fact foreshadowed "the categories of Christian medical ethics" (ibid., p. 344–45). While it is true that pagan ethics lacked "any recognition of social responsibilities on the part of the physician," Edelstein notes that "even the gospel of brotherly love took account only of the relationship between the individual doctor and the individual patient" (ibid.). Even so, as we've observed already, the conception of the dietetics as at once therapeutic, melioristic, and preventive—especially within Galen's works—signifies that even that broader, social perspective has its roots in ancient medicine.

In any case, according to Edelstein's interpretation of the stages of ancient medical morality, Scribonius's "concept of medical ethics goes in fact beyond the demands of the classical period . . . [and] is distinct from the teaching of all the deontological treatises and all the medical sects" within the dogmatic and later empiricist traditions (ibid., p. 340). Although this concept is not explicitly within the oath, Edelstein's argument is quite convincing that it "assumes full significance and dignity only if interpreted in the way in which it was understood by Scribonius and those who came after him" (ibid., p. 347). The oath regards the art as a "sacred" covenant binding the physician to a life of "purity and holiness," which embodies specific and general norms of conduct toward patients and their families, those seeking instruction, and other physicians who have sworn the oath. What Scribonius adds to this is the uniquely lofty ideal that "envisages love of humanity as the professional virtue of the physician." This essentially amounts to the most difficult demand "that the physician should be a citizen of two states, as it were, the one here and now, where he has obligations to his country, the other 'laid up in heaven,' where he is obligated to mankind alone" (ibid.).

THE ETHICS OF METHODISM

While the Stoic roots for Scribonius's remarkable conception of medical morality cannot be denied, our brief historical study suggests that there are other roots as well, specifically those in that movement leading from ancient empiric medicine (the Hippocratics) to the works of the Hellenistic skeptics (the methodists), especially Sextus Empiricus.

It has already been pointed out how these skeptic physicians developed their views, partly from disagreement with the dogmatists and empiricists but even more from what the physician's own medical experience itself requires and demonstrates. They believed that the fundamentals of treatment should be conceived as knowledge and not simply as observation: Therapeutic experience with specific patients is already medical knowledge. The physician is required to know and to treat individuals, and individuals are necessarily different from each other in ways that are medically significant. Thus, the dogmatic and empiricist attempts to comprehend individuals in generalized terms—which presupposes a uniformity among individuals and assumes a license to ignore these differences—cannot but fail. But if the differences among individuals are medically significant, if there is no uniformity, and if the same thing is never repeated, how is the physician to know what he should do in the single, specific case?

Edelstein's conclusion to his analysis of methodism is clear and commanding. Neither dogmatism nor empiricism offered any solution, for the individual patient is ignored, being treated in terms of the "general." Skepticism offered a way out, however, for it included the central tenets of Hippocratic empiricism. Acting on skeptical ideas, the physician made "the afflictions of the human body the law governing his treatment." In so doing, "he was not letting himself be directed by a principle derived from his experience, or from his intellect, and applied to his patient." To the contrary, the physician attended strictly to each specific patient to learn what needed to be done, and in this focus on the *phainomena* "medicine was transformed" from the dogmatic and empiricist theses and renewed the ancient Hippocratic empiric insights (ibid., p. 189).

Methodism incorporates a view of medicine that suggests an underlying moral stance. Medicine is, in the first place, primarily therapeutic, although there is, assuredly, medical knowledge that is gained through its therapeutic efforts. Since the very point of medicine is to help individuals (the unique persons who come to the healer for help), therapy must be guided and governed by "the phenomena," that is, each individual case (and the specific *physies* of the individual's own body). Medical knowledge, furthermore, being derived strictly from therapeutics, must therefore concern individuals as such. Therefore, as far as medicine is concerned, the common Greek preference for the typical and its negligence of the particular, in its conception of knowledge, must be wrong. The skepticism embodied in this view "is discovered in medical practice itself and is derived solely therefrom" (ibid., p. 201). It is, as we saw, "medicine's own creation and . . . its original contribution to the development of Greek thought" (ibid., p. 201, n. 18; see also ibid., pp. 352–53).

It is also perfectly clear that skeptical physicians made a critical distinction between principles "derived from his experience or from his intellect" and those embedded "in the phenomena." To pick up on Eric Cassell's own careful distinction and to depart in a way from Edelstein, the focus of the skeptical physician's work was not only the patient's experience but also his understanding or interpretation of his own experience. To be focused on each unique individual as the very point of medical practice requires proficiency in the ways of the body in health and sickness; it also requires proficiency in cultivating and listening to patients' talk. Cassell's argument that the physician's job concerns both disease and illness, and therefore both curing and healing, is a modern-day way of saying what the ancient Hippocratic empirics and later Hellenistic skeptics knew well and incorporated into medicine as essential ingredients.

Finally, it seems no exaggeration to suggest that this complex view of the nature of the art rests on a fundamentally moral basis. What Scribonius, from mainly Stoic roots, called the love of humanity, seems at once close and yet distant: close, for surely "where there is love of man, there is love of the art"; yet distant, for such a generalization ("humanity") runs directly contrary to the central thrust of the Hippocratic oath and the movement it initiated within empiric and skeptical medicine. It is not the physician's job to "love" in the abstract, any more than it makes sense to adopt the dogmatic and empiricist assumption about the uniformity of individuals. Rather, the physician is "called" to care for each individual in his or her very uniqueness, whether (as Scribonius says) he or she be poor or rich, enemy or friend, slave or free. Thus, to practice genuine medicine is to take on, voluntarily, the responsibility of being attentive and responsive to each and every person who seeks aid and to do so in equal measure, with covenantal regard and respect for each person and his family and household.

Only "in purity and holiness" and within a covenantal understanding of the art as "sacred," it seems to me, could this kind of "love for human beings" at all occur—if, indeed, it is ever really able to be practiced by any of us. Edelstein remarks "that this ideal of professional ethics also is the one most difficult to live up to goes without saying" (ibid., p. 347). For that matter, it may be that inevitable failure is the lot of those who try to commit in any literal way to such a doctrine.

It is an ideal that has nevertheless endured, remarkably, almost unchanged in the history of medicine, an ideal that seems uniquely capable of functioning as the continuing standard of self-criticism for medicine, as William Osler saw so clearly in his last speech, "The Old Humanities and the New Science" (1920, esp. p. 13).

SUMMING UP

Several things should be noted before going any further. First, although methodism became one of the major schools in Galen's time and continued to have serious influence in medicine until the 19th century, the humanistic ideal did not apparently survive beyond the last half of the fourth century A.D., and Stoic philosophy ceased to be very influential in medicine beyond the third (Edelstein, p. 345). There are several major reasons for this, Edelstein argues. First, as Galen came to be established as the unchallenged authority in medicine, the "philosophical ethics of the scientist-physician, which had never quite lost its appeal, came to predominate among the learned" (ibid.), and this ethics was hardly compatible with the methodist's love of mankind.

Second, the ideal most likely was restricted to a small minority of physicians. This program for medicine had no backing from established institutions or organizations with the power to enforce rules of conduct (ibid., p. 347). At the same time, this makes its achievement in ethics all the more impressive, for this moral vision effectively laid the "foundation for all later medical ethics" (ibid.).

It should also be noted that while the humanistic ideal did not survive for very long, the Hippocratic tradition manifestly did survive, although its subsequent history seems to have been rocky. Even though Galen attempted to incorporate Hippocratic medicine in his effort to synthesize medical practice and knowledge, that effort ultimately failed (see Tempkin, 1973).

It seems reasonable to suggest that a good part of the reason for the failure lies in the profound inconsistency between the Galenic and the Hippocratic understanding of the connection between medicine and morality. For the former, ethics is fundamentally extrinsic to the practice of medicine, a matter of mere personal choice and thus incidental. For the latter, ethics is fundamentally intrinsic to medical practice and knowledge, essential to the "will" and "promise" of medicine. Galen thought that practically any of the innumerable philosophical ethics were legitimate for a physician, so long as he did his "outward performance" properly. For the Hippocratic physician, "outward performance" and "inner intention" were an inseparable unity based on the moral character of medicine itself to which each physician owed allegiance, first as a matter of sacred covenant, later as a member of a profession.

Galen himself had, of course, a strong and enduring sense of medical ethics. He demanded that the physician be contemptuous of money, committed to his work, just, and self-controlled. An exalted and demanding enterprise, medicine required that the physician be uncommon in intellectual prowess and drive, morally unbending, personally uncompromising—an altogether superior and meritorious person. The Galenic physician had learned that he had to serve his patient "not only as a master of techniques, but also as a virtuoso in moral conduct (Edelstein, p. 335).

But these virtues, Galen believed, needed to be distinguished from the practice of medicine itself. Fully capable physicians pursued the art for quite different reasons, and, for Galen, a distinction had to be made between "its common characteristics and those belonging to the individual practicing it" (ibid., p. 337). To fail to make that distinction was bad logic. At the same time, to make the distinction required conceiving an individual's specific morality as merely incidental rather than as essential to his practice of medicine.

Harsh as Galen and others like him may have been on themselves, then, they were unwilling to go the route laid out by Scribonius or, if my argument is correct, those empiric and skeptical physicians working to continue the basic tenets of the Hippocratic oath. Galen came to be established as the unchallenged authority in medicine, and the subsequent caste of privileged physicians (who as city officials or court physicians were granted immunity from public duties) was hardly disposed to follow the rigorous precepts of brotherly love. Thus, Edelstein concludes, Galen's "courtly" ethics and view of society "implies principles hardly compatible" with the "love of mankind" or the "brotherhood of men" (ibid., p. 346).

With that development, along with the predominance of the dogmatic ethics of the scientist-physician among the learned, the subsequent history of the Hippocratic theme—that medicine is an inherently moral, indeed sacred, discipline—could only become problematic. As attested by subsequent medical history, of course, that theme nevertheless endured as the primary foundation for all later medical ethics. Yet its very endurance alongside of, or the various attempts to incorporate it within, a Galenic conception of medicine, bequeathed to medicine a profound inconsistency—in Coulter's phrase, though I understand it somewhat differently from him, a "divided legacy," which remains in force even today.

To postulate, we can now say, that medicine is a "fusion" between these two antagonistic traditions (the skeptical-empiric and the dogmatic, or the neo-Hippocratic and the neo-Cartesian), is to adopt an ultimately incoherent view of it. More to the point of this study, such a view must by its own logic make the relationship between medicine and morality quite contingent and incidental. This, on the other hand, is deeply incongruent with the current claim that medicine is an inherently moral enterprise. I cannot rightly say nor am I particularly well qualified to say what a medical theory and practice might look like when conceived as inherently moral, while yet necessarily incorporating its many scientific and technological achievements.

Nevertheless, a serious set of themes does remain for us to explore, themes that have only hovered in the background thus far. In one sense, the question we face is, in rather more precise and direct terms, What is this "love of humanity" or *philia-anthropeia* that seems to have been foundational for medicine? In different terms, What is the moral foundation of medicine, if medicine indeed is "an inherently moral enterprise"? The other side of this issue for us is also pressing: What is an ethics that seeks to be responsive to clinical medicine all about? It is to these themes that we must now turn.

CHAPTER 9

Clinical-Liaison Ethics: Part I

It is probably safe to say that most people in this society have in one way or another had an occasion to deal with the ravages of serious illness or injury—oneself, a family member, or a close friend. On such occasions, each of us has had to contend not only with the effects of the illness or injury, but also with persons in the health professions, the institutions within which they practice, and the technologies and procedures they use. As illness ruptures the integral unity of the person, so does it often fragment families, as well as separate and even alienate people from their established lives, friends, associates, and preoccupations.

The physician, no matter how narrowly focused he or she may be on organic disruptions, thus faces a person undergoing personal, familial, and social disruptions. The organic lesion—its detection, diagnosis, and treatment—is essentially framed by and exists within that broader context. Since each of us lives within a family or a circle of intimates, that family or circle is likewise disrupted; this disruption too is ingredient to the individual's presentation as sick or injured. The facts of a case can no more be neatly compartmentalized (into medical, personal, social, economic) than can the different components of a person be clearly pigeonholed.

For an ethics seeking to be responsive to the actual contexts in which moral issues occur, it is all the more imperative to be fully cognizant of the entire range of facts and interpretations (by each of the participants), as well as the fears and hopes vested in decisions and the aftermaths of these decisions. How should such an ethics be conceived?

"WHY WON'T YOU LET ME DIE?"

As before, we should let a specific case guide our thinking.

Consider, then, the case of a 74-year-old woman, widowed for over ten years. She has two sons, both of whom are married with their own families. One son persuaded her to live in the same small town as he; the other one lives a long distance away. Some years earlier, after the death of her husband, the woman underwent serious surgery, which left her debilitated for some months. No sooner had she begun to recover enough to be up and about, however, than she began to develop serious arthritis—first in her hands and legs, then over the next seven years throughout her body. As she is reported to have said more than once: "I hurt in every joint I've got and in some I never knew I had." She tried every sort of treatment and medication available, went to specialist after specialist, but to no avail. The treatments either caused severe stomach pains ("they all make my stomach act up somethin' awful!") or other debilitating side effects (the gold salts caused extensive shingles lasting over a year, for instance).

Her arthritis became increasingly severe; so did her emphysema, the result of heavy cigarette smoking for over 40 years. It became increasingly difficult for her to get a decent breath, and any activity (walking, taking a bath, dressing) gradually but surely became difficult labor—at times additionally complicated by asthma attacks, some quite severe. Because of the labor of breathing, she grew to need more and more air conditioning in order to be even moderately comfortable.

An intelligent, sensitive, independent, and caring person, outgoing and friendly, she gradually found herself withdrawn, depressed, isolated, and dependent. Visits from her son and daughter-in-law were some compensation; the weekly bridge parties at others' homes also helped and were enjoyed as long as she could manage to get to them (driving her car was increasingly difficult, and she insisted on getting there "on my own"); and visits from her other son and his family, infrequent as they had to be, were eagerly anticipated and enjoyed. During her moments of alertness, however, she noted significant mood changes in herself, which she found personally humiliating and painful. Rare were the times of cheerfulness, happy conversations with her sons, and laughter; more common were gripes, complaints, quarrelsomeness, and spite. Her image of herself as a lively, interesting, and outgoing person deteriorated, and she more and more found herself morose, depressed, bitter—the image of all she had disliked throughout her life. That she had become increasingly reliant on her first son and his wife—for cleaning her apartment, shopping, even cooking—added bitter fuel to her complaining.

Eventually, she found she could do little more than get up from bed and sit on the couch in front of the TV—often, she merely slept on the couch. She had difficulty getting up, turning on the water faucet, opening food packaging, getting into the car. Her world had effectively shrunk to the space of her tiny living room. She had always said to her sons that she would never want to live if she could no longer "do for myself." Fiercely independent, prizing being "beholden to nobody," she now found herself facing what was for her the worst of all possible fates: a nursing home, where she would have few of "my things," little time for herself on her own terms, where everything and everyone is "run" on a schedule dictated by the needs of the home itself and not by her needs and desires. The one time she tried living with her first son proved disastrous for everyone: She was becoming more "an old crone" than the lovely, likeable grandmother she and her family pictured. Her son's family found their lives totally disrupted. With the deep love between them literally on the line, they reached the decision to move her to a nursing home—that dreaded place, symbol of loss and surrender.

Because the local nursing home had no space (nor the town any hospital) and because of the seriousness of her pulmonary function, her arthritis, her asthma, her ulcers, and her dependence on numerous medications and drugs, it was decided—most painfully—to place her in a home in the nearby urban center (30 miles away). The decision seemed the best one: She needed not only to eat regularly (she had reduced her diet to little more than soda crackers and milk while by herself), not only to have medications controlled (she often forgot which, whether, and when), not only to be helped in daily needs, but also to be close to medical help in the event of an emergency (upper respiratory infection was most feared, given her poor lungs).

By this time, she had to be placed on a portable oxygen unit (her breathing was so shallow that she was taking in her own exhaled carbon dioxide) and to have a wheelchair (walking was only barely possible). Almost completely bedridden, she was taken to the dreaded place, even more dreaded for its distance away from her first son. Throughout, her few moments of real lucidity were times when she repeatedly, weepingly, said she saw no reason at all to continue living. Her lungs were almost, and irreversibly, gone; her every joint hurt painfully, was misshapen, and seemed horribly ugly to her; her proud independence was utterly gone and as irrecoverable as her breathing; she had no friends any longer; her second son lived over a thousand miles away; and now she was separated even from her first son. "Why keep up this total charade of life? I'm now," she said again and again, "the very sort of person I've always despised, and I can't seem to help it: I hurt, awfully, all the time, and I can't get a decent breath. I have nothing to look forward to, I can't even look forward to walking to the bathroom without agony, and can barely get my fingers to turn on the TV."

Earlier in her life, she had had to preside over her own mother's slow and painful death from cancer, and she had watched her father fade away, from stroke, in frustrated anger. Then, she had tended her husband's creeping death, from emphysema. She knew full well what was in store for her. Here she was now, in the very same, awful condition, the way she had solemnly sworn never to be caught up in. While dying was dreaded, death seemed a blessing, for it would bring not only relief from her constant pain, constant labored struggle for air, but, far more, relief from her being such a "burden and a trial" to her sons and their families.

One morning, she was found comatose, barely breathing. The nurse on duty quickly called for an ambulance, established temporary pulmonary assist, and sent her to the nearby hospital. The first son was called, and by the time he arrived at the hospital, she was already in the ICU, intubated, mechanically ventilated, with IV and monitor lines in place, and still comatose. Shocked and dismayed, having never before been in such a situation ("like a TV show suddenly become real," he said later), the son waited, not knowing, uncertain, grief stricken, for what he hoped would come—his mother's waking up. She did, soon afterward, and when he saw her, he saw anger, bewilderment, frustration, pleading. Unable to talk because of the intubation, she remained in the ICU for several days before she was stabilized and able to be extubated.

At that point, she seemed suddenly, remarkably, her old self for a time, and for all the still-ominous presence of the medical armamentarium, finding her voice, she said in no uncertain terms that she never wanted to have "those damned machines hooked up to me again, ever." Shortly after, she was discharged and relocated at a nursing home in the town where she had been living, so her son would be close by. Her second son had flown down, and the mother and her sons visited her personal physician. After discussion, the woman and her physician reached agreement, and they signed and properly executed a Directive to Physicians instructing them not to use any "mechanical or other 'artificial methods' " that would serve merely to prolong her dying and pointlessly postpone the moment of her death.

Authorized as the Texas Natural Death Act (1977), this legislation set out certain conditions and guidelines (Figure 1A), among other matters defining whether the directive is to be considered either legally binding or nonbinding on physicians (Figure 1B). In her case, the physician certified that, since her condition was terminal, the directive was legally binding: Physicians were authorized to withhold or withdraw all "life-sustaining procedures" whenever it was additionally determined that death is "imminent," whether or not such procedures are utilized (Figure 1C). The directive was properly witnessed, notarized (Figure 1D), and placed with her medical records as required, with copies delivered to her sons.

Her condition, though somewhat stable, continued to deteriorate slowly. Even though she was encouraged to do modest exercises and to walk a bit in order to regain at least some muscle tone (lost by her recent hospitalization), her depression and bitterness worsened.

At one point, about three months later, she tried to get up from bed to go to the bathroom but succeeded only in falling and breaking her hip (osteoporosis had become generalized). She was taken to the urban hospital for surgery, which successfully replaced the severed bone, and she returned from the hospital in a somewhat more positive mood. This, however, lasted only a few days, and visits from both sons found her increasingly morose, whiny, bitter, angry, and wishing for death. Increasingly forgetful, rarely alert enough to appraise herself any longer, she became known among the home's staff, especially at night, as a griper and whiner.

Early one morning about six months after she had first suffered hypoxia, the night nurse came to her room to check on her. For the first time in a long while, she had not been heard from in over three hours. It was about 4:00 A.M. when the nurse came into her room. She found the woman comatose with very shallow and infrequent breathing; the

TEXAS NATURAL DEATH ACT

Guidelines and Directive

The 65th Legislature enacted the Texas Natural Death Act in 1977 which authorizes use of the attached written directive in accordance with the guidelines set out below.

GUIDELINES FOR SIGNERS

The DIRECTIVE allows you to instruct your doctor not to use artificial methods to extend the natural process of dying.

Before signing the DIRECTIVE, you may ask advice from anyone you wish, but you do not have to see a lawyer.

If you sign the DIRECTIVE, talk it over with your doctor and ask that it be made part of your medical record.

The DIRECTIVE must be WITNESSED by two adults who (1) are not related to you by blood or marriage, (2) are not mentioned in your will, and (3) would have no claim on your estate. It must also be NOTARIZED.

The DIRECTIVE may NOT be witnessed by your doctor or by anyone working for your doctor. If you are in a HEALTH CARE FACILITY at the time you sign the DIRECTIVE, none of its employees or patients may be a witness.

You may sign a DIRECTIVE TO PHYSICIANS if you are at least 18 years old and of sound mind, acting of your own free will in the presence of two qualified witnesses.

No one may force you to sign the DIRECTIVE. No one may deny you insurance or health care services because you have chosen not to sign it. If you do sign the DIRECTIVE, it will not affect your insurance or any other rights you may have to accept or reject medical treatment.

Your doctor is bound by the DIRECTIVE only (1) if he/she is satisfied that your DIRECTIVE is valid, (2) if another doctor has certified your condition as terminal, and (3) at least 14 days have gone by since you were informed of your condition.

If you sign a DIRECTIVE while in good health, your doctor may respect your wishes but is not bound by the DIRECTIVE.

The DIRECTIVE is valid for a period of five years, at which time you may sign a new one.

The DIRECTIVE is not valid during pregnancy.

You may revoke the DIRECTIVE at any time, even in the final stages of a terminal illness. If you revoke the DIRECTIVE, be sure your doctor is told of your decision.

FIGURE 1A.　State of Texas Directive to Physicians.

Summary and Guidelines for Physicians

INTRODUCTION -- A person who is at least 18 years of age and of sound mind may sign a DIRECTIVE TO PHYSICIANS as contained in the Texas "Natural Death Act." This Act permits a person who meets certain qualifications to give legal effect to his/her wishes to avoid artificial prolongation of the dying process. It also imposes certain obligations-- and provides certain protections–for a physician dealing with a person presenting a DIRECTIVE.

SIGNATURE AND WITNESSES -- To be effective, the DIRECTIVE must be signed by the patient, witnessed by two persons who are not related to the patient by blood or marriage, are not mentioned in his/her will, are not potential claimants to his/her estate, and are not involved in the patient's medical care, and notarized. Thus, the DIRECTIVE cannot be witnessed by you or any of your employees. Likewise it should not be witnessed by any other physician or his/her employees, or the employees or patients of any health facility where declarant is a patient.

The DIRECTIVE is effective for five years after which a person may sign a new one. A person signing a DIRECTIVE should, if possible, present the document to his/her physician so that it can be made part of his/her current medical records.

EFFECT OF A DIRECTIVE

Upon receipt of a DIRECTIVE from any patient (qualified or unqualified) the attending physician must determine that the Directive meets legal requirements. Under the Act a "qualified patient" is a person diagnosed and certified in writing to be afflicted with a terminal condition by two physicians, one of whom shall be the attending physician, who have personally examined the patient.

Whether or not a DIRECTIVE is binding depends upon the condition of the patient at the time the DIRECTIVE was signed.

In order for the DIRECTIVE to be binding the patient must be qualified and have signed or re-executed the DIRECTIVE at least 14 days after being notified of his/her terminal condition. If you do not wish to carry out the DIRECTIVE of such a patient, you are required to transfer care of the patient to a physician who is willing to comply with the DIRECTIVE. If you do not transfer such a patient, you may be found guilty of unprofessional conduct. If you do carry out the DIRECTIVE, you are protected from civil and criminal liability.

The DIRECTIVE is not binding if the patient executed the DIRECTIVE while in good health (in anticipation of a terminal illness or injury). However, should the patient be subsequently diagnosed and certified as terminal, you may carry out the DIRECTIVE if, in your judgment, all of the circumstances known to you justify doing so. If you carry out the DIRECTIVE, you are protected from civil and criminal liability.

Regardless of the binding or nonbinding nature of the DIRECTIVE, it is not to be given effect until you have determined that death is imminent, whether or not "life-sustaining procedures" are utilized, and such fact is noted in the patient's medical records. Such procedures include mechanical or other "artificial means" which sustain vital functions only to postpone the moment of death. These do not include medications or procedures deemed necessary to alleviate pain.

The DIRECTIVE is invalid and has no effect if the patient is pregnant at the time it is to be carried out.

REVOCATION – A patient may revoke the DIRECTIVE at any time. Should you receive such revocation from or on behalf of a patient who has previously signed a DIRECTIVE, enter that information promptly and prominently in the patient's current medical record.

SUMMARY -- Withholding "life-sustaining procedures" in compliance with a DIRECTIVE is not euthanasia or "mercy killing." The DIRECTIVE is not a "Living Will." The DIRECTIVE is merely a method recognized under Texas law, by which a physician may respect a patient's instruction to permit an imminent death to proceed naturally. The law authorizing the attached DIRECTIVE does not impair or supercede any legal right or legal responsibility which any person may have to effect the withholding or withdrawal of life-sustaining procedures in any lawful manner.

FIGURE 1B.

Directive to Physicians

Directive made this _____ day _____ (month, year).

I _____ , being of sound mind, willfully, and voluntarily make known my desire that my life shall not be artificially prolonged under the circumstances set forth below, and do hereby declare:

1. If at any time I should have an incurable condition caused by injury, disease, or illness certified to be a terminal condition by two physicians, and where the application of life-sustaining procedures would serve only to artificially prolong the moment of my death and where my attending physician determines that my death is imminent whether or not life-sustaining procedures are utilized, I direct that such procedures be withheld or withdrawn, and that I be permitted to die naturally.

2. In the absence of my ability to give directions regarding the use of such life-sustaining procedures, it is my intention that this directive shall be honored by my family and physicians as the final expression of my legal right to refuse medical or surgical treatment and accept the consequences from such refusal.

3. If I have been diagnosed as pregnant and that diagnosis is known to my physician, this directive shall have no force or effect during the course of my pregnancy.

4. I have been diagnosed and notified at least 14 days ago as having a terminal condition by _____ ,M.D., whose address is _____ , and whose telephone number is _____ . I understand that if I have not filled in the physician's name and address, it shall be presumed that I did not have a terminal condition when I made out this directive.

5. This directive shall have no force or effect five years from the date filled in above.

6. I understand the full import of this directive and I am emotionally and mentally competent to make this directive.

7. I understand that I may revoke this directive at any time.

Signed _____

City, County and State of Residence _____

*Two witnesses and a notary must sign the directive in the spaces provided on back page.

FIGURE 1C.

portable oxygenator's regulator was turned way down. Alarmed, the nurse immediately adjusted the regulator and called the local emergency rescue service (ERS). When the rescue team arrived, the woman was still in a deep coma, but they were able to establish sufficient pulmonary function to take her into the ambulance for the 30-mile drive to the hospital's emergency room. The first son was called and told to go directly to the ER.

Picking up his copy of the directive, he hurriedly drove there, arriv-

The declarant has been personally known to me and I believe him or her to be of sound mind. I am not related to the declarant by blood or marriage, nor would I be entitled to any portion of the declarant's estate on his decease, nor am I the attending physician of declarant or an employee of the attending physician or a health facility in which declarant is a patient, or a patient in the health care facility in which the declarant is a patient, or any person who has a claim against any portion of the estate of the declarant upon his decease.

Witness _____

Witness _____

(After you and the witnesses have signed, each of you must sign the following acknowledgement in the spaces provided, and your signatures must be notarized.)

STATE OF TEXAS

COUNTY OF _____

Before me, the undersigned authority, on this day personally appeared _____ , _____ , and _____ , known to me to be the declarant and witnesses whose names are subscribed to the foregoing instrument in their respective capacities, and, all of said persons being by me duly sworn, the declarant, _____ , declared to me and to the said witnesses in my presence that said instrument is his Directive to Physicians, and that he had willingly and voluntarily made and executed it as his free act and deed for the purposes therein expressed.

Declarant _____

Witness _____

Witness _____

Subscribed and acknowledged before me by the said Declarant, _____ , and by the said witnesses, _____ and _____ , on this _____ day of _____ ,19___ .

_____

Notary Public in and for   County, Texas

FIGURE 1D.

ing shortly after the ERS. He was told by the attending ER physician that if his mother's condition was not promptly stabilized, she would surely die. He showed the directive to the doctor, but he was informed that the ventilator was already in place and that if he (the son) wanted to be responsible for his mother's death by demanding its removal, that was his choice, but he (the doctor) would have no part of that. In effect, the son was told that since "life-saving" measures were already in place, the doctor could not remove them. While they could be "withheld" beforehand, "withdrawal" was, he said a wholly different thing—medically prohibited, morally culpable, and probably illegal. Although this was not consistent with the directive's wording, neither the son nor the ER staff had taken the time to study the document. In any case, the son was told, standard ER procedures had already occurred, as they must be in each case, making the directive inoperative. Now, it was necessary to get the woman to the ICU, do a number of tests, and diagnostically determine whether or not her condition was indeed irreversible, incurable, terminal, and her death imminent.

Emotionally distraught, bleary-eyed from his abrupt awakening, still nervous from his rapid drive into the city, and not fully cognizant of the lengthy and somewhat complex language of the directive, the son felt he had no choice but to go along with the recommendation, even though this amounted to violating his mother's clear and specific wishes never to be on "those damned machines ever again." Besides, since these doctors were not able (or willing) to say whether her death was "imminent," they had to run their tests, didn't they? He then called his brother, who made immediate arrangements to fly down. Soon after the call, the first son met with the physician in charge of his mother's care. He had informed the hospital that Dr. Smith—a pulmonary specialist who had seen her before, including during her first nursing home stay—was her doctor there. Since he was out of town, however, his calls were being taken by his partner, Dr. Jones, whom the son did not know and who knew the mother only through the medical chart.

Communication proved awkward, difficult at best. Upon showing Dr. Jones the directive, the son was told that he shouldn't be in such a hurry; Jones said he fully understood the directive and was willing to comply, but only after he was satisfied that in his own medical judgment the mother's condition was irreversible and terminal. Neurological tests thus far, Jones said, showed slight, but telltale signs of numerous, frequent tiny seizures. His medical response to these came in the form of medication designed to lessen them. Unfortunately, however, medication also muted neurologic activity generally. Thus, he was unable at this time to determine whether there had been brain damage from the hypoxic incident, much less the extent of it or whether recovery of some functioning was still possible. For these determinations, Jones said, time was needed; even if the medication was successful in stopping the seizures, neurologic diagnosis of brain damage would have to wait until the effects of the medication wore off. This would take time, even more time if the seizures continued and additional medication used.

The second son arrived that evening. Going immediately to the ICU, he found his mother behind a set of curtains, intubated, ventilator at work, her face pale and wan, completely comatose. Jones was not there, so the ICU nurse, caring and efficient, told him what she knew. It was as Jones had told his brother, but she went on to say—with words designed as much to elicit his feelings and response as to describe what she knew—that she had noticed what may have been some slight spontaneous leg movements earlier that afternoon as she was turning his mother's body. On the other hand, she said, that was very difficult to know for sure, and there had been nothing else—nothing but the regular, ventilator-induced up-and-down of her frail chest. For anything else, the second son would have to talk to the doctor.

After getting Jones's phone number and making an unsuccessful call to him, the son drove out to be with his brother. Placing another call from there, he got Jones on the line and, expectedly, was told what he knew already. However, Jones agreed to meet him the next morning after rounds, a Sunday. When they met in the ICU waiting room, Jones was brisk but friendly; he restated his findings of the day before and said he'd found little change that morning, except that the seizures were no longer occurring and he had been able to stop the medications. So, he felt, the appropriate tests could be done in about 24 hours. Refusing to let matters stand at that, the son repeated the force of the directive—that his mother had already been determined to be terminally ill by her own physician, that the directive was legally and ethically binding, that it directed that all life-sustaining procedures "be withheld or withdrawn," and that it was his mother's consistently and legally declared wish never to be hooked up to such procedures. Therefore, the son stated, the ventilator must be removed and his mother allowed to die with whatever dignity was left to her now. This was the only morally right thing to do.

Jones's response was swift and harsh. Ethics, he asserted, was irrelevant here and now, as the issue was strictly medical and legal. As he was the physician of record, he had to be satisfied about her condition first and foremost and could not be forced by the Natural Death Act to remove anything from his patient. "But, as legally binding, the thing says you've got to comply or else transfer her to a physician who will comply!" "No way," Jones replied, not unless and until he was himself clear that her medical condition was incurable and terminal even with life-supports in place.

At this point, the first son and his wife joined the argument, insisting that the directive be complied with. Jones reiterated his medical judgment: "Until I can get the right tests, I can't say that she's incurable and terminal." He started to walk off, but was stopped in the hallway by the second son. Urging calmness, the son asked why 24 hours were needed. Jones said that if the first son had not agreed with the ER doctor's recommendation the prior morning—but had demanded removal of the ventilator—none of this discussion would have been necessary. However, since the son did agree, Jones said, and the mother's care was transferred to him, he had the professional obligation to be medically certain before he did anything about the directive—and that will take time. The son pointed out that the feeling about his brother was seriously mistaken, that ventilation had already been effected, and that the urgency and tension of the situation in the ER had in fact been quite coercive influences on his brother. In any event, the son continued, it seemed reasonably clear now that the coma was permanent—or, that a neurological specialist should be consulted about the matter. Jones agreed, and the consultation was arranged with a Dr. Brown.

Brown's examination confirmed the brothers' feeling, but she felt it advisable to have another EEG. As it was Sunday, though, the technician wasn't on duty and had to be located first. In the meantime, the first son and his wife, assured that nothing would be happening for at least 24 hours, returned to their home. Some four hours later, Brown came back and informed the second son that his mother's physical exam had been confirmed by the EEG: The coma was profound and doubtless permanent, there had been massive brain and brain-stem damage, and the ventilator should be removed as she was incurable and terminal. Jones had already been informed and had left instructions with the ICU nurse to remove the ventilator. She asked the son whether he wanted to be with his mother as they withdrew the ventilator, and together they went to his mother's bedside.

The ventilator was removed, but the tube kept in place with an oxygen mask attached. Remarkably, the woman began spontaneous, but very irregular, breathing. After this labored on for a half-hour or so, the son requested extubation. A call to Jones obtained his agreement, and the tube was removed. The mask was kept in place. Sitting there at her side, watching her strain for breath, her emaciated, delicate chest heaving, he watched, awed and trembling, the heart monitor's thin tracing of each beat of her heart as it marked the gradual, final measure of her life, until at last, with awful certainty, her breathing ceased and that monitored line edged to an agonizing, still, stunning flatness. She was finally, surely dead, her face—spare and gaunt and tortured even in her coma—now at ease, reposed, and, somehow, strangely empty.

EVERYONE DID WHAT THEY COULD, RIGHT?

Let's accept that this woman was of sound mind and acted of her own free will when she signed the directive—even that she remained that way for much of the time before the second hypoxic incident, or at least that in more lucid moments she did so and continued to affirm the point of the directive. As she repeatedly said, the "quality" of her life—present and future—was so diminished and compromised that she saw no point at all in continuing to live or for having others fight for her life. Now, several things need to be said right off about her situation, her condition, and the way her condition was managed.

First, the actions of all those involved in her case—sons, nursing home and staff, physicians, hospital and its staffs—can be readily defended without stretching or concealing, even though her clearest and most strongly expressed wishes were violated. Second, the same persons and institutions, however, can also be seriously criticized. Giving some substance to both points will help isolate several key issues in the case, providing insight into how it could have been managed more sensitively, and will eventually help give definition to the place of ethics in such cases.

Everyone did what they could, given the circumstances. Both sons, especially the first (who had been close by for at least eight years, with almost daily contact), knew well how much and why the mother dreaded going into a nursing home. Yet, it was perfectly clear that she could no longer live alone in the apartment. It was not only that she wasn't getting proper nutrition, couldn't clean herself or the place, became unable to get around, but in fact her world had shrunk to the space of the living room. The attempt to have her live in the first son's home was disastrous, however, for both. Conflicts erupted regularly, small upsets were blown all out of proportion, routine family life situations became occasions for major confrontations. Living in her son's home meant for the mother a grievous loss of independence, causing her to become even more bitter and resentful. This caused her to suffer and be dismayed over what she saw herself becoming. Placed on the portable oxygen unit and taking numerous medications, she presented many potentially critical medical problems that simply could not be managed in that setting. In the event of pulmonary failure, for instance, no one in the family was trained, or had the equipment, to respond appropriately. In the end, it was this constant threat of crisis that motivated the move to a nursing home, and it is noteworthy that shortly after the move she did have a pulmonary crisis.

Response to that crisis at the first nursing home was both appropriate and requisite for such institutions. Moreover, its staff provided a controlled environment for medication, nutrition, recreation, physical therapy, and other elements for making life comfortable and interesting for its residents (although the woman's condition and prevailing moodiness meant that she rarely took advantage of any of the recreational or physical therapy opportunities). Its location, proximate to hospitals and pulmonary (and other) specialists, finally, was a positive factor in its selection.

The responses by the hospital's ER and ICU staffs after the first hypoxic incident were also appropriate and professional, especially in light of the fact that the woman had not declared any wish to refuse treatment, neither formally nor in her conversations with physicians, nurses, or other medical personnel up to that time. Everyone did what was professionally expected and legally required of them.

After hospital discharge, the decision was made to relocate her closer to her first son, in a local nursing home, where space was now available. This was done primarily at her own request; she wanted to be closer to her son and his family so they could see one another more frequently. The nursing home was known to be excellent (it was run by an acquaintance of the son), and thus this decision seems quite appropriate. Indeed, the staff's response to her broken hip and their sensitive and attentive care for her before and after this incident provided ample evidence for considerable confidence. Location there, finally, enabled the woman's own personal physician, Dr. White, to see her regularly, discuss the directive with her (and her sons), and be directly involved in the event of a precipating crisis (as with the broken hip).

When the second hypoxic incident occurred, the home's nurse acted promptly to establish temporary but sufficient pulmonary activity (note: the directive is strictly to physicians, not nurses), and the call to the ERS doesn't seem inappropriate. After all, the mother had suffered pulmonary compromise on a number of prior occasions (although not as serious), and resuscitation had been successful and apparently welcomed by the mother. She had broken her hip and had been happy with the surgery. Transfer to the hospital's ER was established policy in any event, as was the ER's immediate use of mechanical resuscitative and ventilatory procedures; stabilization is required in order to effect meaningful evaluation and diagnosis.

Dr. Jones acted in strict accord with standard medical practice in seeking further tests, in what he said to the first son, and in insisting that he had to make his own medical judgment about the mother's condition. Indeed, the directive requires "two physicians" to certify that a patient's condition is incurable and terminal. The directive the mother had signed, of course, had the certification of only one physician, Dr. White (see Figure 1C). While compliance with the directive does protect physicians from "civil and criminal liability" (see Figure 1B), whether it is binding or not, the fact that in this case it was binding did not release Jones from first doing what he deemed medically necessary in order to reach his own judgment about her condition. Finally, after the neurologist, Dr. Brown, consulted, tested, and examined the mother, both she and Jones acted promptly to comply with the directive.

WHAT WENT WRONG?

Yet, despite all those considerations, the woman ended up in the very predicament she had specifically opposed and had legally declared should be prevented. Of course, as she was comatose throughout the last incident, her sons were left with the predicament. Things surely should, and quite likely could, have been very different; alternatives were available but were either ill-considered or not considered at all.

It is hardly news today that more and more people will die of disease in their older years and that society is increasingly aware of this and the accompanying issues it presents (if one judges by the increasing attempts at establishing effective statutory regulations, by the burgeoning membership in "right to die" groups, or by the large number of courses, conferences, seminars, and popular and professional publications on the topic).

A central theme in all this, in clear recognition that how we die is coming increasingly under our own control, is "the challenge of dying well, of living fully and without fear of that last phase of life" (Cassell, 1976, p. 183). As more and more people die in old age, well aware that death is approaching, they ineluctably face the problems of controlling the circumstances of their own deaths (and dying), and, with that, the problems of learning to live their last days constructively and to die well become prominent.

Just these thoughts were frequently on this woman's mind for some years, were known by her sons, and were even explicit topics of their conversations for quite a long time before any of the incidents outlined above. Knowing these issues rather well, then, one can surely wonder why it was that both she and they, each in their own ways, allowed her condition to deteriorate to the point that the dreaded nursing home was eventually the sole reasonable alternative for her remaining life. Surely, one must wonder why alternative living situations were not explored much earlier, or if they were, then why none was acted on. Or, if those discussions were too difficult for them, why was professional counseling not sought (or suggested, by any of them, including physicians and nurses) so that alternatives could have been suggested much earlier on and explored thoroughly, so that the eventual decision(s) could have been more informed and responsible.

We do not know very much about the family prior to these incidents, thus probing such alternatives would be little more than speculation. Still, however difficult and delicate such matters are, it cannot be avoided that the woman herself, and her sons as well, can be faulted for failing to act in responsible ways given the fact that her future prospects should have been perfectly clear to them (especially since her husband died from emphysema, as did she, and she continued to smoke heavily). There was, moreover, ample time for action long before her condition restricted her to the living room couch and TV. We might perhaps find that there were reasons for not acting differently, but in any event, and however complicated the situation, such actions designed to explore productive alternatives are not unreasonable. They will in fact become even more pressing on us all as this clear trend of dying of debilitating illness in our older years continues.

Neither the woman nor her sons took the initiative of obtaining information about the directive authorized by the Natural Death Act, even though the act had been passed some years prior. They surely should have. On the other hand, neither her personal physician, the medical specialists in the city, the first or second nursing homes, nor the hospital staffs took that initiative either. Thus, despite the increasingly widespread public and media discussions of "right to die" issues, thanks to which citizens can or should be expected to be informed, and although the directive had been legislatively authorized some years prior to these events, there seems to have been on everybody's part remarkable ignorance, lethargy, apathy, denial, or at least muting of what the directive terms the person's "legal right to refuse medical or surgical treatment and accept the consequences from such refusal" (see Figure 1C). It can be reasonably argued that such failures are morally culpable. If it is a person's "right," then there must be a corresponding obligation to make good on that right. But whose obligation is this, to inform people about their "right to refuse treatment" and accept the consequences (i.e., to die)?

It cannot be simply presumed that because the Natural Death Act was passed and its passage noted in the public media, people everywhere either know about it or should be left on their own to find out about it. It is probably safe to assume that a good many residents of Texas still to this day do not know about that "right" or the directive. Not even those who face issues like this woman and her family may know about them or know how to go about finding out, much less understand, the full sense and implications of the directive once it is in hand. (It is perfectly clear, for instance, that neither the first son nor the ER doctor had actually thought about it, even though both of them had probably read it, as that business about the supposed difference between "withholding" and "withdrawing" makes clear.)

In any event, it seems equally reasonable to suggest that those who are competent and responsible to diagnose and manage incurable and terminal conditions, and by extension those charged with caring for the people who have such conditions, have a stronger obligation than the patients and their families to be informed about the act and to inform the patients and families about it (and the associated "right to refuse treatment"). The failure of the woman and her sons to inform themselves, to discuss the directive, and possibly even to execute one much earlier, then, seems more understandable and forgivable, than the failure of her physician and nurses to inform and discuss the matter. The latter, after all, knew full well just how bad off she really was and how dim her prognosis was even if there was no precipitating crisis. Her pulmonary function (almost 90 percent loss was reported at least several months prior to the first nursing home) seemed hardly consistent with one physician's suggestion to her first son that she could live another 20 years without further deterioration. Clearly, this physician was unwarrantedly optimistic and had no idea at all of this woman's deeply held values (of independence, for example) and hence of the inevitable despair she continually felt.

The nursing home's failure to inform, discuss, and especially to provide counseling on these issues also seems quite serious, though perhaps less so than that of the woman's own physicians. As noted above, the directive is to physicians, not to nursing homes and staffs. Realistic evaluation of patients' conditions must clearly include ample opportunities for sensitive and candid discussions of, and effective planning for, the likely (if not always inevitable or "imminent") issues faced by this woman and her sons. Had discussions occurred in this case, subsequent events might have been different, even more constructive.

Similarly, at the hospital, while discussion wasn't possible with the woman during the first episode until after extubation and transfer to the floor from the ICU, it was certainly possible at every point with her sons. This did not occur at any time. To the contrary, hospitals seem the least disposed toward candor on such issues; as one physician, J. H. van den Berg, once said, this is hardly surprising, either, in these "palaces of compulsive healing."

Cassell, too, pointedly remarks that despite the growing awareness in society to honesty about death and dying, the real control that dying persons can be taught, and the need for living and dying well, "the attitude of resistance to disease and death permeates the atmosphere of hospitals." In fact, he continues, "the hospital, whatever else it may be, is a tomorrow place. Tomorrow will be a better day; fight for it" (ibid., pp. 201–02). From body markers (reduced fever, less sputum, better bowel movements), flowers, and get well cards, to the attitudes and words of staff, everything and everyone are geared toward curing, hope, winning the battle and thus conspire to mute and repress cognizance of the issues this woman and her sons faced.

The medical setting, thus, tends to reinforce "passivity, resistance, and denial," and not simply because things may run more smoothly that way (ibid., p. 202). This also stems from the way we view diseases "as impersonal forces . . . whose cause in mechanistic terms leave little room for the active participation of the patient," save for the fact that a patient's resistance and efforts to get well aid the doctor in his or her work (ibid.). However, Cassell rightly urges, there is another alternative to this: to help people learn how to die, to help patients, especially in their last days, gain the same kind of control that can be learned in earlier stages of living (ibid., pp. 203ff.).

All I want to note here is that the hospital's failure to provide discussions with the family and even with the woman after transfer to the floor is a grievous flaw in its typical, standardized procedures. Such discussions could well have made the eventual aftermath of this case far different and immeasurably better for this family.

Events at the second nursing home bring us closer to what seems a central issue, given that circumstances before this admission did not include honest discussion of the woman's actual condition and prospects, much less the directive.

It is readily understandable that, finding the woman early that morning in a coma and barely breathing, the nurse on duty promptly established at least some stability and then called the ERS for transport to the ER. However, why was the woman's personal physician not called immediately? Why was the son called only after the ERS had left for the ER? Since a directive had already been signed, why was anything done? The issues, unfortunately, are not altogether clear.

In the first place, it appears that the directive was not discussed with the nursing home personnel, by neither the woman's sons, her physician, nor the woman herself. The directive was made a part of her medical record, as required by law (see Figure 1B). Yet, it seems not to have been a part of her nursing home record, and it became part of her hospital record only when the son brought it to the hospital. As happened in this case and countless others, the first signs of precipitating crisis signifying "an incurable" and "terminal" condition occurred not in the doctor's office and not in the hospital, but in the nursing home (quite expectedly). It is there, then, that knowledge of the directive and the woman's wishes should have been present from the moment it was legally executed.

In the second place, since the document is a "directive to physicians," not to nurses or nursing home personnel or ERS professionals, clear-cut and specifically signed instructions should surely have been placed on record in the home and at the hospital by her personal physician. But even in the absence of a copy of the directive in the nursing home, and with no instructions on what to do in the event of crises such as this, the nurses' actions should certainly have been, first, notification of the personal physician and then the son. Whether a crisis requires transport to an ER is a medical judgment; but, in view of the directive and the woman's condition, transport seems at best difficult to defend.

In the third place, the call to the son after the ERS was already on its way not only precluded his participation in decisions at the moment (including the vital information about the directive, supposing this was not known at the home), it also, predictably, placed the son in the extraordinarily difficult position of confronting the ER doctor and staff with the news of a directive at a vital point. This brings up some final considerations.

The ER is, typically and understandably, not a place to engage in such discussions. Time is often short and every minute vital; all of the procedures are rigidly geared toward immediate stabilization, if not actual rescue. Of course, many people die in the ER. Still, it seems safe to surmise (in the absence of solid data) that few of them die (are allowed to die) because they have in hand such a directive (or a "living will"). They die in ERs because of their diseases or injuries, despite efforts to save them—not because such efforts were withheld or withdrawn as an exercise of the patient's "right to refuse treatment."

While the pulmonary specialist who attended the case in the hospital, Dr. Jones, might be advised to be far more sensitive and ample and less judgmental in his conversations with family members—and to be more alert to the limits of his own competence (it was the second son who asked for the neurological consult)—still, his actions were not inappropriate or unprofessional. The fact is that once he became the attending, he was legally (as well as medically) required by the directive to certify the woman's condition and that death was "imminent." In fact, there is some reason to doubt whether the woman's own personal physician's name on the directive (see Figure 1C) carried any, or much, legal or medical weight: he did not, it should be noted, sign the document, nor is he required to sign it! Hence, the "two physicians" called for were in fact Dr. Jones and Dr. Brown; Dr. White was not part of the issue at the hospital (although he ought to have been the key figure in the case prior to transport).

All things considered, then, while the events in the second nursing home seem central, underlying that is another, more significant problem. The directive is "to physicians." That is, it is not designed so as to instruct hospitals, nor ERs, nor nursing homes. It is not designed even for physicians' use (neither for information nor for action) and does not include any requirement for any physician's signature. Page 3 merely provides space for the patient to give the name of the physician who has diagnosed and informed about the terminal condition—no trivial matter, when on the other hand one looks at the defining conditions for the document to be regarded as legally binding or not.

To be sure, a diagnosis of having a terminal condition (making the document binding) could be readily confirmed. Still, the point is that initiating and even learning about the directive falls to the person wishing to exercise his or her "right to refuse treatment" when death is "imminent" (nor is it irrelevant to note that no indication of what constitutes "imminent" death is given). Therefore, legally, there is no obligation for the physician to initiate a directive for or with a patient. "A person signing a DIRECTIVE should, if possible present the document to his/her physician so that it can be made part of his/her current medical record" (Figure 1B). If the person has been properly notified that his or her condition is terminal, the directive is legally binding; after determining that the condition is incurable and death "imminent," the physician must comply with it or transfer to a physician willing to comply with it. Whichever physician complies is protected from civil or criminal liability. If the person is in good health when signing a directive, it is not legally binding but may be carried out, and, if so, the physician is legally protected.

Now, the crucial point should be quite obvious: This type of directive carries no legal weight at all in the two places where it is by all odds most needed—nursing homes and emergency rooms. We could suppose, after all, that the second nursing home was fully cognizant of and even in complete agreement with the woman's directive. Even so, when the hypoxic crisis occurred, what was the nurse to do? The home's institutional rules require her, in such cases, to attempt temporary stabilization, notify the patient's physician, call the ERS for immediate transport to an appropriate medical facility, and notify next of kin. There is, however, no provision for compliance with a directive, nor could there have been for this document.

While notification of the woman's personal physician was not done (possibly he couldn't be found, and his standing instruction is to transport such patients to the hospital), even if he had come to the home (using up critical time in so doing), his certification of the patient as "incurable and terminal" is not sufficient. The diagnosis and written certification must be done by two physicians, and both of them must "have personally examined the patient," diagnosed the condition as incurable and terminal, and certified that death is *"imminent, whether or not 'life-sustaining procedures' are utilized"* (Figure 1B). Getting two physicians to be immediately present at the bedside of such a patient, having both of them examine the patient, is at best unlikely in such cases. Moreover, because of the nature of this kind of medical crisis and the need for quick response, taking the time for this could well place the patient at considerable additional risk anyway. So far as this case is concerned, finally, it is not without relevance to note that that town had only two doctors in practice, making fulfillment of the directive improbable if not impossible even if the nurse had called the woman's personal physician.

So far as the ER at the hospital is concerned, not only do documents such as this fly in the face of its medically and legally required standard procedures, their fulfillment in that sort of unit seems also improbable if not impossible. The ER physician is not "the attending physician," hence compliance with the directive would require the attending's presence in the ER at the time of the crisis and admission. Even were that unlikely event to have occurred (Which attending physician is in regular attendance in an ER, especially at 4:45 A.M. on a Saturday morning? For that matter, which hospital requires attendings to be in the ER regularly?), the attending would have to examine, diagnose, and certify in writing, along with a second physician (the ER doctor?), while the patient, already critically compromised, awaits crisis interventions. Furthermore, conducting such rigorous and requisite tests for such a patient seems hardly likely or appropriate until stabilization has been established. Obviously in the swift succession of events in the ER and during the wait for differential diagnosis, the patient found herself already in the very situation she desperately sought to avoid at all costs—intubated, ventilated, with other life-supports in place.

The Directive to Physicians, therefore, whatever honorable intentions went into its legislative enactment, is simply a useless document when it comes to medical actions. Its initiation and execution constitute a pointless and painful act, since compliance with it is unlikely, improbable, and in too many cases simply impossible. In our case, the woman's final end, her sons' frustration and despair, seemed foredoomed, even with the best of legislative, legal, and medical intentions.

Other cases, with similar detail, could readily be given. However, in view of the many cases already presented, and especially this one, we probably have enough to go on to begin formulating what ethics must be in order to be responsive to clinical situations.

ETHICS AS CLINICAL LIAISON

Any case presents its own set of issues, moral and other. These are context specific and, as such, require for their identification and delineation an approach and method that are sensitive to what is unique to each case and capable of articulating each in its own terms. Understanding and identifying what these issues are and for whom they are issues; helping the people whose situation it is to develop strategies to manage and resolve them; imaginatively and rationally probing each alternative strategy as far as possible and thus testing each in the only way they can be tested prior to being put into effect; assisting in the eventual decision making (if asked); and providing supports for those involved who must live in and with the aftermath of their decisions—these components of the approach and method rest on three major bases that give shape and definition to an ethics responsive to clinical situations. These bases, or grounds, pick up on many of the themes already disclosed in the course of this study. They also invoke certain fundamental moral values that we must recognize, voice, and explore (as will be done in the last chapter). First things first, however.

Thesis 1: The work of ethics requires strict focus on the specific situational definition of each involved person.

What a particular situation is—which values and what weight are attached to the components of the situation (objects, people, relationships)—is strictly a function of the experiences and interpretations of those whose situation it is. This is, of course, a modification of W. I. Thomas's classic thesis: "If men define situations as real, they are real in their consequences" (Thomas, 1928, p. 572). It requires what Schutz, following Max Weber, called the "subjective interpretation of meaning" (Schutz, 1973, pp. 243–99). If one wants to understand a situation, there is nothing to do but try one's best to get at the ways in which the situational participants themselves understand it and endow its various components with sense and meaning.

To be involved in or be an actual party to a situation is one thing; to be an observer (as is the ethicist, for the most part) is quite another. The problems presented by a case are the problems of those whose case it is, just as are the alternatives, decisions, and aftermaths. Just as the physician is charged with acting on behalf or in the interests of each specific patient within his or her own particular circumstances, so is the work of ethics in clinical situations under the requirement of acting on behalf of the situational participants. That set of persons includes not only the patient and family or circle of intimates, but also the physician or physicians (residents, consultants), nurses, and other care providers, as well as (where appropriate) the hospital and its units, always within the broader context of prevailing legal and governmental policies and prevailing social norms. Whatever contributes to the specific situational definition must be identified, considered, and weighed.

Certain of these contributing components will obviously vary from case to case, and these differences (however slight they may appear from certain perspectives) are critical for the work of ethics. They may well be decisive both medically and morally; no matter how apparently slight, they cannot be ignored without further ado. Furthermore, precisely because each situational participant experiences and interprets things (gestures, language, objects, relationships) from his or her own particular perspective ("autobiographical situation" is Schutz's term for this; see ibid., pp. 92–119), what is viewed as a problem, as alternatives, as decision-points, or as important will also vary. These varying situational definitions themselves require sensitive notice and oftentimes delicate handling in order to arrive at even a modicum of basic agreement.

Often treated as "communication problems" or "breakdowns," such varying situational definitions are clearly that, and much more besides. Communication difficulties will often harbor more serious, deeper conflicts of interpretation, of values, even of life-styles. Without in the least underestimating their significance or frequent occurrence, thus, problems arising or embedded in the talk among situational participants may well be signals indicating other, deeper-lying issues. As a discipline, ethics must be constantly on the alert for these, as has already become clear in our discussions of the many cases presented.

Thesis 2: Moral issues are presented solely within the contexts of their actual occurrence.

In his recently published two-volume study of patient-physician talk, Eric Cassell lucidly shows how critical it is for physicians to learn to be effective listeners as well as speakers. He systematically studies how talk actually works in everyday conversations. Properly understood and utilized, the spoken language "is the most important tool in medicine" (1985, Vol. I, p. 1). Cassell's study brilliantly lays out the dimensions of paralanguage and their interpretation (pause, speech rate, pitch, intonation, among others), the ways by which what is said presents the self who speaks, and the ways to understand the coherence and logic of conversation. Cassell discusses how to establish the intent and credibility of speakers and how to determine the meaning of spoken words; he also presents highly practical proposals for including everyday language within the body of medical knowledge. Of equal interest is his insistence that physicians can and must develop the skills of listening and talking by carefully organized attention to these dimensions.

His central point is that the physician who learns to listen to a patient's paralanguage (the "music of language") and conversation, and especially to distinguish between what is actually heard and what it is interpreted to mean, is far better equipped to find out just what is wrong with each patient and to be far more assured that the patient has been understood. Word choice, intent, and the paralanguage of a speaker are critical since they can and often do "change entirely the meaning of words" used and convey a crucial part of the intent (ibid., p. 15).

Nor is this all. Realizing that when we talk about the world around us, including our bodies, we are at the same time characterizing ourselves and how we relate to the world (what things are for us as situational definers). "Learning to listen skillfully to the patient and to interpret judiciously what is said can be as critical a diagnostic tool as learning to hear and interpret heart sounds" (ibid., p. 45). Attention to these paralinguistic aspects—to word choice and syntax, how conversation moves from one thing to another, and the patient's intent in saying what is said—this, quite as much as the skills of physical diagnosis, is critical to the basic therapeutic aims of medicine.

The same is manifestly true for the understanding and management of the many types of moral issues, conflicts, and dilemmas occasioned by clinical situations. Indeed, to focus on the specific situational definitions that constitute the clinical encounter is in many respects to be focused on the phenomenon of talk, the everyday discourse between patients and providers. Complex and significant as this is, however, it is not the only ingredient. To understand "what's going on" in any case, as Cassell recognizes at one point (ibid., pp. 141–42), one has to be attentive to the actual setting in which the talk goes on (whether it is the ER, the operating room, the office, a waiting room, or the ICU). The setting has its own distinctive features and components, including manners of dress, the general appearance of the people involved, the objects and instrumentalities present, and the various actions being performed or contemplated, as well as what has occasioned the specific encounter and its historical context. Patients, physicians, nurses, and others interact differently in different settings, with different people (and people believed to be, or treated as, different). They also come into these encounters with different histories (what was said or done a moment before or in the further past, what has become habitual for each of them, what is the usual way of doing things in a particular unit, in a particular hospital, and in the culture more broadly and its own historical context).

Thus, to understand in a specific case what's going on, what's troubling people, and what's on their minds—and to know what needs to be clarified, much less resolved—requires careful and cautious probing of the ongoing discourse and attentive awareness of the setting and the other aspects of each specific context.

In the case of the elderly woman just discussed, for instance, the first son was deeply offended by the words and actions (as well as non-actions) of Dr. Jones: Since a directive had been signed, why did Jones refuse to withdraw the ventilator? Only after lengthy discussions (of the rules governing nursing homes, ERs, ICUs, and the document itself) did it become clear that the son was in fact wrong to lay blame on Jones. Jones, too, was at fault for effectively making the son feel guilty for assenting to the ER doctor's recommendation; in fact, for the son to have demanded withdrawal of the ventilator at that point would have exposed him, and the ER staff had they complied, to serious legal risk, since neither the attending nor a second physician had examined and certified the woman's condition. Indeed, the discussions with Jones had first to contend with the heavy guilt the son was already feeling, although it was still silent. He was blaming himself for letting "that damned ER doctor keep her 'hooked up' " to the ventilator, a guilt reinforced by Jones's thoughtless comment that "if you had acted differently, we wouldn't be in this situation now." To probe that guilt required probing the ER setting itself (especially its multiple forms of subtle, but for the most part silent, coercion), the ER doctor's abrupt demeanor, the time of day, the son's physical and linguistic appearance, the nature of ER procedures and standards of practice, the words and actions of the paramedics when they delivered his mother to the ER, and so on. All these needed to be examined, in addition to eliciting the son's attitudes, wishes, values, and his relationship with the mother.

Every clinical case requires the same kinds of paralinguistic, conversational, and contextual probing and assessment. Moral issues are presented solely within the contexts of their actual occurrence and therefore require skillful and sensitive identification, probing, and attention to the fullness of each specific context or setting.

Thesis 3:   The situational participants are the principal resources for the resolution of the moral issues presented.

I was asked once to consult with the parents of a seriously ill infant. Born prematurely and with multiple congenital abnormalities, the nursing and medical staffs became increasingly convinced, as they related to the young parents, that the infant's "many problems are incompatible with life" and "in all probability, though there are some things we can do, even if he survives he will be severely compromised."

The consultation was requested because, I was told, "these parents, especially the father, just won't talk with us." Uncertain whether they understood what they were told, uncertain how to interpret their "stubborn silence" about the "medical alternatives," and especially concerned about their failure to show much "appropriate behavior" when possible withdrawal of life-supports was mentioned, the attending asked me to talk things over with them. "See what you can find out," because "we can't tell what their feelings are, and decisions have to be made very soon."

Meeting with them in a vacant conference room close to the NICU, furnished with several chairs and a table, the conversation opened with small talk—which was encouraged in order to try and gain some sense of these people, revealed by how they talked and what they talked about. This revealed little about the husband, who talked almost not at all; the wife, though, was more willing to talk. This was their first child, and the child had been planned for and wanted very much. The 22-year-old mother was pleasant-looking and cooperative; her conversation articulate, deliberate, and flowing with few pauses. She spoke in even tones and a moderate pitch. Her words were relatively precise, well chosen if somewhat ordinary, and she seemed obviously very bright and intelligent, frank, and outgoing. Definitely a young woman with considerable self-control, she was able to talk rather freely about her severely compromised infant son.

The husband was well-dressed, somewhat ill at ease although intelligent and alert. He was about twenty-five years old. In the early part of the meeting, he struck me as a man who was cautious to the extreme. He talked in a slow, somewhat choppy way with many long pauses (but no "ers," "uhs," and the like—just long silent pauses as if selecting his words with great care), in a sort of monotone. At times his speech was strained and clipped. His words (pronouns, verb tenses) seemed impersonal (not "my" or "our" baby, for instance, but "one's" or "the" infant) and thus seemed evasive, at least in the beginning.

As the conversation progressed (especially after I explained that I was not an M.D. but a Ph.D., there to help them think through their situation and decisions as thoroughly as possible, in light of their own values and beliefs), both of them markedly changed. The wife became more lively and emotional and evidenced considerable concern in her demeanor and words. Her husband became suddenly quite energetic and rather outspoken, clearly very disturbed about something as yet not quite stated.

In substance, they not only fully understood everything they had been told but wanted fervently to save their baby from any further suffering and pain caused by pointlessly prolonging its remaining life. As this came out so swiftly, naturally, and with evidently deep concern and thoughtfulness, I couldn't help blurting out: "But why in the world haven't you said this to Dr. X? He's been very puzzled over how you both feel." The answer was equally surprising: "We *have* told him!" When I pointed out why I had been asked to talk things over with them, the husband said, "Well, maybe not in so many *words*, but we thought it was obvious that Dr. X's recommendation should be followed, and the life-supports removed."

Further talk, about whether they were aware of the Baby Doe regulation (then in its second published version) and its implications for them and the physicians made two things clear. First, as they understood that new regulation, such decisions had been taken away from parents and given to physicians. Parents, the father pointed out, were given no part in such decisions. Both of them deeply resented that and were offended by much of the public discussion of Baby Does, which cast suspicion on the motives of parents like themselves. A second thing also became clear. The husband said that he had felt even more frustrated and not in control since he had seen a recent TV news program devoted to the Baby Jane Doe case. In that case, the girl's parents, after agonizing thought and with much help from their priest and others, decided to refuse surgery, so as to prevent her having to suffer needlessly, only then to die or be massively debilitated. They then found themselves not only at the wrong end of a terrible court suit, but also victims of awful publicity. What had left a lasting impression on him was that picture of the girl's father testifying, in court, with a paper bag over his head, in a last-ditch effort to preserve what little remained of his privacy and dignity.

The husband asserted to me with determined voice that he simply could not allow his baby, his wife, himself, and their families to go through that kind of thing. He was worried that a similar lawsuit might be entered against him and his wife if they were to make any "public" declaration of their earnest wishes to withdraw and cease hurting their baby. Hence, his "silence," which in his own mind was his agreement (perhaps only gestural) with Dr. X. If the life-supports were removed, the "decision" would have been the physician's, not theirs.

The concluding discussion naturally focused on the fact that the Baby Doe ruling had already been thrown out of court several times, was currently being again challenged in court, and did not have quite the legal force it otherwise might have. The question was in fact a moral one. We also explored the unlikelihood of legal suit, given that the attending physician, the primary-care nurses, the residents, and other staff in the NICU were all in agreement. I then pointed out that the long-established policy and practice in this NICU was firm on one relevant point: Parents are viewed as significant partners in all critical decision making. Physicians would not, without parental input, discussion, and agreement, withdraw any life-supports or make any critical intervention decisions.

After a discussion with the attending together with the parents, the decision was made to withdraw. Everyone recognized that continued life-supports were useless, as they served only to prolong suffering and dying. It was then indicated that this kind of action was perfectly in accord with the spirit and letter of the federal guidelines, whatever their legal status at the time.

This consult illustrates the third key point for clinical liaison ethics: It is the people themselves—the parents, the physicians, the primary-care nurses, and the others—and their specific circumstances, that are at once the *sources* of the moral issues and concerns and the primary *resources* for their resolution. In a word, it is they whose problems are at stake, they who must face and make the decisions, and they who must live with the aftermaths of their own decisions.

ENABLEMENT

Methodologically, the central clinical notion of *enablement* is that communicative process whereby situational participants are provided with the understanding, the means, opportunities, power, or authority, already intrinsic to their situation, to effect change by their decisions. The physician must engage in a process of mutual probing, exploring, and testing, together with the other participants, by which their own abilities are fostered, nurtured, and developed so that their decisions can be as responsible and informed as possible within the given circumstances.

In general, the work of the clinical-liaison ethicist is to conduct this process within the complex, highly individual, and variously contextured situations presented by each case. The specific sort of complexity, the specific issues (both explicit and implicit), and the specific range of data definitive of each case must be probed and interpreted, strategies mapped out and imaginatively tested, decisions assisted, and support for their aftermaths provided. As indicated, the communication skills required (especially as detailed in Cassell's fine study and extended to ethics), and the contextural analytic activities each case calls for can be learned, sensitivities acquired, enabling and empowering talents learned—principally within the actual contexts presented by each case, that is, through active clinical involvement and practice.

Those skills, abilities, talents, and sensitivities, being context focused, may well seem too ambiguous, especially for the medical contexts in which they have their place. Still, some further clarification has already begun to appear in the clinical literature. Cassell's work has already been mentioned, and it is of great significance in this connection. Beyond that, as my colleague A. Gene Copello has pointed out (in his unpublished doctoral dissertation [1985]), Germain and Gitterman's interesting study speaks directly to the methodological significance of enablement (although it does not directly concern the medical-ethical implications that Copello brings out). As they indicate, the enabler attempts to "help people move through stressful life transitions" so that "their adaptive capacities are supported or strengthened, and the environment's responsiveness to coping needs is increased" (1980, p. 100). The efforts of the enabler, therefore, are designed to help people gain "at least minimal control over such threatening affects as grief, rage, shame, guilt, and despair that can immobilize them." Enabling or empowering work aims at helping people recognize and utilize their own resources and motivations for dealing with these stresses, through helping them identify and elicit their own feelings and the values these express. By providing them with support and helping them understand their concerns as legitimate, enablers aid them in reducing ambivalence and ambiguity and maintaining a clear focus on the tasks and issues at hand (ibid., p. 101).

Each of the case presentations provided in this study, more clearly the detailed ones, is in a sense designed to give substance to these rather generalized descriptions—to make them become more lively precisely through ongoing probing and interpretation, that is, by trying to show them "in action." What quickly becomes evident in any particular case is that whatever may be, or be seen to be, the moral issues, those who are actually living those issues (and other issues that surface as clinical ethics probing goes on) are, to one or another degree, undergoing some sort of fragmentation, some kind of "deconstruction" in their actual lives. Illness and injury are occasions of stress and are frequently times in which severe moral challenges are faced. Such times of moral crisis, when the persons involved are undergoing hard decisions, are times in which things are not normal. Much often hangs in the balance of the decisions made, and their aftermaths can occasion extreme moral and other difficulties.

As it is these persons themselves whose situation it is, whose lives are (to whatever extent) fragmented or disrupted and who must live with whatever aftermaths then ensue, it is to them, as well as for them, that one must turn as the primary moral resources needed to bring about resolution. These resources, Copello insists in his detailed study of a cancer patient,

> are internal to the relational situation (with particular specifications depending on the case) which the enabler attempts to facilitate, nurture, and encourage. There are times, however, when these internal moral resources are so afflicted or depleted that the enabler must look to external resources to help solve the problem. An example of this might be the introduction of psychological counseling for a family. . . . To say it differently: the enabler is concerned with both the problems and the potentials of the person in his or her situation. In this sense, the enabler attempts to enhance the appropriate decision-making process and management solutions through the *enablement of the moral resolves internal to the situation*—that is, those resolves which structure the relations between the clinical actors. . . . Enablement has the ability *to build community through helping persons* come to terms with their situations. (1985, pp. 44, 47–48.)

To enable, thus, is to help people reconstruct their hitherto deconstructed lives brought on by severe illness or injury: to rebuild community from the threats, and at times the reality, of fragmentation brought on by the moral issues inherent to those situations.

CHAPTER 10

Clinical-Liaison Ethics: Part II

As I have frequently noted throughout, the would-be healer and the person receiving help are typically strangers, and this compromises the very meaning of "helping." Even with the many clues, modes of practice, and acquired communication skills that Cassell details, he is still forced to realize that this social fact in our times makes the already difficult matter of discourse between healers and patients even more so. As has long been recognized, indeed, the prevailing social conditions (fragmentation, pluralism, specialization, mobility) effectively mean that "outside one's immediate family, circle of friends, or stable neighborhood," people are for the most part strangers to one another; they often do not know whether they share values or beliefs, and they do not know what claims they may legitimately make on each other (see Lenrow, in Rubenstein and Block, 1982, p. 43).

THE WORK OF HELPING STRANGERS

When the thing that brings these strangers together is a need for help by one, and the claim of being able to help by the other, their relationship is all the more difficult. And, as was earlier emphasized, when the need is signaled by illness or injury, the situation is ripe for conflicts of many kinds.

Trust by the one and care by the other are at one and the same time structurally required and yet deeply problematic. The uncertainties that are ingredient to illness become structurally enhanced by the very fact of the relationship being between strangers. Add to this the sorts of bodily and personal intimacies demanded by the clinical situation itself, and all the makings for explosive, value-charged conflicts are present and demanding.

In a particularly poignant instance of this in Cassell's study, where he is addressing the "very odd kind of relation between people" that medicine involves—a special and unique relationship—he writes:

> I remember a patient, lying undressed on the examining table, who said quizzically, "Why am I letting you touch me?" It is a very reasonable question. She was a patient new to me, a stranger, and fifteen minutes after our meeting, I was poking at her breasts! Similarly I have access to the homes and darkest secrets of people who are virtual strangers. In other words, the usual boundaries of a person, both physical and emotional, are crossed with impunity by physicians. (Cassell, 1985, Vol. I, p. 119.)

This is only one of many such instances in any physician's daily, routine practice. Relations and conversations in such cases are made comprehensible in many respects by the settings in which they occur (doctor's office, hospital room). The actions and words of the physician—bedecked with white coat, officed in an appropriately titled room, equipped with the recognizable accoutrements of "doctor"—perhaps become more understandable. But they are not for that reason any less difficult to manage, or structurally less incongruous.

Helping, in Lenrow's terms, "refers to social interaction in which the participants are uncoerced, the interaction is intended to benefit at least one of [them], and [they] are in agreement about who is intended to benefit" (in Rubenstein and Block, 1982, p. 44). Given this premise, Lenrow's argument is that it is extremely difficult for those in the helping professions to keep their own beliefs and commitments from becoming compromised, and the very meaning of helping becoming corrupted, because the social situation of the helping professions in relation to strangers seeking help creates two unavoidable kinds of dilemma.

Dilemmas of Interdependence

Lenrow uses this phrase to capture the recurrent experience reported by professionals trying to help strangers. By acquiring training and specialized knowledge designed to prepare a person to help others in need, the professional is thereby encouraged to view this relationship as basically unilateral. For instance, the doctor helps the patient, not vice versa (since helping is what the relationship is all about). Their relationship, however, is necessarily mutual and not unilateral; they are *inter*related and *inter*dependent.

The doctor cannot help the patient unless the patient cooperates, complies, and trusts. Yet, the physician can neither command nor create that mutuality, nor is there anything in the physician's body of specialized knowledge that can in any way guarantee that trust or its conditions, nothing in it that can be utilized to ensure that the patient-stranger feels that his person, his dignity, his worth, is respected simply because the helper is a specialist. Prepared specifically to help, the helper finds that the helping situation is out of his or her complete control and is not unilateral (in the way that the training and specialized knowledge promised). Rather, ensuring that trust, working within that mutuality relationship, requires personal qualities, as we will see, whose source lies outside that training and specialized body of knowledge.

According to Lenrow, there are two main structural characteristics of such relationships that accentuate the dilemmas. First, between strangers there is no set of common, enduring, and mutual obligations—at least, not initially. To encounter a stranger means structurally that "neither the would-be helper nor the person needing help knows what values they have in common nor in what ways their values differ" (ibid., p. 48), nor, it should be added, does their relationship make clear just what to make of, how to assess or interpret, this fact. Is X trustworthy? Does Y mean what he says? Only through mutual collaboration, through learning what is shared and what is not and what meaning is to be attached to those, can the helping relationship proceed. But what can get the necessary collaboration itself going?

The difficulty of establishing some common ground is "made much more difficult by the second structural feature of helping strangers, the asymmetry of power in favor of the helpers" (ibid.). As we've already stressed many times, it is this asymmetry of power (and the inequality of condition—the one being ill, the other not) that is at the center of clinical medicine. Lenrow's analysis, concerning the helping professions more generally, puts the dilemma squarely. The helper can influence the one needing help, but "does not know how his power is regarded by the other person" and thus does not know "to what extent he is trusted to use his power in ways that are in the interests of the person needing help" (ibid.). For the use of power to be regarded as legitimate by the one seeking help, "the helper has to learn what the other's distinctive values are and be responsive to them." Yet, to be seen as trustworthy, the helper must at the same time "use his power according to his own best judgment and take responsibility for his own choices" (ibid.).

At the heart of these structural features of the professional work of helping strangers, thus, is the dilemma of balancing competing demands, claims, and legitimation techniques—ultimately, the structural conflict of different situational definitions, with one of them (that of the helper) being accorded socially approved asymmetry of power.

Obviously, the case of the elderly woman who signed the Directive to Physicians vividly illustrates these issues. Even though she signed the directive, we saw how grievous complications, all understandable and even in a way justifiable, can interfere with the directive's instructions and the right of a patient to refuse treatment, and how her family then found itself in the throes of serious dilemmas.

Clearly, such situations call for the cultivation by helpers of personal qualities such as goodwill, humility, forbearance, empathy, and sympathy—all well known from the earliest stages of medicine's history and its moral traditions. Yet, as is well known, the development and nurturing of these qualities (or virtues), whose source lies outside the specialized training and knowledge of the helping professional, can be compromised. It is not only the development of sophisticated technologies that can "dehumanize," but also the bureaucratization of the work of the health professions (see Pellegrino, 1974; 1979b, pp. 95–116, 141–50). Or, more to the point, Lenrow emphasizes, the very social structure of such work in our times leads unavoidably to another set of inherent dilemmas.

Dilemmas in the Integration of Helping and Work

If a physician did what is necessary to know a patient in the depth and with all the liveliness needed to understand and care for the patient as well as know his or her illness there would be little time left to deal with very many patients in the course of the day.

To spend more time with patients only raises their expectations, and the helper soon is likely to be overwhelmed by their demands. Efforts to cut back only generate additional frustrations by patients, and they then understandably become angry at the helper, the institution, and other helpers. The unending demand for sympathetic attention by those in need, if the helper tries to be responsive to it, only opens the floodgate of still further demands for attention. How can these demands be balanced between realism and the nature of helping work?

There is, after all, much pressure for helpers to be efficient: adequate to the tasks at hand, efficacious in their management, adaptable to the daily round of different jobs and people, productive, expeditious (if not also expedient and quick). But efficiency—easily translatable into quantitative terms (numbers of patients, hours, publications)—can readily conflict with being a decent, caring person. To be a decent, caring person, on the other hand, all too easily means that the helper will be overwhelmed by a bottomless well of patients awaiting responsiveness (Lenrow, in Rubenstein and Block, p. 46).

At the source of these at times overpowering demands and dilemmas of integrating helping with work is what Lenrow terms a "split in our dominant cultural values between impersonal, utilitarian conceptions of work, on the one hand, and caring relationships on the other" (ibid., p. 50). Work is typically understood in terms of utility and efficiency—using impersonal means of achieving predetermined goals. Organized into social bureaucracies, work becomes the channeling of individual self-interests in ways that are structurally intended more to serve organizational productivity and effectiveness than the needs of those seeking help. In tandem with the intense pressures to divide labor, specialize roles, conform to standardized procedures, and centralize control, there has been a tendency to solve this split by relegating the one set of values to the job (utility) and the other to the home (caring, nurturing).

Helping persons who are strangers, as a form of organized work, furthermore, "violates the dominant cultural beliefs and their expression in the specific form of bureaucratic organization" (ibid.). In the first place, to combine some form of caring and nurturing with work (as occurs in medicine, especially within bureaucratically organized and administered institutions such as hospitals) is *ipso facto* to violate that compartmentalization of work values and home values and thus creates the serious dilemma. To combine these dominant values in connection with strangers, moreover, demands a kind of generosity that is difficult at best "in a society and an institutional setting where impersonal relationships and controlled competition are the norms" (ibid.).

In the second place, those who are served by the helping professions are increasingly people whose circumstances, priorities, and values are markedly different from those of the helpers. Yet, "at the same time," Lenrow emphasizes "conditions are least conducive here to recognizing undesirable side effects" intrinsic to the ways in which helpers react to these dilemmas (ibid., p. 51). The result is inevitably defensive behavior that "perpetuates alienation and robs helping work of meaning" for both helper and patient (ibid.).

The social organization of helping professions into bureaucracies (with their dominant values of utility and efficiency) militates against the very qualities needed for helping those in need and for addressing the dilemmas structurally inherent to the work of helping. But just these qualities run counter to the dominant values of our culturally embedded conception of work, and thus these qualities are least encouraged by the values dominating work and its social organization, especially as the organization of work itself becomes more impersonal. The dilemmas emergent from these conflicts of value are even more painful in medicine. This brings up a third set of dilemmas, not analyzed by Lenrow but crucial especially for understanding medicine as a helping profession.

DILEMMAS OF NECESSARY DISTANCING

Addressing the special relationship between physician and patient, in which the accepted boundaries of permissible exchanges are "crossed with impunity," Cassell emphasizes that this "is an inherently benevolent relationship. . . . The sick patient comes to the doctor to get better. This is what the relationship is all about" (Cassell, 1985, I, p. 119). Thus, while the problem of interpreting a speaker's intent can be quite difficult in many situations, especially those involving strangers, the intent of this benevolent relationship seems quite clear: It is the fundamental point of the relationship that th e doctor help the patient get better. Because of this, Cassell remarks, "I cannot think of another conversational sett ing where the underlying intent is so solidly preestablished" (ibid.).

Inherent to this relationship are certain typical expectations regar ding both physician and patient. As for the former, Cassell emphasizes,

> Patients have the right to expect me to be warm, dignified, kind, open, trustworthy, giving (and forgiving), gentle, and perhaps to embody other characteristics usually associated with someone whom we love, or who is a parent, and not usually associated with strangers. The role of physician involves an obligation to behave in this fashion, even when my stomach is upset or I am angry at my spouse. Moreover I am obliged to extend myself in all these ways to many different people day in and day out. (Ibid.)

But as for expectations of patients, Cassell is, oddly, relatively silent. What he does say, however, brief though it is, may point the way to the third dilemma within the social structure of medical situations.

Few things seem to upset physicians more than when a patient is caught lying to the physician. Being angry, fearful, frustrated, unfriendly, sulky, aloof, argumentative, defensive—these and other attitudes and behaviors are neither unusual nor necessarily provocative, even though they can make the relationship complicated and awkward. But a lie from a patient seems not only an offensive act but a downright violation of the very point of the therapeutic dyad.

To be sure, lying by physicians in some form or other has long been thought to be acceptable, since, so it was believed, their centering concern is essentially benevolent and therapeutic. Thus, physicians often believed (and some still do) that telling "bad news" could itself make a patient feel doomed and lose hope and thus compromise care and even the patient's future prospects. The idea that benevolent lying, either by omission or commission, can be justified, however, relates only to the physician; nothing seems similarly to justify lying on the part of the patient—a point that in its way suggests another facet of the asymmetry of this relationship.

What interests me about this matter is not the difficulty involved in determining whether a patient is lying, or being defensive, denying, or expressing fear, although these are surely important issues, as we've seen. Nor am I concerned here to defend so-called benevolent lying by physicians (probably many of these lies cannot be justified). With Cassell, I am convinced that candid and sensitive communication with patients not only avoids the harsh problem of surrounding a patient with still more uncertainties; it also has important positive and therapeutic effects of its own (ibid., pp. 190–91). Finally, I am not concerned here with the difficulties associated with conveying the unavoidable uncertainties of illness (whether by patients or by physicians) (ibid., pp. 116–17).

What rather interests me is Cassell's response to situations in which a patient has unambiguously and evidently told an unmitigated lie to the physician. "The fundamental assumption of medicine is that the mutual relationship between doctor and patient is inherently benevolent. They are not adversaries" (ibid., p. 114). Can lies therefore ever be tolerated? Cassell's response is suggestive:

> If a patient lies to me when I am taking a history, the patient has not lied to *me*, Eric Cassell. People are not supposed to lie to one another. A lie is like cheating, it is a moral offense. The medical setting changes this. The patient has lied to *the doctor*, and in that context the lie has a different meaning. Instead of being something done to me, the lie, once discovered, is a piece of information that can be used to help care for that patient. (Ibid., p. 120.)

Similarly, when a patient behaves seductively, "it is not *me* that is the object of seduction, it is *the doctor*" (ibid.). His point here is to emphasize that the benevolent nature of this relationship radically alters the rules of everyday conversation, as well as the morality of lying. The way a patient behaves toward the doctor "is a part of that patient's relationship to illness and medical care." Thus, deceit, concealing, intimidation, and the like should not be taken personally by the doctor. Rather, this behavior is "medical information . . . facts about the person, as the heart murmur is a fact about the heart" (ibid.). When a patient comes to a doctor, the patient is expected to state why he or she came, but when this doesn't occur and the patient instead talks about everything except his or her complaint, the doctor has to be alert to that. The patient "is not doing those things to *you*, he or she is acting this way in *the doctor's* office. The doctor just happens to be you" (ibid., p. 130).

Accordingly, we can surmise that the expectations regarding patients are quite different from those of the physician or those that are ingredient to any other social situation. Every person who comes to a doctor has a reason for doing so, and when it is not obvious (for whatever reason, including lying) what that reason is, it is the doctor's job to discover it. Whatever the reason may turn out to be, this much seems clear: The person has experienced something wrong or at least believes something has gone wrong, and believes too that the doctor can do something positive (therapeutic) about it—however awkward, fearful, parsimonious, or even dissembling that person may be in his or her talk. In fact, however a person presents, behaves, or talks, the point of the benevolent relationship is that the person himself is presented, or as the case may be, is discovered by the physician as having something wrong, and all the behavior and talk constitutes medical information that serves the end of that relationship.

Cassell's analysis of everyday conversations between doctor and patient is designed to show precisely how sensitivity and skill in listening to and talking with patients can be successful in discovering that "self" of the patient who is in need of care. Problems are not presented; people are, and it is the physician's job to treat people, not problems isolated from the people who have them. If a person lies, that is itself part of what the physician must contend with.

It is significant to note that the reverse is not the case. Whereas the nature of the doctor-patient relation requires the disclosure by the patient of his or her own individuality and circumstances (all the more so as illness is the more serious and life-threatening), it does not for Cassell require the self-disclosure of the physician to the patient. Remarking on what a patient has a right to expect of a doctor, he points out how impossible it would be for doctors to give so personally of themselves all the time "without being pulled to pieces." When doctors express kindness, trust, and warmth, "it is not themselves they are giving" (ibid., p. 119). To be sure, he notes, it takes a long time for students to learn this (and some learn better, and more quickly, than others), "but we physicians do not lose a piece of ourselves when a patient dies or gain when one is born" (ibid., p. 120). While there are things to which patients are indeed entitled, there are also some to which they are not entitled.

And here is the dilemma: How can a physician reconcile this imbalance of expectations within what on the other hand is a mutual relationship? The physician is enjoined by the nature of medicine's fundamental benevolence and therapeutic aims to be "warm, dignified, kind, open, trustworthy, giving (and forgiving), gentle," even to embody qualities usually associated with loved ones or parents. Yet, contrariwise, to attempt to do this "day in and day out" with all sorts of different people, most of whom are strangers, would surely pull the doctor to pieces.

Therefore, the physician must learn to practice a rigorous, subtle, and difficult form of inward *distancing of self* from the social role of "the doctor." This requirement adds another dimension to the dilemma. Not only is the "self" of the physician, unlike that of the patient, not displayed and not at stake; beyond that, the doctor is enjoined to internalize the separation of self from social role while not allowing that separation to go on in his or her own non-medical life or affect the medical relationship. Is it, then, even possible to fulfill what is said to be the right of the patient and to remain an integral person or self? Is it possible to distance oneself inwardly and play a role (the role of warm, caring doctor) without losing oneself or, on the other hand, critically deceiving the patient?

As the point here is vital in grappling with the moral issues occasioned within medical situations, we would be wise to dwell on it further by reflecting on a particular case.

THE AFTERMATH OF DISTANCING:
GOOD TIMES AND BAD

A pediatrician comes to a regional medical center for a short time in order to improve his diagnostic and surgical skills. He arranges to work in conjunction with the center's NICU for part of his time. He performs an umbilical catheterization on an infant, a common procedure for many of these infants, allowing regular access to blood supply so that the regular and frequent blood gases can be readily checked and adjustments made in medications and other procedures. This pediatrician has done the procedure many times in his own practice. Still, it is a difficult and delicate procedure: The umbilical artery is tiny, it goes in different directions in each infant, and the instruments require great skill in their use.

Several hours later, the resident notices that the baby's abdomen is distended and that the swelling seems to be increasing and cannot be stopped. Emergency procedures are instituted, and the attending physician is called in as the infant's condition becomes critical. The efforts are to no avail, and the infant dies. It is felt that the arterial wall was slightly perforated during the catheterization (later confirmed at autopsy).

Of course, the parents were called as soon as their baby's condition became critical; they were not in the hospital at the time (and they lived some distance away, on a farm) and arrived only after the baby had died. The visiting pediatrician was also called at the same time but was able to get to the NICU only at about the time the parents arrived.

Everyone is shocked and dismayed, especially the parents and the visiting pediatrician. While the baby's condition was quite serious, it was expected to survive and do well. Now, the parents and the pediatrician are stunned, remorseful, distressed. The parents are consoled by the NICU staff. It becomes clear to them during the talk with the attending, the visiting pediatrician, the resident, and the primary-care nurse that the baby's death was not due to any negligence but happened as a result of the complications and delicacy of the catheterization. In fact, they are told, the pediatrician had already done the procedure many times before and nothing like this had happened; still, what did happen is one of the clear risks of the procedure, and this was properly communicated to them prior to its being done.

For his part, the visiting pediatrician is obviously grief stricken and feeling considerable guilt. The parents, rural people living among both their extended families, seem to understand, are grateful for the care already given (which, because of their lack of insurance, was provided gratis), and express their concern about the guilt the pediatrician is clearly feeling. They seem satisfied that the medical and nursing staffs are "good folks who wouldn't deliberately harm anyone," and the matter is concluded with the staff's recommendation that the parents participate in the NICU program for parents whose infants have died while in the unit. The parents return to their home, hold a funeral service, and are not heard from again.

The pediatrician, however, is tormented and desolate, mortified at his mistake. The arterial wall was inadvertently nicked, and he held the knife. No one seems particularly anxious to talk about it, though, and anyway he has to return that day to his home, as his time at the center is up. He leaves and, as later becomes known, nothing about this case is conveyed to the hospital with which he is associated in his hometown, nor is any effort made to contact him directly. It is indirectly learned, though, that he continues to feel profound guilt, bitterness, and loss. He apparently does not discuss the matter with anyone in a direct way. He withdraws from many social and professional functions for a long time and only gradually becomes involved again.

Such situations, each with its own uniquely texturing circumstances, are not uncommon, even though patients don't always die as a result of the clinical mistakes. Sometimes, physicians become victims of "burn-out." Some become substance abusers. A few, disillusioned and disheartened, become suicides. Nowadays, some of the more serious aftermaths are addressed through specially designed programs (alcoholism, drug abuse, suicide), but not very many physicians take advantage of such programs. Numerous other aftermaths, equally serious in their way, remain unnoticed and untended—whether from fear of social or professional stigmatization, from beliefs that open discussion is equivalent to admission of personal weakness, or other reasons.

Nor is this surprising. By prior disposition, education, training, and the social structuring of health care—not to mention their position on the favorable end of the asymmetry of power and authority—physicians and nurses are constitutionally disposed toward emphatic values such as inner strength, perseverance, courage, individualism, and resoluteness in the face of accountable decision making and its aftermaths. On the other side of such values is the condemnation of weakness in every form, such as inability to live with stress, being submissive or passive, opening up too much with patients (and colleagues), or taking things too personally.

Cassell's emphasis on what patients have a right to expect is quite naturally a part of this value-nexus, as is his repeated urging that physicians must practice that special type of inner distancing of themselves from their roles. The physician does not give himself, personally; rather, "the doctor" gives, forgives, and is kind, strong, and trustworthy, regardless of what may be going on in his own personal life.

The physician who does "give himself"—what are we, or Cassell, to make of him? How far can Cassell's point be drawn? To be angered or offended when lied to is, perhaps, inappropriate and can damage the benevolent relationship with a patient (temporarily or irreparably). The fact of the lie itself is medically significant, nevertheless, and thus, for the physician to become angry would therefore be medically inappropriate. Additionally, to be taken in by seductive behavior may (but does not always) mean that the doctor has simply confused his rule ("the doctor") with himself. But what about that pediatrician: Is his evidently experienced grief and guilt inappropriate in the same way? Is it grief and guilt only by "the doctor," and are these felt only regarding the "mistake"? Has the pediatrician lost something of himself with the death of this infant? Who, indeed, is suffering here, and over what?

My point is not that the subtle, inner acrobatics of self-distancing are either unfortunate or immoral. It is rather that this act harbors critical consequences that can grievously affect physicians themselves. This becomes especially clear in cases like that of the pediatrician; untended and unresolved aftermaths of living through difficult decisions, actions, and medical errors may themselves become symptomatic of serious conflicts that can create still further problems defeating the aims and purposes of medicine. Such dilemmas and conflicts are only exacerbated when the benevolent relationship is between strangers; questions bearing on trust can then become profoundly aggravated.

There are, obviously, a great many happy aftermaths resulting from helping others, and a great many in between those and the disaster confronting that pediatrician. There are, moreover, definable, teachable ways of working constructively with strangers (for both physicians and patients). Understanding the many subtle features of paralanguage and everyday conversation, along with the contexts of patient-physician encounters, can "heighten one's awareness that one is always a stranger and a guest when another's subjective experience is concerned" (Lenrow, in Rubenstein and Block, p. 52). With that, of course, both patient and physician can be expected to be less presumptuous of one another, more open to their differences, and more aware of ways of managing these differences to everyone's benefit.

As conversations go on, people can and do become less strange to one another. Even if they do not go on to further stages of intimacy, that "temporary intimacy" (Lenrow) can be quite valuable and fruitful for both of them. It may well be, in fact, that the times of happy encounter and fortunate outcome are times in which the otherwise rigorous distancing between the person and the role of "the doctor" is eased, even dissipated and absent altogether (even if only temporarily). No defensive fences are needed with happy aftermaths.

Nevertheless, that very fact only reinforces the point: The less distancing in the one case, the more difficult it must be to maintain that separation of self from role in the other. Suppose, then, that Cassell is correct in saying that "we physicians do not lose a piece of ourselves when a patient dies or gain when one is born" (1985, Vol. I, p. 120). That position is certainly credible and strongly supported by the very social structuring of health care into bureaucratically organized institutions such as hospitals. Still, the dilemma remains intact and exigent.

In the pediatrician's case, it would surely not do to say—neither to him nor to the parents—that it was not *him*, Dr. Q, but "the doctor" who erred and caused the baby to die. It would have been consequential in many ways, obviously, had his error been due to negligence. But even granting that it was not negligence in no way lessens the seriousness of the aftermath for either of them. If anything, that can make the moral character of the aftermath even more difficult to live with—to carry the guilt and remorse silently, without airing, can be devastating.

It is a natural tendency for us to want to know why events occur, seeking the cause of something being one of the prominent ways we do this; and we thereby reduce uncertainties so that we can know how to reckon with things and know what to hold by. But what about this pediatrician's mistake? He was cautious and alert, as usual; the instruments were appropriate and used skillfully; only, the baby's artery either moved at the wrong time or took an ever so slightly different direction than it appeared. The nick in the arterial wall was only ever so slight, the accumulation of fluids in the abdominal cavity so gradual—well, in medicine as in life, sometimes, "that's the way it goes" and nobody, really, is to blame, for none of us can find the cause or reason for the thing's having happened. As there seems no way to blame anyone, however, so there seems to be no good reason for the thing to have happened in the first place. Why then did it happen at all? Of course, as everyone knows, nothing is certain in medicine, all we've got to go on are probabilities, all that we know is relatively uncertain, life is a risky business—do these clichés help ease the pediatrician's aftermath?

There is, then, a glaring feature of that situation. The parents were provided considerable support, not only from their respective families, but also from the NICU's own program designed to assist such parents. The visiting pediatrician, however, received nothing (nor do others, unless they have the good fortune to have extremely close relationships with a knowledgeable colleague). While the NICU medical and nursing staffs talked with the parents in some depth, they talked hardly at all with the pediatrician. Whereas such supports, programs, and consoling talk for parents were initiated by the staff, the pediatrician was left having to take the initiative. That he did not do so is neither surprising nor uncommon, given the prevailing values, attitudes, training, and structural forms of health-care delivery. The fact that this aftermath was the result of a physician's mistake, even if forgivable (and even forgiven by the parents), only underscores the difficulties of taking the initiative to discuss these issues.

As Gorovitz and MacIntyre have observed, physicians—unlike the "touts" of British track betting fame—are least likely to keep records of, much less make public, their errors. That they make mistakes, everyone knows, but few like to admit; admissions are believed to show weakness, increase uncertainty, and lessen confidence, thus damaging relationships with other patients. However that may be, the point is that those values deeply texture these aftermaths, with the result that very little is done to help the helpers themselves when their inner self-distancing is compromised or shaken by the harsh consequences of difficult actions or decisions.

The dilemmas of distancing can be profoundly consequential. They demand (like the dilemmas identified by Lenrow) some positive response, and as these dilemmas are fundamentally moral, quite as much and as difficult as those more usually discussed in the literature, an ethics responsive to clinical medicine must be responsive to these as well.

ADDRESSING AFTERMATHS

We need to consider each of these types of dilemma to see what might be done.

Dilemmas of Interdependence

These dilemmas arise from compromises to the fundamental assumption of medicine: the mutuality of trust and care (benevolence). When patients and physicians are strangers to one another, they initially do not have (or do not know whether they have) any common and enduring system of mutual understanding and obligation, beyond certain generalized typifications of socially accepted roles and functions. The mutuality of the relationship is further compromised by the asymmetry of power and resources (and the inequality of their respective conditions) in favor of the physician.

The physician and patient must find (where and as possible) ways of understanding and trusting one another as these specific individuals they in fact are. They must also reach common understanding about the legitimate forms of intervention and influence for the specific problems being addressed. The initiative naturally falls to the physician. For while it is true that the relationship commences only when the person presents or is presented as an at least potential patient, it is the physician who professes to be able to help, who has access to resources unavailable to the patient, and who has the knowledge and skills required to know "what's wrong" and "what can be done about it." Once initiated, the relationship is quickly transformed into greater mutuality: For among all the things that *can* be done, decisions about what *should* be done require the active participation of the patient (or someone acting in his or her stead).

The dilemmas of interdependence are fundamentally focused on the problems of communication. It is precisely here, I think, that Cassell's study has its greatest value, in its detailed exploration of the subtleties of paralanguage and daily conversation, as well as what has been indicated about the context or setting. As physicians are rightly expected to learn the varieties of heart sounds and to learn to identify and discuss them linguistically, so should they be expected to learn the various features of everyday conversation, paralanguage, and physiognomic gestures. Dilemmas of interdependence are communication issues and are resolvable only by acquired competencies of listening to, interpreting, and speaking with patients.

Dilemmas of Integration of Helping and Work

Here, the basic problems concern what happens to the work of helping patients when the work itself is organized within institutions whose dominant values are at odds with the values inherent to helping. Utility, efficiency, and impersonalized procedures and instrumentalities are basically opposed to the values of nurturing, benevolence, trust, and personal commitment. Moreover, the threat of the social structural organization of medicine is twofold: compromise of the therapeutic dyad of care and trust between physician and patient, on the one hand; erosion of the relationship between helpers in the health professions, on the other.

Here, too, communication is a vital issue, in particular among the health-care professionals themselves and communication between these professionals and institutional administrators and staff. To the extent that one can extrapolate from Cassell's study to these other contexts, as I think one can, it also provides important insight into skills of listening, interpreting, and speaking needed to understand the language and usages among these different conversational forums. It might indeed be suggested that such skills are very much in the interests of these different groups, individually and collectively, and that correctly understood conversations strongly support the values of both utility and benevolence.

Beyond this, Lenrow believes that there is a strong need for what he terms "networks of helpers." Few of us are heroes, even in our own eyes. Although many enter the medical profession with a vision of serving purposes larger than themselves, few are capable of maintaining that vision and benefiting from its sustaining power in times of lonely struggle. We know, too, that people, especially those with such visions, are liable to a sense of self-importance and self-assurance, which can easily mute or even blind them to the darker side of their own efforts—errors, negligence, contradiction, inappropriate intrusion, coercion, findings inconsistent with expectations.

As Lenrow points out, whether a person is charismatic or not, "a solitary mission is unsupportable," and we therefore need a "network" of people for support, criticism, and affirmation of approaches and purposes, not to mention influencing institutions (Lenrow, in Rubenstein and Block, 1982, p. 53). To defuse the negative effects of role conflicts, misunderstanding, misplaced priorities, and mutual defensiveness, which can erode the value of helping and perpetuate still further estrangement between helpers and those helped and among helpers themselves, Lenrow suggests that such networks—like the self-help organizations for different sorts of patients—can be effective.

While such networks run the risk of becoming little more than sub-bureaucracies within the larger one and thus of possibly devolving into promoting the very dilemmas they are conceived to remedy, Lenrow's suggestion is certainly worth taking seriously. In any event, as he seems to recognize, these networks presuppose that their members are concerned and committed enough—to their work, their co-workers, the institution, and to those who are to be helped—to undertake this networking in candid and regular ways.

It seems clear, however, that this idea is more feasible and viable in some of the helping professions (nursing and social work) than in others, medicine in particular. Physicians, as we've noted, embody values like independence and strong individualism to the point where this idea of networking seems somewhat unlikely to be acceptable or, if attempted, effective.

Dilemmas of Distancing

Here, it has seemed to me, is a region of issues quite as pressing and legitimate as Cassell's demarcation of everyday conversation and its place in clinical judgment. The dilemmas of distancing concern physicians themselves. These are generated by a characteristic requirement of being a physician, to be at once intimate yet distanced, gentle yet firm, approachable yet dignified, open yet impervious, giving yet demanding, unbiased yet specialized in knowledge and skill, kind yet directive, personal and appreciative yet impersonal and objective. How to balance these, keep them in constructive equilibrium, is not only a constant daily feature of routine practice; it can also be a formidable task. The inability to do so, or even momentary lapses (for whatever reason), can prove at times catastrophic—the case of that pediatrician—affecting diagnostic and therapeutic skills, relations with patients or colleagues, and the aftermaths of decisions.

Cassell notes that learning this inner distancing takes quite a long time and much concentrated effort. Its difficulties are doubtless part of the core rationale for the lengthy clinical training of students. It is also probably with this very much in mind that ancient physicians (especially in the Hippocratic and skeptical tradition) were so insistent on the need for experience and still more experience with the *phainomena* and so strongly emphasized the uniqueness of each individual patient.

There are dangers implicit to inner distancing (as the ancient skeptics knew well). For instance, one can distance oneself to the point where knowing and curing become emphasized to the exclusion of healing and caring. At the same time, it can also lead the physician to believe in his or her superiority over those "not in the know" (i.e., patients), as happened with the dogmatics and especially Galen. On the other hand, a doctor can feel a patient's needs and suffering so much as to affect his or her medical judgment. Or, like that pediatric surgeon, the physician's inner equilibrium can fail from the consequences of decisions or actions, with the doctor no longer able to maintain that kind of distancing.

What to do about these dilemmas? In the first place, the recognition of their fundamental moral dimension suggests that contending with, much less attempting to resolve, them requires considerable moral sensitivity and competency. In the second place, as students of medicine must come to learn this distancing—and because of the uniqueness of each patient encounter never cease learning it—this initial, ongoing, and never-ending learning must be seriously informed with moral understanding and imagination. Educational and clinical training within medicine has to include moral education and clinical ethics training, quite as much as it includes medical knowledge and skills in the narrower, more usual sense, as well as those linguistic skills Cassell demonstrates. Otherwise, it seems obvious, failure to recognize correctly what one is dealing with (i.e., moral issues) will invariably distort, obfuscate, if not entirely suppress the moral sphere, with consequent and seriously debilitating aftermaths.

In the third place, the act of distancing and maintaining internal balance, or equilibrium, is difficult at any time. It is also constantly challenged by the counterdemands of patients and the discipline of medicine (one's own sense of it, that of one's colleagues, and the accepted standards of the profession). Accordingly, it invariably results in dilemmas and conflicts, and thus of itself demands occasions for candid inquiry, sensitive discussion, and personal support. In plain terms, it was wrong to have left that pediatrician to his own resources, when those were minimal and ineffective. He was in effect abandoned and in consequence impaired, both as an individual person and in his capacity as physician.

As we provide various types of support for patients and their families, so too is it imperative that we provide moral support for physicians and other helpers. The case of that pediatrician clearly illustrates the need for supports regarding the aftermaths of difficult decisions, errors of judgment or skill, and the other facets of clinical life. The physician (and by parity of reasoning, nurses and other helpers) is no less a moral agent than are patients, faces moral dilemmas and quandaries no less than they, and is thus no less deserving of moral address. In part, this implies educational and clinical training reforms; in another sense, it implies the need to establish regular forums for moral discussion of the consequential problems inherent to the act of distancing and yet remaining equiposed.

CLINICAL CONVERSATION: A CLUE

But the issues here are far wider than even that, as we have learned from the central place of the therapeutic dyad.

I take my clue from Cassell. He points out that in teaching physical diagnosis, great importance is placed on accurate listening to and description of what murmurs sound like—location, place in the cardiac cycle, pitch, duration, quality. For instance, terms such as "murmur of aortic insufficiency," "mitral murmur," and "ejection murmur" cannot substitute for clinical *description*. "Someone hearing or reading these phrases does not know what the murmur sounded like," but rather has heard "what the doctor thought," that is, an *interpretation* (Cassell, 1985, I, p. 16). The same is true of every patient encounter. To say of a patient that the elbow demonstrated acute arthritis is already an interpretation. "We want to know whether it was red, hot , tender, or swollen. And if so, how much of each" (ibid.). In precisely the same way, Cassell argues, "we expect trained listeners to remember . . . what the spoken words were and how they sounded . . . separate from any interpretation of meaning" (ibid., p. 17). Thus, before interpreting a patient as "nervous," "saddened," or "depressed," it is imperative to note the rate of speech, the kinds of pauses, and the sort of pitch, as well as be attentive to word choice and intent.

Just these skills of listening to and describing our everyday conversations seem very much what the ancient empiric tradition called *peira*. In the same way, what Cassell carefully distinguishes as "interpretation" expresses very much what the empirics called *semeosis*, and what he terms "judgment" or "decision" seems at least a component of *epilogismos*. There is a critical difference between what is observed, how that is interpreted, and the clinical judgement or decision that combines these together into diagnostics, therapeutics, and moral decisions.

Furthermore, as medicine has accumulated increasingly refined and multiple languages for describing, interpreting, and judging, so too, Cassell in effect argues, it must develop equally refined descriptive, interpretive, and thematic usages pertaining to the paralinguistic, linguistic, and contextual features of everyday conversations between doctor and patient. These skills, like those usually associated with medical competence, are equally an inherent part of medical knowledge, whose goal is helping people get better.

Similarly, I want to suggest, clinical-liaison ethics must be cultivated so as to be equally capable of refined description, interpretation, and thematic judgment regarding each of the complex components of clinical situations. While this discipline is hardly at that stage, it is nevertheless possible to demonstrate the elements of the discipline and their significance for medicine.

DESCRIPTION IN CLINICAL-LIAISON ETHICS

Consider any of the cases thus far presented, for example, the elderly woman who signed the Directive to Physicians.

Because her hands had become so swollen, misshapen, and painful from arthritis, she had been encouraged by her sons to communicate with the one living far away by means of audiotapes. In one of these, she is in the first nursing home, the tape having been made a week or so prior to her first pulmonary crisis. She is by herself, talking to the second son, but at times seems to forget that that is what she's doing.

> I know . . . [clears throat] . . . I know now that no matter . . . how long my sentence is . . . it's gonna be spent in a nursing home, alone . . .'s far as my family is concerned. . . . But I'm glad they don't have to sit and watch me die. I had to sit and watch Mother die, an' it was terrible. I think I'll spare my children that . . . not that I have any choice about it. . . . Can't think of a worse way to spend it th' . . . than in a nursing home. Which is just like bein' in jail, really. You have no rights; you're just a number. A baby. An' all the bodies are old and worn out, an' yours is no different than anybody else's. . . . An' I found out that it's not any advantage at all . . . to have your . . . brains left, because, when you question things, they think you're trying to tell them how to run their business. . . . It's better not to question, it's better just t' go 'n accept their discipline like a child would: no questions, just do [long pause while she tries to turn off the machine, then finally succeeds]

Later, on the same tape, she reflects:

> Well, here's *another* day . . . I'll swear, how slowly they pass . . . and you wonder why I can't be cheerful about things. . . . I'm tryin', I really am tryin', but I'm not gettin' anywhere. . . . When he [her pulmonary specialist] told me that there wasn't any possible chance for me to get out and have another apartment on my own . . . and . . . that I'd always have to live in a place like this . . . that . . . that did somethin' to me . . . I really couldn't shake it. . . . I know I'm gloomy and sad, an' all that. You'll just have to bear with me. . . . I may get used to it, an' I may not . . . 'ts a bad deal. . . .

And, still later on the same tape:

> I sound like ol' gloomy Gus today for sure, don't I? . . . Well, unfortunately that's just the way I feel. . . . I'm gonna stop now. Maybe I'll feel more cheerful another time. . . . Bye-bye.

Throughout, her voice is slow and halting, and there are many pauses, most of them long and none of them filled with "er," "uh," or other such fillers. In part, it seems, the pauses are due to her struggle to get "a decent breath," for we know that her lungs are almost gone. Her tone quality is breathy, at times raspy (again, her lungs); at times it is whiny ("I'll swear, how slowly they pass," and "you have no rights; you're just a number. A body . . .").

Her voice is often weepy and choked ("how long my sentence is," "watch me die," "it was terrible"). The pitch is medium, and the volume has some swings to it from dull and quiet to very low and fading ("no questions, just do," " 'ts a bad deal"). Her articulation is rather precise, though, even when there is some slurring (which may be in part due to her loose false teeth, the lower plate especially). Her word choice is relatively precise and simple, her sentences, even with the pauses, are quite easy to detect (placing of commas, periods) and straightforward, with little syntactic distancing (using "you" when talking about herself, e.g.). Her talk seems quite orderly and consistent, which is striking considering what she is saying and how very poor her health is.

She presents herself in these passages as a rather alert person, even though profoundly sad and depressed. She seems bitter and whiny yet clear-headed. She sees herself as terribly dependent, her reliance a source of grief for her, as having a fate she can't control. Thus she at times seems resigned to her fate, despondent yet dignified as she talks of her death, of what being in the nursing home is doing to her. Her report of being "gloomy and sad" sounds frank and is spoken with a certain dignity. She also seems honest, a bit hostile at times (about the nursing home, for instance) but not actively angered. Her moods seem leveled down; she is pessimistic about her present and future. Somewhat resentful at her fate, she seems at times as if she has recovered a bit of what she once must have been, a spunky, outgoing person. Then, this quickly fades. Once tough, she has now withdrawn.

A RULE OF METHOD

No other recordings of her, her sons, or her physicians (nor any of them together) are available. With such a scant descriptive base, thus, it is difficult to know just what to say about this woman's moral outlook, especially its consistency over long periods. All that is at hand are reports about her (her condition, views, wishes) from her sons and the physicians and other health care personnel. While these are, to be sure, a source of descriptive-observational evidence, they are nonetheless second-hand and thus are not sufficient for anything like definitive interpretations, much less decisive thematic judgments regarding her care and desires. Thus, what we have, while evidence of a kind (by no means original listening, talking, or observing), must be utilized with considerable caution, quite as much as in the case of the patient discourse in Robert C. Hardy's study. Finally, it must be further noted that since none of us were with her at the time of the recording, key descriptive components of the context and physical setting are missing, thus further compromising interpretation and judgment.

What is lacking, then, is left for us to fill in as best we can. We must rather resort to a kind of imaginative speculation (informed by and kept in bounds by what we do know, both from the tape and from the case reports). This lack at the same time points to a crucial rule of method for clinical-liaison ethics: In-person interactions with situational participants are a far better source of evidence for description, interpretation, and thematic judgment than secondhand reports (no matter how trustworthy). In-person interactions coupled with attentive listening, of the sort Cassell delineates, are an even better source, perhaps the best we can hope for. As a corollary, to the extent that ethical commentaries are not based on direct, in-person acquaintance with and observation of the actual participants, their situations, and presented moral issues, they are quite obviously relatively abstract at best, harmful at worst.

INTERPRETATION IN CLINICAL-LIAISON ETHICS

To return to the woman's taped words, with the noted reservations clearly in mind, what can be said? Descriptively, at the time of the recording, her paralanguage and conversational usages seem consistent. She is aware she is never going to get better than she currently is; confined to a nursing home, dependent on mechanically supplied oxygen and numerous medications, she is acutely aware of what this means for her. Her remaining life is a "sentence"; being in a nursing home is "just like being in jail, really." She is "alone"; at best, her family can visit with her for only limited periods, and she is no longer able to visit them on her own.

  She is alone with other patients—"all the bodies are old and worn out, 'n yours is no different"—and with nursing home personnel. Both groups are strangers, and what is "worse" for her is that in such homes "you have no rights; you're just a number. A body." Though she still has her "brains" left, that makes no difference, indeed it is much worse: Your questions simply rebound back to you ("they think you're tryin' to tell them how to run their business"), so it's best not to question, "just accept" and do what you're told.

  Having been told that she could never again live on her own "did somethin' to me . . . I really couldn't shake it." Now, she feels condemned to an awful fate, for herself and for her family. While she never wanted them to "have to sit and watch me die," as she had done with her own mother (and father and husband), she realizes she now has "no choice" even in that. Try as she might to "be cheerful" and not a "gloomy Gus," "I'm not getting anywhere." That is, she knows she is coming off as gloomy and sad, depressed and despondent, and this knowledge is a further source of sadness and depression.

  Each of the paralinguistic aspects of her discourse, along with her word choice, sentence construction, and coherence, confirms the meaning of her words. What we generally know about such settings as nursing homes and their rooms (their typical dimensions and furnishings, as well as the problems of privacy—background noises on the tape can be identified as the voices of people in the hallway, for example) seems congruent with her prevailing mood. These reinforce her being alone (without family) yet surrounded (by strangers, some of whom have authority and power over her, without her having chosen that).

The attempt to interpret so as to understand what she is saying—her intent, credibility, ultimately her self-presentation through her discourse (see ibid., pp. 115–56)—runs into some problems, especially when one tries to figure out which among the available strategies for action could possibly be recommended. On the face of it, not only is she evidently despondent, but this is also perfectly understandable and justified. In light of her bodily condition, available alternatives and strategies seem drastically reduced. While rigorously avoiding giving her false hopes about the future, we might attempt to address the sources of her suffering by suggesting a nursing home closer to her first son (which was later done, though she continued to be profoundly despondent). We might encourage her to get interested in some activities she might still enjoy: playing cards, conversing with other residents and staff, reading books (or having books read to her). (Such encouragement was attempted, but to little avail.)

This "on the face of it" interpretation is just too simplistic, however. Everything known about her confirms that she was, and remained, an intelligent person with a knack for making friends and a strong liking for other people. She was never uncomfortable around strangers. Yet, her recent past indicated that she had gradually withdrawn from most of her contacts (friends and casual contacts alike); she could no longer "get up the effort" to be with others. Her lungs and her arthritis made it increasingly painful to get dressed up (which she always liked to do), move around, or engage in talk. By the time she went to the home her breathing problem was so severe she could hardly sustain more than a few words at a time (as is clear from the tape). She became an embarrassment to herself in appearance and conversation: her limbs misshapen, her face deeply lined from years of deep pain and the struggle to breathe.

Thus, though the "on the face of it" reading is not wrong, there is much more to it—her *history*. Embedded in that history are two centering moral themes, both of which are suggested in the tape. First, she was deeply repulsed by the very idea of having her sons watch her die, as she had watched her own mother (and father and husband) die: painfully, with agonizing and gradual diminishment of alertness. Second, she deeply feared the loss of her ability to "be on her own," to lose her independence and ability to choose. Being compromised in both respects, she wanted to die—a desire she had often expressed in her recent past as well. With her "brains" still intact but her ability to think clearly already becoming impaired, it is not dying or death that are explicitly mentioned so much as her "sentence" to "jail," her "gloominess," and that " 'ts a bad deal." Still, talking of her mother's dying, she says she "can't think of a worse way to spend it" (her remaining life) than in a nursing home. She is "glad" her family won't have to "sit and watch me die," but is also aware that she has "no choice" about that any longer.

A SECOND RULE OF METHOD

From all that is known about this woman, directly and indirectly, there is far more to be told. And this, something obviously true for every person, suggests another rule of method for interpretation: Every life is linguistically inexhaustible, there is always a richer tale to be told that can never be wholly captured in words, no matter how evocative they might be. Interpretation is essentially limited by all that which spills out beyond our words; there is always more to be told, no matter how much we know, hence what is said is always on this side of definitive or certain.

Still, there are certain key themes to any life story. From all we know, one of these is her experience of watching her own mother die. She doesn't mention her father, nor her husband here—apparently, she sees herself as "Mother" like her mother was for her. We know from the sons' reports that her own mother was about the same age when she died in her own home and that their mother was approximately in her middle 40s at the time, that is, about the age of her own sons at the time of the tape. She now sees herself through multiple temporal perspectives: *now* she is (in the position of) her mother; *then* she was (in the position of) her sons *now*. *Then* she witnessed her mother's gradual death from cancer; *now* she fervently wishes her own sons will not have to witness her death.

Now that she is in a nursing home, where she is "sentenced" to die gradually, we can almost hear her say, "at least they won't have to watch me die." She will, she almost seems to say, die there without her sons' presence, so at least they will be spared that awful experience. Her strong protective tendencies toward her sons persist and are immediately affirmed: "I'll spare my children that." But then they are negated by her circumstances: "Not that I have any choice about it." Indeed, one might remark that few of us will have much choice about how we shall die, or where or when: Suicide is not mentioned and was never a positive theme of her prior or subsequent discussions. The only report we have is that she said one time she doubted she "could ever bring myself to do that"; "I'm a coward," she is reported to have said.

In these fuller terms, what can be said about the centering moral themes? There are central values in her life: love for her family, love for her own independence. But these have been compromised at their core. The way she has defined her life and her self is no longer possible; she is apart from her sons, and she is almost completely dependent. Her sons will watch her die despite her fervent wish that they should not have to do that;

she now no longer has any control over what she values most deeply. She has, then, lost her very own core self and is out of control.

UNDERSTANDING MORAL THEMES

What can be done for this woman (or, what could have been done for her, had we had the opportunity to do anything)? The moral themes expressed are her own long-standing love of life as an independent, active woman; the relish of life is now gone, and she faces only the unrelieved struggle for each breath, for each bodily movement. Her love and protective concern for her family, too, have been compromised (by her condition, by distance). Both of these themes are stricken, compromised, and seem unrecoverable.

We are thus compelled to talk of prominent moral themes as the major topic of what has to be understood. To interpret what has been heard and witnessed is to elucidate (explicate: to make explicit) the *thematic moral ordering* of a person's life with a focus on the present in the light of the past and the prospects for the (immediate and long-range) future. Where there are (real or imagined) changes in these themes, these must be explicated and tested, incongruities and congruities alike, against the person's prevailing moods, condition, and values in order to be prepared to think in terms of alternative strategies that might be proposed. The question, thus, is, What can be done to help the person recover some sense of his or her own centering life definition (moral themes)?

For example, is this woman's sense that nursing homes are "jails" (loss of independence, choice, etc.) realistic and informed? In which ways is she "treated like a child"? Or, is her feeling about these homes perhaps as much a reflection of herself and her own losses as it might or might not be an accurate description of actual life in that nursing home? Has her own loss of bodily independence perhaps colored her perceived loss of independence in the nursing home?

There are numerous practical management issues raised by how one answers such thematic questions. For instance, if in fact the nursing home encourages initiative by residents (choice among available alternatives, within de facto limits of personal action), then how can one break through this woman's expression of hopeless dependency? If her sense of herself and her prospects seem well founded (what she can and can no longer do, given her lung problems and arthritis), then what means are available to help her regain a soundly based sense of control, of unconsidered alternatives to her "gloomy Gus" feelings?

Thematic explication of the moral themes of her present life—loss of active independence, threatened familial ties—suggests that she has not become reconciled to her condition and that her life-long moral themes have not undergone any change coordinate with her markedly changed condition and prospects. Hence, her thematic dilemma: What she prizes most of all seems exactly what she can no longer realize, and so long as she continues to value her former independence, for instance, her dilemma only grows more acute and unbearable.

Thematic explication thus shows the need for some sort of *moral transformation*, which can be judged in terms of available alternative strategies: Either she learns to appreciate realistically some ingredients of her actual situation, or she remains gloomy, bitter, depressed. Either she is enabled to see something "worth living for" within her actual condition, or perhaps she must be helped to become reconciled to her losses and ultimately helped to be herself while dying.

On the basis of such thematic understanding, moral judgments and decisions must be framed. Given everything said thus far, what can we say? More particularly, what can be said about her reasons for feeling and acting as she does, and how might these be altered so as to enable her to accomplish a more desirable future (even if it be reconciliation with her dying and eventual death)? Loss of independence is a fact for her. The other side of that loss, however, is loss of control, and this may suggest at least certain moral transformations and strategic alternatives for decision and action. It is crucial for her integrity as the person she is to help her retain control over what can be controlled and realism over what cannot.

Thus, if her condition is indeed terminal (as seems clear, however long it might take before eventual death), the matter seems clear. The approach must be governed by rigorous but sensitive honesty about her condition, her prospects, and what can be rescued of her very own self through forms of control. Cassell's words strike a responsive chord:

> At the time a patient is given the bad news, he is also told how much control over the situation he has. I actually use the words, "You have more control over your body than you have any idea." I point out that the enemy of his control is fear. I then try to find out exactly what he is afraid of in the greatest detail . . . [and] the fears always turn out to be concrete. In equal and explicit detail I show how each problem can be, or will be, handled. . . . Honesty here is rarely difficult, inasmuch as misconceptions about the disease, drugs, or dying make up a large number of the fears. On questions I cannot answer, such as "How long will I live?" I am also honest, but I often point out how much of the outcome is within the patient's power. Having promised the control of the symptoms or situation, it is absolutely essential that the promise be upheld. (Cassell, 1976, p. 222.)

Given what this woman says and what moral themes can be legitimately explicated from that, the basis for honest assessment and judgment are at hand. She can be told that she is actually dying (along with the medical confirmation of that), that she nevertheless can and will be helped to retain important measures of control, over pain or diet, for instance, and that in dying she will not lose herself but rather can become herself fully. If her death is not imminent, she can be helped to retain a sense of her own worth, helped to know that she can be far more in control of her body and her situation than she realizes, and helped to gain that control, hence her deeply valued independence coordinate with her actual condition.

As Cassell rightly recognizes, these descriptions, interpretations, and thematic judgments are based on trust and speak to the patient's reasons for doing something positive about his or her remaining life:

> The process is based on trust. The patient is being told that it is permissible, indeed necessary, to stop doing something that he has done his whole life—namely, battling for life—and he is being told that it will not hurt. To accept that assurance requires a deep trust of one human for another. (Ibid., p. 223.)

This approach has practical implications. Among other things, it requires open, candid discussion of the alternatives presented—for instance, the Directive to Physicians. It requires the same candor in discussions with nursing home staff, family, and hospital personnel. The woman must be assured that these others can be helped to understand, that they will keep the promise of the directive, and that they respect her as this person she is to the very end, thus affirming her need to be in control over as much of her dying and death as possible.

She also needs to be supported relative to her strong value of familial love. She must be reassured that her sons will not go through what she went through with her own mother (for she had to do this alone, without support, as did her own mother), that her sons both understand and will be supported during her dying, that they will not suffer the additional grief she suffered by having to "sit and watch" as she dies. Their mutual love and respect, thus, will not be lost but rewarded and completed.

Finally, some kind of serious reconciliation of the conflicting values of work and helping needs to be carried out within the nursing home itself, among its staff, so as to enable less remoteness and more understanding and caring for such patients as this.

TOPICAL, INTERPRETIVE, AND MOTIVATIONAL SCHEMATA

Our remarks concerned only a part of the woman's case, as was pointed out: that occasioned by the tape-recording of a message to her second son. Obviously, it does not exhaust the descriptive material, the interpretations, or thematic understanding concerning reasons or motives leading to alternative or transformed courses of action, decision, and likely aftermaths. It should also be quite evident that not even that partial commentary was exhaustive nor could it be in any strict sense. As a person's life exceeds the possibility of a strictly complete telling and interpreting, so must that fact be an intimate part of the rules of method governing clinical liaison-ethics commentary.

Those familiar with the seminal work of Alfred Schutz will readily recognize that this methodical framework of descriptive observation, interpretation, and thematization is derived from his conception of *relevancy schemata* (Schutz, 1970; 1973, pp. 182–228). Schutz contended that these schemata, proposed as a phenomenological explication of key structures of everyday social life, must also be principal features of the method for understanding everyday life. Without going into the rich details of his careful explication, his central point can be readily appreciated by means of an illustration.

Suppose you are invited to an NICU case conference along with others—the attending, the primary-care nurses, the resident in charge of the case, the hospital attorney, and the social worker. The conference was called because an infant's condition has suddenly taken a turn for the worse, and it is unclear just what to do. New therapeutic goals have to be set because current therapies are not working—indeed, they seem to be complicating things. As the discussion proceeds, matters become clearer, and eventually sound decisions are reached. The attending, in fact, is delighted with the outcome and the relevant, practical contribution each person made. He then notes how valuable such conferences would be for other cases, and, as people are filing out of the room, he asks the resident to organize a regular, weekly conference for difficult cases. The resident replies, "You know I can't organize a conference." The attending nods, and the matter seems settled.

You have been on rounds in the NICU on many occasions and have talked with these nurses, this attending, residents, and the others on numerous occasions about many different babies. You know, too, that on rounds there have been discussions by such people about the infants and that these have often proved helpful to nurses and physicians, as they have said many times. You have found, though, that discussions on rounds are too brief to permit the kind of detailed discussion in which you have just participated.

So, you naturally wonder why the resident replied as he did, and also why the matter was then dropped. You are tempted to raise the issue, but the group has quickly dispersed and you are left wondering. What was said? The resident was asked. "How about making this a weekly thing? You could organize it," and he replied, "You know I can't organize a conference." Let's consider this in greater detail.

There is the question and the reply, but also a number of contextual matters about that reply: (1) who said it (the resident), (2) to whom it was said (to the attending), (3) where it was said (in the conference room close to the NICU, in the hospital), (4) what the occasion was (in response to a question from the attending, at the conclusion of the meeting, as people were beginning to disperse), (5) the relationship between teller and hearer (a second-year resident to the current attending, who was about to rotate off his month-long rotation), and (6) when it was said (not only at the end of an ad hoc conference, but early in the resident's second year, toward the end of the attending's rotation, when the federal guidelines for Baby Does had been issued but were not yet final).

You know even more than that, for you have just been in the conference yourself, have been on rounds, have studied the federal guidelines and discussed them with the attorney and many of the NICU staff (including those at the conference), and are aware of the sorts of problems such infants present. You have also heard this attending (and others in the unit), this resident (and others currently rotating there), and these nurses talk about such issues before on rounds, in the hallways, and in other conferences. Your knowledge doesn't stop there, of course, but enough is at hand for you to figure out what was said and its meaning.

Strictly, all you actually heard (in fact, overheard) was the question and the reply; all you actually saw was the attending and the resident (the others were more in the background), the room with its furnishings, and the partially opened door. In Schutz's terms, these constitute the schema of *topical* relevance: The topic is the proposal of a weekly conference, along with the resident's reply and the expectable behavior (physiognomic gestures, bodily conducts such as nodding) typically associated with asking-and-replying, then having matters settled.

As was pointed out, your considerable contextual knowledge provides a larger framework for what was seen and heard, including your gradually acquired acquaintance with the work of residents and their relationships with attendings and others in the NICU. Because of that, you have already found yourself thinking of residents' language and behaviors as exhibiting a kind of *code*: There are some things that are "okay" for them to say and do in certain circumstances (e.g., in a meeting of residents) that are decidedly not "okay" in others (e.g., on rounds). As D. L. Wieder points out in his excellent study of the staff and residents of an East Los Angeles halfway house, this code, like the one he found among those residents, "was told 'piecemeal,' came from many sources, and was not necessarily temporally juxtaposed with the objects it was purportedly about." And, like Wieder, you have found that there was always more to it than was being told at the time, thus finding out about this code "required active discovery on the part of the observer" (1974, p. 184).

Hearing the resident's reply on this occasion prompts you to think of that still somewhat unclear code. What you hear at the time is heard in the light of that awareness of the code: "You know" says the resident as you now hear him, "the code for residents does not permit me to organize regular conferences like this, and you know I'm not going to violate that code.

Don't ask me, therefore, but someone else." In the background, as it were, of what the resident has told the attending is something like this: "We residents are already more than preoccupied with everything we have to do in the NICU; even more, I'm new here, and the code is especially tricky and binding on new residents, and we can't appear out of line; other attendings may not agree about the conference, and may see my organizing one as being presumptuous and even arrogant; while such conferences are or can be helpful, neither I nor any other resident can risk offending any attending, for we are evaluated in all manner of ways by all of you; furthermore, as we are in the NICU only for a short time, while others are here permanently, it would be more appropriate to ask one of them rather than a resident."

You realize that the whole situation would have been quite different had the attending asked someone else (the social worker), had someone else (a nurse) asked the question, or had a resident asked another resident. Stripped of its context and of the broader pattern identified as the code, no piece of the talk has a single or self-evident sense.

The gradually acquired knowledge of the code provides you with a schema of *interpretive* relevance: What the resident said is interpretable as an instance of "telling the code." As such, the interpreted piece (reply) functions not only as an example of the code, but also adds to it, elaborates it somewhat, and thus becomes useful in interpreting still other pieces of talk. This interpretive schema is not arbitrarily brought into the situation and then applied by you to the overheard remarks. To the contrary, the schema is spoken or told in the situation itself and at the same time is what enables you to understand the situation. In Wieder's words, the remark heard as an instance of the code "simultaneously elaborated the code and setting as the code was employed by me as a schema" for interpreting the remark (ibid., p. 186). Because of this, it is much more appropriate to think of the code as a continuous, ongoing process, than as a set of stable, enduring elements of culture in the unit.

Since each of the instances of telling the code you have found is relative to specific contextual matters (who said it, to whom, on what occasion, where, when), each is an "indexical expression" (Garfinkle, 1967, pp. 4–7). Wieder in effect argues, correctly I believe, that this indexicality is best understood as the *contextural determination of meaning*. Each instance has its sense and place within its own context, but each is as well an instance of the code, and the code is precisely what is contexturally said or told in each instance.

When the resident says, then, "you know I can't organize a conference," this expresses a normative rule: Show your loyalty to the other residents. This rule is a *moral* norm, which helps to account for this resident's refusal to organize the regular conferences and at the same time helps to account for the general pattern of residents' not doing such things. What you, the observer, have interpretively accomplished is the transformation of a heard remark into the statement of a moral code exhibited in numerous other ways by residents. It is done, moreover, through a process of active discovery and gradual identification: listening to and observing residents within the actual settings of their work and talk. That gradually explicated code is the *interpretive schema* organizing and being elaborated by each *topical occasion* or instance.

You have at hand not only what is topically relevant in the particular setting (the resident's reply to the attending's question, but not, say, the overheard remarks on another topic by a nurse), but also the interpretive scheme (the code) that relevantly accounts for and is further elaborated by that and numerous other topical instances. This permits the observer to know "something of the kinds of motives he would encounter in the setting. Or knowing what kind of motives he might find, an observer would then be able to see the meanings of behaviors he had encountered" (Wieder, 1974, p. 193). This we may recognize as the *motivational schema*, or moral theme: "show loyalty to the residents," and perhaps, "show resident-respect for attendings' authority." This permits the observer to understand otherwise disparate behaviors as coherent types of behavior.

In different terms, the resident's linguistic behavior, seen as an instance of "telling the residents' code," is understood as meaningful behavior insofar as it is understood as motivated by the resident's adherence to that code. In still different terms, paying attention just to what is topically relevant (the organization of a conference), the resident is exhibiting *refusal*; he is making distance between himself and the attending. Paying attention to this talk as an instance of "what residents should and should not do," the resident's talk exhibits or tells a code or theme to which he adheres. The resident is thus motivated in his speech behavior by that moral code.

THE DOCUMENTARY METHOD

This method is termed the "documentary method of interpretation" by Garfinkle (1967, p. 78) and is explicitly adopted in Wieder's excellent study (1974, pp. 184–86). It is dependent on attentive listening to the actual conversations of each situational participant. It is akin, I believe, to Cassell's method of interpreting paralanguage and conversation, and is related to and an expansion of his notion of "the settings" of conversation.

While that method was conceived and developed as a means for conducting social scientific work and study (and as an elaboration of Schutz's methodological delineation of social from natural scientific methods, and his notion of relevancy schemata [1967; 1973]), I believe that it is exactly what must be done in clinical-liaison ethics (and, more generally, within the helping professions). A patient's (or a nurse's, a physician's, etc.) statement ("Can't think of a worse way to spend it th' . . . than in a nursing home") supported by paralinguistic, linguistic, and situational constituents, is an instance of "telling the code." The code here, however, is the person's own *moral life-theme* or outlook: for instance, the elderly woman's theme of independence and the loss of "being able to be on my own." The measure, or moral character (life-theme), of this woman's life has been the governance of that value (among others). Whether she has in fact "lived up to it" (in her own or in others' eyes), it has been the habituated *moral resolve*, the standard by which she has in part judged herself and wanted to be judged and known by others. Her *topic* (going into the nursing home) has its *interpretive schema* (independence) and *motivates* her *thematic judgment* ("can't think of a worse way," "a sentence," "like being in jail").

It is imperative to fasten onto the point that these schemata are not imported into her specific circumstances by me. To the contrary, they are her own implicit, and at times in her life quite explicit, ways of organizing her life, giving it thematic coherence and sense. The clinical-liaison ethicist must actively discover these schemata as they are "at work" in each clinical situation and as the organizing structuring activity of each clinical participant. Only in that way are problems at all identified and apprehended and alternative strategies able to be mapped out and imaginatively explored, much less decisions and resolutions reached and aftermaths made livable.

Although the words used by this woman, or by that resident, are in a sense not completely meaningless when they are extracted from their contextural placement, they can be described in a variety of competing ways when thus abstracted. For instance, the resident could be trying to make a joke: "You know I can't organize a conference," that is, "You know (from past experience) what happens when *I* organize *anything*!" He might be appealing to his own busy schedule, saying that his patients don't need that sort of discussion, suggesting that the next attending physician is ("you know") opposed to such conferences. Only the actual contexts of usage and conversation can fill in what, among the variety of meanings, is the operative one.

Thus, each of the individual parts of conversation (by patients, physicians, nurses, etc.), if abstracted from their respective contexts, is necessarily open to a range of possible interpretations, from among which the observer can find no ground for choosing one over any of the others (see Gurwitsch, 1964, pp. 234–47). Taken as they actually occur in their own respective contexts, however, the talk and behavior mutually determine and fulfill one another. To use a different example, the bodily movement of reaching out with the right arm, hand open and fingers together and extended, acquires its meaning solely within the context of its actual occurrence. The range of possible meanings such a movement could have— handshake, dance movement, karate chop, exercise—becomes narrowed and specified by mutual references to its context and the other constituents, such as the setting, the talk, and the placement and conducts of other people.

However, as Wieder emphasizes, "the ordering of the setting and the definite sense the elements of the setting achieve in their contextural location is contingent and relative" (1974, p. 200). The relativity here was already well known among the empiric and skeptical physicians in ancient times and can be readily specified in our terms. Doing so also helps to make clear what those ancients meant by "the law" within the *phainomena*.

In the first place, those who are observed may have only a more or less clear notion of their own words and conducts and may tend to understress or exaggerate what is called for. The resident may have misunderstood what the attending asked and may have replied without a good understanding of the variability of the code (in the NICU "things are done differently," for instance). In the second place, the sense and order of events are contingent as well on the historical and ongoing experience of the observer, especially in light of the fact that detecting conducts as instances of "telling the code" or "expressing my basic moral outlook"—i.e., the "law" in the *phainomena*—require the active work of discovery by the observer. In simplest terms, what may seem innocent chitchat to a novice will be apprehended by the experienced observer as something quite significant (the "old hand" as opposed to the "rookie"). Hence, observing certain present topics of conversation as ordered instances of "telling the code" or "expressing my moral outlook," that is, as falling within certain interpretive and thematic schemata, is relative to the concrete, prior experiences of each observer.

A third sense in which the specificity of a context's meaningfulness is relative, yet "lawful," should be stated. In Wieder's terms, while the range of these open possibilities of some event "is *narrowed* by its location within a contexture," this does not mean that it is thereby fully specified nor that it precludes encountering "new and startling displays" that might totally change the sense of the original experience (ibid., p. 202).

Any instance of conversation or conduct is always open to further disclosure, can always take on new meanings, in the course of further experience. Thus, were there subsequent conversations between the resident and the attending, or between the resident and another resident, on the same topic, it could well happen that the earlier reply would have to be seen as different, modified, or elaborated still further. Therefore, we are always faced with some degree of uncertainty; we can have only relative specificity in our interpretations and thematic judgments.

Finally, it must be acknowledged that patients, physicians, and others whom the ethicist observes and with whom he or she interacts could at any time be engaged in a form of deliberate or perhaps inadvertent manipulation. For instance, the attending may have been deliberately trying to get this resident into difficulties, or he may have been inattentive in asking his question or testing the resident. Only careful additional observations and acquaintance with these contexts can indicate which direction must be taken in interpretation.

All these suggest that "telling the code" or "expressing my moral outlook," are essentially open and flexible, subject only to relative specification in each case. Therefore, the documentary method—what we earlier termed the detective work of clinical liaison ethics—must incorporate uncommon alertness, caution, and persistence as inherent components of the method. Its purpose is to permit the relevant, sensitive explication of the deeply embedded moral themes (codes or outlooks) on both sides of the therapeutic dyad, or "the law" within the *phainomena*, so as to enable those involved in it to come to responsible and informed decisions.

CHAPTER 11

Trust and Care: Toward a Moral Foundation

A lengthy and somewhat checkered path has been followed in this study. We began with the curiosity of practicing physicians, researchers, and medical educators appealing to persons in the humanities, especially philosophy, for help. Reviewing their initial response, the appearance of a serious backlash against Big Ethics by physicians, and the subsequent efforts to grapple with that, we then found ourselves having to ask an entirely different question, What must ethics in medicine be if it is to be responsive to the actual issues encountered in clinical practice?

REVIEW OF THE TERRAIN

Realizing that the question itself poses a serious need to rethink matters in a thorough way, we were led to a certain initial set of conditions for such an ethics, such as becoming clinically astute, being held accountable, and, in the end, having something positive and responsible to say. To find out what these implied, it was found necessary to come to grips with medicine itself, the physician's specifically complex field of work, and its underlying moral resolve: the fundamental assumption of medicine, or the covenantal relationship inherent to the therapeutic dyad. At the same time, it proved necessary to appreciate the complexity of current medical practice (regarding both sides of the dyad) and the multiple sources of moral conflict inherent to it.

This permitted a somewhat more detailed explication of the conditions for an ethics responsive to clinical medicine—to physicians, to patients and their families, and to the institutional contexts wherein physicians and patients actually meet. Such an ethics, it was suggested, is a kind of *circumstantial understanding*, proceeding in its work rather in the manner of a detective, identifying, interpreting, and assessing clues. Since medicine is focused on patients, it became necessary to study the experience of illness, utilizing the talk of patients themselves to guide this inquiry. This eventually brought home a curious and altogether crucial issue: Close attention to such talk discloses an anomaly in the discourse between patients and physicians. Whereas both of these participants talk to one another and the patient exhibits a discernible communicative intent, the physician seems most often to listen only for the locational index. Once that is at hand, the physician's concern and interest depart from the patient's discourse, proceeding to the work of clinical judgment in its usual sense—diagnosis, therapeutic alternatives, and what Pellegrino calls the prudential decision.

Close attention to this discourse and the direction taken by the physician shows that they have important consequences: the displacement of the patient's interpretation and its replacement by the physician's, a factor that results in a form of displacement of the patient's own self-experience and understanding of self. Inherent to this is especially a view of the human body, specifically the patient's own body and, with it, of the patient's own self—a supposedly Cartesian dualism or, at times, a version of materialism.

That medical view (dualism most often) was found to have a curious and fundamentally misinterpreted history. A close study of Descartes failed to find that well-known dualism (although it did disclose a far more interesting and basic one, centering in the body itself), and this prompted further historical inquiry to discover the origins of the current dominant medical view of body and self (person). Looking into post-Cartesian medicine, we found a widely prevailing notion of the human body as a "machine" composed of inter-functioning material parts. If or when soul is admitted, it is rather awkwardly hung onto that material mechanism. Both body and soul, however, turn out to be abstractions without foundation in concrete human life. The significant thing, however, is not so much the naiveté of the notion of soul (person) as it is the conception of the body. This, along with Descartes's insights and mistakes on the topic, yielded the clue for unraveling further, deeper parts of the puzzle: Why should or can the body be so conceived, especially when this flies in the face of daily, ordinary experience by the one whose body it is? How did medicine come to adopt such a mechanistic view of human life?

Further historical probing was necessary, and the clues at hand led us to look into the history of anatomy (that medical discipline seemingly most intimately acquainted with the human body), both before and after

Descartes's seminal conceptualization of that field. This probing led to the recognition that the post-Cartesian notion of the body (Boyle, Hoffman, Gaub, Morgagni, Bichat) reflects a far more ancient dispute, centering around the practices of dissection and vivisection.

Engaging those ancient themes, it was found that the dispute between the ancient empirics and dogmatics was formative of a "divided legacy," which has haunted medicine ever since, especially in the history of anatomical understanding. At the same time, certain moral and epistemological themes basic to subsequent medical history up to the present were also found. These themes were initiated in early Hippocratic empiric medicine, taken up in later Hellenistic methodism, and then, despite Galen's aversion to talk of the soul, transported into later medical writings with a quite astonishing consistency. Medicine is fundamentally a moral enterprise, says this tradition, and this is affirmed again and again even by those such as Galen or, later, Hoffmann and Gaub, who rejected or compromised much of the basis for that understanding.

After probing these complex themes and the moral understanding of both the dogmatics and the empirics, it then became necessary to reflect on the nature and implications of the Hippocratic tradition itself, after which we could pick up where we had left off: What must ethics be to be responsive to a now more deeply understood clinical medicine?

Utilizing still more cases to guide our thinking about the problems, we were led back into the anomalies of patient-physician discourse and embodied human life from another direction that promised to put these into proper perspective. This was the work of Eric Cassell on everyday language, a theme that has been silently with us since Descartes's letters to Princess Elizabeth (and even since the ancient empirics, as we saw) but that has been studied with astonishing infrequency, not to say lack of depth.

For all its insight and clear merits, Cassell's study leaves the central idea of "setting" largely untouched, especially in methodical, practical terms. To gain purchase on that, we found it helpful to expand on Cassell's work by reference to the important work of Alfred Schutz, Aron Gurwitsch, and D. L. Wieder. The "detective work" or "circumstantial understanding" is an expanded form of the "documentary method of interpretation," a methodical rendering of the central concept of *context* (see Zaner, 1982) and its moral equivalent, *enablement* or empowering.

Now it is time to seek the moral foundations of medicine and the experience of illness.

THE IDEA OF THE AUTONOMOUS MORAL AGENT

If we look into prevailing moral discourse, at the level of either everyday moral life or of ethical theory, a number of common themes can be discovered. There is, for instance, a great deal of talk about rights: of fetuses, infants, children, the young, the elderly, and women; of blacks, Hispanics, and other minorities; of the handicapped, the mentally retarded, and incompetents; of those needing organ transplantations and those with organs to donate; and on and on. If we take these seriously, there are rights to health, birth, life, and death; to equal opportunity, equal access, medical care; to fair trial, protection from crime; and countless others. The list is considerable, and the passion of their various advocates runs high and hot.

The discourse is fueled by such commonly heard moral notions as dignity, respect, personhood, and freedom of choice. As a people, we prize and praise the "self-made" person—independent, self-reliant, self-determining, self-sufficient—the one who "did it *my* way" and "did it on my *own*." Thus, it is widely believed that respect for the individual or person is absolutely essential for understanding, evaluating, and deciding on practically every medical-ethical problem (as well as for many if not most other ethical issues). Theoretically advocated from many points of view, this notion serves as one of the basic rationales for a number of what are commonly believed to be key requirements of decision making, for instance, informed consent or truth telling. It is central in complicated discussions concerning abortion, euthanasia, the use of placebos or double-blind techniques in experimentation, and proxy decision making for incompetents.

The person is said to have the right to his or her own body and, therefore, control over what is done or not done with or to it. If we were to ask why we should respect anyone or what it is that legitimates the idea that each person has the right to choose, the widely accepted response would be that underlying all these ideas and rights is the core concept of the moral order itself—that each individual is a free and autonomous agent, and this alone is what must be presupposed if any talk about human conduct is to make sense (see Engelhardt, 1978, p. 3).

This central thesis of modern individualism was most forcefully asserted by Immanuel Kant:

> The *autonomy* of the will is the sole principle of all moral laws and of the duties conforming to them; *heteronomy* of choice, on the other hand, not only does not establish my obligation but is opposed to the principle of duty and to the morality of the will . . . [The] moral law expresses nothing else than the autonomy of the pure practical reason, i.e., freedom. This autonomy of freedom is itself the formal condition of all maximums, under which alone they can all agree with the supreme practical law. (Kant, 1956, pp. 33–34.)

Morality makes no sense unless the person is free and autonomous. This is the sole formal requirement without which human conduct could not be either moral or immoral.

It has, of course, been pointed out that the sheer formalism of these notions allows them, especially duty or obligation, to "be given almost any content" (MacIntyre, 1966, p. 198). Thus, a common complaint about this view is that it seems unable "to deal effectively with the existence of conflicting ethical duties" (Hunt and Arras, 1977, p. 29). Since most moral difficulties involve precisely such conflicts, serious and perhaps irresolvable dilemmas inevitably emerge. Even so, the moral idea of autonomy is both widely accepted in some form or other and is powerful especially within discussions of the moral issues in medicine, which typically center on duty, obligation, and decision making.

In fact, if we look at the history of medicine, it is impressive how congruent certain of its major themes seem to be with that kind of ethics. The ancient Hippocratic commitment to act in the best interests of the patient, its proscription on abortive remedies and suicide, its strong endorsement of the physician's duty to act justly, its forbidding of "mischief" and sexual relations with patients and members of their families, and its strict adherence to utter silence about them and their affairs—all seem to be early ways of expressing the underlying Kantian idea of autonomy and its valuing of persons (who must always be treated as "ends in themselves" and never merely as means).

If we wonder about the passion generated by dissection and, especially, vivisection, it seems we do not have to look far for the apparent reason—the idea of moral autonomy. In more modern times, after the introduction of the modern world's distinctive individualism, there seems little question but that its rationale was definitively expressed by this idea of autonomy. A key part of Descartes's work may well have prepared the way for it. It seems clear that the idea that the human body can and must be considered "in itself," as if there were no soul attached to it (the discovery of *anatomy*), has its correlate in the idea that the human soul must therefore also be considered "in and by itself," apart from its own embodying body (the idea of *autonomy*).

Thus, the history of medicine since Vesalius's seminal work, aided immensely by Descartes, seems to move directly to the Kantian moral thesis. Indeed, it took only some further work in anatomy to give the final license for medicine's no longer having to be concerned with the patient or person; such concern could then be left to the "moral sciences" (Hume). With that, finally, Bichat's famous dictum—"open up a few corpses" and all will be revealed—seemed fully legitimated once it was accepted that the body can (supposedly) be considered "in itself." Thus, the major direction for medicine became treating the body itself or, as with Gaub and the psychosomatic tradition, the soul only through the body—both of which, however, are mere abstractions, stripped of the rich details of daily embodied life.

This emphasis and exclusivity of focus has its counterpart. Like the body, so the soul is an "in itself" that has its own laws and principles, among them its own moral law of autonomy. Whereas the body (like all material nature) is subject to *causal* determination, the soul is regarded as *free*, self-determining, or autonomous. Anatomy and autonomy thus seem deeply congruent and mutually affirming abstractions, the one preparing the way for the other.

ASSUMPTIONS UNDERLYING AUTONOMY

It is understandably tempting to accept the idea of autonomy as the moral foundation of medicine and the experience of illness, in keeping with the widely accepted view in medical ethics. That is not possible, however. Not only does it fail to capture the basic sense of the therapeutic relationship of trust and care, it also involves several highly dubious assumptions. To get at the latter will require some unavoidable philosophical labor, although I will try to keep this to a minimum.

It has become almost an article of unquestioned faith that one person, as it is often expressed, cannot have any direct awareness of the other person's experience. One cannot see, feel, or hear through the other's organs or senses; therefore, everything the one knows about the other (including that there even is an "other" person) "entails inference from one's own experience of the other to the other's experience of one's self" (Laing, 1969, p. 14).

Whereas "my" own experience is directly or immediately presented to me alone, the other person's experience is given and known by me only indirectly or mediately (i.e., by inference). In a sense, what is asserted here is perfectly obvious: I cannot literally use your eyes or ears to experience the world. If I were to see with your eyes and hear with your ears, I would surely *be* you and not myself.

There are two assumptions here. Expressed most simply, these are:

1. The self is essentially closed in on itself. It is insulated and capable of thinking only its own thoughts and feeling only its own feelings.
2. The only direct experience one self has of another is sensory experience of the other's body. Hence, the other person is not experienced in any direct way, but must rather be somehow inferred on the basis of the self's own sensory experiences (since all that is directly experienced is the other's *body*).

These assumptions, deeply rooted in our history, seem compelling and obviously correct. Cassell, for instance, takes them quite for granted as needing neither argument nor elaboration: "Although we cannot read the 'little black box' of the patient's mind, we can read her words," he says at one point (Cassell, 1985, Vol. I, p. 53). In other words, the only way to "get at" and "know" the other person (the patient) is by way of one's own sensory experiences, in this case, of words.

That assumption, indeed, seems to be the actual reason why Cassell's study of language and conversation seem to him at once difficult and chancy, however necessary and justified. Since none of us can get inside the patient's head ("little black box") and experience directly what's going on (as we presumably can in our own case), we are reduced to reading the other person's language, gestures, and the like. The entire thing is even exacerbated by Cassell, living as he and the rest of us do in the post-Freudian era; when it gets down to it, "no one, not even a speaker, can be certain of the speaker's intent" (ibid., p. 117). Not only can we not directly know a patient's "black box" and its "intent," but even if we had direct access to it we would still not be able to attain certainty, since we don't even really know ourselves!

At the risk of committing a bit of heresy, these assumptions need to be looked at rather carefully, for something is terribly wrong about them—they are profoundly misleading, even mistaken. They do not elucidate and illuminate our actual experience and lives; they distort and mutilate them. Max Scheler's formulation of the issue is apposite: "(1) that it is always *our own self, merely, that is primarily given to us*; (2) that what is primarily given in the case of others is merely the *appearance of the body*" (1954, p. 244). On the basis of the movements and alterations in that appearance we somehow come to accept it as the body of another self or person. These now need to be examined, although it is not possible to probe them in much depth here (see Zaner, 1981, pp. 191–210).

The Autonomy of Self

What's the evidence for this presumption? If we are candid, there seems very little; rather, as Scheler remarks, it is at once too optimistic and too pessimistic. It is too optimistic because it seriously underestimates the extraordinary difficulties of self-awareness and self-knowledge. It is too pessimistic because it equally overestimates the difficulties of knowing other persons.

A part of Cassell's point is surely correct. Not even the speaker can always be certain of his or her own intent in speaking. To be sure, while there are many occasions on which one does know what one means and intends to say, we have to admit how often it is that one knows oneself least of all: one's real motives for doing this or that, one's own feelings at the moment and why one has them, where one's ideas really come from, and the numerous urges and images that constantly bubble up to surprise, embarrass, delight, and even terrorize oneself.

On the other side of it, candor shows ever so clearly just how well we know other persons, their doubts and faiths, their lies and lust, their care and collusion: for example, the subtle but telling glint in that fellow's eye, the way that woman averts her glance, the openly embracing look and aspect of one's lover or child, and the myriad ways of touching, walking, holding the head, shrugging the shoulders, the lift of lip, and grimace of mouth. I am reminded of the wife of the diabetic judge we met earlier, who reported that she "really knew he was ill long before he did. . . . You can tell by looking," she said. "It's like taking one of your children to the pediatrician and saying, 'He doesn't look right to me,' and he didn't. I knew he was ill" (Hardy, 1978, p. 238).

If we really think about these matters, Scheler suggests,

> The only thing we can never perceive in our observation of others is their experience of their own *bodily states*, especially their organic sensations, and the sensory feelings attached thereto. It is these things which account for that particular *kind* of separateness among men which [so many theories] attribute to the *whole* of mental life. (Scheler, 1954, p. 255.)

In other words, my own feeling of my own body is mine alone, my exclusive sphere of private feelings: my inner feelings of bodily movements (kinesthesias), my growling stomach or ache in my leg (coenaesthesias), the smoothness I feel when I run a finger over glass (sensation). But while it is true that only I can experience my own inner bodily states and feelings, it is not these I experience when I see that tree or hold my son's hand. These states and feelings, rather, serve as what functionally orients my seeing the tree, grasping my son's hand, talking with a patient. Thus, simply because my own experience of my own body is my own entirely, it in no way follows that everything I experience by means of these feelings is also my own entirely, private to me alone.

If everything were private to the experiencing self, we would be condemned to what Scheler called a "solipsism of the moment," and everything would be quite exclusive to that self (*solus ipse*) (see ibid., p. 259). This would mean that there would be no basis for distinguishing between mine and thine; the very idea of such a distinction would be quite absurd. The idea that there are things independent of such a solipsistic self could not even occur to that self, much less serve as a basis for inferring or speculating about the existence of other things or other selves. With this first assumption, which undergirds the idea of moral autonomy (the soul considered "in itself" without reference to anything else, its own body included), we face an essentially comic absurdity or farce. The solipsistic self who postulates the assumption could not, after all, postulate anything other than itself, had it not been born, reared, nurtured, and enabled to be the self it is despite its curious and farcical pretense at being alone.

The Alien Other Self

The second assumption is equally wrong-headed, even ludicrous. It states in essence that the autonomous, alone self can be aware of, and come to know, other selves solely on the basis of its own sensory experiences of the other's body (through inference or some such means). There are two matters needing comment here: First, the notion of having to "get outside oneself to" the other person (only indirectly or mediately); second, what our experiences of other people actually are.

Here, too, Scheler has given the lie to one of the most common features of modern thinking about interpersonal life. The idea asserted by this second assumption is that genuine knowledge of one self by another requires something like an argument—an inference, or analogy, the premises of which concern perceptions of another body, which then supposedly lead to the conclusion that there are other (nonmaterial) selves than the one doing the inferring.

Let's be clear. There surely are many times when I or you do in fact infer, impute, and even analogize about other people. For instance, when I encounter a particularly irascible nurse, I may infer that she's having a bad day. When Joe says he's got a headache, I may analogize that what he is feeling is something like what I feel when I have a headache. When I see a physician beat around the bush instead of telling a patient what's wrong, I may impute to him that he is afraid, is denying, or whatever. Of course, in each and every one of such cases, there is never any question but that there are such real, live people there; I already know that these are people, and not, say, mannequins or statues.

Appealing to presumably more basic senses of inference or reasoning by analogy (since what was just pointed out may be thought irrelevant) will not do, either. Any theory that begins with these assumptions and then faces the issue of having to argue that there are other people in the world shows the very same absurdity. Consider, after all, what any such argument must necessarily assume yet must necessarily lack.

1. The premise necessary to yield the conclusion, that the other's bodily movements and features imply another self like me, is simply missing. The ways in which I experience *my own* body (smiling or pointing) are fundamentally and necessarily different from the ways in which I experience *another's* body (smiling or pointing).

2. We all recognize nonhuman but animate creatures (fish, birds, animals, insects), but arguments from analogy or similarity here seem at best peculiar. Yet, such arguments would be quite necessary on the grounds of the two assumptions: We couldn't know there is a dog there without inference (analogy or other) based on the ways we experience our own bodies—which seems outlandish.

3. Every such argument commits the logical fallacy of *quaternio terminorum* (four terms, the fallacy being that only three terms are permissible for a sound conclusion). The only logically correct inference that could be made on the basis of these two assumptions would be when I find bodily gestures analogous to my own (i.e., presented to me in the same or similar ways as are my own), my own self would perforce exist "over there"! The premises yield only my own (not the other) self, since the premises concern strictly and only my own experience of my own body; the other's body is not presented to or experienced by me in the same ways.

The second assumption presumes as well that other people are directly experienced only as regards their bodily attitudes, gestures, and movements. Is this true? If we look candidly at our own experiences, it certainly seems quite false. Scheler observes:

> For we certainly believe ourselves to be directly acquainted with another person's joy in his laughter, with his sorrow and pain in his tears, with his shame in his blushing, with his entreaty in his outstretched hands, with his love in his look of affection, with his rage in the gnashing of his teeth, with his threats in the clenching of his first, and with the tenor of his thoughts in the sound of his words. (Ibid., p. 260.)

I may, as we say, have second thoughts about an old friend when, in contradiction to the sorts of things I have long known him to believe, I learn he has seriously asserted something entirely otherwise. I may not believe my own eyes when I witness a horribly crippled man dance a subtle jig. Such doubts and second thoughts, however, are not about whether there are other people, nor about their joys and sorrows, guilts and shame, delights and desires.

It is quite obvious. I know when my old friend is trying to hide the fact of his pain, when my daughter is feeling badly, when I've bored someone. When I see another person's eyes, it is not just his eyes I see, for I also see that "he is looking at me," indeed, "looking at me as though he wished to avoid my noticing he's looking at me." Although mistakes can and do occur, we notice pretense, lying, and honesty not only through others' words but also in their bodily gestures.

The depths and intimacies of being-with-others, whether strangers or friends, old or young, extend still further (see Zaner, 1981, pp. 210–41), but it is unnecessary to follow these out here to appreciate their implications for the moral foundations of medicine and the experience of being ill. Negatively, the idea of autonomy cannot serve as foundational; at most, it may be a morally coherent idea but hardly the basis for the moral order itself. Positively, if we are neither solipsistic in and for ourselves, nor alien and essentially remote from the lives of other persons, but are instead with others at every point (though in many different ways), then it is not insularity and autonomy that define our being but rather togetherness and mutuality.

Moral life is not first of all a matter of the isolated "rational will" functioning in and of itself to provide itself with self-authorized and self-sufficient governance (autonomy = *auto* + *nomos*), and then, on that basis, relating to other persons in ways dictated by the self-derived moral law. To the contrary, moral life is essentially communal at its root, and it is mutuality (in all its complex forms), not autonomy, that is foundational. Nowhere is this more plainly evident than in the contexts of clinical situations dealing with ill persons.

A CASE IN POINT: THE DIALYSIS PATIENT

We may consider one final type of affliction to help elicit this foundation: end-stage renal disease (ESRD) and kidney hemodialysis (the most common form of treatment, even if only as a stage prior to kidney transplantation).

It was not until the 1960s, with the development of the arterio-venous shunt, that persons with ESRD could hope for even the chance of positive treatment. Before then, they faced a slow and painful death. Today, there are three forms of treatment: hemodialysis, in which the patient's blood is circulated through an artificial kidney machine to maintain the chemical and fluid balances of the body; peritoneal dialysis, less often used, in which the dialysate fluid is introduced into the abdominal cavity; and transplantation of a kidney from a living or cadaverial donor.

The medical problems themselves—both those leading to kidney failure and those arising from dialysis—are complex and difficult. The mortality rate of dialysis is about 5 percent in the first year but increases over time for each patient. The rate is increasing in general as older and sicker people are being dialyzed. Most often the cause of death is cardiovascular failure. But there are numerous other medical complications, including bone degeneration, skin disease, blindness (mainly in diabetics), infection of the shunt or fistula permitting access to the artery and vein, malnutrition, anemia, chronic fatigue, and neurological complications.

What are often called psychological effects also occur and can be equally debilitating: depression, sexual dysfunction, new and damaging forms of dependency-relations (especially among males), separation and divorce, fear, anger, and intense anxiety sometimes edging over into psychosis (Griedman, 1977). So closely intertwined are these that it is always difficult and often impossible to separate the medical from the psychological and social factors (Abrams, 1972). Even when there is agreement over the necessity to utilize hemodialysis for only those patients whose condition is not further complicated by diabetes, cardiovascular problems, or some other disorder, the medical contraindications may not be clear enough to give full confidence in selections even at this stage of the process.

Clearly, as we have seen throughout this study, the interpretation of the "purely medical" problems involve evaluative judgments and issues. But which questions are these, and why are they raised by ESRD and dialysis? Attention has commonly focused on allocation of limited resources, rising medical costs, the impact of life-sustaining technology on patients and their families, the consequences of governmental involvement in the treatment of a particular disease, relationships among various health and other professionals, and the serious attrition among members of dialysis units. (see Rescher, 1969; Levine, 1976). Disciplined attention to ESRD and its main form of treatment, however, reveals another cluster of issues often obscured, if not presupposed, by such discussions.

The ESRD-Dialysis Patient

In few instances is the critical pathos of illness and of modern medicine more clearly seen than in this disease and its treatment. They present *in extremis* certain phenomena that are deeply embedded in almost every medical situation, and it is just this dramatic force that is so intriguing. Harry Abrams has underscored a point that even clinical neophytes can readily recognize: What the dialysis patient faces is not trying to live forever, "but of living with the rigors of the medical regimen which may bring about what Unamuno termed the 'too long' life" (1972, p. 56). It is the dietary restrictions, the dependency imposed by the treatment, and the physical complications that constitute "the major problem" (ibid.).

The regimen here is worth noting briefly. The dialysand must spend between five and eight hours, up to three times a week, on the machine, at a minimum (and if there are no complications with the machine or the patient). However, as Lee Foster, a dialysis patient, reported, the dietary restrictions can be "more onerous than the hours spent hooked up to the machine because of the restrictions on my fluid intake" (1976, p. 7).

Because the kidneys are not functional, no more fluid can be taken in between dialysis sessions than the machine can take off: about 400 cc per day (about 2 cups), including that in fruits, vegetables, and other foods. The dialysand cannot eat salty foods (or use salt) and is allowed very little protein because its breakdown makes waste products in the blood that must be removed. A low-potassium diet is required because only dialysis can get rid of potassium, and too much stops the heart. The dialysand must in general keep weight gain to a minimum (between 1 and 2 lbs per day).

We've already seen how dialysis patients get quite peculiar cravings: for gasoline, pebbles, even a blanket over the head. Foster found that the "hardest of all to resist" was drinking:

> I am tired of little sips of this and that. I would give a year of my life to be able to chug-a-lug a huge schooner of cold, foaming draft beer, to feel it rush down my parched throat like a flood through a desert ravine. I would give another year to slug down an ice cream soda in two huge gulps. And a third year for a whole pitcher of ice water, beaded with little drops of condensation on the outside, cool, crystal clear and a half-gallon deep within. (Ibid., p. 7.)

Foster is among the more fortunate dialysands, having resolved to live with the regimen and not give up. As the patient in Hardy's collection said: "You've gotta look at it that way. You can't feel sorry for yourself or you're going to kick the bucket" (Hardy, 1978, p. 147). Others are not so fortunate; if not undone by the enormity of their condition and prospects, much less the many pressures on themselves and their families, they may easily slide into self-destructive uncaring or psychosis, or become "living vegetables" kept alive not against their will, for their will is what they have lost.

As is true in most medical situations, but is especially striking in ESRD and dialysis, the patient's active participation in his or her own treatment and regimen is central to its success. This can be quite difficult, for the regimen of treatment is punishing, however regular and predictable it may also become. Indeed, as Renée Fox has pointed out, both the transplant patient's and the dialysand's lives are a "chronic way of dying" (Fox, 1976, p. 12). Whether this methodical encounter with death is met with intense despair, depression, or psychosis, or, as in the fortunate few like Lee Foster, whether it "intensifies whatever I am doing . . . sharpens my senses and heightens my appreciation of even such a simple thing as a beautiful spring day" (Foster, p. 8), there is no way the dialysand can forget for very long that with stark regularity a "damnable machine" keeps him alive.

FALLING ILL

Several matters need to be kept very clear, especially what was noted in some detail earlier about the characteristics of being ill. Illness and impairment, as we have noted many times, have a unique way of cutting into the fabric of everyday life, and our lives may sometimes be radically altered (momentarily, or for longer durations). The afflicted person is no longer able to take for granted some of what he or she had hitherto taken for granted, to one degree or another. Affliction not only breaches the person's daily life in clear ways, it also brings into play a special kind of reliance on other persons, as we have seen, whether it be relatively trivial or more serious.

How must it be when what seems the most deeply taken for granted of anything in one's life—namely, that one will continue to be alive—is threatened not just once or now and then but with rigorous regularity? The dialysis patient's very living even from moment to moment is methodically brought into question and can no longer be taken for granted, except, perhaps, momentarily. As Foster said, while "immersed in work or some leisure activity, I completely forget for hours at a time that a kidney machine keeps me alive" (p. 8).

Although dialysands, as Fox points out, invariably "view the machine as miraculously rescuing them from death, they also regard it as a constantly fettering, anthropomorphic presence in their life" (Fox, p. 12). The presence of the machine, methodically filtering your blood, your life, before your very eyes, may be viewed by some as "miraculous" and by others as "damnable." Whichever, the machine invariably seems to have magical qualities for the patient, the regularized three-times-per-week hookup functioning to ritualize optimism in the face of radical uncertainty and emotionally charged risk.

Yet, no matter how well the patient succeeds in becoming accustomed to the ritual and the regimen, these can never be completely taken for granted. As Foster says, "things can go wrong during dialysis, so even when I'm feeling relaxed I can never be completely oblivious to the machine" (Foster, p. 6). Too much liquid beforehand brings on severe cramping and acute pain during subsequent dialysis; the machine might malfunction and inattention to it will prove disastrous; carelessness with the shunt can result in serious infection. At no point is uncertainty far from mind.

Furthermore, whereas in daily life we are all accustomed to being relatively dependent on people and things in various ways and degrees, how must it be to find oneself utterly dependent for one's life on only barely understood technological devices and at times on complete strangers? For some persons, some of this reliance can be ameliorated by home dialysis, but even in these instances there is a critical reliance both on the machine and on others (wife, family, co-workers). For those unable to shift to home dialysis, this complex dependence is more exacerbated, even when undergoing dialysis in a special hospital or private unit where many of the same persons might be regularly found.

Regardless of how accustomed to the regimen the dialysand may become, he cannot take for granted his own continuing to be alive. The very regiment that *rescues* at the same time methodically *reminds* the patient of his own mortality; it makes his own ultimately unrescuable condition continually obvious. These elements, which deeply texture the dialysand's every moment, are, however, by no means all there is to the context of his or her life. Foster's words are helpful to elicit several further elements:

> Yet sometime when I'm feeling fine, and the machine is running perfectly, and I've enjoyed my dinner, and the music is good and the book I'm reading is interesting, and our cat is purring around my feet, and Leslie [his wife] is smiling at me, a thought suddenly runs through my head: "How the hell did I get here?" (Ibid.)

We are not told where this thought leads him, nor which other thoughts pop up along with it. He merely goes on to remark:

> Physicians say I was probably stricken with the disease as a child as the result of some illness or fever. For many years I didn't even know I had a potentially fatal kidney condition although albumin kept showing up in my [urinalysis]. In my mid-forties I developed high blood pressure. After a battery of tests, I got the bad news: my kidneys had degenerated and were continuing to degenerate, slowly but inexorably. (Ibid.)

Though other patients are aware that something has gone wrong at some point and may even be aware that the trouble is with the kidneys, many patients are taken by complete surprise:

> First of all, I didn't know anything was going on. I got sick at work one day and they forced me to go to the hospital. . . . I just got sick, just vomited. All

of a sudden, I got hot and had to go to the bathroom and vomit. We didn't know what caused it. I thought I was all right but they said I looked bad and made me go to the hospital. (Hardy, 1978, p. 141.)

The disease, in other words, just *happens* to the person; the person simply falls ill without knowledge or choice. As we earlier emphasized, this experience of accident or chance is a crucial element of the experience of illness (noting our reservations about factitious illness). The person undergoes the experience of falling ill, of bodily failures. Even when (as with Foster) a patient is told that the disease is known to be located "in the kidneys" or (as with the other patient) is simply told that his kidneys have failed, the experience is wholly intimate: weakness, vertigo, muscle spasms, nosebleeding, vomiting, and pain, vitally affecting the person's lively bond with his embodying organism. The person experiences himself as diminished, out of control, seized upon inwardly by bodily failures—the person is stricken.

The disease, thus, is textured by the prominence of accidental circumstance. "It could have been otherwise" is a dimension of the person's experience of his embodiment, but so likewise is "I had no choice" and "why to *me?*" In other words, to be a patient is to live with the suffusing sense of the utter chance, hence the injustice, the unfairness, of it all. To live as thus falling ill, to be methodically reminded of one's own death, of one's reliance on machines and on other persons for one's very life from moment to moment, deeply texture the chronicity of the person's prolonged living with his or her own death.

This continual and explicit reminder of the sheer precariousness, chance, and rudimentary limits of one's own life is obviously a volatile condition. It has a powerful symbol: the patient's actual connection to and dependence on the dialysis apparatus. Given that, it is little wonder that one witnesses the severe ups and downs of mood, outlook, and sense of prospects with such patients; that there is such rapid turnover on the medical teams; and that the usually mentioned ethical issues have such force for both patients and medical teams.

THE IDEA OF "MORAL CHANCE"

It has been suggested that one of the most widely accepted moral concepts—the autonomy of the person—fails to illuminate the actual experience of illness and medicine as a therapeutic enterprise.

There is, moreover, something peculiarly compelling about such grievously impaired persons (and, in a way, even about those not so grievously afflicted) that emphasis on the will's autonomy fails to grasp. For when confronted with the dialysis patient, most prominently during the times of his most severe impairment, we are faced with a fundamental communal or, in Schutz's term, consociate, phenomenon, which is neither autonomous nor heteronomous in Kant's sense. The person with ESRD and on hemodialysis presents to doctors, nurses, technicians, and family a kind of *entreaty* for help, an appeal that is all the more compelling because the condition was neither deserved nor chosen but simply happened by chance.

This appeal does not have to be expressly stated by a patient to a physician. Just as D. L. Wieder found multiple, indirect (and direct) ways by which inmates were "telling the code," and just as we found that elderly woman's words expressive of her own life-long moral themes, so here. A patient tells his or her moral appeal in physiognomic, gestural, paralinguistic, and conversational ways, which express and methodically require, as we saw, descriptive, interpretive, and thematic (motivational) schemata in order to be appropriately noticed and understood. What is said or told in all these ways by the ESRD (or other) patient is at once the accident of the illness and his and her own human vulnerability. The appeal is a way of making the moral order manifest.

This special phenomenon may perhaps best be elicited in another way. Herbert Spiegelberg, believing that today we are in real need of a fresh start in ethics, proposes a "new approach" that attempts to "face the fact of our existence in all its inexorableness, cosmically and morally" (1974, p. 210). In an early essay exploring the idea of human equality, he maintains that this idea has a fundamental link to that of justice (and injustice). Suggesting that there is a "deeper sense of justice," which concerns the equality both of equals and unequals, he states as premises that (1) *"undeserved discrimination calls for redress"* and (2) *"all inequalities of birth constitute undeserved discriminations"* (1944, p. 113). From these he concludes that *"all inequalities of birth call for redress,"* that is, the effort to cancel such inequalities by some form of "equalization." It therefore also follows, he suggests, that *"equality is a fundamental ethical demand"* (ibid.). He defines "discrimination" as "any kind of unequal lot by way of privilege or handicap." By "undeserved" he means "the lack of legitimating support by a moral title such as moral desert." His argument, then, is that only if inequalities are morally deserved would unequal losts be at all justified; if those inequalities are not deserved, there is no way to justify unequal lots (privileges or handicaps).

To help make this idea a bit more vivid, Spiegelberg invites us to consider our sense of moral outrage when this demand for redress is violated. There is, for instance, a "severe moral disequilibrium" (ibid., p. 114) when we notice that a handicapped person (simply by chance born that way) is forced to struggle up a staircase while non-handicapped persons walk up easily. Undeserved discrimination such as this calls for redress, and when not redressed there is a sense of moral outrage, a severe moral disequilibrium (he leaves open both the "who" and the "how" of such redress).

Spiegelberg's second premise is more difficult to grasp, and it was not until several decades had passed that he came to explicate it more fully. The core idea, however, was already expressed in this early essay: Inequalities of birth are undeserved discriminations. Consider, he advises, that we find ourselves simply born into quite different stations in life, different social environs and groups, and diverse families, nations, denominations, and classes, having neither chosen them nor been consulted about them. Awakening at some point in our lives to self-consciousness, we discover that we are already male or female, white or black, native or foreign, and that we have different physical abilities and biological endowments. None of these was chosen or deserved owing to some action or non-action of our own.

Not only are we born into these different statuses and endowments, we are also born into the fact that some of them are undeservedly unequal. It is one thing to be born a woman; it is quite another to have been born female at a historical time and in a particular culture where being a woman is also a matter for discrimination. As Spiegelberg insists, "the inequality of these endowments is likewise an initial fate into which we find ourselves born," and therefore this inequality is equally undeserved (ibid., p. 115). Hence, the accident of birth expresses a basic aspect of our humanity.

The sense of chance is quite specific, since that which we have at birth is to a considerable extent at the root of what we are and will become. Being born into an already constituted station in life, with specific biological endowments, is "as it were, thrown upon us. . . . Nor is there any objective evidence that they depend upon any moral desert." It is this "lack of a moral title and primarily of any moral desert for our initial shares" that Spiegelberg terms "moral chance" (ibid., p. 116).

Precisely this sense of chance discriminates at birth. As our moral sense "offers no brief for any such discriminations . . . it follows that all initial inequalities in the form of privileges and handicaps are ethically unwarranted" (ibid.).

It then directly follows that our initial factual inequalities "are in an ultimate sense void of moral justification." Thus, Spiegelberg argues, "Our unequal shares constitute an 'unjust enrichment' (or an unjustified deprivation), i.e., undeserved discriminations" (ibid., p. 118). So far as they are unwarranted, they intrinsically call for redress. Though it may be that there are various ways of redressing them, they must always be governed by the following principle: "The common well-being of all those fellow-beings involved in the fate of inequality" (ibid., p. 120).

Along with "moral chance," the key idea, as I understand Spiegelberg, is "well-being." Ultimately, the postulate of equality in the sense at issue here is based "in the demands of a fundamental human justice which requires equal consideration even of unequals who equally owe their factual inequalities to the 'chance of birth' " (ibid.). "Equality," therefore, concerns "ethical status" and not anything merely factual.

"ACCIDENT OF BIRTH" AND MORAL IMBALANCE

The idea of desert or merit is a basic one. If by my own action or decision, or even in view of who and what I am or have become, something is made to happen, then I myself am in some relevant way responsible and either gain credit or blame for that. I deserved or earned it, whatever it may be and however difficult it often is to assess such matters. The notion of the moral order seems to require a close connection between the ideas of desert (or merit) and responsibility. As was pointed out, moreover, the ground for this connection has been commonly thought to be that of freedom. Only if we think of people as individually free does the idea of moral responsibility make sense. If a person is coerced into doing something, it seems utterly unfair, unjust, to hold him or her responsible, to say that he or she deserved or earned praise or blame.

While Spiegelberg seems to agree with this postulate as basic for moral life, however, he does not, like Kant, proceed to interpret it as a matter of the autonomy of the will (pure practical reason). Rather, he suggests that there is an even more fundamental ground for morality: the accident of birth, which he contends is expressive of our essential human condition (ibid.). It is not what we freely do, but, to the contrary, what is *done to us* at the outset of our human careers that constitutes the core of morality.

Accordingly, the connection between desert and responsibility is not freedom or autonomy, at least not in the most basic sense. That connection is grounded in our essential human condition, and this is fundamentally shaped by the accident of birth—that is, by that over which we had no choice, our rudimentary and initial "lot," biological endowment, and social station in life (whether as privilege or handicap).

To put it another way, human freedom is by no means some sort of pure postulate or formal requirement, some sort of abstract ability whose exercise is necessary in order to permit judgments of praise or blame, desert or lack of it. Human freedom is, rather, essentially within the specific context of natal endowment, initial station or estate, and its subsequent exercise is ineluctably shaped and determined by that initial lot. As against the rarified and abstract notion of freedom of choice, I understand Spiegelberg to be suggesting the full, concrete context of actual human life and its ineradicably unchosen endowments as the appropriate context for understanding and variously assessing the exercise of freedom and the ideas of desert and responsibility.

From this perspective, we can more readily appreciate the moral significance of the accident of birth. Each of us is fated by our birth in key ways. Understanding these opens the way to a novel, more adequate approach to morality that relates directly and deeply to the moral foundations of medicine and the experience of illness.

Each of us is fated, that is, we each share certain basic conditions in common, we are "fellows together"; fellowship, then, not autonomy, is basic to human life. But fellowship, as we earlier emphasized, is always a being-with-others in a certain respect, that is, as regards something held or shared in common. This may be trivial (e.g., living on the same city street, riding in the same bus) and may also be more or less extensive (e.g., sharing the same country, living on the same planet).

Terming these types of fellowship "same-fated," Spiegelberg carefully distinguishes these from what he calls "like-fated," or "parallel-fated," fellowships—sharing similar but otherwise unconnected characteristics (e.g., height, skin color, sex, social class). Noting that we are not always consciously aware of these similarities—indeed becoming aware of them invariably requires effort—Spiegelberg points out that while some of them are trivial, some are quite momentous (being afflicted with the same disease, having the same good fortune) and may give rise to fellowships exhibiting special bonds (disease advocacy groups, e.g.).

Cautiously probing such "like-fated fellowships," we can begin to detect some quite significant fates that we all share in common, of which we are rarely conscious, and all of which are accidents of our respective births. Unchosen and unearned, these constitute that with which we are each initially "gifted" or endowed. Each of us has the common fate of belonging to one rather than another grouping—one or another sex, generation, race, historical time and place, nationality, and religious denomination or social class. Each of us, more basically, born as an alive human being and, even more basically, as an existent being who is this or that specific person or self (see Zaner, 1981, pp. 144–64).

The issue here is whether and why such fates, especially the second sort, have any moral significance. We know that companionship, friendship, and even partnership are morally close and binding types of fellowship. But is "being born as an alive human being" also close and binding in any moral way? After all, most of us are rarely if ever even conscious of such "common fates"; rather, we have to be forced or be brought to awareness of them. The key here is the "accident of birth." To become aware at some point in one's life that one has certain native endowments or talents: Is this morally significant?

Earlier, in the course of trying to find the historical roots of the idea of accident of birth, Spiegelberg came across a surprising place in the work of John Stuart Mill (Spiegelberg, 1961). Mill was concerned with such accidents as sex, skin color, race, and health as examples of congenital conditions or specific hereditary circumstances of birth. These phrases occur in passages discussing justice in the distribution of advantages and benefits in the social order, and they serve as examples of a kind of social injustice connected to privileges certain people enjoy simply because of noble birth.

Mill was concerned that the social order should not allow any person "one fraction of unearned distinction or unearned importance" (Mill, 1942, p. 33). He regarded it as "a flagrant social injustice" for there to be no option for women, for example, "except in the humbler departments of life" (Mill, 1923, p. 187). He called for equalizing the "injuries of nature" (ibid., p. 202) and the abolition of any unearned enrichment or advantages such as what accrues to a man simply in view of his having been accidentally born male. Showing that such accidents function as basic moral categories in Mill's works, Spiegelberg then points out that they are quite independent of Mill's utilitarianism.

It was over a decade before Spiegelberg returned to this theme (1974), contending then that just as what Mill identified as the unearned advantages and disadvantages of sex, class, etc., are "flagrant" injustices, so the more fundamental "fates" or "accidents" of birth disclose a moral concept of existential justice and injustice. Existence itself invokes certain moral claims for people, whether or to whatever extent these can be fulfilled.

1. That I am born as "me myself" is not of my own choosing; therefore, I can take neither blame nor credit for this. At best, I can be held responsible only for my further becoming, for what I make of my basic endowment. Being myself is a fate and an accident of which the person may or may not become aware as such, but which was an accident happening without his or her knowledge, consent, or choice. Whatever is done to a person without consent or choice is, Spiegelberg suggests, an "*existential wrong*" regardless of whether it is an objective benefit, harm, or even neutral. It is something morally incongruous (Spiegelberg, 1974, p. 199).

2. Similarly, that I am born as a human being, having to contend with this, my life and all it includes (e.g., being embodied by this specific body and its various abilities and limitations), without a prior hearing or choice, is an accident. In this sense, to be born at all is to be "an innocent victim, a pawn, at least at the start of one's career" (ibid., p. 201).

3. To be born is to be endowed with a certain congenital and genetic heritage to some extent determining my intellectual and emotional constitution: what, why, and how well or poorly I think, remember, feel, and anticipate. This is morally telling precisely because we really should have had a say about such critical matters—our lot, character, abilities, and talents.

4. To these must be added that by birth each of us is male or female, sound or handicapped (in whatever way), of one race or another, and with one or another temperament and bodily form (beauty or ugliness, e.g.). The conclusion clearly suggests itself: Our initial, unchosen stations and endowments constitute "an essential moral imbalance," whether these involve privileges or disadvantages (ibid., p. 202).

Therefore, neither pride nor blame regarding our initial stations and endowments can be morally justified. There is then something deeply wrong if people who share similar situations are subject to discrimination that favors the more "fortunate" by the mere happenstance of good luck and disfavors the "unfortunate" as mere victims of bad luck (ibid., p. 206). Not only is something wrong about this, but in addition something ought to be done about it. The accident of birth has positive moral force, as Spiegelberg had appreciated in his earlier essay on human equality (1944); undeserved discrimination is wrong and calls for redress.

It is not freedom, then, that is the foundation for moral life; it is rather the compromise to, or imbalance of, that freedom signified by the accident of birth. Similarly, it is not justice that is basic, but rather injustice, the injustice inherent to our unchosen initial lots in life. Our common natal privileges and handicaps are void of moral justification, deserve redress, and thus imply an equality of *moral status.*

Insofar as one is either privileged or handicapped (by genetic, mental, cultural, or historical endowments), by "moral chance," one had no choice in these crucial matters, nor was one consulted or advised in advance of them. It is not only the fact of having been born as one sex, skin color, or race; it is in addition the fact that these inequalities are themselves subjects of discrimination, different moral assessments, relative cultural values, and subsequent forms of unequal treatment. Together, these constitute the foundation of moral life.

AWAKENING A MORAL SENSE: "GOOD FORTUNE OBLIGATES"

The phrase "good fortune obligates" was coined by Spiegelberg to express what Albert Schweitzer had called his "other thought" about ethics—that is, other than his profound and sweeping reverence for life (Spiegelberg, 1975). This "thought" is that, having been born into a well-situated and loving family, "I must not accept this good fortune as a matter of course but had to give something in return" (in ibid., p. 228). This led to Schweitzer's decision to become a missionary physician. Much later in life, Schweitzer stressed again that none of us should take for granted "his own advantages over others in health, talents, in ability, in success, in a happy childhood and congenial home conditions" (ibid., p. 228n6). These "good fortunes" carry a "special responsibility" for other, less fortunate people.

As Spiegelberg formulates this idea, "the more fortunate owe to those less fortunate a compensation in proportion to their handicaps" (ibid., p. 231). Schweitzer, Spiegelberg argues, was not so much formulating a principle as he was appealing to modern man to broaden and deepen his moral sense, to awaken "a moral sense that is usually dormant but that on special occasions can be brought to the surface" (ibid., p. 232).

What are these "special occasions"? How are they connected to that "special responsibility for other lives," to Schweitzer's idea that "good fortune obligates"? Following Spiegelberg and Schweitzer, my suggestion is that the awakening of "a moral sense that is usually dormant" comes as a response to an appeal for redress of an injustice or undeserved wrong suffered without choice. It is this idea, in short, that underlies and gives moral force to such notions as informed consent.

More concretely, the experience of illness, handicap, or injury is precisely one (but not the only one) of those "special occasions." Of itself, the experience is an appeal for relief, help, or restoration, to whatever extent and in whichever way possible. The core of the appeal is twofold: On the one hand, it is addressed to anyone directly or indirectly witnessing the ill person and his or her plea for help; on the other, it is for a response, in whatever ways are available, that can somehow redress the harm, thus neither taking advantage of the already disadvantaged person nor causing further harms.

To elicit illness as an appeal requires brief rehearsal of the experience while keeping in mind the special issues raised by various types of factitious illness (as we have seen). Illness occurs as a threat (relatively minor or more grievous, as the case may be), even as an "assault" or "insult" to the person (see Pellegrino, 1982, p. 124). To be ill in these terms is, first, to find one's sense of bodily integrity afflicted. Being in pain or being disabled, one's body takes center stage and consumes one's attention and energies; in this respect the embodying organism is no longer (or at least for many of one's usual activities) capable of functioning in its usual ways.

Second, affliction impairs one's ability to make a variety of choices and decisions in the light of alternatives and free from coercion. Third, with the illness or injury continually preoccupying one's attention, one must place himself or herself in the hands of other persons, often total strangers, for that help. Not only is there unusual reliance here, but many of the actions required for help are among the most intimate between persons. Finally, illness deprives the patient of a crucial sense of self, of bodily and personal integrity, and places the patient in a relationship of inequality (of physical condition) and asymmetry (of power and resources), with the advantage on the helpers' side. Hence, the pathos of trust is understandable; its context is the critical and unique vulnerability we noted before.

This vulnerability has two main sources. On the one hand, particular features of illness diminish or impair a person's abilities to think and feel, much less to live to the fullest. The physician, nurses, and other helpers, to the contrary, are (or ought to be) in full possession of their faculties and skills. On the other hand, this inequality of condition is enhanced by the structural asymmetry inherent to the helping professions: the understanding of illness, the knowledge and power to heal, the legal and social legitimation of the helping professions (especially medicine), and the access to the considerable resources of health care (technologies, medications, drugs) are all on the side of the helper. To fall ill, thus, is to suffer an accident that threatens one's integrity and being as this person or self; the patient is vulnerable, exposed to an essentially unequal and asymmetrical relation to other persons who possess faculties, abilities, skills, power, and authority and whose actions bring them into the most intimate actions in and knowledge of the patient and the patient's family and household.

Illness is an appeal for responsive help or comfort. More particularly, it is an appeal for these others to take care of and to care for the ill person: that is, for them to appreciate and keep constantly in mind this very inequality and asymmetry of the relationship. This, I take it, is the core meaning of the widely used term "appropriate" in clinical discourse. What is appealed for is the exercise of the multiple powers in an appropriate, or responsive, manner. The appeal, to put it still differently, is from a vulnerable person (patient) whose very exposure to others is an appeal not to be additionally disadvantaged by the very fact of this asymmetry of the relationship, not to be taken advantage of by those who surely can take advantage. The helpers most surely can, but most surely ought not, additionally disadvantage the ill person (already disadvantaged by illness).

What is "special" about the occasion of illness is that it is by nature open in many different ways to violation of the vulnerable. To be responsive to the ill person, not giving in to the inherent temptation to take advantage, is to have had one's moral sense awakened, to have encountered and responded to a "special occasion."

AWAKENING A MORAL SENSE: GRATITUDE AND RESPONSE

Each of us in some way or other has felt and known the vulnerability intrinsic to affliction. For the most part, our sundry ailments, abrasions, breaks, cuts and fevers pass away or become healed, often leaving us with a sense of profound relief at their passing. And with relief there often passes away, too, the sense of vulnerability and urgency, fear and apprehension. That is, even though we each have suffered in some ways, we do not always maintain a clear memory of the events—partly because, of course, memorial functions may also be impaired by the affliction and partly because the relieved return to our usual lives itself plays a role in forgetting.

Thus, it may well be that we need reminding of the inner, intimate experience of illness in order to appreciate anew that it is indeed a "special occasion" appealing for and compellingly evoking a "moral sense" that is usually "dormant." For this awakening, and short of another bout with illness, the encounter with other afflicted persons seems to have a unique recalling force. The encounter with an ill person can function to awaken a moral sense, to evoke a response to help without additionally disadvantaging or harming the ill person.

But there is a rarely noticed side to the experience of being ill or maimed that points to Schweitzer's emphasis on the "fraternity of those marked by pain." Illness diminishes our bodily activities, our abilities to choose and feel, our self-image and bodily integrity. It increases our reliance on others and places us in an unequal and asymmetrical relationship in favor of these others. At the same time, when we are in fact helped by these others, the experience of being ill and then recovering is marked also by an evident sense of gratitude. The relief at getting well again, of feeling the pain lessen and then disappear, is not merely a sense of "having done with" the illness. It is also and more importantly a sense of gratefulness or indebtedness, that, moreover, needs to be expressed. Although we may believe (and even be encouraged in this by prevailing social norms) that repayment in the form, say, of fee-for-service is the right way to show gratitude, it doesn't take much to realize that that is rarely felt to be either altogether appropriate or adequate relative to the sense of relief and gratitude. While expressions of gratitude are characteristic of post-illness experience, they are felt to be (if I understand patients' talk rightly) woefully inadequate to the experience.

This phenomenon is quite elusive; it can and often is taken as a kind of momentary sentimentalism. Yet the experience of being ill and then gaining relief is marked by that complex sense: With the easing of pain, the healing of a wound, the cooling of fever, the abatement of disease, there comes the relief, the elation, the gratitude, the sense of indebtedness seeking a way to be expressed.

Looked at more carefully, this experience of relief and gratitude is, I think, one of those special occasions through which a moral sense is awakened and can be reawakened. Schweitzer insists, for instance, that there is a "special league of those who have known anxiety and physical suffering." Indeed, there seems to be a "mysterious bond" connecting them. "They know the terrible things man can undergo; they know the longing to be free of pain." Yet, once relieved of the pain and suffering, they "must not think they are now completely free . . . [to] return to life as it was before" (in Spiegelberg, 1975, p. 228, n. 6).

Having experienced the accident of illness with its grief, pain, loss— and beneath it all death—leaves its mark on the person. Yet the insult of the accident of illness, the urgent wanting to get well, the elation when cured, tend to lose their dramatic and vivid force. Even so, Schweitzer insists, the "fraternity of those marked by pain" should not forget the "terrible things" they have suffered and think that they can now "calmly return to life as it was before." People who get well, or even experience some relief and comfort even while their impairment continues, people who have been cared for and liberated from pain—these people are not now completely free to forget their experience, even though it understandably tends to fade in memory and lose its lively force.

For those who have been relieved from pain and anxiety, it is not enough to be grateful to those whose responsive care was given. Rather, this complex experience seems to be intrinsically obligatory; that is, here as elsewhere for Schweitzer, "good fortune obligates." As those born in good circumstances, with advantages of body and culture, must realize their lack of moral entitlement to these accidents of fortune and are obligated to help redress the no less unjustified inequities of the less fortunate, so, too, for those who have recovered from the experience of illness. To get well is no less a matter of "good fortune" than is being born into good circumstances with a loving family.

If relief from the uncertainties, vulnerabilities, even humiliations of illness happens (as it often does, even for some who are chronically ill), the experience is also (although far more subtly) to have the "good fortune" of being helped or healed. This, I suggest, is a source of moral responsibility. It is an awakable sense that others also stand in need of help, especially those who are undergoing the same kind of thing as did the one who is now healed, well, or better. This awakened (and awakable) moral sense seems to be directed first of all to those who are similarly afflicted, because the experience itself (as we saw in our study of ancient medical skepticism) is a form of knowledge and because having had the same type of illness is precisely what establishes a communal bond or "fate".

THE TWOFOLD MEANING OF AWAKENING A MORAL SENSE

The experience of illness, then, constitutes a special occasion for awakening our moral sense in two distinct but closely related ways. First, to witness affliction, and even more to find oneself called upon or appealed to by an afflicted person for help, is to encounter what Spiegelberg in another respect calls a "moral imbalance" that is compelling and demanding. To be responsive to that appeal is to have experienced that "moral awakening." To be sure, one may well refuse, be blind to, betray, demean, take advantage of, or ignore that appeal. No appeal necessitates responsiveness, for here, Kant is in a sense quite right: Being free—which means, however, being free to refuse, betray, demean, as well as to be responsive—is indeed a condition for moral responsibility. It is a condition, not of the appeal, but rather for the response. But, being free is not the only condition for moral responsibility, since prior to response must be a recognition of the appeal as such and a felt affiliation, a kind of fellow-feeling or a bond of kinship with the one who is ill and is suffering (we return to this later). Within that recognition and affiliation, one is indeed still free to refuse, demean, or betray. But then, having undergone this concrete affiliative experience and thereby having come within the evoked moral order, moral guilt, blame, or censure come into play.

The second way in which illness is a special occasion for awakening a moral sense concerns the ill person. Being stricken by chance with illness, living through its uncertainties and pain, longing to be free of pain, undergoing relief, and eventually experiencing the gratitude and indebtedness of getting well—this is as well to have learned, to have gained a form of vital knowledge. Precisely this is a special occasion awakening our moral sense.

I am especially struck by the phenomenon of felt gratitude here. Sick people who get well are rarely if ever satisfied by expressing their thanks to their healers (although this is surely called for and appropriate). Their sense of indebtedness is rarely gratified merely by paying their bills and saying their thankful adieus. Like that woman with the apron we met earlier, who tangibly felt it right to help that fellow patient (informing her of the need to keep those bandages in place), patients seem to relate with remarkable naturalness and directness to others who are sick like they were sick. They feel a vital affiliation, a connectedness, with others suffering like they suffered. "I know what it's like, what you're going through, and maybe I can help you get through it, too!" Of course, the experience of illness fades, and its moral grip relaxes in time. Some persons may never have experienced an illness or injury severe enough to have evoked that moral imbalance. Even so, witnessing illness and being ill oneself are both special occasions evoking an affiliative sense of obligation to be responsive to those marked by pain. There is here one of the "like-fated fellowships" Spiegelberg mentions or a "fraternity of those marked by pain," as Schweitzer says.

THE ESRD-DIALYSIS PATIENT'S "GOOD FORTUNE"

A dialysand lives with the daily awareness of being near death and being kept from death by those "damned machines" and by all those people whose work made the machines possible and keep them running. Dialysands who are able to live with their illnesses do so for basically two crucial reasons.

First, they have been able successfully to blend the otherwise counter-attitudes of (passive) compliance and (active) collaboration. Their treatment requires at times utter dependence and passivity, most obviously on the machine and on those who maintain it but also on physicians, surgeons, nurses and family. However, it has been well established that the more a patient actively collaborates in his own treatment and the more he makes the effort to pursue as normal life as possible (with job, family, friends), the better are the chances he will respond to dialysis and have psychological problems. Thus, taking treatments in a special clinic is far better for the patient than remaining hospitalized and passively receiving dialysis in bed; home dialysis is the most successful.

Second, it is clear that patients on home dialysis have the literal good fortune to be able to rely on supportive, responsible, and responsive others.

This comes through clearly in Roger Coene's talk about his own experience:

> On home dialysis I have been able to pursue my career as well as most of my outside interests with only slightly less vigor than I would have under other circumstances. This achievement has been a direct result of the determined effort my wife and I have made to pursue as normal a lifestyle as possible. We have reorganized our personal schedules around dialysis, designed our daily menu around its dietary restrictions, and organized our household with dialysis as a primary thread. Most important, the supportiveness of my wife has been an essential factor in my success. (Coene, 1978, p. 7.)

The good fortune here, however, must include as well such things as the kind of profession or job (only some can be adjusted to fit the regimen) and the support of employers (not all of them make the necessary allowances), fellow workers, and children and spouse, not to mention the happenstance of being stricken within the historical and social circumstances when dialysis technology is available and funded by federal monies. Others, with different afflictions, different jobs, and so on, are not so fortunate, nor are those who live alone, are divorced, or have no responsive friends.

Thus, the few successful dialysis patients are able to "take for granted" and "forget" that "a kidney machine keeps me alive" (Foster), because of their compliance-collaboration and their quite fortunate personal and social circumstances. Even so, as we have seen, the forgetting is never fully possible here, and death is ever present with methodical chronicity.

Furthermore, it is evident, even with such fortunate patients, that their critical awareness is by no means self-centered. Precisely in their compliant collaboration, for example, they are continually aware of the serious impact and drain they have on their families. They live with a constant sense of gratitude toward others, both family and medical, research and technological persons (and experience this even though they cannot be cured). Literally everything in their lives must be reorganized around the centering presence of their own conditions which is thereby the "primary threat" (Coene) and constant reminder (Foster) of precisely what on the other hand enables them, if only momentarily now and then, to forget that organizing focus.

The greater a person's awareness of his condition and the more able (and enabled) he, like Coene or Foster, is to live as normally as possible, the greater is his intimate alertness that he had no part in having been so stricken and rendered vulnerable. At the same time, the greater is his awareness that, while he was by chance singled out ("why me?"), other afflicted persons do not have even this own good fortune. Others may have been denied even this treatment (for medical or other reasons), whereas he was able to get it: "Why am I so lucky and not others . . .?" "I am deeply grateful," Roger Coene states, as do others, "that I am offered two possible methods of survival [dialysis and transplantation]" (ibid.). The very regimen that enables even relatively successful continued living is just what brings dramatically home to the patient his or her own affliction and its double happenstance and luck of occurrence and treatment.

ILLNESS AND THE MORAL ORDER

If, as I have urged, human affliction is an appeal to be cared for and taken care of, it thereby requires the afflicted person to put himself or herself (or to "find" himself or herself) in the hands of others. It is essentially a trust relationship that is evoked, and it is trust in a special sense: namely, trust in the context of initial, vital vulnerability and diminishment of selfhood. On the other hand, those to whom this appeal is addressed, in whom trust is to be given—whether it be stranger, friend, family, or physician—are called on precisely to be responsive to just this specific afflicted person in his or her very condition and responsible for his or her actual well-being and life (in whatever respect it may be).

Affliction is a fundamental disclosure of the moral order in a deeply poignant and vivid form. The fact of illness is evidently a moral phenomenon, precisely because it is the contextual presentation of a special kind of "moral chance," the core form of which is the accident of birth and its undeserved inequalities calling for redress and justice. Good fortune obligates; it obligates at once to awaken and cultivate a more demanding than usual moral response to those marked by pain and affliction—both from those to whom the appeal is addressed and by those who, having been ill, know the terrible things that illness can bring and thus ought not return to "life as it was."

The moral order is fundamentally a communal phenomenon. Even though it is clear enough that freedom is in a crucial sense prerequisite for there being moral responsibility, this freedom is not a matter of autonomy but rather a matter of affiliative appealing and responding on behalf of the accidents of birth and circumstance and their "moral chance."

For the patient stricken with ESRD (or other disease) and for those treating the patient, the central issues are trust and care. So important to patient relations and family ties and so essential in gaining the compliant collaboration without which treatment cannot usually be more than minimally successful, trust and care present the physician, nurses, and others with the basic problem: How can the patient with ESRD be effectively led to understand and enjoined to adhere to the rigorous regimen required by dialysis? For the family, too, that problem is the continual, actual fabric of daily life.

What, in truth, is the patient being asked to do when he is informed of his condition, of the regimen, and of the importance of following it? To tell the patient these things is to tell him that he must trust the medical team, the medications, the machine and its paraphernalia; in short, that the patient should trust their intentions, actions, and words even if these are not fully understood or even understandable. At just this point the crucial pathos of dialysis (and transplantation) becomes evident. To tell the regimen and its importance is to tell the patient, already critically afflicted in his or her humanity and selfhood, that this affliction and its associated regimen must be regularly and methodically borne—with all that that implies, including the continual presence of crisis, dependency, accidents, good fortune, and social, familial, psychological, and medical complications.

Within this complex affliction, regularly made evident to the patient, the dialysand is told that the most important thing to do is to follow the regimen with unprecedented rigorousness. As Roger Coene expresses it, successful dialysis "requires a strength of character and determination from both the patient and his family" (ibid.). What the medical talk in truth says, thus, is that the patient must be "strong and determined": The need to have moral strength and courage constitutes the basic meaning and intent of such talk.

This is the case, it must be noted, even though many of these patients are notably unable to understand precisely that kind of talk and even though these persons have been deeply afflicted in their very selfhood (in their ability to comprehend, judge, choose, compare, and even to feel and will beyond the immediacy of their condition, and thus in their ability to grasp the kind of moral requirements and virtues their condition itself manifestly demands of them). We must also remind ourselves that such talk goes on at a historical time when the sense of what constitutes us as moral beings has been under unprecedented attack and controversy, when our moral resources seem if anything at low ebb.

Dialysis patients and their families are faced with the unyielding necessity to trust, to be courageous, to bear up strongly and with determination under a strenuous and difficult regimen. They must be or become, then, morally strong in the most rigorous sense. This illness is especially illustrative because the dialysand, in his or her singularly compelling condition, helps to mark out the essential features of our own common condition as moral beings. The patient's very presence is a clear appeal to us to call on our own most profound moral resources.

Thus the very phenomenon of illness, especially those such as ESRD, unequivocally presents those who must respond to it with their own critical need for moral strength. To respond is not merely to care in any simple sense. It is to find oneself appealed to for help, called upon to "be with" and "feel with" (to affiliate). It also includes the need to understand the full circumstances of the patient and the patient's family and to act with care and a strong sense of the art and of disease in a fitting and just manner—as the ancient Hippocratics expressed it, with *sophrosyne* and *dike* foremost in thought and action. Hence, the response and not only the affliction is fundamentally moral.

To help or respond to such patients (whether by physicians, or by other patients similarly afflicted) is thus a venture, not always happy, in moral awakening or education. The ethical dimensions of ESRD and other illnesses thus have their root in that mutual, affiliative appealing and responding in the context of moral chance. This is, in all its complexity, a profound reminder of our own essential character as moral beings. Such afflictions and their treatments allow us to catch a glimpse of what ultimately makes us all human and defines our common condition.

INTENT IN PATIENT-PHYSICIAN DISCOURSE

"Clinical medicine," Cassell writes, "with the aid of medical science, has become a profession of effective action" (1985, Vol. II, p. 8). The whole point of it, from diagnosis to developing therapeutic plans of action, "is that the patient be better, not that the physician be proved correct" (ibid., p. 7). Accordingly, medicine's long-standing focus on diagnostic thinking, "talking and teaching as though the greatest achievement for physicians is to make a diagnosis of disease" (ibid., p. 8), is misleading for both patients and physicians. Clinical medicine has since the 1930s increasingly become a profession of intervention, and, with that, serious changes in our understanding of it are needed. Three such changes are primary:

1. Since the best thing to do for sick people is to help make them better, the most useful knowledge concerns understanding the embodied person in health and sickness. Diagnosis must be conceived, then, as serving that end. In terms we used earlier, clinical medicine today is primarily a therapeutic discipline and only secondarily a diagnostic, epistemic science. It is a human enterprise that is fundamentally within the moral order.

2. The attempt to discover the process by which a well person became sick, in order then to devise another process to help the person return to maximum possible function, is never (or, very rarely) a matter of certainty. Therefore, Cassell maintains, what distinguishes medicine from most other professions is the "constant possibility of error, and thus of doing terrible harm to someone" (ibid., p. 7). No matter how well a history is taken, how scrupulous the diagnostic assessment or how certain it appears, the physician must keep a centering question constantly alive: *"What if I am wrong?"* (Ibid.) Precisely for that reason there must always be a plan in case an error has in fact occurred. Similarly, an ethics responsive to clinical medicine must be an ethics of uncertainty.

This constant possibility of error, while surely present in any discipline dealing with such naturally unpredictable, diverse, and variable objects as human beings, is a qualitatively different matter for medicine. The concern, to repeat, is not being right, but making the patient better; hence, cognizance of uncertainty and error are vital concerns at every point in caring for a patient.

3. Clinical medicine is a profession of effective action. Any intervention on behalf of a sick person therefore "implies that you know what is best for that person" (ibid., p. 8). Although there are many situations (such as acute trauma or infectious disease) where "what is best" is not very difficult to determine, there are just as many where it is not at all clear what that "best" is. In the latter cases especially, the emphasis has to be on learning as much as possible about the specific patient (who the patient is and how he or she interacts with the pathophysiology to produce this specific ailment); determining whether and to what extent other factors (environmental, familial, occupational) have had a part in that illness; and determining how the patient defines the problems and what should be done for him or her to consider it resolved (see ibid., pp. 86–147).

In each of these three areas of change, it is clearly vital for the physician to reach a sound understanding of the specific patient: his or her own particular body (as well as human biology more generally); habitual patterns of bodily attitudes and movements; how the body, organs, and sensations are experienced and interpreted by the person whose body it is; the ability to handle uncertainty and error; his or her life circumstances, occupation, family. Obtaining this information is in the service of the effort to find out what's wrong, what can be done about it, and settling on what should be done—that is trying to help the person get well, feel better, or become healed.

This unique relationship, as we've seen many times, is one of the most intimate, and certainly most delicate, among persons. Because of its inherent inequality (of condition and awareness) and structural asymmetry (of power and resources), both in favor of the physician, the relationship is essentially fragile and exposed to constant dangers—manipulation and coercion, improper intimacies, therapeutically compromising forms of remoteness or distancing, to mention but a few.

Historically, these decisive features of the relationship have been clearly recognized. Indeed, as we saw, they have been understood as being at the heart of medical morality and were conceived as intrinsic to medicine as a therapeutic enterprise. If these features tended to be muted, or even ignored, in medicine's more recent history (from Bichat on), with the physician being taught to focus solely on the locational indexes of patient discourse, and on the body abstracted from its intimate union with the person, in an effort to conduct physical diagnosis, Cassell's work serves as a clear indication that those days have become problematic and perhaps are gone. As it has become an interventionist enterprise, careful listening to and talking with patients has become of central importance again, along with the need for good patient history taking and sound clinical techniques.

Perhaps the most significant feature of such patient-physician conversations, however, is what Cassell terms "intent": What do people mean when they say what they say, especially those people who have become sick and are now patients (along with their families or circle of intimates)? Correlatively, perhaps the single most important skill the physician must acquire is learning to describe, interpret, and understand what a patient's intent actually is. It can also be among the more difficult matters to get straight in interactions with patients and their families and among the easiest to misjudge, hence is a ready source of communication difficulties and, thereby, conflicts that, left unnoticed and untended, can too easily blossom into outright public and legal battles. This issue, then, is of immense importance, and errors can be costly.

The physician's scientific training demands a number of formal requirements for diagnostic tests. When ordering a laboratory serum test, for instance (the example is Cassell's), the physician has to know whether the results are accurate, including the statistical range of error for each test in each laboratory used. For example, plus or minus 14 percent range for a reading at one level could mean that the serum is either normal or it could be evidence of a disease. Accuracy is but one requirement; degree of precision is another. In addition, it is increasingly necessary to know the specificity (number of false positives) and sensitivity (number of false negatives) for each test and measurement. All these together indicate the confidence about or degree of probability for these diagnostic tests. To our point here, these same requirements are necessary for interpreting what patients tell doctors about their complaints, themselves, events, relationships, and their bodies. To understand the patient's talk—its intent, what is meant by what is said—the physician needs to know how accurate and precise it is, its specificity and sensitivity, and to what extent it is adequate and true (see ibid., pp. 116–17).

For all the difficulties of establishing a patient's intent in saying what he or she says to the physician—conversely, a patient's understanding the physician's intent—the matter is vital to their relationship and, ultimately, to its whole point: helping the patient get better. Obviously, as Cassell has made wonderfully clear, the primary way we have of finding out what someone "has in mind" is through the person's words: paralanguage, word choice, conversational coherence, and the like. Establishing intent is partly a matter of recognizing the typified ways we commonly express ourselves in everyday conversation, usages that are governed in some part by social conventions and in some part by idiosyncrasies of the individual speaker. It also requires cautious and sensitive description, interpretation, and thematic judgment, as we've argued. But there seems to be a good deal more to this complex process.

AFFILIATIVE FEELING: "PUT YOURSELF IN MY SHOES"

Vital as those methods are, they are not enough. We are, after all, attempting to understand what a unique individual person means by what he or she says, in a specific context definitively textured by the characteristics we've explicated about sick people and governed by the aims of therapeutic intervention. The fact that these relationships so frequently involve strangers not only further complicates the encounter, it also harbors certain distinctive dangers.

To deal with a stranger, after all, is to be faced with the constant, nagging temptation to interpret the talk in abstract and typified (i.e., "distancing") ways. It also harbors the real temptation for the physician to be predisposed in "reading" the patient's talk: to interpret the talk and its intent as what the physician would have meant if he or she had said it. Both of these dangers, as well as others, can be devastating, can lead to inappropriate medications (for pain, e.g.), and can lead away from "this" individual patient to some standardized, even stereotypical notion of "a" patient.

How, then, can the issue of intent be settled, from either the physician's or the patient's point of view? To repeat, it is a vital part of the physician's work to help patients maintain control over their worlds, to help them remain or recover as much as possible the persons they and their significant others recognize and cherish. To accomplish this, understanding the patient in his or her own individuality and specific circumstances is an essential (although not the only) task, for which the matter of intent is central.

In a very brief section of the first volume of his study, Cassell mentions several things that, I want to suggest, are most directly to the point here (ibid., pp. 136–39). In ordinary conversations, listeners interpret a speaker's intent in part by means of a certain kind of self-knowledge. When someone tells me, for example, that he had a great time at a party I missed, I know what having a great time at such affairs is like: I've been to parties and have had a great time myself. An acquaintance complains that her boss is hard to get along with, and I know what she means and intends, partly by my own experience with difficult people. Similarly, someone remarks how hot it is in Phoenix, or how hard it is to swallow capsules, or how bad a headache is. As listeners, we understand what's being said and meant in part on the basis of our own particular experiences: how things would be for us were we to have been in Phoenix, swallowed a capsule, and the like. This knowledge, as Schutz has marvelously shown, is the typified "stock of knowledge" at hand for each of us as social beings living in the common life-world we all share in various ways (see Schutz, 1973, pp. 99–181).

Obviously, errors happen in interpreting intent in this typified way, even though they often don't have particularly serious consequences (though of course they might). Uncertainties abound. In medical encounters, however, major problems can arise if errors and uncertainty in interpretation occur. On the other hand, Cassell remarks,

> the benefits of such assumptions to the attentive listener may also be considerable. When I am in doubt about the meaning of a symptom report, I attempt to elicit the description of pain or other symptom to the point where I can *actually almost feel the physical distress.* (1985, Vol. I, p. 137.)

To reach this point, he continues, reporting a case where this occurred to him, may require repeated descriptions by the patient or approaching examination in more than one way. Similarly, as we've noted above, having experienced an illness or distress yourself can make understanding easier.

Cassell then concludes this brief section (in part): By continually asking questions and learning "what things feel like to the patient," the physician will be better able to find out just "what's wrong" and whether the patient has been actually understood. "This comprehension will be genuine," he continues, for getting at the "intent" of a speaker is most simply to understand that person. Now, while it is surely not necessary for the physician to have every disease patients may have ("although it might be useful"), it is most assuredly "desperately necessary that you try to comprehend what they are trying to tell you" (ibid., p. 138). A crucial part of "intent," after all, is how important something is to the patient (whatever it may be for the doctor).

One thing to note right off: When Cassell seeks "to elicit the description," these words suggest that this is not the same thing as what is often done in ordinary conversations. In the latter, we tend to take it for granted that we and the speaker share the same intent and meaning; in the former, the listener (Cassell) is "attentive" and actively "elicits" the description of the pain or other symptom. Thus, if I understand it correctly, to be "attentive" is precisely not to take it for granted, not to assume that the intent of word usages is the same. Rather, the "attentive listener" is expressly aware of this tendency to "take for granted" but instead of giving in to it (and becoming inattentive) actively "elicits" again and again until the pain or symptom is actually almost felt.

The next thing to note is that actually having had a specific illness enables one to understand what a patient is going through, thus to understand what the patient is telling you about pain and distress. As was already suggested, this is so because undergoing illness (e.g., ESRD) and treatment (e.g., dialysis) is itself a kind of knowledge. Here, "I know what you're going through," has the bite of reality: "I've been through it, too, know what it's like, and maybe I can therefore not only understand you but possibly help."

Finally, we should carefully note the rest of what Cassell says: Continually "asking questions" teaches "what things feel like to the patient" and thus makes it more readily possible to understand what is actually wrong. Although the physician doesn't have to have every disease his or her patients have, even that is "useful" (it is a kind of knowledge). But the main thing is the importance of comprehending what the patient tells you, which includes how important something is, what it means to this patient. Cassell continues, "To empathize with her [the patient] is to understand not only the factual implications of her words, but also the importance to her of what she is describing" (ibid.).

Thus, the "attentive listener" who "elicits" and actually almost "feels," who may also have experiential knowledge, and who "asks questions" comes to "empathize" and thereby "know" what things feel like and what they mean to the patient. Clearly, it seems to me, what is being proposed here is by no means strictly included in the list of paralinguistic and conversational characteristics Cassell analyzes—lengthy and excellent though that list surely is. At most, noting these characteristics, especially the words used and everything noted about the patient using them, serve as the means for something else, a different sort of act. On the other hand, Cassell's very sharply focused question about, and the significance of, intent seems to be most directly addressed here, albeit only briefly and even almost in passing. What is it, we have to ask, which is, so to speak, set in motion by this eliciting, this almost actual feeling, asking questions, and empathizing?

My reason for pressing the point at such length is simply this: Quite in spite of his taken-for-granted assumption that one can never gain access to the other person's "little black box," the person's own interior life, Cassell is here approaching, awkwardly and almost without realizing it, an insight that fundamentally challenges that very assumption. To put it differently, he assumes (along with most everyone else for the past several centuries) the utter inaccessibility of the patient's own subjective life. For, as he states at one point:

> Words can be perceived; they are "things;" and one can prove they existed. Not so for intentions; they can never be known, measured, or their existence proved, in any objective fashion. Intentions are irreducibly subjective—they totally and completely depend on their possessor. (Ibid., p. 117.)

Hard, firm, unequivocal words, these; even so, Cassell goes right on to urge that it is the physician's critical job to get at how "things feel like to the patient," including not only "factual implications" but "the importance to her of what she is describing." By eliciting and empathizing ("feeling with"), he believes physicians can and must (it would seem) almost actually feel what things are like for the patient, what is important to the patient, what things mean for the patient. Yet, were we to take Cassell seriously in the passage just cited, this eliciting and empathizing could only be the sheerest of fantastic figments. Fortunately, however, he is too fine a clinician to let such assumptions get in the way of the very significant point at issue here.

Furthermore, as was urged earlier, on closer inspection these assumptions fly in the face of our actual experience and knowledge, for they completely distort and underestimate our actual knowledge of other persons. At the very least, clearing the air of those presumptions permits and even requires us to reassess this issue of intent, its apprehension and understanding.

While it is surely true that we often presume that we share the same intent and meanings with speakers, a presumption that is often quite correct (as subsequent conversation shows, we did indeed understand), that is not the only thing accomplished in these conversations. Even in everyday conversations, it should be noted, "attentive listening" is no stranger; we are often very attentive indeed. Nor is "asking questions" alien to ordinary life; again, we often engage in this, as a result of which we, like Cassell, do indeed come to see how things feel to the speaker, as well as what import they have for him or her. In daily life, we even have intriguing ways of describing this common, but largely ignored, act: "put yourself in my shoes" "try to see things from my point of view," to mention only two of them.

It seems quite true that we do indeed know far more about other persons than those assumptions can admit, and sometimes even know more about them than they do themselves (and conversely). What Cassell is trying to tell us, I think, is that the clinician has to engage in this act of putting yourself in the patient's shoes in a disciplined manner, where discipline has its grounds and rationale in the very point of the interaction: helping the patient get better and rigorously refusing the temptation to take advantage inherent to their asymmetrical relationship. That Cassell laces his words with qualifiers only shows the surreptitious power of those assumptions. Without them, however, there is no reason to beat around the bush, and every reason to be quite straightforward. What is needed is the clear recognition that this act must be sternly disciplined and that it is a, if not *the*, fundamental moral act.

A more exotic-sounding name for it might be "imaginative self-transposal" (Spiegelberg, 1955, 1964), or even my own "affiliative feeling." However it be labeled, its point is the same: A vital component of actual clinical thinking is appreciating what the patient is going through, what things feel like to the patient, including what is experienced and its significance for him or her, without in any way taking advantage of one who is already disadvantaged.

The real limit to this act has also been pointed out. In Scheler's terms, the only exclusively private sphere in the self's own experiences of its own bodily sensations. To gain access to this dimension, however, we are not restricted just to the patient's words, though these are clearly a most fruitful source of information. We also have a rich resource in the patient's physiognomic gestures, postures, and quasi-linguistic phenomena (groans, grimaces, grunts)—precisely because of which we do indeed "see the other's joy in his laughter . . . his sorrow and pain in his tears . . . his shame in his blushing" (Scheler, 1954, p. 260). Thus, while it is true that we do not have direct access to the bodily sensations of the patient, we do indeed have direct access to what things mean and in that sense what they "feel like," to the patient. (What is gained from physical diagnoses, tests, and radiological techniques may in these terms be viewed as supplements, albeit critical ones, to what has been stated.)

In everyday life and in many of our various enterprises, this access to the patient's experiences may not be called for. Nor is it necessarily done with particular skill or purpose on many occasions, by different people. Here, as elsewhere, training, practice, and guidance are essential in developing and nurturing a requisite skill. In clinical medicine, a disciplined understanding of the patient, as fully as circumstances and time permit, is a positive moral responsibility, requiring the physician to utilize every available resource to that end, in order thereby to reach, together with the patient and the patient's family or circle of intimates, the right decision enabling the patient to return to maximum functioning with integrity intact. What else is involved in this critical act, and what its philosophic roots and conditions are, will have to be considered on another occasion.

A FINAL WORD

The moral foundations of clinical medicine and of the experience of illness, not surprisingly, turn out to be profoundly interrelated and mutually determining. The therapeutic dyad of trust and care has its basis, on the one hand, in the "moral chance" of illness and in the scientifically and linguistically informed clinical act of affiliative feeling, on the other. Because of the uniqueness of this relationship and the conversations and actions by which it is carried out as a process, it is an essentially moral relationship showing all the characteristics of being fundamental to moral life. On the one side, the vulnerability and *appeal* of the ill person; on the other, the *response* from would-be healer. Their relationship, deeply textured in our times by complex forms of social norms and institutions, complicated by strangers engaging in multiple forms of intimacy, is an essentially tenuous, unequal, and asymmetrical one, the very fact of which constitutes a complex and altogether special set of occasions for awakening our sense of morality in its core form.

To respond within this set of special occasions to the appeal of the person who has suffered the accident of illness (ultimately reminding us of our common fate and condition—the accident of birth) is to seek to help sick people preserve themselves while suffering impairment, by helping them maintain control over themselves and become restored and whole again as far as circumstances allow. The role of clinical-liaison ethics is to assist in this complex process, to enable and empower both those who take care and those who must trust, and the various contextual features pertaining to both, to maintain their respective integrities, thereby to become better, morally responsive and responsible persons.

That is the central theme that I believe can be gained from the history of medicine and must remain the centering concern within the remarkably complex technological and social institutionalization of health care. In the end, it is not only the patient's "getting better" that counts; it is equally, though perhaps more subtly, that the physician, no less than the patient, morally benefits from the relationship.

Bibliography

Abrams, H. S.: 1972, "Psychological Dilemmas of Medical Progress," *Psychiatry in Medicine*, 3, pp. 51–58.

Agich, G. J. (ed.): 1982, *Responsibility in Health Care*, D. Reidel Publishing Co., Boston and Dordrecht.

Agle, D. P., et al.: 1970, "The Anticoagulant Malingerer: Psychiatric Studies of Three Patients," *Annals of Internal Medicine* 73, pp. 67–72.

Aristotle: 1941, *De partibus animalium*, in R. McKeon (ed.), *The Basic Works of Aristotle*, Random House, New York.

Aristotle: 1941, *Posterior Analytics*, in R. McKeon (ed.), *The Basic Works of Aristotle*, Random House, New York.

Aristotle: 1962, *Nicomachean Ethics*, Library of Liberal Arts, Bobbs-Merrill, New York.

Avorn, J.: 1982, "A Physician's Perspective," *Hastings Center Report* 12, pp. 11–12.

Beauchamp, T. L.: 1982, "What Philosophers Can Offer," *Hastings Center Report* 12, pp. 13–14.

Beauchamp, T. L., and Childress, J. F.: 1979, *Principles of Biomedical Ethics*, Oxford University Press, New York and London (2nd ed. 1983).

Beauchamp, T. L., and Walters, L. (eds.): 1982, *Contemporary Issues in Bioethics*, 2nd ed., Wadsworth Publishing Co., Belmont, Calif.

Blane, C. E., et al.: 1983, "Nonobstructive Fetal Hydronephrosis: Sonographic Recognition and Therapeutic Implications," *Radiology* 147, p. 95.

Brody, H.: 1980, *Placebos and the Philosophy of Medicine*, University of Chicago Press, Chicago.

Burnet, M.: 1978, *Endurance of Life: The Implications of Genetics for Human Life*, Cambridge University Press, New York and London.

Callahan, D.: 1975, "The Ethics Backlash," *Hastings Center Report* 5, p. 18.

Callahan, D.: 1981, "Minimalist Ethics," *Hastings Center Report* 11, pp. 19–25.

Caplan, A.: 1982, "Applying Morality to Advances in Biomedicine: Can and Should This Be Done?" in W. Bondeson et al. (eds.), *New Knowledge in the Biomedical Sciences*, D. Reidel Publishing Co., Boston and Dordrecht, pp. 155–68.

Carrodus, J. L., et al.: 1971, "Haematuria as a Feature of the Munchausen Syndrome: Report of a Case." *Australian New Zealand Journal of Surgery* 40, pp. 365–67.

Cassell, E. J.: 1973, "Making and Escaping Moral Decisions," *Hastings Center Report* 1, pp. 53–62.
Cassell, E. J.: 1976, *The Healer's Art: A New Approach to the Doctor-Patient Relationship*, J. B. Lippincott Company, Philadelphia. (1985, MIT Press, Boston.)
Cassell, E. J.: 1979, "The Subjective in Clinical Judgment," in H. T. Engelhardt, Jr., et al. (eds.), *Clinical Judgment: A Critical Appraisal*, D. Reidel Publishing Co., Boston and Dordrecht, pp. 199–215.
Cassell, E. J.: 1982, "The Nature of Suffering and the Goals of Medicine," *New England Journal of Medicine* 306, pp. 639–45.
Cassell, E. J.: 1985, *Talking With Patients*, 2 vols., MIT Press, Boston.
Clark, K. B.: 1973, "Psychotechnology and the Pathos of Power," in F. W. Matson (ed.), *Without/Within: Behaviorism and Humanism*, Brooks/Cole Publishing Company, Monterey, Calif., pp. 92–98.
Clements, C. D.: 1982, *Medical Genetics Casebook: A Clinical Introduction to Medical Ethics Systems Theory*, The Humana Press, Clifton, N.J.
Clements, C. D., and Sider, R. C.: 1983, " 'Medical Ethics' Assault Upon Medical Values," *Journal of American Medical Association* 250, pp. 2011–15.
Clewell, W. H., et al.: 1982, "A Surgical Approach to the Treatment of Fetal Hydrocephalus," *New England Journal of Medicine* 306, pp. 1320–25.
Clouser, K. D.: 1972, "Philosophy and Medicine: The Clinical Management of a Mixed Marriage," *Proceedings of the 1st Session, Institute on Human Values in Medicine*, Society for Health and Human Values, Philadelphia, pp. 10–21.
Coene, R. E.: 1978, "Dialysis or Transplant: One Patient's Choice," *Hastings Center Report* 8, p. 7.
Copello, A. G.: 1985, "The Case of X: A Commentary on the Utility of Clinical Ethics Practice Methodology," D.D. diss. (Vanderbilt University).
Coulter, H. l.: 1975, 1977, 1973 *The Divided Legacy*, 3 vols., Wehawken Book Co., Washington, D.C.
Curlender v. Bioscience Laboratories, 165 Cal. 477, 488 (Cal. App. 1980).
Department of Health and Human Services: 1985, "Child Abuse and Neglect Prevention and Treatment Program: Final Rule," *Federal Register* 45 C.F.R. pt. 1340 § 72 (Apr. 15), pp. 14878–14901.
Descartes, R.: 1931, *The Philosophical Works of Descartes* (in 2 vols.), trans. E. S. Haldane and G. R. T. Ross, Cambridge University Press, London; Dover Publishing Co., New York.
Descartes, R.: 1963, 1967, 1973, *Oeuvres philosophiques*, 3 vols., Ed. F. Alquié, Editions Garner Fréres, Paris.
Descartes, R.: 1976, *Conversations with Burman*, trans. J. Cottingham, Oxford University Press, London and New York.
Dijksterhuis, E. J.: 1964, *The Mechanization of the World Picture*, Oxford University Press, London and New York.
Dolan, J. P., and Adams-Smith, W. N.: 1978, *Health and Society: A Documentary History of Medicine*, Seabury Press, New York.
Donnelly, W. J.: 1986, "Medical Language as Symptom: Doctor Talk in Teaching Hospitals," *Perspectives in Biology and Medicine* 30, no. 1, pp. 81–94.
Dubos, R.: 1965, *Man Adapting*, Yale University Press, New Haven and London.
Eccles, J. C.: 1970, *Facing Reality: Philosophical Adventures by a Brain Scientist*, Springer-Verlag, New York and Heidelberg.
Eccles, J. C.: 1979, *The Human Mystery*, The Gifford Lectures, University of Edinburgh (1977–78), Springer International, New York and Heidelberg.
Edelstein, L.: 1967, *Ancient Medicine*, Johns Hopkins University Press, Baltimore, Md.
Engelhardt, H. T., Jr.: 1973, "The Philosophy of Medicine: A New Endeavor," *Texas Reports on Biology and Medicine* 3, pp. 443–52.
Engelhardt, H. T., Jr.: 1975, "Bioethics and the Process of Embodiment," *Perspectives in Biology and Medicine* 18, pp. 486–500.
Engelhardt, H. T. Jr.: 1978, "Basic Ethical Principles in the Conduct of Biomedical and Behavioral Research Involving Human Subjects," *Belmont Report*, Appendix, Vol. 1, DHEW Pub. No. [OS] 78-0013.
Engelhardt, H. T., Jr.: 1982, "Introduction," in Bondeson, et al. (eds.), *New Knowledge in the Biomedical Sciences*, D. Reidel Publishing Co., Boston and Dordrecht, pp. xi–xviii. Also, "Why New Technology is More Problematic than Old Technology," pp. 179–184.

Engelhardt, H. T., Jr.: 1985, "Current Controversies in Obstetrics: Wrongful Life and Forced Fetal Surgical Procedures," *American Journal of Obstetrics and Gynecology* 151, pp. 313–18.

Farber, S. M., and Wilson, R. H. L.: 1961, *Control of the Mind*, 2 vols., McGraw-Hill Book Co., New York.

Fleischman, A.: 1981a, "A Physician's View," *Hastings Center Report* 11, pp. 18–19.

Fleischman, A.: 1981b, "Teaching Medical Ethics in a Pediatric Training Program," *Pediatric Annals* 10, pp. 51–53.

Ford, C. V.: 1983, *The Somatizing Disorders: Illness as a Way of Life*, Elsevier, New York.

Fost, N., Chudwin, D., and Wikler, D.: 1980, "The Limited Moral Significance of Fetal Viability," *Hastings Center Report* 10:6, pp. 12–13.

Foster, L.: 1976, "Man and Machine: Life Without Kidneys," *Hastings Center Report* 6, pp. 6–8.

Foucault, M.: 1973, *The Birth of the Clinic*, Pantheon books, New York.

Fox, R.: 1976, "Long-term Dialysis Programs: New Selection Criteria, New Problems," *Hastings Center Report* 6, pp. 11–12.

Garfinkle, H.: 1967, *Studies in Ethnomethodology*, Prentice-Hall, Englewood Cliffs, N.J.

Germaine, C. B., and Gitterman, A.: 1980, *The Life Model of Social Work Practice*, Columbia University Press, New York.

Gleitman v. Cosgrove 227 A.2d 689 (N.J. 1967).

Goldstein, K.: 1947, *Language and Language Disturbances*, Grune and Stratton, New York.

Gorovitz, S.: 1982, *Doctors' Dilemmas: Moral Conflict and Medical Care*, Macmillan Publishing Co., New York.

Gorovitz, S., and MacIntyre, A.: 1976, "Toward a Theory of Medical Fallibility," *Journal of Medicine and Philosophy* 1, pp. 51–71.

Gorovitz, S., et al. (eds.): 1976, *Moral Problems in Medicine*, Prentice-Hall, Englewood Cliffs, N.J.

Greenblatt, S. H.: 1976, "Round-Table Discussion," in S. F. Spicker and H. T. Engelhardt, Jr. (eds.), *Philosophical Dimensions of the Neuro-Medical Sciences*, D. Reidel Publishing Co., Boston and Dordrecht, pp. 241–45.

Grene, M.: 1974, *The Understanding of Nature: Essays in the Philosophy of Biology*, Boston Studies in the Philosophy of Science, Vol. XXIII, D. Reidel Publishing Co., Boston and Dordrecht.

Griedman, E. (ed.): 1977, *Strategies in Renal Failure*, Wiley and Sons, New York.

Gurwitsch, A.: 1964, *Field of Consciousness*, Duquesne University Press, Pittsburgh, Pa.

Guttentag, O. E.: 1968, "Ethical Problems in Human Experimentation," in E. F. Torrey (ed.), *Ethical Issues in Medicine*, Little, Brown, Boston.

Harbeson v. Parke-Davis, Inc., 656 P.2d 483 (1983).

Hardy, R. C.: 1978, *Sick: How People Feel About Being Sick and What They Think of Those Who Care For Them*, Teach 'em, Inc., Chicago.

Hare, R. M.: 1977, "Medical Ethics: Can the Moral Philosopher Help?" in S. F. Spicker and H. T. Engelhardt, Jr. (eds.), *Philosophical Medical Ethics; Its Nature and Significance*, D. Reidel Publishing Co., Boston and Dordrecht, pp. 49–62.

Harrod, H.: 1981, *The Human Center: Moral Agency in the Social World*, Fortress Press, Philadelphia.

Harvey, W.: 1961, *Lectures on the Whole of Anatomy*. Annotated and translated by C. D. O'Malley et al., University of California Press, Berkeley and Los Angeles.

Hauerwas, S. M.: 1982, "Authority and the Profession of Medicine," in G. J. Agich (ed.), *Responsibility in Health Care*, D. Reidel Publishing Co., Boston and Dordrecht, pp. 83–104.

Hobbins et al.: 1984, "Antenatal Diagnosis of Renal Anomalies with Ultrasound," *American Journal of Obstetrics and Gynecology* 148, pp. 868–77.

Hoffer, E.: 1958, *The True Believer*, The New American Library of World Literature, New York.

Hunt, R., and Arras, J.: 1977, *Ethical Issues in Modern Medicine*, Mayfield Publishing Co., Palo Alto, Ca.

Illich, I.: 1976, *Medical Nemesis: The Expropriation of Health*, Bantam Books, Inc., New York.

Ingelfinger, F. J.: 1975, "Ethics and High Blood Pressure," *New England Journal of Medicine* 292, pp. 43–44.

Jonas, H.: 1966, *The Phenomenon of Life: Toward a Philosophical Biology*, Delta Books, Dell Publishing Co., New York.

Jonas, H.: 1974, *Philosophical Essays: From Ancient Creed to Technological Man*, Prentice-Hall, Englewood-Cliffs, N.J.

Jonas, H.: 1984, *The Imperative of Responsibility: In Search of an Ethics for the Technological Age*, Chicago University Press, Chicago.

Jonsen, A. R.: 1983, "Watching the Doctor," *New England Journal of Medicine* 308, pp. 1531–35.

Jonsen, A. R., Siegler, M., and Winslade, W. J.: 1982, *Clinical Ethics*, Macmillan Publishing Co., New York.

Kant, I.: 1956, *Critique of Practical Reason*, trans. L. W. Beck, Bobbs-Merrill, Indianapolis, Ind.

Kennington, R.: 1978, "Descartes and Mastery of Nature," in S. F. Spicker (ed.), *Organism, Medicine, and Metaphysics: Essays in Honor of Hans Jonas*, D. Reidel Publishing Co., Boston and Dordrecht, pp. 201–24.

Kierkegaard, S.: 1978, "Thoughts on Crucial Situations in Human Life," in T. C. Oden (ed.), *Parables of Kierkegaard*, Princeton University Press, Princeton, N.J.

King, L. S.: 1963, *The Growth of Medical Thought*, The University of Chicago Press, Chicago.

King, L. S.: 1978, *The Philosophy of Medicine: The Early Eighteenth Century*, Harvard University Press, Cambridge, Mass.

Kluge, E-H. W.: 1975, *The Practice of Death*, Yale University Press, New Haven, Conn.

Koyré, A.: 1957, *From the Closed World to the Infinite Universe*, Harper and Row, New York.

Kramer, S. A.: 1983, "Current Status of Fetal Intervention for Congenital Hydronephrosis," *Journal of Urology* 130, pp. 375–77.

Lain-Entralgo, P.: 1963, *Historia de la Medicina Moderna y Contemporánea*, Ed. Cientifico-Medica, Barcelona.

Lain-Entralgo, P.: 1969, *Doctor and Patient*, World University Library, London.

Laing, R. D.: 1969, *Self and Others*, Pantheon Books, New York.

Langer, S.: 1942, *Philosophy in a New Key*, The New American Library, New York.

Leake, C. D.: 1976, *What Are We Living For? Practical Philosophy*, PJD Publications, Westbury, N.Y.

LeBaron, C.: 1981, *Gentle Vengeance: An Account of the First Year at Harvard Medical School*, Richard Marek Publishers, New York.

Lenrow, P. B.: 1982, "The Work of Helping Strangers," in H. Rubenstein and M. H. Bloch (eds.), *Things That Matter: Influences on Helping Relationships*, Macmillan Publishing Co., New York, pp. 42–57.

Levine, C.: 1976, "Home Dialysis and the Medicare Gap," *Hastings Center Report* 6, pp. 5–6.

Liddle, G. W.: 1967, "The Mores of Clinical Investigation," *Journal of Clinical Investigation* 46, pp. 1028–30.

Lindeboom, G. A.: 1978, *Descartes and Medicine*, Rodopi NV, Amsterdam.

MacIntyre, A.: 1966, *A Short History of Ethics*, Macmillan Publishing Co., New York.

MacIntyre, A.: 1977, "Patients as Agents," in S. F. Spicker and H. T Engelhardt, Jr. (eds.), *Philosophical Medical Ethics: Its Nature and Significance*, D. Reidel Publishing Co., Boston and Dordrecht, pp. 197–212.

MacIntyre, A.: 1978, "How to Identify Ethical Principles," *The Belmont Report*, Appendix, Vol. I, DHEW Pub. No. [OS] 78-0013, Washington, D.C.

MacIntyre, A.: 1981, *After Virtue*, University of Notre Dame Press, Notre Dame, Ind.

MacIntyre, A.: 1984, "Does Applied Ethics Rest on a Mistake?" *The Monist* 67, pp. 498–513.

Majno, G.: 1975, *The Healing Hand: Man and Wound in the Ancient World*, Harvard University Press, Cambridge, Mass.

Martin, S. P.: 1972, "The New Healer," *Proceedings of the 1st Session, Institute on Human Values in Medicine*, Society for Health and Human Values, Philadelphia, Pa., pp. 5–27.

Mendelsohn, S.: 1978, Introduction to *Sick*, by R. C. Hardy, Teach'em Inc., Chicago.

Meropol, N. J., Ford, C. V., and Zaner, R. M.: 1985, "Factitious Illness: An Exploration in Ethics," *Perspectives in Biology and Medicine* 28, pp. 269–81.

Mill, J. S.: 1838 (1923), *Principles of Political Economy*, W. J. Ashby (ed.), Longmans, Green and Company, London.

Mill, J. S.: 1942, *The Spirit of the Age*, Chicago University Press, Chicago.

Morison, R. S.: 1981, "Bioethics After Two Decades," *Hastings Center Report* 11, pp. 8–12.

Mumford, L.: 1970, *The Myth of the Machine: The Pentagon of Power*, Harcourt, Brace, Jovanovich, New York.

Nadelson, T.: 1979, "The Munchausen Spectrum," *General Hospital Psychiatry* 1, pp. 11–17.

Noble, C. N.: 1982, "Ethics and Experts," *Hastings Center Reports* 12, pp. 7–9, 15.

Ortega y Gasset, J.: 1957, *Man and People*, W. W. Norton and Company, New York.

Peabody, F. W.: [1927] 1985, "The Care of the Patient," in D. Rabin and P. L. Rabin (eds.), *To Provide Safe Passage: The Humanistic Aspects of Medicine*, Philosophical Library, New York, pp. 1–21.

Pellegrino, E. D.: 1970, "The Most Humane of the Sciences; the Most Scientific of the Humanities," *The Sanger Lecture*, Medical College of Virginia, Virginia Commonwealth University (Apr. 10, 1970). (In E. D. Pellegrino, 1979b, *Humanism and the Physician.*)

Pellegrino, E. D.: 1973, "The Hippocratic Ethics Revisited," in R. Bulger (ed.), *Hippocrates Revisited*, The Williams and Wilkins Company, New York, pp. 133–47. (In E. D. Pellegrino, 1979b)

Pellegrino, E. D.: 1974, "Medicine and Philosophy: Some Notes on the Flirtations of Minerva and Aescupalius," Presidential Address, Society for Health and Human Values, Philadelphia.

Pellegrino, E. D.: 1979a, "The Anatomy of Clinical Judgments: Some Notes on Right Reason and Right Action," in H. T. Engelhardt, Jr. et al. (eds.), *Clinical Judgment: A Critical Appraisal*, D. Reidel Publishing Co., Boston and Dordrecht, pp. 169–94.

Pellegrino, E. D.: 1979b, *Humanism and the Physician*, University of Tennessee Press, Knoxville, Tenn.

Pellegrino, E. D.: 1982, "Being Ill and Being Healed: Some Reflections on the Grounds of Medical Morality," in V. Kestenbaum (ed.), *The Humanity of the Ill: Phenomenological Perspectives*, University of Tennessee Press, Knoxville, Tenn. pp. 157–66.

Pellegrino, E. D., et al.: 1985, "Relevance and Utility of Courses in Medical Ethics: A Survey of Physicians' Perceptions," *Journal of the American Medical Association* 253, pp. 49–53.

Pellegrino, E. D., and McElhiney, T. K.: 1981, *Teaching Ethics, the Humanities, and Human Values in Medical Schools: A Ten-Year Overview*, Institute on Human Values in Medicine, Society for Health and Human Values, Washington, D.C.

Pellegrino, E. D., and Thomasma, D. C.: 1981, *A Philosophical Basis of Medical Practice: Toward a Philosophy and Ethic of the Healing Professions*, Oxford University Press, London and New York.

Penfield, W.: 1975, *The Mystery of the Mind*, Princeton University Press, Princeton, N.J.

Perone, N. et al.: 1984, "Legal Liability in the Use of Ultrasound by Office-based Obstetricians," *American Journal of Obstetrics and Gynecology* 150, pp. 801–04.

Plato: 1961, *The Collected Dialogues of Plato*, Bollingen Series LXXI, Eds. E. Hamilton and H. Cairns, Princeton University Press, Princeton, N.J.

Plügge, H.: 1970, "Man and his Body," in S. F. Spicker (ed.), *The Philosophy of the Body*, Quadrangle Books, Chicago, pp. 293–311. (From H. Plügge, *Der Mensch und sein Leib*, Max Niemeyer Verlag, Tübingen, 1967, pp. 34–42, 57–68.)

Portmann, A.: 1954, "Biology and the Phenomenon of the Spiritual," in J. Campbell (ed.), *Spirit and Nature: Papers from the Eranos Yearbooks*, Vol. I, Bollingen Series XXX, Princeton University Press, Princeton, N.J. pp. 342–70.

Purtillo, R. B.: 1984, "Ethics Consultations in the Hospital," *New England Journal of Medicine* 311, pp. 983–86.

Ramsey, P.: 1970, *The Patient as Person*, Yale University Press, New Haven and London.

Ramsey, P.: 1974, "The Indignity of 'Death with Dignity,' " *Hastings Center Report* 2, pp. 47–62.

Rather, L. J.: 1965, *Mind and Body in Eighteenth Century Medicine*, University of California Press, Berkeley and Los Angeles.

Rawlinson, M. C.: 1982, "Medicine's Discourse and the Practice of Medicine," in V. Kestenbaum (ed.), *The Humanity of the Ill: Phenomenological Perspectives*, University of Tennessee Press, Knoxville, Tenn. pp. 69–85.

Rawls, J.: 1971, *A Theory of Justice*, Harvard University Press, Cambridge, Mass.

Rescher, N.: 1969, "The Allocation of Exotic Medical Life-saving Therapy," *Ethics* 79, pp. 173–86.

Riese, W.: 1966, "Descartes as a Psychotherapist: The Uses of Rational Philosophy in the Treatment of Discomfort and Disease," *Medical History* 10, pp. 237–44.

Roe v. Wade, 410 U.S. 113 (1973).

Romanell, P.: 1956, "Morals and Medicine: A Critique," *Humanist* 16, pp. 33–34.

Romanell, P.: 1972, "Medical Ethics in Philosophical Perspective," in M. B. Visscher (ed.), *Humanistic Perspectives in Medical Ethics*, Prometheus Books, Buffalo, N.Y. pp. 24–38.

Romanell, P.: 1974, "A Philosophic Preface to Morals in Medicine," *Bulletin of the New York Academy of Medicine* 50, pp. 3–27.

Rothman, D. J.: 1982, "Were Tuskegee and Willowbrook 'Studies in Nature?" *Hastings Center Report* 12, pp. 5–7.

Ruddick, W.: 1981, "Can Doctors and Philosophers Work Together? *Hastings Center Report* 11, pp. 12–17.

Scheler, M.: 1954, *The Nature of Sympathy*, trans. P. Heath, Yale University Press, New Haven.
Scheler, M.: 1973, *Formalism in Ethics and Non-Formal Ethics of Values*, trans. M. S. Frings and R. L. Funk, Northwestern University Press, Evanston, Ill.
Schutz, A.: 1964, *Collected Papers, II: Studies in Social Theory*, Phaenomenologica 15, Martinus Nijhoff, The Hague.
Schutz, A.: 1967, *Collected Papers, I: The Problem of Social Reality*, Phaenomenologica 11 (2nd ed.), Martinus Nijhoff, The Hague.
Schutz, A.: 1970, *Reflections on the Problem of Relevance*. Edited and with an introduction by R. M. Zaner, Yale University Press, New Haven.
Schutz, A.: 1973, *The Structure of the Life-World*, trans. H. T. Engelhardt, Jr., and R. M. Zaner, Northwestern University Press, Evanston, Ill.
Shaffer, J.: 1975, "Round-Table Discussion," in H. T. Engelhardt, Jr., and S. F. Spicker (eds.), *Evaluation and Explanation in the Biomedical Sciences*, D. Reidel Publishing Co., Boston and Dordrecht, pp. 215–19.
Siegler, M.: 1979, "Clinical Ethics and Clinical Medicine," *Archives of Internal Medicine* 139, pp. 914–15.
Siegler, M.: 1985, "MDs to be the Principal Teachers of Clinical Ethics at Chicago Center," *Medical Ethics Advisor* 1, p. 41.
Silber, T.: 1981, "Introduction: Bioethics and the Pediatrician" (a special issue devoted to bioethics), *Pediatric Annals* 10, pp. 381–82.
Singer, C.: 1925, *Evolution of Anatomy*, Alfred Knopf Publishers, New York.
Singer, P.: 1982, "How Do We Decide?" *Hastings Center Report* 12, pp. 9–11.
Spicker, S. F., and Engelhardt, H. T., Jr. (eds.): 1976, Introduction, *Philosophical Dimensions of the Neuro-Medical Sciences*, D. Reidel Publishing Co., Boston and Dordrecht, pp. 1–11.
Spiegelberg, H.: 1944, "A Defense of Human Equality," *Philosophical Review* 53, pp. 101–24.
Spiegelberg, H.: 1955, "Toward a Phenomenology of Imaginative Understanding of Others," *Proceedings of the XIIth International Congress of Philosophy*, Vol. VII, Brussels, pp. 235–39.
Spiegelberg, H.: 1961, " 'Accident of Birth': A Non-Utilitarian Motif in Mill's Philosophy," *Journal of the History of Ideas* 22, pp. 475–92.
Spiegelberg, H.: 1964, "Phenomenology Through Vicarious Experience," in E. Straus (ed.), *Phenomenology: Pure and Applied*, Duquesne University Press, Pittsburgh, Pa. pp. 105–26.
Spiegelberg, H.: 1974, "Ethics for Fellows in the Fate of Existence," in P. Bertocci (ed.), *Mid-Century American Philosophy: Personal Statements*, Humanities Press, New York, pp. 193–210.
Spiegelberg, H.: 1975, "Good Fortune Obligates: Albert Schweitzer's Second Ethical Principle," *Ethics* 85, pp. 227–34.
Starr, P.: 1982, *The Social Transformation of American Medicine*, Basic Books, New York.
Steinbeck, A. W.: 1967, "Hemonhagica Histrionica—The Bleeding Munchausen Syndrome," *Medical Journal of Australia* 1, pp. 451–56.
Stevens, R.: 1971, *American Medicine and the Public Interest*, Yale University Press, New Haven and London.
Stewart v. Long Island College Hospital, 196 N.Y.S.2d 41 (1968), aff'd, 283 N.E.2d 616 (N.Y. 1972).
Sullivan, M.: 1985, "In What Sense is Contemporary Medicine Cartesian?" paper based on author's doctoral dissertation (Vanderbilt University, 1983).
Taylor, G. R.: 1968, *The Biological Time Bomb*, World Publishing Co., New York and Cleveland.
Tempkin, O: 1973, *Galenism: Rise and Decline of a Medical Philosophy*, Cornell University Press, Ithaca and London.
Thomas, W. I.: 1928, *The Child in America: Behavior Problems and Programs*, Alfred Knopf, New York.
Titmuss, R. M.: 1971, *The Gift Relationship: From Human Blood to Social Policy*, Vintage Books, New York.
Toulmin, S.: 1958, *The Uses of Argument*, Cambridge University Press, London and New York.
Toulmin, S.: 1982, "How Medicine Saved the Life of Ethics," *Perspectives in Biology and Medicine* 25, pp. 736–50.
Turpin v. Sortini, 643 P.2d 954 (Cal. 1982).
Untersteiner, M.: 1954, *The Sophists*, trans. K. Freeman, Basil Blackwell, Oxford.
Van den Berg, J. L.: 1978, *Medical Power and Medical Ethics*, Duquesne University Press, Pittsburgh, Pa.
Veatch, R. M.: 1981, *A Theory of Medical Ethics*, Basic Books, New York.
Veatch, R. M.: 1982, "Medical Authority and Professional Medical Authority: The Nature of Au-

thority in Medicine for Decisions by Lay Persons and Professionals," in G. J. Agich (ed.), *Responsibility in Health Care*, D. Reidel Publishing Co., Boston and Dordrecht, pp. 127–37.

Von Uexküll, J.: 1953, *Der Mensch und die Natur: Grundzüge einer Naturphilosophie*, Munich.

Von Uexküll, J.: 1956, *Streifzüge durch die Umwelten von Tieren und Menschen*, Rowohlt, Hamburg.

Weber, M.: 1947, *The Theory of Social and Economic Organization*, trans. A. M. Henderson and T. Parsons, Oxford University Press, New York and London.

Wieder, D. L.: 1974, *Language and Social Reality*, Mouton, The Hague and Paris.

Wikler, D.: 1982, "Ethicists, Critics, and Expertise," *Hastings Center Report* 12, pp. 12–13.

Wolff, K. H.: 1976, *Surrender and Catch: Experience and Inquiry Today*, D. Reidel Publishing Co., Boston and Dordrecht.

Zaner, R. M.: 1981, *The Context of Self: A Phenomenological Inquiry Using Medicine as a Clue*, Ohio University Press, Athens, Ohio.

Zaner, R. M.: 1982, "Chance and Morality: The Dialysis Phenomenon," in V. Kestenbaum (ed.), *The Humanity of the Ill: Phenomenological Perspectives*, University of Tennessee Press, Knoxville, Tenn. pp. 39–68.

Zaner, R. M.: 1986, "Soundings From Uncertain Places: Difficult Pregnancies and Imperiled Infants," in P. R. Dokecki and R. M. Zaner (eds.), *Ethics of Dealing with Persons with Severe Handicaps: Toward a Research Agenda*, Paul H. Brookes Publishing Co., pp. 71–92.

Acknowledgments continued from page ii

E. J. Cassell, *Talking with Patients* (Cambridge, Mass.: MIT Press, 1985). Excerpts reprinted by permission of the publisher, © 1985 by The Massachusetts Institute of Technology.

H. L. Coulter, *Divided Legacy*, Vol. I: *The Patterns Emerge: Hippocrates to Paracelsus* (Washington, D.C.: Wehawken Book Company, 1975). Excerpts reprinted by permission of the publisher.

R. Descartes, *The Philosophical Works of Descartes,* Vol. I, Elizabeth S. Haldaine and G.R.T. Ross (New York: Cambridge University Press [1931] 1955). Excerpts reprinted by permission of the publisher. Copyright © 1931, 1955 by Cambridge University Press.

L. Foster, "Man and Machine: Life Without Kidneys," *Hastings Center Report,* 6 (1976): 6–8. Excerpts reproduced by permission of the publisher, © The Hastings Center.

E. D. Pellegrino, "The Anatomy of Clinical Judgments: Some Notes on Right Reason and Right Action," in H. T. Engelhardt, Jr., et al. (eds.), *Clinical Judgment: A Critical Appraisal* (Boston and Dordrecht, Holland: D. Reidel Publishing Company, 1979), pp. 169–194. Excerpts reprinted by permission of the publisher. Copyright © 1979 by D. Reidel Publishing Company, Dordrecht, Holland.

L. Edelstein, *Ancient Medicine,* ed. O. Tempkin and C. L. Tempkin (Baltimore, Md.: The Johns Hopkins University Press, 1967). Excerpts reprinted by permission of the publisher.

R. C. Hardy, *Sick: How People Feel About Being Sick and What They Think of Those Who Care for Them* (Chicago: Teach 'Em, Inc., 1978). Excerpts reprinted by permission of the publisher.

Index

Abortion, 47–50, 207, 217. *See also*
　　Case discussions: "Baby Doe";
　　Case discussions: fetal anomalies
Abrams, Harry, 293, 294
Analogismos, 149–150, 172. *See also*
　　Diagnosis; Dogmatics
Anatomy, 110, 112–114, 118–119,
　　122, 124, 129, 132–137, 147,
　　151–153, 158–159, 164–170,
　　185–189, 190–197, 284–285,
　　287–288
Aristotle, 6, 36, 144, 189, 192,
　　193–194, 209
Autonomy, 285–292, 297, 310. *See
　　also* Freedom; Mutuality
Autopsy, 129, 132–137, 151, 153,
　　196–197

"Baby Doe" amendment, 21–27
Bacon, Francis, 116, 126, 199, 201
Beauchamp, Tom L., 11, 19
Berg, J. H. van den, 165–168, 198,
　　238

Bichat, Xavier, 80, 119, 133–137, 144,
　　150–153, 175, 186, 285, 287, 313
Biomedical model, 98, 103, 105–106.
　　See also Medicine
Birth, accident of, 299, 300–303, 310,
　　320. *See also* Chance, moral
Blood
　　circulation, 113–114, 121
　　transfusion, 113
Bloodletting, 111, 112
Body, human, 105–129, 135,
　　157–172, 185–188. *See also*
　　Corpse; Descartes, René;
　　Dissection; Embodiment
　　brain, 106, 108, 119, 132–133
　　living, 120–124, 127, 135, 154,
　　　158–170, 185–188, 195–196.
　　　See also Embodiment; Life
　　machine analogy and, 117–120,
　　　152, 168, 186, 197
　　relationship of, with mind. *See*
　　　Dualism; Embodiment; Mind-
　　　body relation

Body, human (*cont.*)
  restorative powers of. *See* Empirics,
    ancient; Skepticism
Boyle, Thomas, 119, 151, 168, 285
Burnet, Macfarlane, 2, 155, 157,
  160–161, 170, 172

Cadaver, 120–124, 159, 167. *See also*
  Corpse
Callahan, Daniel, 10
Care, moral idea of, 254–255,
  283–320. *See also* Case
  discussions; Illness
  contrasted to cure, 204
Case discussions
  adult respiratory distress syndrome
    (ARDS), 14–16
  "Baby Doe," 21–27, 30, 31, 42, 48,
    50, 246–248
  breast cancer, 71–73
  cancer, 56–58, 65, 70
  coronary bypass, 88–89, 90
  fallen arches, 73–74
  fetal anomalies, 44–50
  gall bladder, 61–62, 63, 65, 75
  kidney disease (ESRD), 86, 90,
    293–297, 298, 308–311
  missed diagnosis, 86, 90
  muscular dystrophy, 76–77
  obesity, 58–61, 65, 69, 91, 308
  parents of "Baby Doe," 246–248
  pediatric neural disease, 33
  pediatric surgeon, 259–263
  resident and attending physician,
    276–279, 281
  terminal illness, ("living will"),
    225–242, 245–246, 254,
    267–269, 270–274, 280, 281
Cassell, Eric
  Cartesian dualism, 106, 107, 110
  clinical medicine and diagnosis, 78,
    266–267, 312–313, 314
  death and dying, 88, 236, 238–239,
    274–275
  deficiency of traditional medicine,
    95, 99, 102, 103
  doctor-patient relationship, 252,
    255–257, 260, 261, 265–266,
    315, 316–317, 318
  healing vs. curing, 204, 220–221
  illness vs. disease, 204, 220–221
  individual person, 78–79, 80
  medical morality, 3, 7, 13, 27,
    37, 65

  pain and suffering, 71–73, 74, 83,
    128
  patient's scale of values, 105
  patient vs. physician experience,
    220–221
  talking with patients, 96–97, 114,
    244–245, 249, 251, 258, 263,
    271, 279, 285, 288–289, 315,
    316–317
  trust, 274–275
Cause, proximate. *See* Dogmatics,
  ancient
Celsus, 146, 191–196
Chance, moral, 297–299, 300–303,
  310, 319. *See also* Case
  discussions: kidney disease; Case
  discussions: parents of "Baby
  Doe"
Cicero, 218
Circumstantiality. *See* Ethics: clinical
  methods; Skepticism
Clark, Kenneth B., 155–157, 161, 163
Coene, Roger, 89, 309, 311. *See also*
  Case discussions: kidney disease
Committee on Costs of Medical Care,
  128–129, 151
Context, 244–246, 275–282, 285. *See
  also* Conversation; Interpretation
Conversation
  clinical, 75–80, 97–106, 108,
    266–267, 275–279, 310–311,
    314
  communicative intent in, 97–99,
    102, 104, 284, 312–314. *See also*
    Case discussions
  interpretation of, 244–248,
    267–282, 310–311, 315–319.
    See also Case discussions
  locational index in, 97, 102–105,
    128, 137, 284
  ordinary, 78–79, 82–84, 88–91,
    135–137, 244–246, 258, 315.
    See also Descartes, René
Copello, A. Gene, 249–250
Corpse, 158–170, 185–188, 193, 194.
  See also Cadaver
Correlation, clinico-pathological, 129,
  132–137, 152–153, 196–197. *See
  also* Anatomy; Dissection
Coulter, Harrison B., 38, 112,
  137-138, 139, 142, 145, 149, 150,
  151, 212–213
Cure, 204. *See also* Care, moral idea
  of; Diagnosis; Medicine

Curlender v. Bio-Science Laboratories, 48, 49
Cusa, Nicholas of, 198–199

Death, 67, 86–88, 98, 122–123, 135, 150–153, 158–170, 186–188, 192, 195, 309
  and dying, 225–242, 274–275. *See also* Case discussions: terminal illness
Descartes, René
  anatomy and physiology, 112–114, 121–122, 151–152, 185–188, 196
  body-machine analogy, 110, 117–120, 121, 123, 124, 159, 188, 198, 284, 287
  circulation of blood, 113–114, 121–122. *See also* Harvey, William
  clinical medicine, 110–112, 117, 120, 121, 124, 201
  issue of dualism or mind-body dichotomy, 106–122, 135, 136, 156–157, 166, 175, 186, 187, 197, 284. *See also* Dualism; Mind-body relation
  mastery of nature, 161, 199. *See also* Nature
  medical consultant, 110–112
  medicine as goal of knowledge, 112, 136
  ordinary life and conversation, 110, 115–118, 125–126, 127, 135, 186, 188, 285, 287. *See also* Conversation
  relation to subsequent medicine, 80, 126, 127, 135, 136, 137, 163, 172, 284
  two senses of nature, 115–119, 122–123, 124, 167, 168, 186, 188
Desert, idea of moral, 298–303
Diagnosis, 75–78, 97, 99, 104–105, 312–313, 314. *See also* Medicine; Pellegrino, Edmund D.
  and classificatory pattern of disease, 100–101, 103
  fetal, 44–50
Dialysis, 84, 86, 90, 109, 293–297, 298, 308–311
Dietetics, 148, 189–190, 199–201, 205, 207, 208, 211. *See also* Empirics, ancient; Galen

Disease. *See also* Illness
  humoral theory of, 143–146, 178, 189, 191. *See also* Dogmatics
  logical classification of, 144–145, 203. *See also* Diagnosis
Dissection, 112, 121–123, 152, 164–165, 167, 184–188, 189–197. *See also* Anatomy; Autopsy; Corpse
Distancing, 255–263, 265–266, 315. *See also* Helping, dilemmas in; Physician-patient relationship
Dogmatics, ancient, 138–146, 148–152, 157, 173, 175–176, 178, 189, 191, 194, 195–196, 217, 220. *See also* Empiricists, Hellenistic; Skepticism
  contrast with empirics, 170–172, 178–180, 194–196, 203
Donnelly, William, 97–98, 103
Dualism, 106–110, 114–129, 135–137, 151–152, 155–157, 168, 175, 186–188, 197–199, 284–285
Dyad, therapeutic, 38, 40–41, 53, 83, 87, 88, 91, 93–96, 108, 172–176, 283–284, 319–320. *See also* Experience: therapeutic; Therapeutics

Eccles, John, 2, 107, 109, 161, 162
Edelstein, Ludwig, 177–184, 190–196, 200, 201, 205–210, 212, 213, 215, 216, 217, 219, 220, 221, 223
Elizabeth, Princess of Bohemia, 109, 110, 111, 115, 119, 124, 125, 156, 187, 285
Embodiment, 66–67, 69, 79, 104–105, 157–164, 168–170, 173, 185–198, 290. *See also* Body, human; Mind-body relation
Empiricism, Hippocratic. *See* Empirics, ancient
Empiricists, Hellenistic, 148–150, 170–172, 191–196, 203, 217, 220, 285
  contrast with empirics, 177–180
Empirics, ancient, 138–142, 146–150, 151–152, 154, 173, 175–177, 183, 191, 200–201, 203, 205, 212, 285
  contrast with dogmatics, 170–172, 179–180, 189, 194–196
  contrast with empiricists, 177–180
Empiricus, Sextus, 179, 183, 219
Enablement, 248–250, 285

Engelhardt, H. Tristram, Jr., 48, 49,
    108, 162, 163, 286
Epilogismos, 149–150, 172, 267. *See
    also* Empirics, ancient; Skepticism
Equality. *See* Chance, moral
Erasistratus, 147, 190–193, 195
Ethics
    applied, 6–17, 40
    awakening moral sense, 90,
        303–310, 319
    backlash, 9–13, 15
    biomedical, 1–20
    clinical, 13–14, 27–28, 31–41, 52,
        91, 93, 94, 108, 114, 224–282,
        315–320. *See also* Case
        discussions; Conversation
    clinical consultation, 246–248,
        259–263. *See also* Case
        discussions
    clinical liaison, 242–248, 320
    clinical methods, 31–32, 36, 40, 69,
        242–243, 267–282
    clinical theses, 243–248
    complexity of issues, 20, 30–36, 38.
        See also Interpretation;
        Physician–patient relationship
    feelings, 38, 41–42, 50, 54, 55–56,
        65, 71–74, 300–303, 316. *See
        also* Case discussions;
        Gratitude; Illness; Intimacy;
        Power, medical
    pluralism, 12, 16–19, 41–43, 93–94
    sources of conflict, 41–44, 52, 70,
        71, 94. *See also* Case discussions
    uncertainty. *See* Illness: uncertainty
        in
Eugenics, ancient, 199–201
Experience
    interpretation of. *See* Interpretation
    therapeutic, 38, 42, 93, 94,
        137–138, 150, 170–171. *See also*
        Therapeutics

Feeling, affiliative, 308, 315–319
Fellowship, 300–310. *See also*
    Mutuality
Fetus
    diagnosis of, 44–50
    viability of, 48–50. *See also*
        Abortion; Case discussions:
        fetal anomalies
Fleischman, Alan, R., 5, 6, 7, 14
Fortune, good. *See* Luck

Foster, Lee, 86, 90, 294, 295,
    296–297. *See also* Case
    discussions: kidney disease
Foucault, Michel, 129, 133, 135, 152.
    See also Anatomy; Gaze,
    anatomical
Fox, Renée, 295
Freedom, 286–287, 300, 303, 307,
    310. *See also* Autonomy;
    Mutuality

Galen, 114, 188–190, 192, 194, 196,
    198, 199–201, 205, 213, 216, 217,
    219, 221–223, 265, 285
Garfinkle, Harold, 278, 279
Gaub, Jerome, 126–127, 151, 152,
    156, 157, 172, 186, 187, 285, 287
Gaze, anatomical, 153, 154. *See also*
    Anatomy
Gleitman v. Cosgrove, 48
Goldstein, Kurt, 168
Gorovitz, Samuel, 2, 27, 37
Gratitude, 65, 88–91, 305–310. *See
    also* Case discussions; Ethics
Greenblat, Samuel H., 107, 108, 110,
    187
Gurwitsch, Aron, 280, 285

Harbeson v. Parke-Davis, Inc., 49
Hardy, Robert C., 56, 62–63, 64, 76
Hare, Richard M., 10, 11, 19
Harvey, William, 113–114, 121, 166,
    185, 196
Hauerwas, Stanley, 87, 88
Healing, 204, 220–221. *See also* Illness
Helping, dilemmas in, 252–266. *See
    also* Illness; Power, medical
Hemodialysis. *See* Dialysis
Hermeneutics. *See* Ethics;
    Interpretation
Herophilus, 147, 190–193, 195
Hippocrates
    oath of. *See* Oath, Hippocratic
    tradition of, 13, 14, 38, 50, 51, 107,
        138, 170, 172, 187, 285, 287
    works of, cited, 112, 139, 142, 143,
        146, 200, 212, 213, 214, 221
History, medical, 92–129, 136–223.
    See also Descartes, René;
    Dogmatics, ancient; Empiricists,
    Hellenistic; Empirics, ancient;
    Medicine; Skepticism
    irony in, 94–96, 188. *See also*
        Ludibrium materiae

Hobbins, J. C., 47, 48
Hoffer, Eric, 131
Hoffman, Friedrich, 119, 151, 168, 186, 197, 285
Hospitals, 29–30, 34–38, 40, 42, 43, 78–79, 80–84, 92, 238–239. *See also* Case discussions
emergency rooms of, 226–227, 230–232, 235, 237–242, 245–246
Humanities, 3, 4, 20
Humor, gallows, 157–158, 169–170
Hyperaspistes, 110, 115

Illness. *See also* Case discussions
appeal in, 62–65, 93, 304–305
care and, 88, 236, 238–239, 252, 255–257, 265–266, 274–275, 315–317. *See also* Care, moral idea of
contrast to disease, 204
effect on person's humanity, 55, 85, 87, 128–129, 295–297, 304–305
experience of, 40–41, 53–91, 93–94, 98–99, 104–106, 115, 120, 172–174, 204, 225–242, 295–297, 305–307
factitious, 67
moral order in, 310–312
phenomenology of, 53–56, 65–91
power and vulnerability in, 55, 67–68, 80–84, 85, 94, 105, 303, 304, 305, 319
promise in, 86–88
as special occasion, 303–310, 319
strangers and, 54–55, 80–84, 85, 94, 105, 251–258, 315. *See also* Physician-patient relationship; Power, medical
"telling" about, 88–91, 97. *See also* Conversation
trust and, 54, 55, 63, 65, 69–71, 80–84, 85, 87, 89, 90, 91, 93, 94, 105, 308–312. *See also* Care, moral idea of; Physician-patient relationship
uncertainty in, 54, 55, 72–74, 75–80, 94, 100–101, 105, 316
Inequality. *See* Chance, moral
Infant survival. *See* Case discussions: "Baby Doe"; Case discussions: fetal anomalies

Interpretation
in ancient medicine, conflict of, 137–140, 180–184, 203
clinical ethics and, 31, 32, 40, 93, 94–96, 243–248, 270–273, 275–282. *See also* Ethics
conflict of, 244
patient, 56–62, 62–65, 98–99, 105–106, 172–174, 220. *See also* Case discussions
physician, 68–69, 79–80, 96–98, 172–174, 220, 312–314. *See also* Diagnosis
of symptoms. *See* Symptoms, interpretation of
Intersubjectivity, 290–292, 315–319
Intimacy, 54–55, 81–84, 261, 319. *See also* Care, moral idea of; Illness; Physician-patient relationship
Power, medical

Jonas, Hans, 107–108, 123, 124, 159–161, 163, 170, 188, 197
Jonsen, Albert, 14, 15, 39, 50–52
Judgment, clinical, 36–38, 75–80, 93, 97, 98–103, 154–156, 194
Justice. *See* Chance, moral; Empirics, ancient; Oath, Hippocratic

Kant, Immanuel, 286–287, 298, 300, 307
Kennington, Richard, 117–118, 119, 120, 199
King, Lester, 119, 129, 132–133, 136, 186

Lain-Entralgo, Pedro, 129, 134, 136, 151
Laing, Ronald D., 288
La Mettrie, Julien Offrey de, 119, 151, 172
Langer, Suzanne, 139–140
Lenrow, Peter B., 55, 85, 251–255, 261, 264, 265
Lesion, organic, 132–134, 151, 152, 224. *See also* Autopsy; Bichat, Xavier
Liddle, Grant, 39
Life
everyday, 53–54, 55, 66–69, 81, 86, 116–118, 120–129, 151–152, 295–297, 315–319. *See also* Conversation; Descartes, René

Life (*cont.*)
    taken-for-grantedness of, 66–69,
        295–297. *See also* Case
        discussions
    theories of biological, 159–161
Lindeboom, G. A., 111, 112, 113,
    118, 121, 123, 124
Luck, 88–91, 302–305, 308–310
Ludibrium materiae, 123, 159–162, 167,
    188, 197–199

MacIntyre, Alasdair, 8, 16–18, 37, 42,
    51–52, 94, 214, 286
Majno, Guido, 112, 191
Martin, Samuel P., 3, 4, 5
Materialism, 107–108, 124, 168–170,
    187–188, 190, 195, 197, 284. *See
    also* Mechanism
Matter. *See Ludibrium materiae*
Meaning. *See* Interpretation
Mechanism, 106, 108, 117–125, 127,
    135–137, 151–152, 187, 197–198
Medicine
    ancient, 136–223, 284–285
    ancient philosophy and, 181–182,
        193–196, 221–222
    anomalies in traditional, 96–99,
        104–106, 108–109, 126–129,
        152, 157–165, 175, 186–188,
        285
    as challenge to ethics, 1–28
    clinical, 36–38, 75–80, 97–108, 134,
        312–319. *See also* Diagnosis;
        Judgment, clinical;
        Therapeutics
    complexity of practice in, 20,
        31–34, 36–38, 40–43, 80–81,
        85, 92, 128–129, 243, 283–284
    deficiencies in traditional, 95, 99,
        102–104
    divided legacy in, 151–153, 203,
        223, 285
    errors in, 73–74, 76–77, 100–101,
        259–263, 312–313
    historical thematic of, 162–164,
        168–170, 187–188, 198–199,
        283–285
    moral dimensions of, 51–96, 100,
        199–201, 252–266, 276–279,
        315–320
    moral resolve and. *See* Therapeutics
    need for critique of, 130–131

    as profession, 52, 88, 218–219,
        253–255
    psychosomatic, 126–127, 136,
        151–152, 156–157, 172,
        186–187, 287
    reasoning in, 75–80, 88, 93, 96–97,
        99–102, 144–145, 148–150. *See
        also* Diagnosis; Judgment,
        clinical
    social legitimation and, 55, 85, 105
    social organization of, 20, 51–52,
        252–255, 263–265, 276–279,
        284. *See also* Hospitals; Illness
    values in, 76–80, 93–96, 99–102,
        105–106, 109
Mendelsohn, Robert S., 64
Mersenne, Father Marin, 111, 112,
    113, 125
Metaphysics, 109, 110, 114, 115, 117,
    120, 125
Methodists. *See* Skepticism
Mill, John Stuart, 301–302
Mind, management of. *See* Gaub,
    Jerome
Mind-body relation, 106–110,
    114–126, 135–137, 151–152,
    168–170, 175, 185–188, 197–199.
    See also Descartes, René;
    Embodiment
Morgagni, John Baptist, 119,
    132–133, 152, 175, 186, 285
Morison, Robert S., 12, 14, 15
Mutuality, 292, 310–312. *See also*
    Fellowship; Intersubjectivity

Nature. *See also* Descartes; René;
    Mechanism
    mastery of, 116–119, 199–201
    two senses of, 114–120, 122–125,
        185–188
Neonatology, 21–27, 30, 31, 246–248,
    259–263
Networking, 264–266
Neuroscience, 76, 106–108

Oath, Hippocratic, 200, 202–223. *See
    also* Hippocrates
    covenant, 209–210, 221
    date, 206
    entrusted wisdom, 207–208, 210,
        211–214

ethical code, 206–209, 216–217. *See also* Power, medical
  origins, 206, 207, 208, 209, 216
  sacred relationship, 210–211, 215–219, 221
  virtues, 209, 210–212, 214–215, 218–219, 223

Obstetrics, 44–50
Ortega y Gasset, José, 78, 159

Pain, 71–74, 83, 89, 106–107, 114, 117, 118, 128, 308. *See also* Illness
Patients
  best interests of, 42, 43, 44, 51, 78–79, 94. *See also* Case discussions; Oath, Hippocratic; Physician-patient relationship
  care for. *See* Care, moral idea of: Illness
  displacement of, 79–80, 97–99, 104–106, 109, 284–285
  locational index in discourse by. *See* Conversation: locational index in
  loss of control by, 68, 72–74, 78, 81, 88–88
  moral response of. *See* Gratitude
  social context of, 34–36, 42, 78–79, 80–84, 92–93, 224, 284, 295–297, 309, 310–311
  talk of, 56–65, 70, 71, 73–76, 96–99, 102, 106–109, 115, 116, 128, 129, 294, 296–297. *See also* Conversation; Interpretation
  unique individuals vs. classes of, 79–80, 87, 93, 100–104, 144–150, 178–184, 220–221, 315
Pellegrino, Edmund D.
  clinical judgment, 37, 38, 75, 76–78, 93, 99–102, 103, 154–156. *See also* Judgment, clinical
  contemporary medicine, 107, 157, 170, 172, 174
  dehumanization, 254
  illness, 85, 86, 304
  medical morality, 3, 5, 6, 55, 92
Penfield, Wilder, 2, 106–107, 109, 156, 158, 170, 172, 180

Person, 78–83, 87–88, 95–96, 97, 105–106, 107–127, 151
Philanthropy, 217–219, 220
Philosophers in Medical Centers Project, 6–9
Physician-patient relationship, 31–37, 41, 54–55, 62–65, 70–74, 75–80, 83–85, 87–88, 91, 94–99, 100, 102, 104–106, 128–129, 252–266. *See also* Care, moral idea of: Diagnosis; Illness; Therapeutics
  asymmetry of power in, 63, 84–86, 253–255, 304–305, 311–313
  communication in, 34, 63–65, 70, 74, 76, 244–246, 285. *See also* Conversation; Interpretation
  covenant in, 93–94
  as helping relation, 54–55, 84–88, 90, 251–266, 312–315. *See also* Therapeutics
  lying in, 255–258
Physiology, 106, 107, 108, 110, 112–114, 118, 119
Plato, 125, 190, 192, 195, 209
Plemp, Vopiscus Fortunatus, 113, 114, 121–122
Plügge, Herbert, 168
Power, medical, 55, 63, 84–86, 105, 116, 128–129, 162–163, 199–205, 213–215, 253–255
Probabilism. *See* Empiricists, Hellenistic
Prudence. *See* Judgment, clinical

Ramsey, Paul, 157–158, 169, 188
Rather, L. D., 119, 126, 127, 134, 135, 136
Rawlinson, Mary, 66, 67, 68, 72
Reductivism, 106–107, 109, 155–157. *See also* Dualism
Relevance, schemata of. *See* Ethics
Reliance, 54, 67, 69–71, 80–85, 89–91, 308–309. *See also* Illness; Trust
Rights, moral, 285–286
Roe v. Wade, 48, 49, 50

Scheler, Max, 289–290, 291, 318, 319
Schutz, Alfred, 31, 53, 54, 65, 83, 92, 243, 275–279, 285, 298, 315
Schweitzer, Albert, 303–308

Scribonius, 217-219, 221, 223
Self, autonomy of. *See* Autonomy
Semeiosis and signs, 139, 146, 147, 148, 267. *See also* Empiric, ancient; Skepticism
Sickness, 71-74, 78, 110, 115. *See also* Illness
Siegler, Mark, 12, 13, 14, 15, 19, 27, 39, 160
Silber, Tomas, 5, 6
Singer, Charles, 122, 164
Singer, Peter, 12, 17
Skepticism, 148, 151, 177-201, 205, 212-213, 219, 285
  contrasted to empiricists and dogmatics, 180, 181, 183-184, 219-220
  ethics and, 219-221, 223. *See also* Oath, Hippocratic
  medical method of, 180, 182-184
  originality of, 180, 181, 220
  rationale of, 179-180, 183-184, 220
  related to empirics, 182-184, 203
Society, need for critique of, 131-132
Spiegelberg, Herbert, 298-305, 307, 308, 318
Starr, Paul, 32, 128-129
Stenson, Niels, 121, 186
Stewart v. Long Island College Hospital, 48
Strangers. *See* Illness: strangers and; Physician-patient relationship; Power, medical
Suffering, 71-74, 83, 106, 107, 128, 308. *See also* Illness; Pain
Sullivan, Mark, 134
Symptoms, interpretation of, 38, 42, 43, 68-69, 79-80, 97-101, 133-134, 138-150, 170-174, 187, 203. *See also* Diagnosis; Illness

Talk. *See* Conversation; Illness: "telling" about

Technology, medical, 162-163, 199, 293-297. *See also* Power, medical
Texas Natural Death Act, 227, 228-231, 233-237, 240-242, 275. *See also* Case discussions: terminal illness
Therapeutics. *See also* Dyad, therapeutic
  moral resolve and, 38-41, 42, 52, 88, 93, 94
  moral theme in, 39-42, 52, 77-80, 88, 93, 96-97, 101. *See also* Care, moral idea of: Illness
Thomas, W. I., 243
Titmuss, Richard, 54, 113
Trust, 54, 69-71, 283-320. *See also* Care, moral idea of
Truth-telling, 62-65, 70, 74, 76, 78-79, 81-84, 87. *See also* Illness; Physician-patient relationship
Turpin v. Sortini, 48

Uncertainty. *See* Illness: uncertainty in

Veatch, Robert, 16, 17, 39
Vesalius, Andreas, 112, 121, 122, 165, 167, 185, 189, 287
Vivisection, 121, 122, 152, 190-197. *See also* Anatomy; Autopsy; Dissection
Vulnerability. *See* Illness: power and vulnerability in; Physician-patient relationship; Power, medical

Wieder, D. Lawrence, 31, 277, 278-282, 285, 298

Zaner, Richard M., 53, 67, 84, 158, 168, 285, 289, 292, 301